ORGANISING KNOWLEDGE IN A GLOBAL SOCIETY

REVISED EDITION

Topics in Australasian Library and Information Studies

Series editor: Dr Stuart Ferguson

This series provides detailed, formally refereed works on a wide range of topics and issues relevant to professionals and para-professionals in the library and information industry and to students of library and information studies. All titles are written from an Australasian perspective, drawing on professional experience and research in Australia, New Zealand and the wider Pacific region. Proposals for publications should be addressed to the series editor (sferguson@csu.edu.au).

Recent publications include:

ORGANISING KNOWLEDGE IN A GLOBAL SOCIETY

principles and practice in libraries and information centres

Revised edition

Philip Hider with Ross Harvey

Topics in Australasian Library and Information Studies, Number 29

 Centre for Information Studies

 Charles Sturt University
Wagga Wagga New South Wales

ISBN 9781876938673 (pbk.)

ISSN: 1030-5009

National Library of Australia cataloguing-in-publication data

---

Hider, Philip, 1971-
   Organising knowledge in a global society / Philip Hider with Ross Harvey. – Rev. ed. – Wagga Wagga: Centre for Information Studies, Charles Sturt University, 2008.

   Includes index.
   Previous ed. published 2003.
   9781876938673 (pbk.)

   1. Information organization 2. Information storage and retrieval systems. 3. Cataloguing--Standards. 4. Electronic information resources. 5. Metadata. I. Harvey, D.R. (Douglas Ross), 1951- . II. Charles Sturt University. Centre for Information Studies. III. Title (Series: Topics in Australasian library and information studies ; no. 29).

025.3

Published in 2008

Series editor: S. Ferguson
Copy editor: R. Crease
Indexer: R. Salmond
Cover editors: T. O'Neill and M. McNicol
Printer: On-Demand, Southbank VIC

Centre for Information Studies
Locked Bag 660
Wagga Wagga NSW 2678
Australia
Phone: + 61 (0)2 6933 2325
Fax: +61 (0)2 6933 2733
Email: cis@csu.edu.au
http://www.csu.edu.au/cis/

Contents

Organising knowledge in a global society

Figures

Preface to the first edition

This book is based, in large part, on *Organising Knowledge in Australia*, published in 1999 by the Centre for Information Studies. *Organising Knowledge in Australia* aimed to provide an introduction to bibliographic organisation and information retrieval practice in Australian libraries and information centres. There was, accordingly, an emphasis on Australian practice. The title change for this book to *Organising Knowledge in a Global Society* is intended to reflect the fact that bibliographic organisation is now a global activity, with increasing levels of international collaboration and higher dependence on international communications.

The writing of this book is also prompted by the growing realisation that information accessible on the web needs better organisation. We are, states Elaine Svenonius, 'at a time when intelligent life on the internet desperately needs to be jump-started by graduates knowledgeable about the principles and objectives of information organization' (McGarry 2000, p.15). We need to take account of how the web is searched, and of the tools (such as Google) used to search it, and to apply some of the lessons learned to improving our practice in organising bibliographic information.

Organising Knowledge in a Global Society provides an introduction to bibliographic organisation and information retrieval practice in libraries and information centres. It is written for professionals and paraprofessionals in all types of libraries and information agencies, and for students of library and information studies. It has two primary aims: to provide an overview of the field of bibliographic organisation and information retrieval practice in libraries and information centres; and to present a conceptual framework within which information professionals can consider the subject and upon which they might build during their professional careers. Its global perspective is complemented by case studies taken largely from Australian practice, although examples from other countries are also provided.

It is important to note that this book is *not* intended to be a guide to *how* to apply standards and tools used in bibliographic organisation in libraries. It is less about *how* to organise information, and more about *why* to do it. It examines and elucidates the question of *why* bibliographic organisation is necessary, describes significant concepts of bibliographic organisation at the national and international level, and notes what mechanisms and means are currently available to, and applied in, libraries and information agencies to carry it out effectively. Sources which do teach how to apply commonly-used standards are plentiful, with examples such as *CatSkill* on CD-ROM (Mortimer, Lochhead & Hyland 1994), Davis's Dewey workbooks (Davis 1997; Davis & New 1997), Mortimer's cataloguing and classification workbooks (Mortimer 2002, 1997), Dittman and Hardy's classification workbook (Dittman & Hardy 1999), Millsap and Ferl's workbook on AACR2 and MARC (Millsap & Ferl 1997) and Manheimer's workbook (Saye 2000) deserving mention.

What is meant here by *bibliographic organisation*? Our brief definition, sufficient for this preliminary section, is *the process of making accessible to those who seek it the information present in information resources (documents in any form, and digital objects) which can be accessed through libraries and information centres, and also of making the information resources themselves accessible.* This definition is amplified in the first chapter and is explained further as the book proceeds.

As libraries move further and further into the digital age, the importance of conventional bibliographic organisation practice is lessening. While it will not disappear in its present form, conventional practice will become marginalised as we enter a new context for bibliographic organisation, one defined by the availability of massive amounts of content in digital form rather than print. As Jennifer Younger puts it, 'resource description, known more familiarly within the library community as cataloging or indexing, is undergoing intense scrutiny with the rapid proliferation of, and access to, digital resources' (Younger 1997, p.462). More specifically, the information resources used in libraries are changing from primarily print-based media owned by the library to digital objects which may not be owned by the library; library practice is converging with practice in other kinds of information organisations, such as archives and museums; and other mechanisms for organising and controlling these 'new' information sources will become standard practice. It should be noted, too, that some aspects of 'traditional' library knowledge organisation practice, such as thesauri and classification schemes, are being investigated and adopted by organisations that are realising that they need to structure the information they provide through the internet to their users. We are convinced that current practice will remain a significant part – but not the only part – of a wider field of organising knowledge for the effective dissemination of information, in which libraries are but one of many agents. This book, then, is concerned primarily with *library* practice, although it recognises that such practice is only a part of a wider milieu.

Organising Knowledge in a Global Society examines techniques, such as cataloguing, abstracting, indexing, thesaurus construction and applying metadata, by which information is organised in information centres. Information centres of every kind depend on efficient retrieval of information so that they can fulfil their primary mission of serving their users; a crucial factor for efficient retrieval is the way in which information is organised. Traditional information centres such as libraries have developed complex systems for organising information. Recently, the widespread application of computers to information-handling tasks, and in particular the use of the internet and the world wide web, have changed the ways in which information is used, and, consequently, has also changed the ways in which information is organised so that it can be effectively retrieved and used. Knowledge both of the traditional techniques and of the more recently developed techniques is essential for all information workers.

Although we are fully aware that library practice is changing rapidly, we are convinced that the traditions of that practice are still worth upholding. One focus of this book is, therefore, on the user. It is worth reminding the reader here of Ranganathan's five laws of library science, which are relevant to this focus:

- books are for use,
- to every reader his book,
- to every book its reader,
- save the time of the reader, and
- a library is a growing organism.

If *book, reader* and *library* are replaced by *information resource, user* and *information centre* then (despite the loss of elegance in the wording) Ranganathan's laws still hold good today.

We have made five basic assumptions about bibliographic organisation:

- that knowledge of bibliographic organisation is at the heart of all professional knowledge in library and information studies;
- that a high quality catalogue is the foundation of an effective information delivery system;
- that libraries maintain a catalogue containing surrogate records of the information resources they acquire, or provide access to, to assist them in their role as information providers;
- that dictionary card catalogues have been superseded in most libraries by computerised catalogues; and
- that catalogues are compiled according to international bibliographic standards which facilitate the national and international exchange of bibliographic data.

This book owes much in conception to Jennifer Rowley's *Organizing Knowledge* (2nd ed. 1992; 3rd ed. by Rowley & Farrow 2000). Its authors have also been influenced by other widely available texts on bibliographic organisation, including *Wynar's Introduction to Cataloging and Classification* (9th ed. by Taylor, 2000),

Lois Mai Chan's *Cataloging and Classification: An Introduction* (2nd ed. 1994), Ronald Hagler's *The Bibliographic Record and Information Technology* (3rd ed. 1997), Mary Piggott's *A Topography of Cataloguing: Showing the Most Important Landmarks, Communications and Perilous Places* (Piggott 1988), Arlene Taylor's *The Organization of Information* (Taylor 1999), and Elaine Svenonius's *The Intellectual Foundation of Information Organization* (Svenonius 2000). These texts are laudable in large part, but are not wholly satisfactory. Piggott, for example, emphasises a British view of cataloguing history, not entirely applicable to an increasingly internationalised information environment, and some of the books which originate from the United States emphasise the minutiae of cataloguing codes and, perhaps, represent a narrow North American concept of the field.

As well as providing a global perspective, *Organising Knowledge in a Global Society* contains case studies and examples taken largely from Australian practice. Some of these case studies and examples have been selected because they illustrate aspects of practice that are applicable in a wide range of environments, regardless of the country. Others have been selected because they describe aspects of practice that are distinctively Australian. The field of bibliographic organisation includes some notable success stories from Australia. The country has, for instance, by far the largest truly national bibliographic database in the world. And, historically, the contributions made by Australians to bibliographic organisation practice have been significant: H.C.L. Anderson's contributions to the development of the Library of Congress subject headings, Andrew Osborn's to the development of modern cataloguing rules, John Metcalfe's to the theory of subject access, and more recently the Enhanced Subject Project at the Australian Defence Force Academy Library, indicate that the contributions have spanned at least a century.

Organising Knowledge in a Global Society has five parts. *Part I: Overview* introduces the subject and provides a conceptual framework for more detailed examination of specific topics. *Part II: Bibliographic Description* examines the standards used in bibliographic organisation: standards for describing documents and digital objects, for providing access to them, and for ensuring consistency (such as authority control standards). *Part III: Subject Access* addresses the question of how access to documents is provided through their subject contents. The chapters in this part address classification, alphabetical subject access systems, and subject access to web content. *Part IV: Bibliographic Data Exchange and Management* covers the technical and organisational standards required to exchange bibliographic data globally; the major bibliographic utilities OCLC and RLIN; an extended case study illustrating bibliographic data exchange in Australia; and local systems. *Part V: Current Issues in Organising Knowledge* is concerned with current and future issues in the organisation of knowledge in libraries and information centres.

Many people have contributed, sometimes unwittingly, to this book and to its predecessor, *Organising Knowledge in Australia*. Although they are too numerous to list here, some need special acknowledgment in relation to this book. Ross Harvey acknowledges students and tutors in bibliographic organisation subjects in Charles Sturt University's School of Information Studies who have contributed to the development of many of the ideas. Students in Nanyang Technological University's Division of Information Studies have also contributed, especially by helping to clarify ideas by confronting us with different traditions of organising information. Leonie Bourke has kindly shared her wide experience of the field and, most recently, her knowledge of SCIS. Rona Wade, Director of UNILINC, provided updated information about UNILINC. Anne Robertson, Australian representative on the Dewey Decimal Classification Editorial Policy Committee, provided examples. Staff at the National Library of Australia answered numerous queries, especially about Kinetica. The support of Charles Sturt University and the hospitality of the National Library of Australia, where Ross Harvey was based as a National Library Fellow from March to June 2003, are also gratefully acknowledged. Students and other users of *Organising Knowledge in Australia* have alerted us to inconsistencies and errors and their contribution is welcomed; the assistance of Brigitte Dostie is especially acknowledged.

Philip Hider wishes to give special mention to several people who responded to specific queries: Ann Huthwaite and the Australian Committee on Cataloguing, the staff at Kinetica, Göran Berntsson and Professor Sulistyo-Basuki. He also wishes to thank those people who have given him their support, without which he would not have been in a position to undertake this project, including his former colleagues at SILAS, Choy Fatt Cheong, Anthony Gooderham, and, most of all, his wife, Hongmin.

The main acknowledgment must, however, go to Rachel Salmond. From her experience as a cataloguer and educator, and more recently as an information architect, she has contributed very significantly to the content of this book. She has also assisted immeasurably with the multitudinous tasks of preparing the text for publication.

The reader should be aware of the propensity for URLs (universal resource locators, that is, world wide web addresses) to change. All were correct at the time of writing.

Preface to the revised edition

Knowledge and information organisation is dependent on the environment in which knowledge and information is shared. As this environment continues to evolve, so too do developments in the way information and knowledge resources are organised and made accessible. Since the first edition, written in 2003 and published in 2004, the information environment has undergone what some might call a revolution, namely, the transition to 'Web 2.0'. Others might view the phenomenon more as a trend, an increasing use of the online environment as a social environment. Such an environment is not merely for visiting, but for participating in and for contributing to. The information organisation part of this trend is exemplified by the rise of social tagging, and by new approaches to search interface design that emphasise the users' role in information retrieval. The last word of the book's title is thus now all the more apposite: the Web 2.0 environment is more than just a global network, it is highly social, in which virtual realities are constructed and negotiated through the mostly voluntary and enthusiastic participation of millions of people.

The revised edition of this book aims to cover this trend, as it pertains to the field of information organisation, and also to update the reader on those trends already identified in the previous edition, such as the development of more flexible and web-friendly metadata standards, of which the prospective *Resource Description and Access* standard is perhaps the paradigm case. Examples and case studies have also been updated, as appropriate. The basic structure of the book has not been altered, however, as the fundamental components of information and knowledge organisation, which this structure reflects, have not, in my view, drastically changed over the past five years.

I wish to thank Charles Sturt University for allowing me sabbatical leave in which I completed the revision, and my students and colleagues in the School of Information Studies. I would like to convey special thanks to two great champions of bibliographic organisation: Saralee Turner and Ashley Freeman. I also acknowledge the kind assistance provided by members of the Australian Committee on Cataloguing, and by staff in CSU's Division of Library Services. Very significant contributions were made by Rachel Crease, who performed the copy editing, and, once again, by Rachel Salmond, who re-indexed the book. For their wonderful support and forbearance, I thank Hongmin and Lawrence.

Philip Hider, School of Information Studies, Charles Sturt University

PART I: OVERVIEW

CHAPTER 1
Definitions and introductory concepts

Chapter 1 provides an overview of bibliographic organisation. Terms are defined and basic concepts introduced, the need for bibliographic organisation is explained, and the methods by which it is achieved are noted. The systems that are used to enable effective bibliographic organisation are described and their requirements are outlined. The building blocks and structure of metadata are introduced and the sources of this data are noted, as are the physical forms in which metadata is presented. Briefly noted are the requirements for exchanging metadata among different systems.

Definitions

The first definition to consider is *library collection*. In the pre-digital, pre-computer-networked past the library collection consisted only of information resources that the library owned and housed. These information resources were usually printed physical objects such as books, manuscripts and maps. Today, library collections also include other information resources to which the library gives access, and encompass:

1. documents owned by the library;
2. intangible electronic documents (digital objects) owned by the library;
3. documents owned by other libraries but available to the library's users through inter-library loan, faxing arrangements, and so on; and
4. remote electronic documents (digital objects) available through the library's online systems.

Other key terms are *information* and *knowledge*. No functional distinction is made between information and knowledge in this book. Information is potential knowledge, and there is often no clear difference between them in terms of their embodiment in documents. For example, the word information is commonly used in terms such as *information resource* and *information retrieval*. The terms *knowledge resource* and *knowledge retrieval* could be used equally validly, but the more commonly used terms are preferred in this book.

Many of the terms used in this book have different meanings in other contexts. It is not uncommon for words and phrases applied primarily in the context of information service provision to be used to describe new concepts, practices and procedures elsewhere, and especially in the field of computing. It is therefore important that we establish the meaning of some terms used throughout this text at the outset. Current terminology is at times inadequate for our purposes. For example, the phrases *library information retrieval system* or *information retrieval system* are used here to describe any total system in an information centre used for performing the tasks associated with the intellectual organisation of information resources so that they can be retrieved when required. However, some information professionals use the phrase *information retrieval system* to describe a more specialised system, and do not include in it the OPAC (online public access catalogue) or other standard library systems.

The four broadest terms requiring definition are:

- *resource description* – the description of information resources for the purposes of their retrieval and selection;
- *bibliographic organisation* – the organising of the bibliographic information that users of libraries and information centres need in order to find and select the information resources that allow them to acquire the knowledge they seek; sometimes called *bibliographic control*;
- *information centre* – an organisation which has as its primary function the provision of information (in the context of this book the term refers mostly to libraries, although occasional reference will be made to other information centres such as archives and records management units); and
- *abstracting and indexing services* – services, usually offered on a commercial basis, that provide access to surrogate records of information resources (and increasingly to the information resources themselves). The techniques these services apply are closely related to, or often the same as, those used in information centres. Some examples of well-known established services include ERIC (Educational Resources Information Center), PAIS (Public Affairs Information Service), RILM *Abstracts of Music Literature* and AEI (*Australian Education Index*).

Terms describing the contents of libraries and information centres and some of the products of those who organise them are:

- *information resources* – the *documents* and *digital objects* that are present in the collection of a library or information centre, or to which the library or information centre provides access;
- *document* – used here in the broad sense of an information-bearing medium. The term has traditionally been applied to printed media, but in this book is also used to include non-print media. Information in digital form is encompassed by the term, but is also referred to more specifically in this book as *digital objects*;
- *digital object* – an object that can be represented by a computer. Digital objects commonly of interest to libraries and information centres include web pages, databases, word-processed documents, and digital video, audio, images, and maps; newer forms of digital object include blogs and wikis;
- *metadata* – a set of metadata elements that describes an information resource, for example catalogue records, index entries, and metatags on web pages; sometimes called *bibliographic data*;
- *bibliographic records* – metadata produced by cataloguers according to defined standards and included in a library catalogue or bibliographic database;
- *metadata elements* – the building blocks of metadata; they are the attributes of the information resource considered necessary to describe it succinctly. For example, for a

printed book the conventional data elements include its title, name(s) of its author or authors (or other people who have contributed to the book's intellectual or artistic content, such as illustrators), the name of its publisher, its date of publication, and its ISBN (International Standard Book Number). For a digital object, the data elements will include many in common with a book (title, name(s) of people involved in its creation, subject, name of its publisher, date of publication) and others specific to digital objects such as format and resource identifier (for example, a uniform resource locator), or of particular importance in the digital environment, such as information about rights held in and over the resource (for example, intellectual property rights, copyright).

 Metadata usually makes access to information possible in two ways:

- it provides *intellectual access* to the information contained in an information resource by allowing the seeker of that information to locate a reference to the information resource where it is present; and

- it provides *physical access* to an information resource by indicating where it is located (for instance, its location on the library shelf as indicated by a call number, or its electronic address as indicated by its uniform resource locator.

The processes that information professionals involved in bibliographic organisation engage in include:

- *cataloguing* – the process of compiling bibliographic records for information resources by identifying and recording certain attributes of those information resources, such as title, authorship, publication and contents. This process can be divided into two parts: *descriptive cataloguing* by which information resources are described in sufficient detail to distinguish them from other similar information resources, and *subject cataloguing* by which the subject content of information resources is described. These terms, as defined here, are usually used in a library context and imply adherence to defined library standards, such as cataloguing rules;

- *classification* – the process of identifying the subject content of an information resource and of allocating a classification number from a bibliographic classification scheme to that information resource; such bibliographic classification schemes are based on a systematic arrangement of entities and concepts into categories. Classification is closely related to subject indexing;

- *indexing* – the process of describing an information resource according to specific data elements (such as author, title or subject) in order to provide access to that information resource. The term is used in different ways, but is used here to encompass more than the term *cataloguing*: it includes not only the largely library-specific process already noted, but also the processes, often less standardised, which are used to build up the metadata records used by indexing and abstracting services; and

- *abstracting* – the process of concisely and accurately summarising the content of an information resource, usually in the context of indexing and abstracting services.

Cataloguing and indexing have very similar aims, the difference being largely that cataloguing is concerned with providing summary access to composite information resources (*all* of a book, *all* issues of a serial) in the context of the library catalogue, whereas indexing and abstracting is primarily concerned with providing access to parts of an information resource (*a chapter* in a book, *one article* in an issue of a serial). Both sets of techniques have much in common, and both will be examined and described in this book. The differences between them and the contexts in which they are applied are diminishing, and this point will be amplified as the book progresses.

The *cataloguer*, then, performs certain tasks in order to provide effective access to information resources. He or she:

- *creates descriptions of information resources* – this is done by selecting metadata elements and recording them according to agreed standards; and
- *provides access to information resources* – this is traditionally carried out by assigning access points, or index entries, for associated personal names, names of corporate bodies and titles in the case of descriptive cataloguing; and classification numbers and subject terms in the case of subject cataloguing.

These tasks are very similar, and in part identical, to the tasks that are carried out by *indexers* – those who create the large computerised databases of indexes and abstracts which provide access to periodicals, patents, technical reports and other information resources. The common ground includes principles of authority control, access points and description. It also includes subject access, where library cataloguing practice is slowly but surely adopting some of the techniques initially developed and applied in the indexing and abstracting arena. We must never forget that the ultimate aim of these activities is *service* (see figure 1.1).

Need for bibliographic organisation

Michael Gorman, one of the editors of AACR2 (*Anglo-American Cataloguing Rules*, 2nd ed.), a key standard in the field of organising information, has exerted a major influence on the development and current practice of bibliographic organisation in libraries. His opinions have been challenged in recent years, in the context of new environments, but few would deny the success of AACR2 and Gorman's approach during the last two decades of the twentieth century. Here is Gorman on why bibliographic organisation (which he terms *bibliographic control*) is essential to the effective practice of librarianship (and by analogy those other professions whose task it is to organise and make recorded information accessible):

> Bibliographic control is central to librarianship in a realistic and functional manner. It is impossible to imagine anything called 'librarianship' without the structures and patterns of thought that we find in bibliographic control. While it is not necessarily important for librarians to know individual cataloguing rules or the bases of the major classifications, it is vital that librarians think logically, understand the ways in which knowledge and information are organized for retrieval, and be able to communicate their knowledge of these structures to the library user (Gorman 1992, p.694).

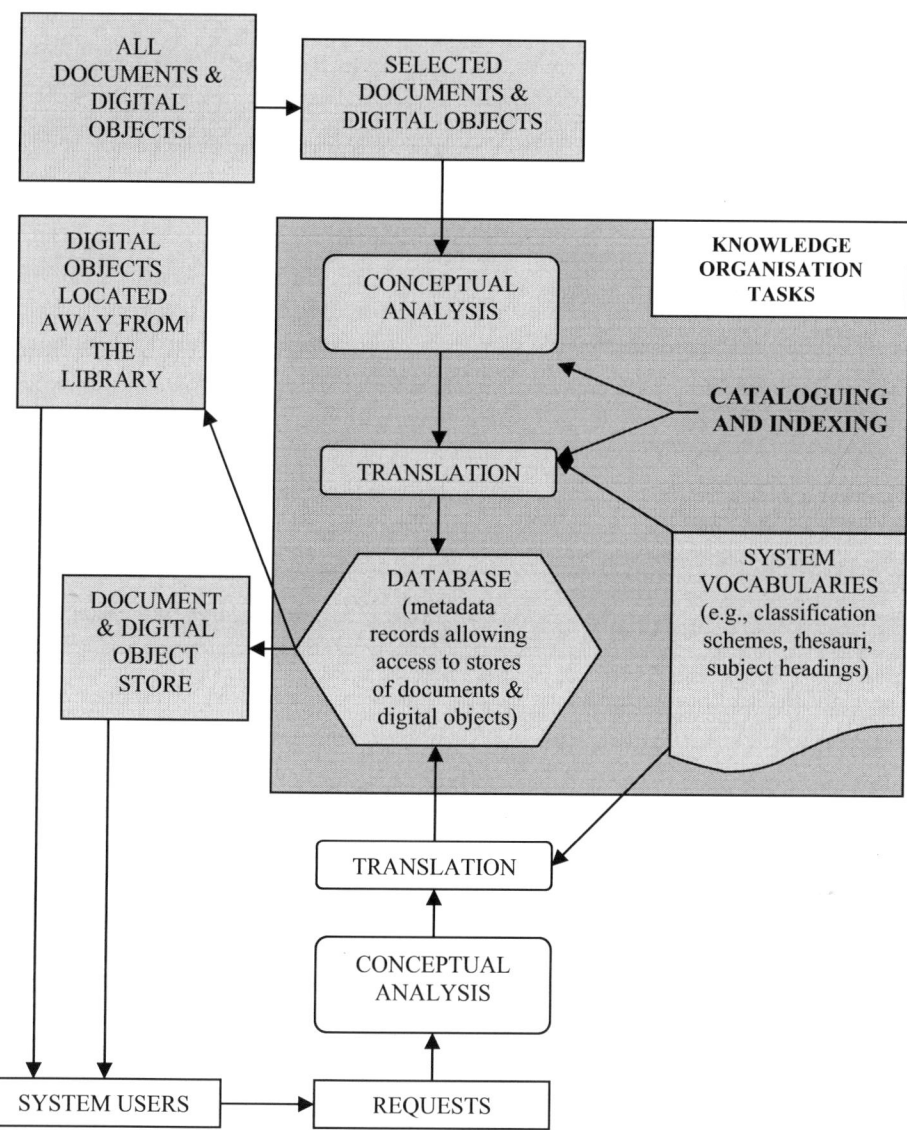

Figure 1.1 Knowledge organisation tasks performed in information centres. Adapted from Lancaster 1979, figure 3, p.8

In a paper presented in Melbourne at the 9th Australian Cataloguers Conference, Gorman also noted his opposition to the view that cataloguing is becoming irrelevant as a result of the widespread use of library computer networks and the digital library. While he acknowledged that these factors have considerably altered the way cataloguing is carried out, he argued that:

> cataloguing and the kind of imposition of order on the flow of knowledge and information that it represents may be all that separates us from becoming electronic neanderthals … If electronic documents are to become the predominant or … only form, then cataloguing will be the only activity for professionals in whatever we then call librarianship (Gorman 1991, p.132).

While the traditional cataloguing approach, as exemplified by standards such as AACR2, may not be the only way of tackling the great explosion of digital information that we are currently witnessing, it is certainly true that efforts to impose some sort of order on this information are seen as critical to the internet's future, and are the preoccupation of many both inside and outside of librarianship. As such, the highly-developed skills and practices of cataloguers and indexers are increasingly recognised and sought in the online environment.

Elsewhere Gorman comments more specifically on the role of bibliographic organisation in providing effective user services:

> The fact is that the bibliographies, catalogues and other materials that are the stock-in-trade of the reference librarian are products of the world of bibliographic control. In order to use them well, one has to have an understanding of that context and of the history and evolution of the structures of which they are a product. One small example: there can be no dispute that the British Museum Department of Printed Books *Catalogue* is a bibliographic resource of great importance. The fact is that, without a knowledge of Panizzi's cataloguing rules (set out most recently in the British Museum Rules of 1936), it is very difficult to use that important resource. What may seem to be arcane beyond belief (the study of the anglicized Italian cataloguing prophet of the 19th century) turns out to be of immediate practical moment (Gorman 1993, pp.120-121).

While Gorman uses a very specific example, his general point – that it is essential for every effective professional *in every branch of information provision* to master an understanding of how knowledge is organised – is entirely valid. An Australian author, Margaret Cameron, made a similar point in a public lecture titled 'A Catalogue is a Reader Service', described as 'a plea for recognition of the work of cataloguers as providing a fundamental reader service: access to the collection' (Cameron 1992, p.18).

Users of bibliographic data

In addition to the requirements that need to be considered when we develop a library information retrieval system (such as standards for constructing bibliographic records), we also need to consider the output of the system. A library information retrieval system is only effective if it allows the information that has been entered to be retrieved when required. In addition, it should be straightforward to use by the seekers of the information, without the need for an intermediary such as a librarian or other information professional. Therefore, important questions we must ask when we construct or alter our library information retrieval systems (our catalogues, indexes and bibliographies) include:

- who are the users?
- what do they need?
- how can our systems be improved to meet their needs?

There have been many studies of library catalogue users, so we do know, with some degree of accuracy, some things about them and their requirements – although still not enough.

From these studies we know many of the attributes of the 'typical' catalogue user and the way he or she uses the catalogue, for example:

- most people avoid using the catalogues if possible, especially in public libraries where many do not use it at all;
- most people know little about how the catalogue is organised;
- the catalogue is used mostly for *known item searches* (to determine whether or not the library owns or can provide access to a particular information resource) or for *subject searches* (to identify information resources the library owns or can provide access to about a particular subject);
- for known item searches, the user's success or failure in locating entries in the catalogue relates to:
  a) previous experience with library catalogues, including the one being studied;
  b) his or her general intelligence and perseverance;
  c) the information (how much, and its accuracy) which the user brings to the catalogue. Information about the title of a document is more likely to be complete and accurate than is information about the author. Keywords in titles are often remembered, but few users recall complete bibliographic information, and what they do remember is often inaccurate. Written bibliographic information is only a little more likely to be accurate than is memorised information;
  d) how the user searches the catalogue. Most users will search under names of authors despite the fact that their title information may well be better; and
  e) the number of access points which the catalogue provides;
- many known item searches are, in fact, subject searches in which the user is using the known item only as an entry to a subject area;
- more than 50 per cent of catalogue users will look up only one entry and then stop, even if they have not found what they are looking for; and
- most subject searches are attempted under a single subject heading (Lancaster 1993; Ayres 1983).

To these points we can add the one that is causing perhaps the most concern amongst librarians at present: many people are now used to searching the world wide web through search engines like Google and Yahoo and find these alternative tools of information retrieval very helpful, in many situations, and more user-friendly than the typical library catalogue. Thus the tendency to avoid the library catalogue has become, if anything, even more pronounced.

More research is needed on the way in which users search library information retrieval systems as part of their wider online information-seeking activities, but it appears that many observations based on stand-alone catalogues are still applicable to web-based catalogues (Bates 2002; Roe 1999). For example, research has indicated that the reasons for failure in online catalogues include lack of user perseverance, and inaccuracy (such as spelling mistakes) of the terms used to search the online catalogue (Drabenstott & Weller 1996), the user's inability to match the terms they use to search with the terms used in the online catalogue for subject retrieval (and they are frequently not aware of the source of the terms used in the catalogue, such as the *Library of Congress Subject Headings*), and lack of knowledge of how to use the online catalogue well (Long 2000, p.162). One important lesson to always keep in mind when we develop and implement library information retrieval systems, therefore, is that we constantly need to seek feedback from users on how well our systems are working, to take note of research into information-seeking behaviour, and to use the results to design better systems. That is what has been happening with the design of some OPACs, but not nearly enough of the lessons learned have been fully applied (Borgman 1996). We have taken some notice of the users, but not enough: for example, queries are easier to input, and user interfaces have adopted many of the conventions of the seemingly ubiquitous Windows operating system, but there are still many issues in OPAC design. Some of these are noted in chapter 14.

 ## Meeting users' needs

Objectives of library information retrieval systems

How do we attempt to meet the requirements of the users of our library information retrieval systems? An old, but still eminently workable, definition of the objectives of these systems is that stated by Charles Cutter in 1876. He defined the objectives of a catalogue as being:

> 1. To enable a person to find a book of which either
> A) the author
> B) the title
> C) the subject is known.
> 2. To show what the library has
> D) by a given author
> E) on a given subject
> F) in a given kind of literature.
> 3. To assist in the choice of a book
> G) as to its edition (bibliographically)
> H) as to its character (literary or topical) (Cutter 1904, p.12).

The important factors in Cutter's statement are that the catalogue (or other information retrieval system) allows its users to determine the existence of a document and to physically locate a document, and it provides guidance on the relevance and currency of a document.

Although Cutter's definition was developed for the card or book catalogues of more than a century ago it has stood the test of time, but not without revision to better meet today's needs. It was amplified by an international committee of cataloguing experts which met in Paris in 1961 to develop principles on which a standardised code of cataloguing practice could be based; and these *Paris Principles* have themselves recently been superseded by the *Frankfurt Principles* (see chapter 3). Later rewritings of Cutter's definition have attempted to take account of online systems for organising information, with their different needs and different procedures. Patrick Wilson has put on record a powerful argument for redefinition. He considered that the 'organizing devices' of the bibliographical universe ('the big independent periodical indexes, abstracting services, published catalogs, national bibliographies, comprehensive subject bibliographies') are 'instruments of bibliographical control ... allowing first the discovery of the very existence of a text or book and then the discovery of where copies can be found.' Wilson questioned Cutter's statement that the catalogue should enable us to find a book of which either the author or the title or the subject is known. Does it? – no; it tells us where a book ought to be, its theoretical location, not whether it is on loan, in process, or lost. This situation has changed with online catalogues. Why, asked Wilson, 'limit the catalog to things owned [by the library] but perhaps not actually available? Why not extend it to cover things available through the library, whether or not owned by the library? ... the local catalog should list everything that anyone is willing to lend'. Wilson also amplified Cutter's objective regarding 'book': why limit it to book? And why not extend it to text (regardless of format)? He also argued for access through the catalogue to parts of texts (for example, a chapter or discrete section in a book or other format) (Wilson 1983, pp.5-7). He did not, however, extend his argument to the next logical step: the catalogue as access mechanism to full texts of documents, a concept which is currently being energetically explored in library information retrieval systems.

In a similar vein Michael Buckland has redefined the library catalogue. The library user, he considers, wants 'convenient access to texts' (Buckland 1988, p.306) not merely a guide to local holdings. The technological means are now available to deliver this, so we need to aim at 'a bibliography of what is conveniently accessible rather than the much narrower concept of a catalog of what happens to be locally owned' (Buckland 1988, p.307).

Cutter's definition, if expanded, is appropriate for use with a virtual collection of information resources, that is, a collection which is dispersed through a number of different physical locations. In this book we consider that the functions of a library information retrieval system are:

- to enable a person to find an information resource, regardless of format, of which the author, the title, the subject, or other specified characteristics are known;

- to show what information resources by a given author, on a given subject (and related subjects), or in a given kind (or form) of literature can be delivered to the user, by whatever delivery mechanism is appropriate;

- to assist in the choice of an information resource which meets the information needs of the user; and
- to deliver a copy of a required information resource to the user, or (where appropriate) to provide the user with access to a copy of the information resource.

It should be noted that no current library information retrieval system delivers all of these functions. At present the more advanced of them achieve only some of the goals, to the extent that they indicate whether the information resource is held in the information centre and whether it is available (on the shelves, on loan, or available as hard copy or in electronic form). Most do not provide a copy of the information resource on screen, although some allow for online ordering of a document to be delivered to the user (perhaps by fax) at a convenient site. However, more and more of them provide access to a digital object (such as the full text of a journal) on screen. This topic is explored further in chapter 14.

Three primary tasks are required to achieve the objectives of library information retrieval systems:

- to uniquely identify information resources so that they cannot be confused with other similar information resources;
- to provide the user with access to information resources if he or she knows the name or names of a person or organisation associated with those information resources; and
- to provide the user with details of the subjects of information resources.

We examine each of these tasks below.

Describing the information resource

Unique identification of an information resource is achieved by isolating distinctive and significant attributes of it and combining them in a metadata record of the document. The selection of these attributes (or metadata elements) is guided by various standards, which, in turn, are based on conventions established over many years of practice in libraries.

What does metadata do?

We have already defined metadata as a description, or summary, of an information resource. This is used to represent, that is, stand in place of, the information resource itself. Hence bibliographic records are sometimes referred to as surrogates. The elements of metadata are therefore those attributes of the information resource which are considered necessary to represent the information resource accurately and usefully. One significant reason for constructing a bibliographic record, or set of metadata, is that it is very much smaller than the information resource itself: for example, a library catalogue record for a book may be only ten lines long, whereas the book itself could easily be several hundred pages in length. This allows for economy of storage in information retrieval systems. More important, perhaps, in the online context, it allows for economy of the search process. That is, the user can narrow down, or zoom in, on far fewer resources than they might otherwise need to examine.

In some systems, metadata is taken from the source itself. For instance, users may search on keywords derived from the actual text (full-text retrieval). If they are indexed, then they are still, in a sense, metadata, if not necessarily very differentiated metadata. Other systems may use more specific metadata that are *embedded* in an online resource. Many systems, particularly search engines, employ a combination of methods in their retrieval processes (also known as algorithms). In very few cases do systems not use some sort of metadata, that is, rarely do they simply scan a resource's content directly for each search query entered by the user. Metadata, in some form or other, is usually the key to retrieval.

However, by no means all information retrieval systems lead the user directly to the resource; we have already noted this as a drawback of many library catalogues. There are a couple of important reasons for this: first, many resources still have no digital version, and cannot readily be made available digitally; and, second, the retrieval system may not have the rights to provide the resource itself, only the metadata. When the user needs to follow up on the metadata by physically visiting the shelves, or another library, or setting up a subscription to another online resource, then it becomes all the more important that the metadata is accurate. Good metadata saves the user a lot of time; bad metadata wastes the user's time.

The metadata elements on which the surrogate record is constructed are based on conventions developed over a period of time. In the case of the bibliographic records used as document surrogates in the library catalogue, the rules and conventions have been developed over many centuries. For another kind of document surrogate, the abstract, the conventions used are more recent. For yet another kind of document surrogate, the ISBN (a very brief and cryptic, or coded, surrogate) the rules were developed only in the 1960s. Many conventions for the metadata of online resources are still being developed.

Metadata versus bibliographic data

We have defined metadata as a set of metadata elements that describes an information resource. Metadata is a term that is currently being used in a number of different ways. In its most general usage it applies to all data that is about data, its literal meaning, which certainly includes bibliographic records for books and other types of documents that make up the collections of traditional libraries. A more specific use of the term often encountered is that metadata is structured data that describes information resources in digital form (digital objects). In this sense, it may be contrasted with bibliographic data, that is usually the product of traditional library cataloguing. However, as the old and new ways of creating and using metadata merge with each other in today's increasingly online world, these distinctions blur. In this book we normally use the term metadata in its most general definition, as applying to all information resources.

The term metadata is often associated with the standard, 'Dublin Core' (or simply DC). This is a specific set of metadata elements initially developed for resource discovery (locating information resources) for the internet. The basic Dublin Core set of metadata elements was designed to be simple to apply and use, but has been found to be too limited for many kinds of information resources. It has been further developed and expanded for a wide variety of information resources, for example digital government information resources on the web. We will look in more detail at some of these DC-based metadata element sets (known as schemas) in chapter 10. Information professionals working in the library context increasingly need to know about these new standards that have until recently been outside the normal library areas of interest.

Which attributes are selected?

The attributes used for the metadata elements, or the bibliographic record, are primarily those elements of an information resource that have been traditionally used to describe that information resource and that are those commonly used to find and evaluate that resource. Some elements may also be recorded so that the resource can be obtained and managed (the latter are called administrative metadata). For a book, some of the key elements are the author's name, title, date of publication; for a music CD (compact disc) the attributes might include name of performer and composer of the music, date it was recorded, date on which the disc was manufactured (if different), and name of the company which issued the disc. Some attributes of an information resource are not usually selected because it is considered that they do not provide useful identification of that information resource, or they do not assist in providing access to it. Examples of attributes not usually selected for a book include the colour of binding (books are often rebound) and the type font in which it is printed (of interest to only a small number of users).

The roots of these conventions can be found in the history of library catalogues and other kinds of indexes, and also the development of the book and other information media. The book in printed form has been available in the Western world for more than 500 years, with the result that knowledge of this medium is widespread. It has become, therefore, a standardised commodity. Take as an example the title-page. If we pick a printed book at random we expect to find a page at the front of the book containing certain pieces of information: title of the book, author's name, who published the book, where the publisher is located, and probably the date of publication. The conventions of the title-page did not arrive fully-fledged, but developed over several centuries. At first, some of the information which is now presented on the title-page appeared at the end of the book; it gradually moved to the front, but even as recently as early in the twentieth century it was still common practice for some of this information (details about the printer, for example) to be placed at the end of the book. These conventions have developed because they are useful, and those who construct bibliographic records for library information retrieval systems select metadata based on them because they are well known and widely applied by the publishers of books. For many media which are not printed the conventions are not nearly as uniform or standard, because these media have not existed for very long. As an example, on a CD the information that we need to construct a useful bibliographic record might be present on the CD itself, or on the printed insert, or both; in some cases the information is not on the CD or its accompanying material at all.

The ideal set of metadata

Any set of metadata we create must meet certain requirements:

- it must uniquely identify the information resource. It must contain sufficient details to distinguish that information resource from another which is similar, for instance to distinguish a second edition from a third edition of a book, or a journal article on one subject from another by a different author on the same topic.

- it must tell us what the information resource is about (what its subject is).

- it should be as brief as possible. Reasons for this include the cost of constructing the metadata record, and the cost of storing it (which can be very high in some kinds of library information retrieval systems).

- it should be able to be easily duplicated. This allows more than one user to have access to a metadata record at the same time.

- it should be constructed according to standards which are widely understood and readily recognised.

- it should be constructed in a form in which it can be easily transferred to another information retrieval system. For example, the MARC format is a widely adopted standard for bibliographic data exchange which allows computerised library catalogues around the world to incorporate bibliographic records from a wide range of sources.

All of these requirements are addressed in detail in following chapters.

Providing access by names of people and organisations

One attribute of information resources conventionally included in their metadata is the names of people or organisations associated with their creation. Users of information retrieval systems commonly seek to identify and locate an information resource for which they know only the name of a person or organisation associated with it. This convention has historical precedent which has significantly influenced current practice.

Before the twentieth century, the primary information resource which information centres (mainly libraries) handled was the printed book. Books were, in almost every instance, the work of a single author, and this characteristic resulted in the convention that the name of the author was the single most important attribute by which an information resource could be identified. This notion of authorship became entrenched to the extent that standards for library cataloguing have given it the status of an unalterable law. The concept of *main entry* (or *chief access point*) as implemented in library catalogues involves the selection of a person, or in some instances of an organisation, as the primary attribute by which the information resource can be identified and located. This concept raises considerable difficulties when it is applied to anything other than information resources written by a single person. For example, to what extent can an organisation (a group of people) be considered to be the author? – for, clearly, all of the members of, say, a large business organisation cannot be the authors of its annual report. And is the performer of music recorded on a compact disc the author? Or the cartographer the author? Or the director of a film? The standards in common use for constructing metadata do not recognise fully the reality of the characteristics of the information resources they seek to describe, or the full diversity of the roles people and organisations can play in their creation. The artificial construct of the *main entry* is a good example of this failure to recognise diversity and cooperation in the creation of many information resources.

There is, however, no doubt that most of the names of persons and organisations which play some part in the intellectual and physical existence of an information resource are important characteristics that assist greatly in identifying that information resource and which are sought by users of information retrieval systems. For these reasons they need to be included as access points. The two questions which need to be resolved in relation to names used as metadata are:

- is the name important enough to note? For example, the name of the author of the text of an information resource is, but the name of an illustrator who contributed a few decorations to it is probably not; and
- if we decide to record the name, in what form should it be noted?

Chapter 4 covers these topics in detail.

Providing subject access

The question 'what is the subject of an information resource' is the most difficult question to address when constructing metadata. The main mechanisms by which subject access is provided can be grouped into three types:

- controlled language indexing schemes (subdivided into alphabetical indexing languages and classification schemes),
- derived indexing, and
- free indexing.

Many information retrieval systems offer a combination of means for subject access. Library catalogues commonly use two or more controlled vocabularies – terms selected from one or more list of subject headings, and a classification scheme. They usually also offer 'keyword searching' of titles, contents lists, and so forth, which can be another powerful way of finding resources covering particular topics.

Controlled language indexing schemes

Subject access mechanisms use terms (usually words or numbers) to summarise and describe the subject of an information resource. These terms are the *vocabulary* of the indexing language. A controlled indexing language scheme uses predefined terms which are selected from an authority list by the indexer (who includes them in a bibliographic record) and by the user (who uses them to locate information resources about a particular subject). Because such lists are made up of selected, predefined terms, they have limitations which may affect their usefulness. For lists used to describe the wide subject range of information resources in a public, state or academic library, the question of comprehensiveness is an obvious concern: how can the vocabulary be comprehensive enough to represent all recorded knowledge? The great expansion of recorded knowledge brought about by the internet makes this question all the more important. Even within a clearly defined subject field (such as engineering) it is impossible to provide a fully comprehensive list. Another concern is the need to keep the vocabulary up-to-date as words and their usage change. To be useful, controlled vocabularies require constant updating so that they match the users' vocabulary, experience and knowledge. Despite these limitations, controlled vocabularies in the form of lists of subject headings, classification schemes and thesauri are currently the primary tools used to provide subject access in information centres, although other techniques are being introduced either to supplement, or in some cases to replace, the use of controlled vocabularies.

Controlled language indexing schemes appear in two forms: *alphabetical indexing languages*, and *classification schemes*. Examples of alphabetical indexing languages include thesauri and subject headings lists. The subject terms selected and defined are represented by a word or phrase in common use in the literature of whatever subject field is being described. These schemes rely on the order of the alphabet, which is an arbitrary order in the sense that subject terms cannot be meaningfully related to each other: for instance, *aborigines* are not related to *abodes* in any particular way but are juxtaposed simply because of alphabetical order. Alphabetical indexing languages do, though, have one significant advantage over classification schemes: they are easy to use because they are based on words and phrases in common use and, thus, accessible to the user. But such familiarity can also pose a major problem: the apparent ease of use – 'we all know what the word means' – disguises differences of meaning which may be significant but are not always easy to distinguish. Synonyms, homonyms, homographs and other 'nyms' and 'graphs' also raise problems which need to be addressed in alphabetical indexing languages.

Classification schemes group concepts with other related concepts, so that the placing of a concept in the scheme bears a meaning, rather than being an arbitrary location. Each subject concept is assigned a notation which can be entirely numerical (familiar in the commonly used Dewey Decimal Classification (DDC) scheme), limited to letters of the alphabet, or a combination of numbers and letters (such as in the Library of Congress Classification (LCC) scheme). The use of notation removes potential concerns, such as the user not fully comprehending differences of meaning of words, but the notation needs to be learnt, at least at a broad level. As with alphabetical indexing languages, the currency of classification schemes is of considerable importance.

Derived indexing languages

With derived indexing languages there is no predetermination or control of the vocabulary used; instead, terms used in the information resource itself are selected as subject access points. This is a form of *natural language indexing*, as is free language indexing (see below). That is, the words and terms naturally occur, they are not taken from an artificial list. In the case of derived indexing, they naturally occur in the resource itself. Such words and terms are typically selected from the title, abstract, or full text of a document. Sometimes there is in fact no conscious effort to select terms – the title, for example, is often recorded as a matter of course, whether or not it is a good representation of a resource's subject. Nevertheless, these metadata can still be used to provide subject access. For instance, it is quite common for library catalogue users to perform a title search as a subject search. The advantages of derived indexing include the fact that little or no intellectual input is required to determine and select the terms. In KWIC (KeyWord In Context) and KWOC (KeyWord Out of Context) indexes, for example, the terms used are automatically selected from the title of the information resource by a computer program. Despite the obvious advantages, such as the reduced need for intellectual input by the indexer when selecting terms (expensive because time-consuming), derived indexing languages have many disadvantages: there is no control over synonyms, and there may be a reduction in access when the authors of documents use vague or idiosyncratic terminology.

Free indexing languages

Free indexing languages are closely related to derived indexing languages, in that there is no attempt to predetermine terms and control the vocabulary. Hence they are also a form of natural language. However, in the case of free language indexing, the indexer is free to use *any* term to describe the subject of an information resource, whether found in the information resource or not. If the indexers who assign the subject terms are very familiar with the vocabulary of their users, then they can assign more useful terms with consistency.

The educational research database AEI (*Australian Education Index*) provides subject access using all three approaches outlined above. Its descriptors (terms denoting subjects of information resources) are of three kinds: descriptors selected from a controlled vocabulary based on its own thesaurus (*Australian Thesaurus of Education Descriptors*); derived language indexing terms provided in the citation and abstract (which together form the bibliographic record); and additional terms selected from any source by the indexer.

These topics, as well as some of the major mechanisms used in libraries to provide subject access, are examined in following chapters.

Systems for bibliographic organisation

As already noted, we require our library information retrieval systems to find an information resource about which the user has some information, to indicate what information resources can be delivered to the user and by what delivery mechanism, to assist in the choice of an information resource, and to deliver a copy of a required information resource to the user. The information retrieval systems in current use in libraries exist in a variety of physical formats, but all share certain characteristics.

Forms of information retrieval systems

Examples of information retrieval systems in common use abound: the library catalogue, the printed bibliography, a finding aid in an archives, an indexing and abstracting database operated by a commercial service, and a museum registry system are just some of them. The traditional typology of the subset of information retrieval systems most closely identified with libraries was the distinction between bibliography, catalogue and index:

- a *bibliography* is a list (usually exhaustive or comprehensive) of information resources in a specified field or by a particular author, usually with no geographical limitation on the location of the information resources;

- a *catalogue* is a list of information resources gathered in a single collection or set of locations, for example, in one library, or accessible from that location; and
- *index* is a term applied very widely; here it is used to mean a list of information resources with a specified limitation, such as on one subject, or in one collection, and this definition includes both bibliographies and catalogues as examples of indexes. The most specific case might be the 'back of the book' index – which refers the reader to particular pages in a single book.

To this traditional typology we now add the internet. The availability of large numbers of information resources through the world wide web has resulted in these distinctions breaking down, as computers and communications networks are integrated into library practice and as the OPAC divests itself of the traditional location functions of the catalogue, and takes on more of the characteristics of the bibliography (Buckland 1992). Despite this complicating factor, the distinction between bibliography and catalogue can still be useful.

Library information retrieval systems have existed in a large number of physical forms over many centuries. Early forms of catalogue included the codex (a manuscript book), the printed book (and its variations such as the sheaf catalogue, loose-leafed to simplify updating), and the card catalogue. Although such forms, and many others, can still be found in countries where information centres have flourished for many centuries, they are rapidly disappearing. The current predominant form of library information retrieval system is the OPAC, although the printed book catalogue, the microfiche catalogue and the card catalogue will also sometimes be found.

Essential requirements for an ideal library information retrieval system are that it:

- can be updated rapidly so that it can be kept current,
- is easy to use,
- is easily scanned (it is easy to view a number of entries on one screen or page), and
- is able to be used simultaneously by as many users as possible.

Other requirements, formerly significant in the era when card catalogues were the dominant form of library information retrieval system, but now of much less significance with the almost complete takeover by OPACs, are that they should be:

- compact (space is money to the manager of an information centre, and card catalogues can take up considerable amount of space), and
- able to be duplicated easily (for instance, for security reasons: the catalogue represents a major investment and management tool for the information centre).

Although some information centres in developed countries still have card-based information retrieval systems (often for documents catalogued before they introduced a computerised system) almost all now have their collections organised in a computerised system. By the 1950s there was considerable concern in the large research libraries of the United States and Britain about many aspects of card catalogues, especially their ever-increasing space requirements as library collections rapidly grew, and about the security aspects, as most of these catalogues existed only in one complete copy because of the difficulty of duplication. The need to address such issues resulted in much analysis of the need for catalogues and considerable research into the possibility of machine-readable catalogues (Grose & Line 1968; Line 1969). This activity culminated in the development of a data format for catalogue records, the Machine-Readable Cataloguing (MARC) format, in the United States, followed rapidly by the introduction, and gradual takeover, of the card catalogue by the computerised catalogue. By 1976 it could be asked 'Is the card catalogue's unquestioned sway in North America ending?' (Elrod 1976).

While it is easy to see why the card catalogue was supplanted, its successor, the OPAC, is not without problems. Although the OPAC can be rapidly updated by bulk loading of new records, is now familiar to most library users, can be used by users at one time (both in the library and remotely), and allows several records to be scanned at one view, it does, however, depend heavily on expensive and complex computing equipment which becomes outdated rapidly.

More about the forms of information retrieval systems, especially those used in the library context, can be found in other standard textbooks about bibliographic organisation (Hunter & Bakewell 1991; Taylor 2006; Chan 2007; Rowley & Farrow 2000).

OPACs

The OPAC has established itself as the dominant form of library information retrieval system, although this dominance is diminishing as other database systems provided by libraries are able to deliver more and more information resources to the user's desktop. The pervasiveness of web search engines such as Google has also challenged this dominance, and OPACs continue to evolve to meet this challenge (though not necessarily as fast as some would like). Indeed, in recent years OPACs have become much more integrated parts of larger retrieval systems that connect catalogues and other databases allowing users to conduct what are known as *federated searches*, that is, searches across a range of databases, including library catalogues.

The OPAC has already evolved considerably over the thirty or so years it has been in use. At first the computer was adopted merely as a more efficient tool for producing catalogue cards, but as computers and telecommunications became more affordable, powerful and widespread, and as library-specific software systems became commercially available, librarians began to see the new possibilities. By the early 1980s it was widely recognised that the days of the card catalogue were numbered, although some vocal supporters still championed them (Baker 1994). The new possibilities offered by the online catalogue were rapidly adopted: greatly improved searching possibilities such as post-coordinated Boolean searching on keywords, instead of access only by the initial word of the title, access through data elements such as ISBN, access to the catalogue at any time, and access to the bibliographic information of other libraries (Kilgour 1984; Malinconico 1984; Fattahi 1996). By 1990 it was possible to state that the online catalogue would have at least 'a machine-readable bibliographic database mounted on a computer with a number of terminals', and also 'powerful searching capacities … links to a circulation system with detailed holdings and status information, an integrated authority control system … [and] information on titles that are "on-order" or "in-process"' (Potter 1990, p.157). Also desirable were transaction monitoring (the ability of a computer catalogue to record how it has been used and therefore to use this data to improve its service), the ability to act as a gateway to other systems and to other machine-readable files, and the ability to mount and make accessible the full texts of some documents. This still reads as the core of a useful specification for a library information retrieval system for today.

More than thirty years of OPAC development has meant that many libraries are implementing perhaps their third or fourth online catalogue, and the new web-based OPACs are often referred to as third or fourth 'generation', or in the case of the more avant-garde models, 'next generation'. Probably the most notable change in the more recent OPACs, or WebPACs as they are sometimes called, is that they provide direct access to information resources as well as the bibliographic data, commonly through hyperlinks from records in the library's catalogues to a full-text document or to an information source on the web, with one click of the mouse. Increasingly, related web resources, such as tables of contents and reviews, are also accessible through the catalogue record. The vast majority of OPACs are now accessible through the web.

The new generation of OPACs offers a wide choice of searching possibilities, ranging from keyword searches in any part of the bibliographic record to precise searches on combinations of specified metadata elements. They can be customised to meet the library's requirements: figures 1.2 and 1.3 show two implementations of the same OPAC software. To varying extents, they can also be customised by the user, particularly in terms of the interface – for instance, the way in which results are presented. On the more advanced catalogues, results can be ranked by relevance in a similar way that search engines rank hits; a user's 'search history' is available; bibliographies can be generated; even set searches can be automatically performed by the system and new results sent electronically to the user. Most OPACs are developed by commercial companies that specialise in library management systems.

What makes information retrieval systems effective?

To make information retrieval systems work effectively, three issues assume considerable importance. These are:

- standards for organising information;
- participation in an agreement for exchanging metadata; and
- participation in cooperatives to gain maximum benefit from exchanging metadata.

Systems that do not address these issues will become increasingly ineffective and decreasingly cost-effective in a global information environment where the paramount consideration is currency of information potentially sourced from any part of the world. Effective library information retrieval systems need to meet certain requirements, categorised here into input requirements and output requirements.

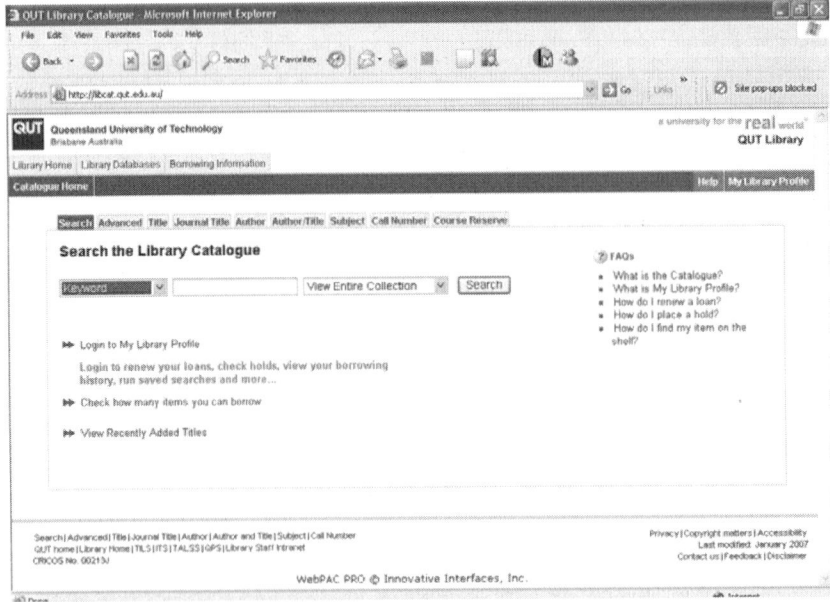

Figure 1.2 Library catalogue, Stockholm School of Economics, Sweden
http://inn.hhs.se/search/Y (accessed 12 December 2007)

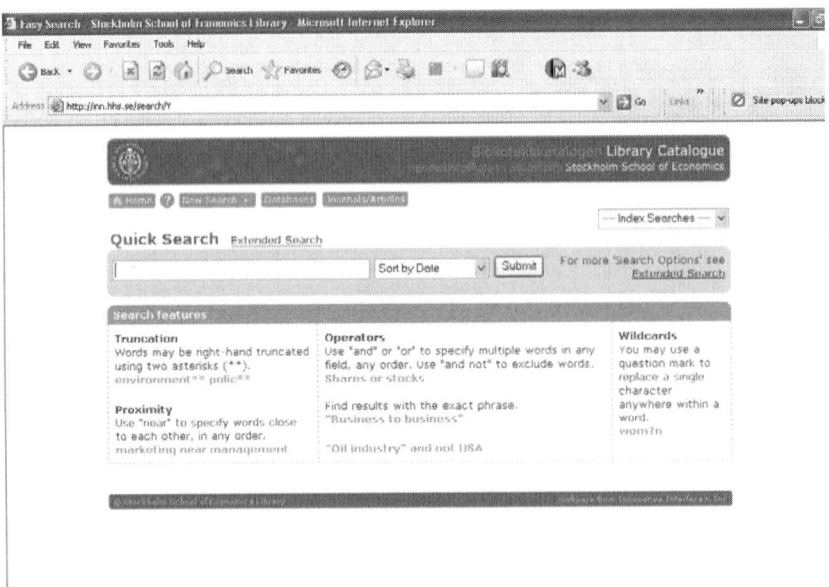

Figure 1.3 Library catalogue, Queensland University of Technology, Australia.
http://libcat.qut.edu.au/ (accessed 12 December 2007)

Some input requirements

Effective information retrieval systems need to satisfy the following requirements in relation to data input:

- data input must adhere to widely-understood standards, so that the resulting records can be widely and readily comprehended;
- data input must require minimal effort (for example, importing already-formatted data is better than intensive keyboarding);
- data input must meet the minimum requirements of the system (for example, it must adequately distinguish between similar information resources such as different editions of the same document); and
- data input must maintain a high level of accuracy and consistency.

Some output requirements

The following are requirements in relation to data output if an information retrieval system is to be effective:

- data output must be readily understandable to the user;
- data output must match users' requests as closely as possible;
- the system must be user-friendly;
- the system should respond to users' requests as rapidly as possible; and
- output must not be restricted to a limited number of terminals, but should be capable of being used simultaneously by all users who require it.

Sources of bibliographic records

Library information retrieval systems rely on two sources for the bibliographic records that are put into the system. Either the information centre that operates the information retrieval system creates the bibliographic records, or they are imported. In practice the bibliographic records for most library catalogues are drawn from both sources, the precise mix depending on the needs and resources of the information centre. For instance, a library with responsibility for bibliographic control of the national imprint will almost certainly produce bibliographic records for most of that nation's printed output. A public library, however, will import almost all of its records; and an information centre in a business environment may fall somewhere in between and create bibliographic records for its parent organisation's technical reports and other publications, but import records for other information resources.

Creating the records in-house

Metadata created by an information centre need to meet certain standards so that the users of the information retrieval system will be offered the best result. As one example, if the vocabulary used for subject access is not fully and regularly checked for consistency, then the system will not distinguish between synonyms and will thus not perform as effectively as it should. Another example is the consequence of not checking the spelling of titles, for here any errors directly affect the ability of the system to retrieve all relevant information resources by keyword title searches.

Importing the data

Although in the past information centres created most of their own bibliographic records, in current practice much of this data is imported. Why has this change occurred? The reasons for importing metadata records in preference to creating them locally fall into two categories:

- the cost savings which can occur, and
- the benefits of sharing data created to the same standards for improving the service which the information centre offers.

Not all agree with the widespread importing of bibliographic records, often with little or no editing. Critics base their objections on the inflexibility that they perceive is imposed by accepting records created by other institutions that may have different aims. Other information professionals, however, believe that not enough use is made of externally created metadata, and call for more use of publishers' information, author-generated metadata, and metadata created by computers. In reality, there are still many resources for which few metadata exist, and libraries have little choice but to create their own records, particularly in the case of many non-print media such as music, computer software, and interactive multimedia, and also in the case of archival and unpublished materials.

Exchange of bibliographic records

Universal bibliographic control has been an aim of libraries for many centuries. It is the concept that all of the world's published output can be listed and thus controlled. If all bibliographic records were constructed according to the same standards, and if there were some way in which these standardised bibliographic records could be shared, then every information resource in the world would have to be catalogued only once; others who wanted a copy of that record could then procure it for use in their own information retrieval system. If this arrangement could be made to work, the outcome would be greatly increased efficiency in organising information, for cataloguing is a time-consuming, skilled and therefore expensive process. There would also be opportunities to improve greatly the service offered to users by being able to access and understand bibliographic records in the information retrieval systems of other libraries, because they were based on the same standards, and therefore to expand the quantity of information resources which could be offered to the user from the collections of other information centres as well as from one's own centre.

To this end many schemes have been implemented, with varying degrees of success. In recent decades one scheme, the UBCIM (previously UBC) Core Programme of IFLA (International Federation of Library Associations and Institutions) achieved remarkable success. The UBCIM Programme, which was closed in 2003 and superseded by the IFLA-CDNL Alliance for Bibliographic Standards (ICABS), was organised through a series of international agreements, so that one agency in each country (usually a national library) took responsibility for preparing, or coordinating the preparation of, the bibliographic records for that country's publications, and then sent copies of these bibliographic records to agencies in other countries. It also ensured that libraries in their own country had access to these records. This is international cooperation on a large scale. For the exchange of bibliographic records to operate successfully there are two main requirements:

* the use of agreed standards, and

* agreements about who accepts responsibility for which tasks.

Standards

International agreement about two sets of standards is needed for UBC (Universal Bibliographic Control) to work. The first requirement is for standards for the creation of bibliographic records (for example, AACR and ISBD (International Standard Bibliographic Description)); the second is for standards for exchanging bibliographic records (for example a common data format for exchanging records in electronic form, such as the MARC format). We examine these standards in later chapters.

Responsibilities

Also essential are agreements about which agency, or agencies, in each country takes responsibility for providing bibliographic records for that country's published output and for disseminating records from other countries to information centres within that country.

In Australia the National Library of Australia assumes general responsibility for universal bibliographic control. That role is considered at greater length in chapter 13.

Conclusion

Part I has set the scene for the rest of the book. Chapter 1 has provided an overview of bibliographic organisation: an outline of the processes which are carried out, why we carry out these processes, who the users of the products of the bibliographic organisation tasks are, and how we meet the needs of those users. The main tasks of bibliographic organisation are identified: describing information resources so that they can be uniquely identified, providing access to these information resources through various attributes such as names of people and organisations, and providing access to them through their subjects. Finally, the computer-based systems we use for bibliographic organisation are briefly noted.

Part II is concerned with the many different standards that form the basis of effective bibliographic organisation. It begins with an examination of some general aspects of standards for bibliographic data, in chapter 2.

PART II: BIBLIOGRAPHIC DESCRIPTION

Introduction

The second part of this book covers bibliographic description. This term is normally employed to mean the process, and product, of describing non-subject aspects of information resources, and that is how it is used here. Non-subject aspects include titles, authors, dates of publication, size, edition statements, and many other things – anything, in fact, worth noting that is not concerned, or at least not specifically, with the subject of a resource.

Bibliographic description is normally based on certain *standards*. Much of its form and content is the result of the cataloguer following a particular set of standards, and so we need to examine why these standards are followed, what sort of bibliographic descriptions result, and what impact they have on the end-user.

Chapter 2 examines how standards in the field of bibliographic organisation assist libraries and other information providers to meet their objectives, and what kinds of standards are applied. Chapters 3 to 5 relate some specific examples of standards for bibliographic data. Chapter 3 covers standards for the description itself. Chapter 4 considers standards for indexing certain elements of the description. Chapter 5 looks at authority control, a way of ensuring that the indexes to the bibliographic data enable optimal retrieval – for which there are also certain standards.

CHAPTER 2
Standards for bibliographic data

This chapter examines how standards in the field of bibliographic organisation assist libraries and other information services meet their objectives. It notes one specific category of bibliographic standard: those necessary to ensure international uniformity in the construction of databases of bibliographic information, including library catalogues. The characteristics of bibliographic data (or metadata) are identified; also discussed is the conventional division of bibliographic data elements into those that *describe* the item, for example, its size, and those that allow *access* to the data and thus the item, for example, author name or title.

Why standards are necessary

'The value of standardization as a means to avoid the duplication of cataloging effort and to facilitate the exchange of bibliographic data has long been recognized' (Svenonius 1989, p.41). Standards are vital for organising information. The many advantages that come from using standards include:

- *economies* can be achieved through the exchange of standardised bibliographic records among information centres,

- *quality control* is maintained, and

- users become *familiar* with standardised structures and formats employed by information retrieval systems throughout the world.

There are in fact various levels of standardisation. Most information retrieval systems aim at *internal* standardisation, so that each record of bibliographic data contains many of the same elements, formatted in a similar fashion. However, many systems also adhere to standards that are adhered to in other systems. This higher level of standardisation allows users, who increasingly interact on a regular basis with a string of separate information retrieval systems, to become familiar with all of them more quickly. It also makes it easier to systems to 'talk' to each other so that federated, that is, all-in-one, searches can be performed across different databases and institutions.

Apart from end-users, cataloguers and other metadata creators also benefit from standards, for they often find it easier to work with rules, or at least guidelines, which advise them how to record the various elements of metadata, and which elements to record. Cataloguers still have to make decisions, according to these guidelines, but many of the more basic decisions are already there for them to follow, speeding up the cataloguing process. Should the bibliographic description include the dimensions of the item? How about the name of the fourth author? Where and how should a statement about a video's playing time be recorded?

Such questions – and there are thousands of other, similar questions – can be answered by consulting the standard rules and guidelines.

There is, however, an even more important reason why libraries and other information centres welcome standardisation of bibliographic data: economics. If they wish the bibliographic information in their database to include particular elements and to be set out in a particular format, then it saves them a lot of work if other databases are based on the same standards, for it means that bibliographic records for the same or similar resources can be shared. From such sharing flow real economies, as well as greatly enhanced opportunities for meeting the needs of users.

Standards have become more important than ever before with the use of computers for bibliographic organisation. Although some commentators have argued that as computing increases in effectiveness (faster processing speeds, full-text searching capabilities), so the need for bibliographic standards will decrease, it is becoming increasingly clear that if the information riches of the internet are to be effectively harnessed for serious information seekers, then certain kinds of standards are critical, and although certain standards may need to adapt, the process of standardisation is if anything becoming more intense.

Standardisation in Australia

The value of standardisation has long been recognised in Australian libraries. Early references to standardisation are found in the proceedings of the First Australasian Library Conference held in Melbourne in 1896. H.C.L. Anderson, of the Public Library of New South Wales, remarked that 'the compilation of a recognised list of ... [subject] index headings seems to me a fit subject for cooperation among the librarians of Australia' (Library Association of Australasia 1896, p.16) and Caleb Hardy of the University of Sydney deplored 'the enormous waste of time and energy' expended in developing classification schemes and argued for the adoption of 'some universal system ... the Decimal Classification of M. Dewey ... seems to meet these requirements' (Library Association of Australasia 1896, p.56). Somewhat more recently, Janet Hine's 1973 survey of cataloguing practices in Australian libraries demonstrated that 'most libraries are operating according to standards which are compatible with those developing internationally, and that they are prepared to keep up-to-date in most areas of standardization' (Hine 1973, p.12). In the decades since Hine's survey the situation has become even more uniform with widespread participation in Libraries Australia, formerly known as Kinetica, and before that, the Australian Bibliographic Network (ABN).

The consequences of not using standards

What happens if an information centre does not follow common standards for bibliographic control? It effectively removes itself from the mainstream: there are reduced – perhaps no – opportunities to download external bibliographic data, and the resulting economies and other advantages will not be available. Perhaps most critically, the information centre will not have access to the massive quantities of bibliographic records available in the MARC format. This is of particular concern since most of the commercially available computer systems and software for automating library processes still rely on the MARC format as a standard for importing, maintaining and exporting bibliographic data, although other, newer exchange formats, such as RDF/XML, are beginning to be taken up by some of the system vendors.

However, there is sometimes a need for an information centre to deviate from the common standards. This may be in order to accommodate local needs and local variations in bibliographic organisation practice. It is important that the need to deviate from the standards is genuine – it is all too often merely an elitist urge to be different for its own sake. The implications of developing local standards must be fully understood: for instance, there may be increased costs incurred because of the need to edit imported bibliographic records to make them conform to the local standards.

This dilemma – of standards versus cataloguing tailored to local needs – has been present for well over a century of centralised library practice, and is difficult to resolve satisfactorily, as Donald Cook points out. He notes that it is important to:

> question seriously all local variations with a view to eliminating those which result simply from the inertia of existing records, from purely economic considerations, and from 'whims' or resentment at being told what to do. At the international level, we need to ask these questions of our own national practices as we compare these with the practices of other countries with which we wish to cooperate (Cook 1986, p.25).

However, the standards used for bibliographic organisation are often criticised by managers of information centres who frequently face the need to contain, or even reduce, costs. Their argument is based on the belief that the local information centre does not need the level of detail required by current international standards. Consequently, they argue, the standards should be simplified, in order to save time and other resources in the construction, storage and manipulation of bibliographic records. This is a powerful (if self-centred) argument, which can only be countered by appreciating the value brought to the information centre by adhering to internationally-agreed standards. As indicated later in this chapter, those who develop such standards are well aware of this issue, and the standards continue to be actively examined to see if they are indeed too complex and contain too many unnecessary requirements.

Who sets the standards

A question of some significance is: who sets bibliographic standards? They are not developed by nameless bureaucrats remote from the day-to-day concerns of information centres, but rather by numerous practitioners throughout the world who provide input based on their actual concerns and everyday practice. The process by which this advice is finally reflected in the standards is effective, but often slow and cumbersome.

Standards are essentially *agreements*. The more parties involved, the more difficult it is to come to an agreement, or to a new agreement. However, standards do need to be revised, particularly as the types of information resource continue to diversify. Although the process may be slow, eventually it happens. To take only one example, the *International Standard*

Bibliographic Description (ISBD), established in the 1970s, initially took no account of CD-ROMs and online resources, because these information media had not yet been developed and were not to be found in libraries. The ISBD could still be applied when describing these resources, since the standard was developed from a set of general principles in a framework that could accommodate new media, but these particular media have now become so prominent that a specific treatment of them was incorporated in the *ISBD for Electronic Resources*, ISBD(ER), published in 1997. This could be done quite smoothly because procedures have always been in place for regular updates of ISBD.

Emerging standards

There has been concern expressed, however, that some of the older standards have been adapting too slowly to the new information technology, and that, instead, a paradigm shift is required on the part of the standards' setters. Modern computing power and networking have made *digital libraries* feasible, consisting of digital objects that may be derived from the physical collections not only of libraries, but also of other kinds of information centres, such as archives, museums, educational institutions, and government departments, or that may have been 'born digital'. Indeed, it is now possible for many people to contribute their own resources to the largest (albeit poorly organised) 'digital library' of all – the internet – by establishing their own personal websites. Such convergence of information resources requires convergence of metadata for these resources, and this means new frameworks that accommodate metadata derived from the different bibliographic standards applied by the various information communities. It may also mean that existing standards will have to make greater efforts to fit into these new frameworks.

The most popular alternative to the older standards is currently Dublin Core (DC). This standard provides a framework for metadata creators to describe the essential bibliographic data for all types of resources, including new kinds of digital object. It is designed to accommodate the primary metadata needs across domains and has been developed with inputs from a wide variety of metadata specialists, not just librarians. As its name suggests, Dublin Core aims to include the core elements of metadata only. Additional elements may be, and often are, recorded according to the local context. Furthermore, DC gives the cataloguer the freedom to adopt different styles and vocabularies *within* its framework.

DC is therefore considered by many to be more flexible than many of the older, pre-digital standards. This flexibility allows for the *interoperability* among different information retrieval systems and databases that is necessary, or at least desirable, in the networked world of today. The fact that Dublin Core pays special attention to the types and nature of the metadata required for the organisation and administration of digital information resources demonstrates the forward-looking approach of its authors. Other emerging standards are discussed further in following chapters, in particular, chapter 10.

Characteristics of bibliographic data

As noted in chapter 1, information resources in the collections of information centres are often represented by databases of *surrogate* records containing bibliographic data, or metadata. Access to the information resources is achieved by providing access to the surrogate records that represent them. For information retrieval purposes, surrogate records have many advantages over the full text (or image, video, and so on) of the resources themselves: for example, they take up less storage space than the actual resource, yet if appropriately constructed they represent as many of the resource's characteristics as are necessary to provide effective access. Surrogate records can work in this context because information resources in the collections of libraries and other information centres are usually constructed according to well-established conventions and standards, with readily identifiable characteristics.

Bibliographic conventions

What are the characteristics, or *bibliographic conventions*, of information resources that have traditionally been used to describe the resource and on which the standards for bibliographic records are based? Why have they arisen? And are these conventions still valid?

As noted in chapter 1, the metadata elements usually used to describe books include:

- title,
- name of author, and
- details of publication (place of publication, name of publisher, date of publication).

For resources other than books, these metadata elements may have less, or perhaps no, relevance. Many graphic materials, for instance, are unpublished and thus have no details of publication, and many do not have an explicit title. Conversely, descriptions of non-print items often include other data elements not applicable to books. For example, for an information resource (such as a computer file) that relies on a mechanical or electronic device to make the data it contains accessible, an essential metadata element may be information about the playback equipment. These issues are examined in more detail in chapter 3.

Why have these conventions arisen? The answer lies in the development of the information storage media themselves, as well as in the history of library catalogues and other kinds of library information retrieval systems.

The key point here is that the conventions have developed over many decades, even centuries, because they are useful, and they form the basis of the standards we use to build bibliographic records in our library information retrieval systems. However, we find that the more recent the media, the less settled are the conventions, with the consequence that the bibliographic standards are less comprehensive and not nearly as uniform. For example, the standards for remote access computer files (such as internet files) are still evolving and, as such, there is considerable debate about the composition of their metadata.

How much metadata?

Not every type of information centre needs the same amount of metadata. For example, a national library, which carries responsibility for providing metadata for all documents published in that country, and also for making the records available internationally, will develop very full bibliographic records. But a smaller information centre (a special library, say, with only a small collection of books) will probably not need so much metadata. To accommodate differing needs the concept of different levels of bibliographic record has been developed; these levels are sometimes referred to as full, medium (or core), and brief. Three *levels of description* are thus set out in the first part of the *Anglo-American Cataloguing Rules* (AACR). Whether cataloguers using AACR create full, medium, or brief bibliographic records, they are still adhering to the same basic standard.

So, one important question to examine is: how brief should a bibliographic record be? We can answer this question by looking again at the reasons we create bibliographic records. Cutter's objectives, noted in chapter 1, suggest that the information resource needs to be described only as fully as is necessary to set it apart from other resources, and only as fully as will make it easy to find. After many decades where internationally-agreed library cataloguing codes insisted on full records, almost regardless of the use for which these records were intended, the question of record size was the focus of considerable research. Some of the most significant research was conducted by the Centre for Catalogue Research in Bath, England, which focused on 'the effectiveness of library catalogues with regard to the level of content of the entries', with special emphasis on users' needs and how usable catalogues with different levels of content are. This research noted: 'The conclusion suggests that much of the information normally included in the catalogue entry is very rarely used by readers, and its inclusion makes catalogues difficult to use with the result that some items may not be found' (Seal 1983, p.144).

The question of 'how brief' is an issue in the context of economic constraints in library and information centres, and in many cases the costs of constructing bibliographic records and of maintaining them in an online database have been questioned. One illustration is the attention paid by national bibliographic agencies to 'minimal-level cataloguing' (Horny 1991; Lambrecht 1992). Recently, the Library of Congress in the United States has established a new 'access level' for remote access electronic resources, which focuses on those bibliographic elements needed for resource discovery, that is, those that are searched on, rather than those used primarily for selection. The theory is that for such resources, display elements are much less important as the resource itself is just one click away.

Paradoxically, at the same time as there is an interest in reducing the amount of metadata, there is also an interest in the benefits which can result from including more metadata, especially the kind of metadata required to provide *subject* access to information resources. The addition of more than the traditional metadata elements is common in contemporary digital library projects, and is by no means uncommon in today's WebPACs. Three examples of expanding record content are:

- the addition of an abstract to a standard library bibliographic record to make that record more useful to the user – for example, adding a summary of the plot for fiction, or of a film;

- the addition of keywords from the contents page or index of a book to a standard library bibliographic record to improve subject access; and

- links to related material on the web, such as book reviews, author biodata and cover images.

So, while there has been a trend to 'downsize' many parts of bibliographic description, there is also something of a counter-trend to enhance those parts of bibliographic records that provide subject access, or that significantly assist users in selecting the most useful and relevant resources. This counter-trend will be discussed further in chapter 14.

Are the conventions still valid?

Are the standards used for constructing bibliographic records in the library context still valid? After all, they are based on cataloguing rules which have been established according to principles developed many years – in some cases centuries – ago. Do they still meet the requirements of organising information and information retrieval in the digital age?

The reasons for retaining these standards, and the conventions on which they are based, are many and include:

- their use is widespread: users of library information retrieval systems either know them, or can easily find out what they are;

- they allow users of library information retrieval systems to readily transfer their knowledge of one system to another, if both are based on the same conventions, increasing the usability of these systems;

- they improve the ease with which bibliographic records created for one system can be transferred to another system; and

- there exists huge amounts of bibliographic data based on these standards that represent enormous numbers of valuable resources – probably the majority of items in the world's library collections.

Perhaps it is this last point that is most critical here. To recatalogue all these resources, or even just to digitise them, is obviously not a task that is going to be accomplished any time soon (despite the best efforts of Google Books, etc.), and so libraries are not really in a position to simply disregard the traditional bibliographic data – it would be far too wasteful, and would be a monumental step *backwards* for the cause of Universal Bibliographic Control. An alternative is to move to new standards but to devise ways in which the old metadata can still be utilised – in other words, address the issue, in a positive way, of *legacy data* (the data based on the old conventions).

There are, however, in certain situations, reasons for discarding old conventions (or parts of them) and for adopting new conventions, particularly if issues concerning legacy data can be successfully addressed. These include:

- some conventions were developed for earlier situations which are no longer valid. For example, is the height of a book useful to note in the modern bibliographic record? Most books published now fall within a narrow range of sizes, because standard paper sizes are widely adopted (and e-books have no dimensions at all). Instead of noting the height, we could perhaps assume that a physical book will fall within the range of standard sizes and only note it if it comes outside the range; and

- the conventions, although still valid, may cost too much to implement without noticeably improving the effectiveness with which an information resource can be retrieved. As mentioned above, research has indicated that fuller level bibliographic records do not add much value for the average catalogue user, yet they are much more expensive to produce than are brief records, since they require much more expertise and time to create.

Despite recent questioning of the conventions, the *standards* for constructing metadata records – whether the older, well-established ones, such as ISBD, or the newer ones, such as Dublin Core – are still the key to organising information in libraries.

It should be noted that, while some of these standards are officially ratified and adopted by national and international cataloguing agencies and library associations, others are *de facto* standards – that is, they are standards only by virtue of being widely used and they have no official status. And there are other tools which cannot be called standards except in a very general sense: they are sets of precedents which tend to be followed, but from which there is often considerable deviation.

Conclusion

Chapter 2 has examined some general aspects of standards used in the field of bibliographic organisation: why standards are necessary, what happens if we do not use them, who sets the standards, and some of the primary characteristics of bibliographic data which determine what kinds of standards are necessary.

Chapter 3 notes one important set of standards, those used for bibliographic description. Two international standards for description, ISBD and Part I of AACR2, are examined in detail.

CHAPTER 3
Standards for description

Bibliographic description forms the basis of any document retrieval system. In whatever way users may search the database of surrogate records, on whichever metadata elements (subject, title, name, etc.), once they have retrieved a set of records, users will often select (or eliminate) a particular document (represented by one of those records) according to certain elements of the bibliographic description; or, in the case of a known-item search, users will identify the particular document (or eliminate others) according to the bibliographic description. Even in the case of full-text databases, the user will be presented with titles and authors and other bibliographic information, and will normally consider these (as well as abstracts and subject descriptors) before downloading the whole document. Even when the 'document' is of an audiovisual nature, basic elements of bibliographic description will still usually be required by the user.

Chapter 3 considers standards which *describe* the bibliographic characteristics of information resources: in particular ISBD and Part I of AACR2. ISBD is the main international standard applied to the selection and formatting of metadata elements in bibliographic records, although there are various alternative standards quite often used for certain types of special material. Part I of AACR2, which (largely) follows ISBD, is extensively used in the English-speaking library cataloguing world, as indeed is the other part of AACR2 (Part II), but this deals with *access* to the descriptive elements, and is examined in chapter 4. Chapter 3 concludes with a brief discussion of other standards used to describe information resources.

Before we examine the development of ISBD, it is worth noting that conventions for constructing bibliographic records in library catalogues have remained relatively stable over many years. Figure 3.1 illustrates this point – and, in particular, shows that the selection of metadata elements to describe a document has remained remarkably consistent for one and a half centuries. These examples of bibliographic records for the same item have been constructed using different library cataloguing standards published between 1841 and 2002.

ISBD

Origins of ISBD

The *International Standard Bibliographic Description* is one example of a standard in common use for describing information resources. It was developed following the International Conference on Cataloguing Principles, organised by IFLA in 1961 to try to reach international agreement on cataloguing standards. In 1966 and 1967 Michael Gorman (who later became the editor of AACR2) conducted a study for IFLA on the descriptive

Anglo-American Cataloguing Rules, 2nd ed. (2002 rev.)
New rules for an old game : proceedings of a workshop on the 1967 Anglo-American cataloguing code held by the School of Librarianship, the University of British Columbia, April 13 and 14, 1967 / edited by Thelma E. Allen, Daryl Ann Dickman. – Melbourne [Vic.] : F.W. Cheshire, 1968.
175 p. ; 24 cm.
Bibliography: p. 161-165.
Includes index.

Anglo-American Cataloguing Rules (1967)
Allen, Thelma E., ed.
New rules for an old game; proceedings of a workshop on the 1967 Anglo-American cataloguing code held by the School of Librarianship, the University of British Columbia, April 13 and 14, 1967. Edited by Thelma E. Allen [and] Daryl Ann Dickman. Melbourne: F.W. Cheshire [1968].
175 p. 24 cm.
Bibliography: p. 161-165.

Rules for Descriptive Cataloging in the Library of Congress (1949)
Workshop on the 1967 Anglo-American Cataloguing Code, University of British Columbia, 1967.
New rules for an old game. Edited by Thelma E. Allen [and] Daryl Ann Dickman. Melbourne, F.W. Cheshire, [1968].
175 p. 24 cm.
'Proceedings of a workshop on the 1967 Anglo-American cataloguing code held by the School of Librarianship, The University of British Columbia, April 13 and 14, 1967.'
'Bibliography': p. 161-165.

Cataloguing Rules: Author and Title Entries (1908)
Allen, Thelma E., *and* Dickman, Daryl Ann, eds.
New rules for an old game; proceedings of a workshop on the 1967 Anglo-American cataloguing code held by the School of Librarianship, The University of British Columbia, April 13 and 14, 1967, edited by Thelma E. Allen [and] Daryl Ann Dickman. Melbourne, F.W. Cheshire, [1968].
175 p. 23.5 cm.
'Bibliography': p. 161-165.

British Museum. Rules for Compiling the Catalogues ... (1841)
CANADA. – *Workshop on the 1967 Anglo-American Cataloguing Code.*
New Rules for an Old Game : proceedings of a workshop ... School of Librarianship, The University of British Columbia, April 13 and 14, 1967. Edited by Thelma E. Allen [and] Daryl Ann Dickman. pp. 175. *F.W. Cheshire: Melbourne*, 1968. 8°.

Figure 3.1 Bibliographic descriptions constructed according to five cataloguing standards

cataloguing practice of eight national bibliographic agencies. His report was discussed at the International Meeting of Cataloguing Experts in Copenhagen in 1969. A draft version of ISBD was developed, circulated internationally for comment, and published in December 1971. After further revision a first standard edition of ISBD(M) (the 'M' indicating monographs) was published in 1974 (ISBD(M) 1974).

The ISBD(M) was followed quickly by ISBDs for other formats, as well as ISBD(G) (the 'G' indicating general) in 1977. ISBD(G) was developed as a framework to be used for

ISBDs for specific formats. It was necessary because the earlier ISBDs had discrepancies which it was deemed important to bring into line.

ISBD rapidly found favour. It was adopted immediately after the draft edition appeared in December 1971 by the *British National Bibliography* (BNB) (in 1972) and in the 1972 cumulation of the *Australian National Bibliography* (ANB) (Langker 1974a). It was eventually implemented by the Library of Congress in September 1974, and its future was assured when it was adopted as the basis for Part I (Description) of the second edition of AACR (i.e., AACR2) published in 1978. This meant that its use became widespread internationally, for AACR2 found favour in many places across the world and was quite widely translated.

In 2007, the 'family' of ISBDs for various formats was superseded by a consolidated version that, like the former ISBD(G), is intended to apply to all forms of material. The new standard is also aligned with the influential *Functional Requirements for Bibliographic Records* (more on FRBR later in the chapter). The consolidation recognises the increasing convergence of media in the online environment: websites, for example, are often a mix of text, images, sound and video, and do not readily fit into one particular category.

Aims of ISBD

The primary purpose of the ISBD is to standardise descriptive cataloguing practice throughout the world in order 'to aid the international communication of bibliographic information' (ISBD(M) 1974, p.1). It achieves this by:

- making records from different sources interchangeable, so that records produced in one country can be easily accepted in library catalogues or other bibliographic lists in any other country;

- assisting in the interpretation of records across language barriers, so that records produced for users of one language can be interpreted by users of other languages; and

- assisting in the conversion of bibliographic records to machine-readable form.

The ISBD defines the elements of the description part of the bibliographic record precisely and prescribes both the order in which these elements are presented and how they are demarcated.

Features of ISBD

The most important characteristics of ISBD are:

- its comprehensiveness – it aims to provide a uniform descriptive framework for all types of library material, including formats not yet devised;

- its fixed order of data elements; and

- its use of punctuation as delimiters or dividers between the different bibliographic elements.

ISBD achieves its aim of international standardisation of practice by using a framework of eight *areas*, which is to be applied to all resources:

1. title and statement of responsibility area,
2. edition area,
3. material or type of resource specific area,
4. publication, production, distribution, etc. area,
5. physical description area,
6. series area,
7. note area, and
8. resource identifier and terms of availability area.

Figure 3.2 illustrates the application of the eight ISBD areas.

Example 1: English-language item with ISBD areas marked
Trees and shrubs of New Zealand [text] / A.L. Poole and Nancy M. Adams. *[Area 1]* – Rev. ed. *[Area 2]* – Wellington : DSIR, 1990. *[Area 4]* – iv, 256 p. : ill., map ; 25 cm. *[Area 5]* – (DSIR field guide). *[Area 6]* – First ed. published Wellington : Govt. Printer, 1963. – Includes index. *[Area 7]* – ISBN 0477026036 *[Area 8]*

Example 2: Non-English language item with ISBD areas marked
Kisah-kisah sufi [text] / oleh Idries Shah ; penerjemah: Sapardi Djoko Darmano. *[Area 1]* – Cet. 3. *[Area 3]* – Jakarta : Pustaka Firdaus, 1989. *[Area 4]* – x, 149 p. ; 19 cm. *[Area 5]*

Example 3: Non-print item with ISBD areas marked
Computer Centre handbook [electronic resource] / Nanyang Technological University. *[Area 1]* – 1992- . *[Area 3]* – Singapore : Nanyang Technological University Computer Centre, [1992-] *[Area 4]*. – computer disks : col. ; 3½ in. *[Area 5]* – Annual. – Title from title screen. – Title on disk label: Electronic handbook. – Description based on 1994 issue. *[Area 7]*

Figure 3.2 The areas of ISBD, with ISBD punctuation

1) *Title and statement of responsibility area*. Most information resources have a title and some indication of the person, people or groups responsible for its content. These data elements are recorded in the first of the ISBD areas, the *title and statement of responsibility area*. Although the emphasis here (as elsewhere in the ISBDs) is on transcribing the wording and spelling of the title and statement of responsibility exactly from the resource, on rare occasions the cataloguer is obliged to supply a title (say, for a manuscript). Statements of responsibility include those such as 'written by', 'edited by', 'illustrated by', 'performed by', 'produced by'. This area is also the place to record what is termed *other title information*, that is, subtitles, and also *parallel titles* (those which are a translation of the title in another language, sometimes found in multilingual publications).

2) *Edition area.* Any information relating to the edition of an information resource is recorded in this area. This information is often straightforward (for example, 2nd ed., 4th rev. ed., 1st Australian ed.) but is occasionally more complex. The concept of edition has had to be revisited for the non-traditional media, most notably for electronic resources, where different versions may be issued simultaneously (e.g., Windows and Mac versions) or may be issued 'on top' of its previous version, and constantly, as in the case of most websites. The series of revisions that occur in many online resources are, in fact, treated not as new editions, but as *iterations* of 'integrating resources', more akin to issues of a serial.

3) *Material or type of resource specific details area.* The third ISBD area is not applied to the description of all types of media. It is used only for cartographic materials (maps, charts, globes and such like), music scores, and serials. This area performs different functions and takes different names for each of the media to which it applies: for instance, for maps the data recorded in this area – the *mathematical data area* – is scale (for example, 1:50,000) and projection, so that the user can determine whether the map is the right kind to suit the intended purpose, and to differentiate one map from another covering the same area but at a different scale. For serials, the *numbering area* is used to provide information about issue numbering. A typical statement of this kind is in the form: Vol. 1, no. 1 (Feb. 1974)-v. 5, no. 4 (Dec. 1978).

4) *Publication, production, distribution, etc. area.* This area applies to all media. It is the area in which to record information about the place from where the information resource comes (such as place of publication, and sometimes the place of manufacture), the name of the publisher or other body responsible for the information resource's production and distribution, and the date of publication, issue or manufacture/creation. For commercially published books, this area usually presents few problems (typical examples are Adelaide : Libraries Board of South Australia, 1992; Ringwood, Vic. : McPhee Gribble, 1991). For other media these metadata elements can be more difficult to identify. Indeed, in some cases, they are not applicable – for example, for unpublished manuscripts, only a date of creation is recorded (and even that often has to be inferred or estimated).

5) *Physical description area.* Formerly called the *Physical description area*, this now applies also to non-physical, remote access resources. Most of the information recorded in this area is divided into three general sections: extent of item, other physical details, and dimensions. The *extent of item* section answers the question 'how many?': examples are 135 pages; 2 microfilm reels; 1 piano roll. Information recorded in the *other physical details* section varies according to the medium. Some examples are of illustrations in books (25 col. ill.); of the colour of a graphic item (b&w or col.); of the nature of a graphic item (engraving, tinted); of characteristics of videorecordings and films (Panavision); and of projection speed for a film, if non-standard (25 fps). The *dimensions* of each medium are also usually recorded: for example, for books the height (19 cm.); for computer disks the size (3½ in., 5¼ in.); and for videodiscs the diameter (12 in.).

6) *Series area.* Publishers and distributors often group together related items and supply a collective title to the group. Because this collective title (series title) often indicates useful information about the standard or authority of the individual titles in the series, or about the style, subject coverage, or intended audience of the information resources, it is usually

included in the description of the resource. Like titles in the first ISBD area, the series title is transcribed exactly, and any numbering in the series is also included. Typical examples are: (Topics in Australasian library and information studies ; no. 7); (Lonely planet travel survival kit). Note how parentheses are used in ISBD to identify this metadata as series statements.

7) *Note area.* The note area is where you place everything else you need to record to describe the item, but for which there is no clearly defined place in any of the other ISBD areas. The notes can cover a very wide range of aspects. Typical categories of notes are: *mode of access* – Online access via AUSINET; *nature and scope or artistic form* – Comedy in two acts, Spreadsheet with word processing and graphic capabilities; *language of item* – English dialogue, Japanese subtitles; *accompanying material and supplements* – Accompanied by installation instructions; *summary* – Eight versions of a video game for 1-2 players. To survive, players use laser cannons to destroy flying demons; and, *contents* – Includes index, Statistical tables cover period 1849-1960.

8) *Resource identifier and terms of availability area.* The final ISBD area is used to record the resource identifiers such as standard numbers if they are present on an item: for books this is likely to be an ISBN (International Standard Book Number), which has recently changed from a 10-digit to a 13-digit number, and for serials, an ISSN (International Standard Serial Number). Additionally, *terms of availability* (for example: $10.00; For hire) can be recorded in this area after the standard number.

For each of these eight areas further conventions are specified in ISBD:

- 'sources of information': from where the cataloguer should take the information, and in what order, for each of the eight areas and for each of the different media covered by ISBDs (e.g., for books, primarily the title page, then other sources such as the cover and the back of the title page, known as the title page verso); and

- the punctuation which should be used within each area and also to delineate each area: examples can be seen in figure 3.2.

Future of ISBD

Are the three aims of ISBD outlined earlier still relevant today? Have they become unnecessary or obsolete because of changing technology?

The first aim (making records from different sources interchangeable) has been achieved, as shown by the widespread exchange of bibliographic records that use this standard (mainly through AACR2). Whether the second aim (to assist in the interpretation of records across language barriers) has been achieved is perhaps less clear-cut. There is little doubt that ISBD punctuation assists in comprehending records in unfamiliar languages by marking the metadata elements clearly. We can, for instance, look at a record in ISBD format in a language and, perhaps, a script with which we are unfamiliar, and easily determine which part of it is, say, the statement of responsibility. To illustrate this, examine the second example in figure 3.2. You might not be able to read the language, yet you can still deduce much of the description's bibliographic information because it is based on ISBD. However, ISBD is no longer the only means of achieving this goal, as labels for metadata elements can easily be translated into different languages that can then be displayed by a computer according to a user's preferences. Such labels consist of words, which are more readily intelligible to users than are colons and semi-colons. In fact, even online library catalogues that could display the full ISBD punctuation usually do not, and instead use various (non-standard) terms to introduce particular elements.

ISBD did not really fulfil its third aim (to assist in the conversion of bibliographic records to machine-readable form), which was based on what are now superseded ideas of how computer data had to be structured so that computers could process it, for example that databases could only work with data formatted in fixed field lengths. It was also based on the prophecy, which proved to fall into the 'pious wish' rather than the 'about to be fulfilled' category, that OCR (optical character recognition) techniques were just around the corner and it would soon be easy to convert bibliographic records in card catalogues into computer data. This was not the case and it took almost two decades before OCR technology became reliable and viable. Now that computer software has become more flexible in its ability to handle data structures, and card catalogues have, for the most part, been converted manually, this aim has become redundant.

In terms of providing the basis for the international exchange of bibliographic data, ISBD has succeeded in the library context. It has encouraged standardisation, so that bibliographic records constructed according to its prescriptions are readily understandable by anyone familiar with the conventions. However, this does not mean that its future is totally secure. Although it has continued to develop as new information media have become established, there are those that see some of its prescriptions as irrelevant in the online world of today, particular the punctuation and the fixed order of elements. Even when it was first introduced, not everyone appreciated its 'somewhat baroque notation' (Langker 1974a, p.100). Three decades later, and still many catalogue users fail to fully comprehend the meaning of all the brackets and dashes, colons and semi-colons. Newer standards, such as Dublin Core, offer much greater flexibility, having been developed specifically for the online environment and computer manipulation. Although they still depend on particular encoding formats so that the computer can read and display the metadata, these can be readily applied by software, rather than humans. If neither computers nor users much like the punctuation, nor necessarily require bibliographic elements in a particular order, then it may well be that these aspects of ISBD will be increasingly less applied in the coming years. Indeed, the writing may be on the wall, as AACR2's successor, the forthcoming *Resource Description and Access* (RDA) standard, has already disengaged itself from ISBD, leaving the cataloguer the freedom to omit the punctuation marks altogether.

Given that the success of ISBD has largely been achieved in the English-speaking world through the wholesale adoption of AACR2, this recently declared independence on the part of the AACR revisers does not bode well for the future of ISBD. On the other hand, most of the elements in the proposed RDA standard ('AACR3') mirror those stipulated by ISBD. The great strength of ISBD is that it has been successfully applied by many libraries over many years, and has the backing of the principal international body for librarianship, the International Federation of Library Associations and Institutions (IFLA); indeed, it is managed by IFLA. Unlike some of the competing standards, it is specifically for libraries and their catalogues. Librarians may question the relevance of the punctuation, but most of the ISBD elements are well-known to end-users and continue to be used for retrieval and selection of resources. Although the standard might not be moving as fast as some might wish, it continues to be applied by libraries throughout the world; few metadata standards enjoy this kind of support. For the short and medium term, therefore, ISBD looks set to remain a key standard, even if some aspects of it diminish in importance.

AACR2

AACR2 is one of the most widely used library standards in the English-speaking world; it is also used, or is influential, in many other countries. Specifically, it is a standard for constructing library catalogue records. Part I of AACR2 is concerned with the metadata elements that describe the bibliographic characteristics of information resources in library collections, that is, their *bibliographic description*. This book does *not* teach the reader to become expert in applying AACR2 – guides to AACR2 are plentiful. Rather, it aims to provide enough knowledge about the standard to decide in which situations it can be suitably applied, and why its application can improve information retrieval.

The second edition of AACR was first published in 1978; subsequent revisions were published in 1988, 1998 and 2002. The current version of AACR is referred to here as AACR2 (2002 revision). The last update of this version was in 2005 – updates consist of amendments and minor changes, affecting a relatively small amount of the content. According to its developers, this will be the *final* update. Instead, a new standard will be published, scheduled for 2009 at the time of writing, to replace AACR2, namely *Resource Description and Access* (RDA). It will perform some of the same functions as AACR2, but with some important differences. This new departure will be outlined and discussed later in the chapter, but first we need to learn more about the current standard, AACR, and how we have got to where we are with it.

Predecessors of AACR2: a brief history

AACR2 (2002 revision) is based on more than a century of international cooperation, initially between Britain and the United States, and later with other countries participating. Australian librarians, for example, became formally recognised as partners in the revision process for AACR2 in 1981, and had been contributing comments and suggestions for improving cataloguing codes before this date. The first Anglo-American code, or set of rules, was developed by committees of the American Library Association and the (British) Library Association, and was published in 1908. That code was, in turn, based on the principles established in the *British Museum Rules* (1841) and Cutter's *Rules for a Dictionary Catalog* (1876). The 1908 code was in widespread use in the United Kingdom until 1967.

Meanwhile, the Americans produced revisions of the Anglo-American code in 1941 and 1949, but these were sharply criticised, most notably by the Australian Andrew Osborn (at that time working in the United States) in his influential article 'The Crisis in Cataloging' (Osborn 1941; Gorman 1975) and by Seymour Lubetzky, chief cataloguer at the Library of Congress from 1943–1960, in his seminal work, *Cataloging Rules and Principles* (Lubetzky 1953). The codes contained elaborate edifices of rules and counter-rules (in some instances downright contradictions) which had grown without the benefit of consistent principles behind their construction. The rules were difficult to apply and did not reflect the bibliographic realities of libraries' collections. They were often over-specific, with many applicable to only small categories of material. One infamous rule in the 1949 code for author and title entries, 116A(3), is devoted to the Basilian Monastery at Mount Sinai (*ALA Cataloging Rules for Author and Title Entries* 1949).

Seymour Lubetzky drafted a new revision of one part of the American code, and this was used as the basis for the so-called 'Paris Principles' established at the International Conference on Cataloguing, held in Paris in 1961. These principles formed the basis of Part I of AACR1, which became Part II of AACR2 – these rules are discussed in chapter 4. The Paris conference led to a new push towards another Anglo-American code, involving American, British and Canadian librarians. This culminated in the publication of the *Anglo-American Cataloguing Rules* in 1967, by the American and British Library Associations. Since it was the first edition, it is now known as AACR1.

AACR1 did not, however, truly represent Anglo-American thinking. Two versions, one British and the other North American, contained significant differences. Both were based to a large degree on the same principles, but these were not thoroughly or consistently applied. Further difficulties to the widespread adoption of AACR1 were caused by the decision of some major libraries, one being the Library of Congress, not to fully adopt the code. 'The result', noted Michael Gorman, 'was bibliographic anarchy' (Gorman 1987, p.111).

Revised chapters of AACR1, incorporating ISBD, followed: Chapter 6 for description of monographs, Chapter 12 for description of audiovisual materials and Chapter 14 for description of sound recordings. In addition, numerous official rule revisions ratified by the editorial board responsible for oversight of AACR were issued. By the mid-1970s a fully updated copy of AACR1 was unwieldy: not only did it consist of the original 1967 volume, plus the revised chapters in separate volumes, but it also contained many crossings-out and additions of revised words, sentences, paragraphs and frequently whole pages pasted in. Copies tended to have their spines broken as a result of the thickness of these added pages.

Adoption and revision of AACR2

This set the scene for the publication of the second edition of AACR in 1978. Known as AACR2, it not only incorporated the numerous amendments to the first edition, but also other significant changes. The second edition was, in effect, a highly transformed work. AACR2 was not immediately popular, as its adoption required many changes to existing practice, which many large libraries considered too expensive to implement in their catalogues. For example, implementing the changes in forms of names required significant re-cataloguing, an expensive process in large libraries. The Library of Congress did not adopt AACR2 until January 1981 (Gorman 1987, p.112).

By about 1982, however, the international library community had realised that the enormous advantages of adopting AACR2, in particular with respect to the standardisation of library cataloguing in the English-speaking world, overrode the local disadvantages of adopting it. AACR2 became well and truly ensconced in mainstream bibliographic organisation practice.

History of cataloguing codes in Australia

Until AACR, there was no nationwide cataloguing standard in Australia. Some libraries used their own in-house code: for example, the State Library of New South Wales (formerly known as the Free Public Library of New South Wales and by various other names) used a *Guide to the System of Cataloguing of the Reference Library* developed in 1902 by its Principal Librarian, H.C.L. Anderson, until it adopted AACR2 in 1980.

Despite its inconsistencies, AACR1 was enthusiastically received in Australia. In a 1967 review Jack Nelson strongly urged its adoption:

> The new code is so obviously better organized and in every way superior to the 1949 code that non-adoption would be virtual professional suicide ... a library retaining the 1949 code ... would be cutting itself off from a progressive, new approach to library cataloguing and, ultimately, from the possibility of contributing to a standardization, both nationally and internationally, of cataloguing practice and policy (Nelson 1967, p.123).

The Library Association of Australia's General Council recommended that AACR be adopted for use in Australian libraries. The Hine survey of cataloguing practices in Australian libraries indicated that, by 1972, AACR1 had been widely adopted, especially the North American version, but that about half of the Australian libraries who had adopted it felt that modifications were necessary (Hine 1973, pp.4-5).

The National Library of Australia announced in early 1979 that it would implement AACR2 in January 1981, in line with the Library of Congress's decision. Australian librarians participated in a program of familiarisation and consciousness-raising in the many months between the National Library's announcement and the 1981 implementation (Osborn 1979; Ramsden 1979). Since the early eighties, AACR has remained the standard for descriptive cataloguing in almost all Australian libraries.

As expertise in using AACR2 grew, amendments were issued to address anomalies and to interpret some of the more obscure rules. The rules were, in other words, fine-tuned for maximum effectiveness. Three sets of official amendments appeared: in 1982, 1983 and 1985. These were official in the sense that they were sanctioned by the Joint Steering Committee (JSC) for Revision of AACR. Eventually, the need to produce a version which consolidated these changes became apparent, and so in 1988 a revision of AACR2 appeared. This was not, the editors insisted, a new edition: the Australian Committee on Cataloguing, one of the six members of the JSC, was at pains to point this out, advising that:

> the revision is not a new edition as such; it has not changed basic concepts. Rather, what the revision does is incorporate corrections to obvious errors, modifications to wording to improve understanding, and changes to rules which have proved inadequate, as well as give additional rules and examples to cover new types of materials (McMillan 1989, p.7).

To many practitioners, however, AACR2 (1988 revision) should have been designated 'third edition'. One American commentator was critical of the timidity of those who did not allow it to be called a third edition, for in his view it contained differences significant enough to qualify (Smiraglia 1987). These differences included the incorporation of rules for the description of two new media, CDs and microcomputer software.

There have been two further revisions published since the 1988 one: in 1998 and 2002. Again, these revisions contain some radical developments, including new rules to cover new classes of material, most notably other types of computer file (which are now called 'electronic recourses'). In the 2002 revision the chapter covering serials was greatly expanded so as to cover all 'continuing resources', including so-called 'integrating resources' such as updating websites, online databases and loose-leaf materials. There were also changes to the rules covering electronic resources, new rules for the treatment of cartographic materials in electronic format, and some changes to the rules for serials.

While the pace of AACR2's development might not have been particularly fast, it has been relatively sure, with most of the changes having been widely adopted, if not always fully (the Library of Congress leading the way in this respect, with its sometimes diverging *Rule Interpretations*). The reason for its continuing success, in terms of its adoption, is primarily due to the involvement in its revision of the key stakeholders – the national libraries, and the other major record producing libraries represented by their respective library associations. The title page of the 2002 revision notes that it was 'prepared under the direction of the Joint Steering Committee for Revision of AACR'. JSC-AACR (now JSC-RDA) consists of representatives from six organisations: the American Library Association, the Australian Committee on Cataloguing, the British Library, the Canadian Committee on Cataloguing, the (British) Chartered Institute of Library and Information Professionals and the Library of Congress. One commentator considers AACR2 to be:

> a monumental tribute to bibliographic democracy, for its every nook and cranny is constantly pored over by hundreds of experts in the four member countries of the Anglo-American cataloging alliance – the United States, the United Kingdom, Canada and Australia (Smiraglia 1987, p.5).

However, there are also those who question the 'democratic' nature of the decision-making process. In reality the views of the national bibliographic agencies carry the most weight on the Joint Steering Committee (JSC) – after all, they produce the most records – and these views are based largely on the context of the national libraries' own particular circumstances, at that time. Certainly other cataloguing experts are able to voice their opinions and submit their own proposals – increasingly so, through email and the web – but at the end of the day, it is the JSC that makes the decisions. How systematically and objectively each proposal for revision is reviewed is thus debatable. There is a question of balance here, as the more open is the revision process, the more difficult it is to obtain consensus and to move forward; yet without the support of most of the library community, developments run the risk of rejection. This issue has assumed particular importance in the last couple of years with progress towards the new RDA standard having been less than smooth. This time around, drafts have been made available on the JSC website for everyone to examine, giving rise to much electronic discussion, and, in some cases, consternation. The trouble is that for every cataloguer with a certain view on an issue, there appears to be another with the opposite opinion. JSC is under considerable pressure to keep as many people as possible 'on board', but at the same time need to produce *something* – the 2002 revision of AACR2 is beginning to look seriously out of date, particular given the recent rise of Web 2.0. The choice between 'getting it right' and 'getting it out' is a tough one.

Contents of AACR2

AACR2 is a heavy tome, running to a few hundred pages. In its current revision, it is difficult to say exactly how many pages, as its only available in loose-leaf format and online – the number of leaves in the loose-leaf binder depends on the update. The online version is part of *Cataloger's Desktop*, issued by the Library of Congress. Unlike some of the other standards, it is not *gratis*. There is also a concise edition intended for use in small general libraries, prepared by Michael Gorman (Gorman 2004). This conveys the basic principles to those who do not need to know or apply AACR2 in detail, such as librarians managing small collections and paraprofessionals involved in copy cataloguing. However, almost all exchange of bibliographic records between libraries is based on the full edition.

AACR2 consists of two parts plus appendices (see figure 3.3). Part II: Headings, Uniform Titles, and References contains six chapters which cover choice of access points, headings for persons, geographic names, headings for corporate bodies, uniform titles, and references, and is discussed in more detail in chapter 4. The appendices cover capitalisation, abbreviations, numerals, glossary and initial articles. Of most interest to us here is Part I: Description.

Part I of AACR2 (2002 revision) has 13 chapters. Space was left for additional chapters (there are no Chapters 14 to 20, Part II starting with Chapter 21), as new types of information resource came to light. After the prefatory material comes Chapter 1, a general (and key) chapter that applies to the description of all types of information resource in every format. This chapter is used in conjunction with the following Chapters 2-11, which cover specific types of media, and Chapter 12, which covers continuing resources such as serials. The rules in Chapters 2-12 often refer back to Chapter 1.

More than one of these other chapters can, in fact, be used for some kinds of resource, since although AACR2 treats materials primarily according to their physical form, increasingly resources appear in new formats of the traditional forms, especially electronic format, which combine features of more than one of the traditional forms. For example, serials need no longer be printed – they could well be published as e-journals. In such cases, the chapter for electronic resources (Chapter 9) as well as the chapter for serials (Chapter 12) needs to be consulted. It should be noted that the electronic resources chapter should only be used where rules in other chapters do not apply. For example, a video compact disc is in a sense an electronic resource (it requires a player powered by electricity), but it counts as a videorecording as far as AACR2 is concerned – thus Chapter 7 for videorecordings, and not Chapter 9 for electronic resources, is applied.

Chapter 13 does not fit the pattern of the chapters that precede it, because it does not deal with a specific kind of resource, but instead notes how to describe parts of individual resources, for instance, volumes in a multi-volume set.

CONTENTS

Committees
Preface to the 2002 Revision
Summary of Rule Revisions since AACR Second Edition (1998 Revision)
General Introduction

PART I

Description

PART II

Headings, Uniform Titles, and References

APPENDICES

Figure 3.3 Contents of AACR2 (2002 revision)

Main characteristics of AACR2

1) *AACR2 is developed from general principles.* This feature is especially noticeable in Part II, which, by comparison with AACR1 and especially by comparison with the ALA code of 1949, is straightforward to apply. This is because it is based on principles as far as possible, in contrast to the earlier cataloguing codes which were based on cases: that is, every time a new instance arose which needed a decision, another rule was developed. Consequently there was little consistency and a very large number of rules, each with exceptions to it, and they were extremely complex.

2) *Options are present in AACR2.* AACR2 provides some choice through optional rules, in cases where there are genuinely different practices and conventions that need to be accommodated. In some cases, an option allows for extra detail to be put in should it be required by a particular library's users; in other cases, it provides for alternative terminology or another way of recording a particular piece of information. An example of the former, is the optional addition of a statement of coordinates that a map covers – something more for the map specialist than, say, the average public library user. An example of alternative terminologies is the option to describe a CD specifically as a 'compact disc' instead of the more generic 'sound disc'. This is also an example, it has to be said, of how AACR2 can be a little behind the times – the option to allow for terms in common usage, such as compact disc, DVD and CD-ROM, was introduced a long time after these terms had become well used.

3) *AACR2 gives equal status to all resource types.* Within the structural framework of AACR2, all resource types are treated alike. Chapter 1 contains 'those rules that apply to all library materials' (AACR2 (2002) 0.23). The following chapters with rules for specific 'classes' of material are used in conjunction with Chapter 1. For example, in cataloguing a map, the general rules in Chapter 1 are used in conjunction with the rules governing cartographic materials in Chapter 3, for all parts of the description. A basic premise of AACR2 is that general precepts can be identified which apply to the description of all materials. It is assumed that elements of description such as title, edition, publisher, and date are common to all materials, and that detailed rules can be specified in the general chapter which will apply to most materials. (The history of how non-book media have been treated in cataloguing codes is long and not directly relevant here, because AACR2 successfully resolved many of the issues (Hoffmann 1977).) The ability of AACR2 to accommodate a wide range of media is illustrated by the persistent rumour that a bibliographic record for a packet of biscuits, constructed according to AACR2 rules, is held on the Te Puna database, formerly known as NZBN (New Zealand Bibliographic Network), and that a record for a motorcycle, once owned by former Australian prime minister Bob Hawke, can be found on the Libraries Australia database.

4) *AACR2 has a consistent system of numbering of rules.* The consistent system of rule numbering in AACR2 enhances its use. For example, rule 1.1B in the general chapter (Chapter 1) deals with recording the title proper in all materials; 2.1B deals with the same topic for monographs, 3.1B the same topic for cartographic materials, and so on.

5) *AACR2 incorporates ISBD.* As noted earlier in this chapter, ISBD prescribes a particular set of elements, their presentation in a consistent order for data elements, particular punctuation, and particular sources of information. That AACR2 incorporates ISBD has contributed strongly to the widespread use of both standards.

6) *AACR2 allows three levels of bibliographic description*. This allows AACR2 to be used in a wide variety of situations, from small libraries that need only relatively brief records to the largest of national libraries, and other libraries with specialised, research collections, where very detailed cataloguing is often carried out.

International use of AACR2

The clearly-articulated principles on which AACR2 is based have been the most significant factor in its international adoption as the basis for standardised cataloguing practice, a prerequisite for exchange programs for bibliographic data. According to a list on the JSC website, AACR2, or its concise version, has been translated into Arabic, Catalan, Chinese, Czech, Estonian, Finnish, French, German, Greek, Italian, Japanese, Latvian, Malay, Norwegian, Portuguese, Russian, Slovakian, Serbian, Spanish, Swedish, Tagalog, Ukrainian, Urdu and Vietnamese.

How widespread is AACR2's international use? We must not forget that these are the *Anglo-American* cataloguing rules, for this is a significant point. They are widely used in the United Kingdom, North America, Australasia, and in some other places with a British colonial past, such as Hong Kong, Malaysia and Singapore. AACR2 is based on an Anglo-American view of fundamental matters such as corporate authorship, legal structures and bodies, government sadministrative systems and religious bodies. This makes its rules sometimes difficult to apply in countries where this view is less accepted. Germany and France (and also those countries which have been, or are still, under their jurisdiction) have their own traditions of cataloguing, developed over a long period of time, which do not always coincide with the Anglo-American tradition and AACR2 (Jeffreys 1993). Other traditions, especially non-European traditions, have different ways again. So we have to say that AACR2 is not fully accepted internationally, although it is certainly the most widespread cataloguing code in use today, and its influence is increasing as efforts to unify cataloguing codes continue. There are, in fact, signs that other cataloguing traditions might be sidelined as the economic benefits of being part of the AACR2 community – savings resulting from the lack of need to edit copy created by AACR2-based libraries, who together produce millions of new records each year – prove irresistible. German librarians, for example, are seriously considering abandoning their RAK (*Regeln für die alphabetische Katalogisierung*) code in favour of AACR (Gömpel & Niggemann 2002).

Levels allowed in AACR2 (brief, medium, full)

One general principle for bibliographic description is to make the description as brief as possible – as long as the aims of the information retrieval system are met.

> How brief? It all depends. In a small public library, for instance, the edition of a book on physics may mean a great deal, but for a novel it may be enough to know that a library has five copies without bothering about the edition of each. In a large research library, however, the editions, printings, and issues of a great many books may be worth knowing (Dunkin 1969, p.51).

That is, we cannot answer the question 'how brief?' unless we have a context, a specific library or information centre, in mind when we construct bibliographic records. It is often felt that users do not require as much detail as the cataloguing rules, even when interpreted minimally, require. For instance, the WAIT (Western Australian Institute of Technology, now Curtin University of Technology) Library's policy was articulated in this way:

> Although AACR2 is used for cataloguing monographs, rules are not necessarily followed in their entirety. Descriptive elements are kept to a minimum ... in the belief that such details ... are not required by WAIT Library users (Hayward 1985, p.2).

1.0D1 First level of description. For the first level of description, include at least the elements set out in this schematic illustration:

Title proper / first statement of responsibility, if different from main entry heading in form or number or if there is no main entry heading. – Edition statement. – Material (or type of publication) specific details. – First publisher, etc., date of publication, etc. – Extent of item. – Note(s). – Standard number.

1.0D2 Second level of description. For the second level of description, include at least the elements set out in this schematic illustration:

Title proper (general material designation) = Parallel title : other title information / first statement of responsibility ; each subsequent statement of responsibility. – Edition statement / first statement of responsibility relating to edition. – Material (or type of publication) specific details. – First place of publication, etc. : first publisher, etc., date of publication, etc. – Extent of item : other physical details ; dimensions. – (Title proper of series / statement of responsibility relating to series, ISSN of series ; numbering within the series. Title of subseries, ISSN of subseries, numbering within subseries). – Note(s). – Standard number.

1.0D3 Third level of description. For the third level of description, include all elements set out in the following rules [that is, AACR2 (2002 revision) Chapters 1-13] that are applicable to the item being described.

Figure 3.4 The three levels of description in AACR2 (2002 revision), pp.1-5

First level of description
Majurakura Wangka ngaanya / [collected] by Bruce Thomas. – Wangka Maya Pilbara Aboriginal Language Centre, 1994. – 29 p. – Text in Martu Wangka with English translation. – ISBN 064220578

Second level of description
Majurakura Wangka ngaanya = Majura's stories / [collected] by Bruce Thomas. – South Hedland, W.A. : Wangka Maya Pilbara Aboriginal Language Centre, 1994. – 29 p. : col. ill. ; 22 x 29 cm. – Text in Martu Wangka with English translation. – ISBN 064220578

Figure 3.5 Different levels of description in AACR2 (2002 revision) applied

AACR2 recognises different user requirements in its idea of levels of description: brief, medium, full; or, first, second, and third level (see Figures 3.4 and 3.5). This idea is not new – it was initially used by Charles Cutter in his *Rules for a Dictionary Catalog* in 1876 – but until AACR2 was not a formal part of cataloguing codes. As indicated in chapter 2, there have been moves to reduce the amount of data in bibliographic records because of the cost implications of creating, and to a lesser extent storing, longer records. Although the first level of description – the minimum amount – is considered to minimal for most larger libraries, particularly national and academic libraries, very few libraries can afford to apply the third level in their routine cataloguing, opting for something around the second level in many cases instead.

Australian input to AACR2 and RDA

Although Australian input had been invited as early as 1970, specifically to assist with integrating the British and North American versions of AACR1, Australian cataloguers only became formerly involved in the development of the standard in 1981, when, as the Preface to the 1988 revision states:

> because Australian cataloguers had for some time been contributing to code revision and to the review of draft documents … the Australian Committee on Cataloguing [was] invited … to send a representative to Joint Steering Committee meetings (p.xiii).

The Australian Committee on Cataloguing became a full participant of the Joint Steering Committee for Revision of AACR in 1986. The National Library of Australia is now also represented on the standard's governing body, its 'Committee of Principals'.

Australian librarians may submit proposals concerning AACR/RDA development to the Australian Committee on Cataloguing (ACOC), whose current representative on the Joint Steering Committee for Revision of RDA (formerly JSC-AACR) is Deirdre Kiorgaard, who is also Chair of JSC. Given that JSC consists of only six members in total, Australian librarians are, in fact, relatively well represented. The former ACOC representative, Ann Huthwaite, was also Chair of JSC for several years.

The process is not simply one way, either, for ACOC also has the role of keeping the Australian library community advised of developments. To this end, it has instituted a series of yearly seminars, which have been held in various cities across the country. ACOC's membership is made up of representatives from the National Library of Australia and the Australian Library and Information Association (ALIA), and meets on a regular basis to discuss not only the latest news from JSC-RDA, but also other developments in the world of cataloguing, particularly those most affecting Australian libraries.

The role of the Library of Congress

As noted earlier, the Library of Congress was dilatory in adopting AACR2, with widespread consequences. Its influence extends far beyond this, however. Because the Library of Congress creates and distributes a very significant number of the catalogue records used in libraries around the world, any decisions it makes about cataloguing are widely followed internationally. For example, the Library of Congress's interpretations of optional rules in AACR2 are followed closely by many other libraries, particularly those in North America, to the extent they have become a *de facto* standard in their own right. Thus the Library records its decisions and promulgates them as the *Library of Congress Rule Interpretations* (LCRI), which many cataloguers in the larger libraries use in conjunction with AACR2. Current LCRI are available as part of the Library's *Cataloger's Desktop* product, available online by subscription.

Library of Congress influence on Australian cataloguing

The availability of bibliographic records from the Library of Congress has powerfully influenced cataloguing practice worldwide, including Australian practice. During the 1960s and 1970s Australian library journals carried significant debate on whether that influence was beneficial or harmful. A 1971 issue of the *Australian Library Journal* presented the various arguments. While the predominant feeling was that the Library of Congress services (in the form of printed cards and catalogues) were 'of inestimable value' to Australian libraries, because they enabled savings of time and money in the cataloguing process, it was felt they also presented a 'danger for the future of Australian cataloguing' (Dobrovits 1971, p.17). The reasons given to support this contention were that the cataloguing records were too specific to the Library of Congress's particular requirements and were, therefore, unsuitable for Australian needs. There was, it was felt, a need to adapt 'LC copy' for local conditions. Even in the 1990s the same arguments were still voiced occasionally, but Australian cataloguing practice is now almost totally dependent on receiving bibliographic records from the Library of Congress and other cataloguing agencies based outside of the country (Byrum 1992). This dependence is described in more detail in chapter 13.

FRBR

Although AACR2 is generally based on clearly thought-out underlying concepts, one quite recent publication has demonstrated that some areas would benefit from a rethink. This publication, *Functional Requirements for Bibliographic Records* (FRBR), has proved very influential in the AACR and MARC communities, and is one of the main drivers of the new RDA standard. Indeed, the 'FRBR cause' has also been taken up by others outside the traditional cataloguing community, some of whom have made use of it in the design of databases which use other metadata standards, such as Dublin Core and its related schemas.

FRBR was produced by an IFLA study group whose final report was published in 1998. Following an analysis of what users require of a national bibliographic database, a list of metadata elements is recommended as the 'basic data requirements for records created by national bibliographic agencies' (IFLA Study Group on the Functional Requirements for Bibliographic Records 1998). These elements are very similar to those defined in ISBD and AACR. What is different, however, is the way in which they are derived, that is, by analysing the requirements of the basic catalogue user tasks – to *find*, *identify*, *select* and *obtain* resources – according to a conceptual model of the information resource and its relationships with other resources and other entities, such as people and organisations, concepts and objects.

One of the key achievements of FRBR is that it defines 'information resource' in a much clearer way than previously by using a four-tier hierarchy to express the concept: *item*, *manifestation*, *expression* and *work*. A resource may thus be viewed at each of the four levels: for example, a book is, simultaneously, a particular copy (item), a particular publication (manifestation), a particular edition (expression), and a particular piece of work (work). In contrast, AACR2 has had a tendency to muddle these different levels, so that terms such as 'edition' and 'work' are defined inconsistently. RDA will employ such terms 'in a manner consistent with their definitions in FRBR' (Lindlan, Beacom & Attig 2003).

By applying this distinction between levels of a resource, in a systematic way, the catalogue user is able to group together different expressions of a work, different manifestations of an expression, and different items of a manifestation. Thus another dimension is added to the catalogue, through which the user can drill down from a work all the way through to particular items that contain the work. Adding this new dimension to the library catalogue has been termed 'FRBRisation', and has now become a goal of bibliographic database design. However, it can only be fully implemented if the metadata fully distinguishes between these different levels, something that AACR2-based data fails to do. It is hoped that RDA will address this shortcoming, although it should also be noted that creating records for each level, instead of just the single record as is presently done, is likely to create extra work at a time when cataloguing is already often considered too expensive. It is also worth noting that the value of FRBRisation may vary according to subject field and type of user. Some early attempts at FRBRisation, based on the metadata currently available in MARC records, have demonstrated its usefulness for researchers in the humanities and the arts; it appears to be less worthwhile in, say, the sciences or for the general public library user (chapter 14 includes more on FRBRised catalogues).

Although FRBR can be criticised for its lack of empiricism and for certain AACR-based presuppositions, its systematic and clear analysis has been seen by many as a breath of fresh air. The document, which itself is in the process of being revised, has already had an impact of the development of various metadata standards, and not just AACR/RDA. ISBD has been aligned with the FRBR model, while the Dublin Core community has been busy building application profiles based on it. A companion to FRBR, the *Functional Requirements for Authority Data* (FRAD, formerly FRAR) is also being drafted. It was also very influential in the development of the new *Statement of International Cataloguing Principles* by IFLA (see below). The importance of FRBR is underlined by the existence of a blog devoted to it.

RDA – the new AACR

In 1997 an International Conference on the Principles and Future Development of AACR was held in Toronto. Items for immediate action arising from the conference included several which aimed to clarify the underlying principles of AACR2, such as determining the extent to which it should be internationalised, and its relationship to other standards such as MARC and ISBD. Soon afterwards, FRBR was published, a document that pointed to some serious shortcomings in AACR2. Also at this time, new metadata standards, such as Dublin Core, were emerging, specifically designed for modern programming and the web, and in sharp contrast to an AACR that was still partly based on the workings of the card catalogue. Further, the NACO project (see chapter 5) highlighted a gap in AACR2's coverage of descriptive cataloguing: there were no rules in AACR dealing specifically with the construction and content of authority records; instead, the NACO Participants' Manual serves as a *de facto* standard. A new *Statement of International Cataloguing Principles*, originally drafted at the First IFLA Meeting of Experts on an International Cataloguing Code, held at Frankfurt in 2003, also demonstrated the need for a fresh approach; the Frankfurt Principles thus superseded the Paris

Principles of the 1960s, emphasising the modern context of the online information environment and dealing with a much wider definition of bibliographic organisation.

Eventually, it became clear that the time had come for a radical overhaul of AACR2 as a whole, and not just the periodic incremental revisions. JSC began work on a new edition of AACR in 2003. At that time, the plan included:

- incorporating FRBR terminology and concepts,
- revised, conceptual introductions to the rules,
- increasing consistency and reducing repetition in rules in Part I,
- reconceptualising the scope of Chapter 9 (Electronic resources),
- thorough revision of Chapter 21 (dealing with main and added entries, see next chapter), and
- creating a new Part Three on authority records (Lindlan, Beacom & Attig 2003).

Looking at the latest drafts of RDA, we can see how far this journey has taken JSC. It was not long before the Committee realised that what they were attempting was going to be so radically different from AACR2, that it was going to amount to a new work, not just a new expression (to use FRBR terminology). Thus the new 'AACR3' became the new 'RDA' – Resource Description and Access. This signalled two important changes in perspective. First, the new code is not just for the Anglo-American world, it is for the global community, for anyone who wishes to share bibliographic data. Second, the new code is not just for those who perform cataloguing, in the traditional sense of the word, but for the wider metadata community, anyone who might be interested in generating metadata that will allow information seekers to find, identify, select and obtain the information resources they need. Of course, the reality is likely to be that the *primary* users of the standard will continue to be cataloguers based in libraries, even those who now go by such job titles as 'metadata specialists'.

The journey towards RDA has also led to a reassessment of the relationship with ISBD. Up until now, revisions to the two standards were largely coordinated, so that, for example, revised chapters in AACR2 dealing with particular materials were published shortly after new ISBDs had been issued for those materials. However, JSC has decided that AACR's primary contribution to the new metadata environment lay in its use as a *content* standard, rather than as a format standard. As a content standard, it prescribes the bibliographic elements and the content of those elements. Its adherence to ISBD in prescribing a particular order of elements, and particular punctuation around those elements, is now considered something of a handicap that limits its use outside the ISBD-based communities. Thus JSC has taken the radical step of divorcing RDA from ISBD, so that the former is independent of any particular format standard, and can thus, in theory at least, be used together with any format standard, and not just ISBD. In other words, RDA will no longer deal with the formatting of elements (neither their encoding in mark-up language, nor the way in which they are displayed on the screen or printed on paper).

During the past four years, the proposed structure of RDA has been revised several times, as the differences between it and the old AACR2 grow ever wider. While new rules are being incorporated to cover authority control work, some of the detailed rules pertaining to particular categories of resources have been eliminated through a process referred to as 'generalisation'. Of course, not all specialists are convinced that the slimed-down rules will suffice, but there remains the option of supplementing this general standard with more specific standards, covering maps, music, rare books, and so on. Indeed, such standards are sometimes used already, to supplement AACR2 and LCRI.

There are those (including the original editor of AACR2, Michael Gorman) who are skeptical about the 'RDA revolution'. Some are concerned about the usability of the standard for day-to-day cataloguing. Only time will tell. But even if AACR2 disappears off cataloguers' shelves over the next few years, it is unlikely to be forgotten in a hurry, and its legacy will be no doubt be manifest in the new standards that take its place. In the words of Raya Fidel and Michael Crandall, it represents 'the cumulative history of the activities of the cataloging community [and] is the largest pool of documented experience in database design we have available in the modern world' (Fidel & Crandall 1988, pp.123-124).

Other standards for bibliographic description

Many other standards for description of information resources are in use, although most are not as comprehensive as ISBD or AACR2, nor have they been as widely adopted. As well as codes based on other national cataloguing traditions, they include standards issued by standards associations of countries or by bodies such as the ISO (International Organization for Standardization), and those devised by other information-handling communities, such as archives and museums. Some examples are provided in figure 3.6.

BS 1629: 1989 Recommendations for References to Published Materials

The Foreword to the standard BS 1629: 1989 *Recommendations for References to Published Materials* refers to both AACR2 and ISBD, and the standard has been significantly influenced by them. For example, it incorporates provisions for 'not only printed matter, but also for audio, graphic, video, computer and other non-print material'. Section 4 (Elements of a reference) indicates which data elements are used, and the order in which the elements should be placed, a clear influence from AACR2. As another example, Section 6 (Title) deals with such matters as preferred form (6.1.1: 'The wording and spelling of the title should be in the form in which they appear in the preferred source'), and what to do with alternative titles (6.1.3: 'give a widely known alternative title in square brackets if necessary') and subtitles (6.1.5: 'should be included if they furnish essential information … otherwise they may be omitted'). Section 11 (Production) prescribes that production details should be given in the order place, publisher or equivalent, date. Some examples of completed citations are given in an appendix to the standard (BS 1629 1989).

ISO 690 : 1987 Documentation – Bibliographic References – Content, Form, and Structure

The ISO standard for citations is similar to the British standard and has influenced citation practice since its establishment in 1987. This standard demonstrates an even stronger influence of ISBD. There are the same eight areas of description, in the same order, and entry is according to 'primary responsibility'. There is even the 'issue designation' to be recorded between edition and publication statements for serials, mirroring ISBD/AACR

(ISO 690 1987). An edition of the standard covering electronic resources was produced in 1997, the same year that ISBD(ER) came out.

National cataloguing rules

Regeln für die alphabetische Katalogisierung, RAK (Germany)

Reglas de catalogación (Spain)

Pravila sostavleniia bibliograficheskogo opisaniia (Rules of Composition of Bibliographic Description, Russian)

Nihon mokuroku kisoku (Nippon cataloging rules)

Rules from standards organisations

BS 1629 : 1989	*Recommendation for References to Published Materials*
BS 5605 : 1990	*Recommendation for Citing and Referencing Published Materials*
BS 6371 : 1983	*Recommendations for Citation of Unpublished Documents*
ANSI/NISO Z39.14 - 1997	*Guidelines for Abstracts*
NF Z 44-050 Déc. 1989	*Documentation – Catalogage des monographies – Rédaction de la description bibliographique*
ISO 690 : 1987	*Documentation – Bibliographic References – Content, Form, and Structure*
ISO 690-2 : 1997	*Information and Documentation – Bibliographic References – Part 2: Electronic Documents or Parts thereof*

Rules from non-library communities

General International Standard for Archival Description (ISAD-G)

Rules for Archival Description (RAD, Canada)

Content Standard for Digital Geospatial Metadata (CSDGM)

Archives, Personal Papers, and Manuscripts: A Cataloging Manual for Archival Repositories, Historical Societies, and Manuscript Libraries (APPM)

Categories for the Description of Works of Art (CDWA)

Archival Moving Image Materials (AMIM)

Descriptive Cataloging of Rare Books (Library of Congress)

Figure 3.6 Examples of other standards for bibliographic description

ISAD(G) General International Standard Archival Description

Another example of a standard for description is the attempt to apply some of the principles of ISBD to archival material, in the ISAD(G) *General International Standard Archival Description*. Archivists had been trying for some decades to develop standards that can be used in more than one archive. Until recently they had little success because archival material, by its very nature, is unique. If we compare this with material in libraries, which is mostly published and is typically not unique, we can see that such issues as standardisation of metadata (which are significant in libraries in order to achieve economies of cataloguing) were not quite so relevant. However, as the archival profession has become more user-oriented, its members have come to realise the advantages of standardising metadata records. For instance, mounting records from many archives on the same database would have major benefits to users because of the increased ease of locating material. In the past there was little or no alternative for users of archives but to write to or visit each archive that might have relevant material.

The International Council on Archives produced the first edition of ISAD(G) in 1994 and a second edition was adopted in 1999 (International Council on Archives 2000). ISAD(G), which is a general framework, like the former ISBD(G), may be used to develop ISADs for specific archival media. The influence of ISBD can be clearly seen in the structure and some of the rules of ISAD(G). In the Table of Contents, for instance, the order of areas and such other features as the numbering of sections are similar to ISBD. There is a Notes area, which is, as in ISBD, the penultimate area of description. There are seven areas of description in all, each subdivided into different elements. An example of a similar rule is Rule 3.1.5 (Extent and medium of the unit of description (quantity, bulk, or size)): compare ISBD's 'extent of item' rule in area 5. Librarians who are familiar with ISBD would, however, be mistaken in thinking that a knowledge of that library standard would automatically make them expert users of ISAD. The archives standard can only be applied by those who have considerable knowledge of the nature of archives and the precepts and practices of archivists.

ISAD(G) is a relatively new standard and the extent to which it will be adopted and used as the basis for large databases, and especially for sharing metadata, remains to be seen. However, it has already heavily influenced the development of another new standard, Encoded Archival Description (EAD), which facilitates the exchange of online metadata for archival materials. Within EAD, at least, ISAD looks to be a standard with a healthy future (*Development of the Encoded Archival Description DTD* 2003). It should also be remembered that, in libraries, ISBD took some years to be accepted and was never fully adopted internationally until it was incorporated into AACR2 in 1978 – almost ten years after it first appeared.

Categories for the Description of Works of Art (CDWA)

Another example of a guide to description used in another domain is *Categories for the Description of Works of Art*, used by curators and librarians working with art objects, particularly in North America. It sets out what and how attributes of art works are described, and is supplemented by *Cataloging Cultural Objects: A Guide to Describing Cultural Works and Their Images* (CCO). Unlike most of the other standards mentioned in this chapter, CDWA also covers subject description, that is., the subject matter of the art works.

Conclusion

We can fittingly close this chapter with a summary of the characteristics of a 'good' standard for description:

- its product (the description) should be as brief as possible,
- it should be easily understood by the user,
- it should be easy to apply by the information professional,
- it should be applicable to all information resources,
- it should be widely accepted and used (internationally if possible), and
- it should be economical to apply.

The historical tendency in descriptive cataloguing has been to move from producing perfect records to producing useful records. As Anthony Curwen notes

> There is no point whatsoever in creating the most perfectly polished descriptions, each a masterpiece of the cataloguer's art, if they take far too long to produce … or if, when created, they cannot be found in the catalogue when they are needed (Curwen 1991, p.81).

Chapter 4 examines how bibliographic records are constructed so that they can be found in the database – that is, through their *access points* – and the standards used for selecting and constructing them.

CHAPTER 4
Standards for access points

Chapter 3 discussed standards for the description of information resources. However, compiling a description of the bibliographic characteristics of a resource and putting it into a standard format is only part of the process of constructing a bibliographic record. The record also needs to be *accessed*, that is, retrieved by the database user. When users search in a catalogue or other bibliographic database, they are searching on various indexes. In a card catalogue, an index consists of the headings and references at the top of the cards. (Standards such as AACR2 still use the term *heading*, even though there are, of course, no physical 'headings' in online databases.) In a computerised catalogue, an index consists of metadata derived from the bibliographic records and, possibly, references linked to these terms. Only by searching on these indexes, are users able to retrieve the records, and, in turn, the items they represent.

In large bibliographic databases, it is not normal for every element of the description to be indexed. For example, the '123 p.' for the number of pages in a book is not usually going to be searched on – people rarely require a book of exactly 123 pages. To index such metadata is a waste of disk space, and, perhaps more importantly, a distraction, producing false hits (for example, users might retrieve the record when they are looking for a title with '123' in it), or a redundant search option (hardly ever would they utilise a 'page number' search function). It is also not normal to have only one index, and modern OPACs are able to offer users several different searches: by author, title, subject, series, general keyword, and so on.

Those parts of the bibliographic description that usually require indexing are known as access points: they allow access to the record. However, the way in which they are entered as access points is not a straightforward matter. It may be that in the description, the name of the author is transcribed from the title page as 'Jean P. Whyte', but this is not necessarily the best way to have the name in the database. Users who browse on the list of authors will be more familiar with the surname coming first. Thus, the name may need to be inverted to: 'Whyte, Jean P.'

Even then, the name might not be in the best form. This is because in more effective databases access points are *controlled*, so that a particular name is used in a consistent form and style. In the descriptions of various works by the same author, variations of a name may have been used, but only one particular form is used in the document retrieval system. For example, in the case of *Jean P. Whyte*, the author's name might also be cited as *Jean Whyte, J. P. Whyte, J. Primrose Whyte, Jean Primrose Whyte, Jeannie Whyte, Jen Whyte,* or *J. Whyte*. If this name is properly controlled, only one of these forms will be used in the system.

As we are often dealing with databases containing many hundreds of thousands, even many millions, of records, such issues of consistency become very significant. Without consistency, the user may have a hard time finding all the relevant records, and may also retrieve many more false hits. Fortunately, there are standards that deal with the way to construct access points in bibliographic databases, followed by many cataloguers and other metadata creators. Part II of AACR2 deals with access points for the non-subject, descriptive metadata elements, and this is followed, just like Part I of AACR, by most libraries in the English-speaking world. The primary focus of consistency efforts with respect to descriptive metadata revolves around *names*, and names are what much of Part II of AACR2 is concerned with. This chapter considers Part II in some detail and also briefly examines some other standards for non-subject access points. Standards for subject index terms are covered in chapter 8.

Using names as access points

There are four main issues to be addressed when using names as access points in library information retrieval systems:

- deciding which name (or names) to provide access to;
- if there is more than one version of a name, deciding which one to use;
- selecting how much of the name to use; and
- linking the name to other names which are related (e.g., different forms of a name used by the same person).

Which name or names to choose?

There are many conventions which help us to decide who is the author, or authors, of an information resource. But what is an *author*? Normally – for a very high percentage of information resources – there is no great problem in deciding this. Although definitions of *author* in library cataloguing practice have changed over the last century, we will note here only the current definition of personal author as: 'the person chiefly responsible for the creation of the intellectual or artistic content of a work' (*Anglo-American Cataloguing Rules* 2002, Appendix D-1).

Note that the author need not be a *writer*: he or she could be a photographer, composer of music, painter, or be acting in other roles in relation to a resource, whoever is responsible for the intellectual content of the work – whose thought or creativity is encapsulated in the work.

The document with a single author is a clear-cut case. But what about other cases: editor, compiler, translator and so on. They can all claim to have some input into the work, so sometimes, where there is more than one person responsible, we have to try to determine which person put in the most effort – which person, that is, was most responsible for the intellectual content of the work. This decision is obviously more difficult, and that is the reason why we need to apply standards to ensure such decisions are made consistently.

Corporate responsibility

Another complicating factor is the concept of *corporate responsibility*. Here we pretend that a group of people (a corporate body) can act together as one entity and be responsible for creating the intellectual content of a document. This pretence is, clearly, nonsensical.

Even in an official document from a business company (an annual report, for instance), it is very likely that one person, or just possibly a very small number of people, was responsible for the appearance of the document in its final form. This person collected the data in the report, edited it and perhaps also designed the final product. It is rare indeed that a large group of people act in accord as one body.

The concept of corporate responsibility, and of its earlier manifestation, corporate authorship, has a long history in the Anglo-American cataloguing tradition. Enormous amounts of energy have been spent in defining it, attacking and defending it, attempting to apply it, and sorting out the ensuing mess. Its popularity in the past suggests that it was thought necessary for effective organisation of knowledge. It has, however, caused a lot of problems in library standards for bibliographic records, and it is now applied in a more limited number of cases. Nevertheless, it is still applied, and is incorporated into the FRBR and FRAD models (see chapter 3 for more about these models).

Primary responsibility and main entry

The question 'who is responsible?' is one which has been of considerable importance in library cataloguing, but less so in other areas of information practice: archivists do not, for example, worry about this so much, preferring the idea of transaction (which government department, company or individual used the documents in the course of their business and caused them to be grouped together); and to other information professionals the question is simply not important. But library practice still requires that we have at least an understanding of the idea, and cataloguers require considerably more detailed knowledge. Most of Chapter 21 of AACR2 (around ten per cent of Part II) is devoted to the question. Not all librarians are pleased about this state of affairs. 'The concept …' says Alan Jeffreys, 'is irrelevant to the users of an automated catalogue. Some cataloguers still waste time in worrying about a 'correct' interpretation of a rule in Chapter 21, but for the rest these 70 pages can be scrapped' (Jeffreys 1993, p.56).

A strong lobby is pushing for abandoning the concept of primary responsibility, instead advocating rules which are considerably simpler to apply because they do not require a high level of decision-making. An example might be a rule which directs simply: 'indicate in the bibliographic record all names which are prominent in the document. Do not attempt to indicate the role they played in relation to the document'. One of the editors of AACR2, Michael Gorman, has himself suggested such a rule in his 'The Most Concise AACR2': 'Make as many copies of the description as are necessary and add to each the names of the author and of other persons or bodies associated with the work' (Gorman 1981, p.499).

Not content with grappling with the myriad problems caused by attempting to determine primary responsibility for information resources, librarians have further extended the concept. They have introduced the concept of *main entry* – the notion that one person or body has to be singled out, whenever it can be, as bearing more of the responsibility for creating and producing an information resource and, therefore, its name is granted a status above, and treated in the library information retrieval system in a manner different from, the other names of persons and bodies also significant in that resource.

Main entry is partly a result of old technology and has much less relevance in computerised library information retrieval systems. In a card catalogue or printed book catalogue, there is a strong imperative to save space and to be as concise as possible. For example, making a copy of a catalogue record involved retyping the catalogue card, or, in a book catalogue, it meant that the book had more pages and, therefore, cost more to produce. To minimise expense, the full catalogue record was *entered* at one place only (this was called the main entry) and only a short version of the record (the added entries) was *entered* at other places where needed, such as for second author's name, or for the title of the document. These practices were carried over into computerised library catalogues and are still with us today – the computer does not make added entries as such, but cataloguers do assign on access point as the main entry so that it can be displayed at the top of the screen, and so on.

To the disappointment of many, AACR2 has retained the requirement to differentiate between main entry and added entries despite plentiful evidence that there is little need in computerised library information retrieval systems to do so. Michael Gorman has put it strongly:

> The main entry is a bibliographic ghost that haunts current and future machine systems … In the real world of the electronic catalog, there is no practical difference between main and added access points *and* there is no practical difference between an access point and a reference to that access point (Gorman 1989, pp.630-631).

There may be an argument, however, for indicating a name or names primarily associated with a resource if the resource is usually cited through the element (e.g., 'Gorman' in the above citation). In any case, AACR2 does at least recognise that not all libraries may wish to apply the concept, and advises such libraries to 'use Chapter 21 as guidance in determining *all the entries* required in particular instances'. It is worth noting that AACR2 goes on to point out that '[i]t will be necessary, however, for all libraries to distinguish the main entry from the others when: a) making a single entry listing *or* b) making a single citation for a work' (*Anglo-American Cataloguing Rules* 2002, p.2). Here we see that AACR2 still aims to be applicable to pre-automation cataloguing as well as online library information retrieval systems – there are still many libraries in the developing world with no automated system, some of which use AACR2.

Which form of the name?

As well as the conventions which have been developed about which name to choose (where there is a choice, that is), there are other conventions connected with selecting the form of the name to be used and the order in which the elements of a name are cited. The conventions about the forms of names have developed over many thousands of years, and we understand them automatically for the society we were born in, but need to learn them when we move to a new society. For example, the Chinese convention is to use the surname (family name) as the first element of the name, confusing to Westerners who place it as the last element of the name. Thus, for instance, a Hong Kong person with the name 'Chan Wai Ming' might be accidentally addressed as Ms Ming, instead of Ms Chan.

Pseudonym or real name?

Once we are clear about the order of the elements in a name, there is more we have to decide on. It is quite common for authors to use different names – pseudonyms, noms-de-plume or pen-names – for different kinds of material they write. For example, Thomas Keneally writes most of his novels using this name, but he has also used the name William Coyle for two novels in a different style. Keneally and Coyle are different names for one person and, to acknowledge this, earlier codes of library cataloguing rules encouraged cataloguers to choose one name (say Thomas Keneally) as the valid name, and then make a reference from William Coyle to Keneally. Considerable detective work was often required to establish the relationship. The current convention is to use the name which the author uses, and not to spend time looking for any connections. So today we would have both Keneally and Coyle in the catalogue. Only if we happen to know that they are the same person could we make a connecting reference between them.

Another example is where a person goes to some length to keep their real name secret and to write or record music or take photographs under another name because they want to maintain a distinction between their private name and their public name. Again, earlier sets of cataloguing rules expected the cataloguer to go looking for a connection between names. Luckily, in modern library cataloguing codes there is much less expectation, saving a lot of time and effort.

Changes of name

Name changes are another instance where the question 'which name to select?' needs to be posed. Name changes are common in many cultures and societies, for example when women marry and decide to take the name of their husband, either in place of their unmarried family name, or as well as it. Another example is when someone converts to another religion, such as Islam, and adopts a new name as a result. Standards for access points sometimes need to take such name changes into account. As with our other examples, we find in this case that earlier library cataloguing rules directed the cataloguer to do some detective work: using our example of a married woman as author, the form of name selected could on occasion be the husband's name (such as Mrs Humphrey Ward). Currently, we simply accept that the name the author uses on the document is the name by which the author wants to be known: who are we to change their name without their permission? But for the cases where authors change their own names in their publications, then our standards and information retrieval systems need to cope with this, by providing references from each name, or by providing access to the bibliographic record directly (i.e., automatically) from each name.

How much of the name to use?

Another common case where we have to make decisions about names is to answer the question 'how much of the name do we include'? In other words, what are the essential elements of a name? One of the authors of the first edition of this book could use these forms of his name:

> *D.R. Harvey; D. Ross Harvey; Douglas R. Harvey; Douglas Ross Harvey;*
> *Douglas Harvey; or Ross Harvey*

or any of the above forms plus his qualifications and professional affiliations:

> *D.R. Harvey, B.Mus(Hons), Ph.D., DipNZLS, ANZLA, AALIA*

or he could add, in place of, or as well as his qualifications, his position:

> *D.R. Harvey, Professor, School of Information Studies, Charles Sturt University.*

So there are obviously many possibilities to select from for even a straightforward name. The situation can get a lot more complicated; for instance in the case of a member of a royal family, who writes under a family name as well as under his or her royal name.

In cases like the Harvey example the library convention is to use as little as possible of the name, and ideally to use the version of the name found on the publications, ensuring that this briefest form of the name still uniquely identifies that name. So, using the same example, the briefest form of the name we could select is *Harvey*, but this is obviously too brief, as it could be confused with any other Harvey who has been an author, and so on, of a document. We need more: *Ross Harvey* (the form he uses on the documents he writes) is probably sufficient. However, if there was in our information retrieval system a record for another author who uses the same name, another Ross Harvey, then we would need to use additional parts of the name to distinguish between them, perhaps even resorting to using date of birth or academic qualifications to further distinguish between the two names.

One important point to note is that the briefest form of the name can vary depending on which information retrieval system is used. For example, in a very small database of bibliographic records the short version – Ross Harvey – is all that is required to distinguish that name from others in the database, but, in a larger information retrieval system (a large online library catalogue, say), more elements may be needed to distinguish between identical, or very similar, names.

Some general principles about standards for using names as access points in information retrieval systems can be identified:

- use the name in the form it appears on the information resource;
- if the form of the name changes, that is, appears in different forms on different resources, use one particular form consistently (the most common form or the form already established);
- if the name itself changes, that is, the person uses a new name for another publications, use the name on the resource being catalogued;
- if different names or forms of name are definitely used by the same person, then *link* them in the database, for example, by providing references; and
- be as brief as possible: select as little of the name as is needed to uniquely identify the author.

Titles as access points

Titles of information resources can be used for two different purposes in document retrieval systems:

- as access points for an information resource where the user knows the full title already, or (more likely) knows some keywords in the title; and
- as a source of keywords to provide subject access to a resource.

In this chapter we are concerned only with the first of these. The second purpose is addressed in chapter 8. Using titles to provide access points to information resources raises some issues similar to those already examined for names as access points. For instance, we need to know how to deal with resources where:

- the title varies between one volume and another volume in a multi-volume work;
- the title differs from one edition of a work to another; or
- the resource has different titles in different countries, either in the same language or in different languages.

The same kinds of general principles apply to providing access by titles and access by names. Such general principles include:

- copy the title exactly as it appears on the resource;
- if a title changes, use the title on the resource being catalogued, but, if necessary link, the two different forms of the title; and
- be as brief as possible: select as little of the subtitle as is needed to uniquely identify the resource.

In the case where we have a choice of titles on the same resource, standards and conventions suggest that we choose the most official-looking, or otherwise the most obvious one: the one on the 'title page' or, perhaps, the one printed in the largest size of type, or the one that appears at the top of each page of the document. If, however, there is no title at all, we might supply one, though this is uncommon. If we do this, we follow the same conventions as for providing access through names, that is, the title we make up is both as brief as possible and as descriptive as possible.

Multiscript access points

Of particular interest in countries where many languages are in common use is the question of how to deal with names and titles in multilingual information retrieval systems. This is especially difficult to answer when more than one script is used. For example, the information retrieval system may need to handle roman script (the script in which English is written) plus Chinese, and perhaps also Greek and Arabic. Unfortunately some online information retrieval systems cannot yet handle more than one script, though the situation is steadily improving, thanks to such standards as Unicode (see chapter 10). This means that Western cataloguers have often romanised names in non-roman scripts, giving rise to questions such as:

- how is consistency ensured in the romanisation process?
- which romanisation scheme should be used? (For instance, two romanisation schemes are used for Chinese; many North American metadata records have been converted recently from one, the Wade-Giles (Chung-kuo) scheme, to the other, Pinyin (Zhongguo) scheme, which is the scheme used in China and elsewhere.)
- is romanisation understood by users? and
- is romanisation acceptable to users?

The application of diverse romanisation standards can result in names appearing quite differently in different sources. For example, the renowned Russian singer can be listed in a dictionary of music as 'Chaliapine, Feodor Ivanovich', but variants of all the words in this name may appear: Chaliapin, Shaliapin, Shaliapine, Saljapin; Fedor, Fyodor; Ivanovic, Ivanovitch. This can certainly affect the retrieval of this name in information retrieval systems.

Standards for access points

All the early library cataloguing codes provided standards for access points and are of interest to anyone who wants to understand why our current practice has developed the way it has. Summaries can be found in many places (see Rowley & Hartley 2007).

Currently the major standard for access points used in libraries and information centres in the English-speaking world is Part II of AACR2, examined in more detail later in this chapter. Many other sets of conventions about access points, some not formalised enough to be considered as standards, are also in common use. Many of these are limited to quite explicit situations, for instance the conventions used by a company in its in-house filing system. These are often not clearly articulated or formally recorded, so that it is difficult to find out on what basis decisions about access points have been made.

A more widely used set of conventions is found in telephone directories. Figure 4.1 reproduces part of the instructions for using Australia's Telstra *White Pages*. Some of these instructions imply that data is input as it is received and are not processed to comply with any explicit rules. For example, it is still up to the user to conduct more than one search in the alphabetical sequence for business names such as John Smith Motors and for names beginning with 'The'.

AACR2 Part II

Part II of AACR2 is widely used in library catalogues, but its standards for access points, and particularly for deciding on what form of name to use, are much more widely applicable. They are used in many different information retrieval systems, not just library catalogues, for example in indexing and abstracting services, in some archival finding aids, and no doubt in other places. As soon as an information retrieval system grows to a reasonable size, there needs to be some mechanism for ensuring consistency about names, otherwise the quantity and quality of the records the user can retrieve will be seriously diminished.

How To Find Names in This Directory

Names are divided into two parts for sorting. The first part, or the first word, determines the place to find the name. The second part, all the initials or remaining words (including locality and telephone number),

- If there are *several surnames* in determine the order within that group. a business name such as "Burke, Jones, Smith & Co", look under the first name.
- Names such as "John Smith Motors" may also appear as "Smith John Motors". **Check both places**.
- Business names which begin with "The" are generally sorted under the next word. **Check both places**.
- Punctuation and special characters within a name will generally not alter their alphabetical position and should be ignored.
- When **initials** precede a name, they will be treated as the first name, regardless of punctuation.

If the name contains a **number**, the numeric character will be sorted as though it is a word (i.e., 1 = one)

A Able Pest Control
A One Aircraft Hire
A1 Industries
A-1 Kitchens Pty Ltd
A 24 Hour Printing

In some cases, names commencing with numerals will be found under the name as it is pronounced.

Twentieth Century Products Ltd
21 Club (*pronounced Twenty One Club*)
Twentyman R …

Mc and Mac

"Mc" is treated as though spelt "Mac". Names such as "Mace" and Mack" are sorted with those names commencing with "Mc" and "Mac".

McDonald Carriers
MacDonald G & Co
Mace Hiring Ltd
Macey P R
McFarlane Kennels
Mack W D …

Mt and Mount

Names beginning with "Mt" are treated as though spelt "Mount". Names such as "Mount" appear first, followed by names which have "Mt" or "Mount" as the first part of the name.

Mount A F
Mt Abercrombie Rest Home
Mountain S
Mountford G N
Mt Hutt Ski Resort
Mount Macedon Lodge

St and Saint

Names beginning with "St" are treated as though spelt "Saint". Names such as "Saint" appear first, followed by names which have "St" or "Saint" as the first part of the name.

Saint A M
St Elena's Hostel
Saintford L R
Saint John Council

Figure 4.1 Telstra *White Pages, Perth* (1997–1998), p.52

Part II of AACR2, titled 'Headings, Uniform Titles, and References', has six chapters, which apply to all types of information resource. They are:

- Chapter 21   Choice of Access Points
- Chapter 22   Headings for Persons
- Chapter 23   Geographic Names
- Chapter 24   Headings for Corporate Bodies
- Chapter 25   Uniform Titles
- Chapter 26   References

AACR2: deciding the names to which access should be provided

Chapter 21 of AACR2 provides guidance on the question of the name (or names) on the information resource to which we should provide access (see figure 4.2). Two definitions are important here:

> *Personal author.* The person chiefly responsible for the creation of the intellectual or artistic content of a work, [and]
> *Corporate body*. An organization or group of persons that is identified by a particular name and that acts, or may act, as an entity. Typical examples of corporate bodies are associations, institutions, business firms, nonprofit enterprises, governments, government agencies, religious bodies, local churches, and conferences (*Anglo-American Cataloguing Rules* 2002, Appendix D-2, D-6).

Chapter 21 is based on the concept of *main entry*, that is, on the principle that *one* feature of an information resource is selected as its identifying access point. It instructs us to decide on a main entry (called here a *chief access point*) and other entries that are subservient to the main entry – these are *added entries* (also called *other access points*). As noted earlier in this chapter, this concept is now partially outmoded because of the possibilities offered by computerised information retrieval systems, but it is nevertheless commonly applied.

Chapter 21 first states some general rules. The first step in using this chapter is to determine which condition of intellectual responsibility applies:

- a single personal author,
- shared responsibility,
- mixed responsibility, or
- corporate body.

If none of these conditions apply, then the chief access point is the resource's title.

To cover the most commonly occurring case, that of the document which has a *single personal author*, Rule 21.4A directs the cataloguer to select as the chief access point for that document the name of the single author.

Works of *shared responsibility* are works produced by the collaboration of two or more persons who performed the same kind of activity such as writing, designing, or performing.

Works of single personal authorship: chief access point is the author (Rule 21.4A)

Works of shared responsibility: (i.e., works produced by the collaboration of two or more persons who performed the same kind of activity such as writing, adapting, or performing) chief access point is:

- *Principal author if indicated (Rule 21.6B)*
- *Author named first if responsibility is shared between two or three persons and no principal author is indicated (Rule 21.6C)*

Works of mixed responsibility: (i.e., adaptations, revisions of previously existing works; or new works in which different persons or bodies perform different kinds of activities, for example collaborative work by an author and an artist) chief access point is:

- *Adaptor for a paraphrase, rewriting, adaptation for children, version in a different literary form (Rule 21.10)*
- *Writer of the text for a work that consists of a text for which an author has provided illustrations (Rule 21.11A)*
- *Original author of an edition that has been revised, enlarged, etc. by another person if the original author is still considered to be responsible for the work (Rule 21.12A)*
- *Reviser of an edition if the original author is no longer considered to be responsible for the work (Rule 21.12B)*
- *Original author of a translation (Rule 21.14A)*

Entry under corporate body: selecting a corporate body as chief access point is restricted to those works which emanate from (i.e., are issued by or have originated with) a corporate body *and* fall into one or more of the following categories (Rule 21.1B2):

- *Works of an administrative nature dealing with the corporate body itself or its internal policies, procedures, and/or operations; its finances; its officers and/or staff; or its resources (for example catalogues, membership directories)*
- *Some specified legal and governmental works (for example laws – Rule 21.31, constitutions – Rule 21.33; court decisions – Rule 21.36)*
- *Works that record the collective thought of the body (for example reports of commissions, committees, etc.)*
- *Works that report the collective activity of a conference (for example conference proceedings) provided that the conference is prominently named in the item being catalogued*
- *Sound recordings, films, videorecordings resulting from the collective activity of a performing group as a whole.*
- *Cartographic materials emanating from a corporate body if the body is not merely the publisher*

Entry under title: the title is the chief access point for works where a person or corporate body is not selected as chief access point (Rule 21.1C). Title is selected as chief access point when:

- *The personal authorship is unknown and the work does not emanate from a corporate body*
- *It is the work of more than three personal authors (Rule 21.6C2)*
- *It is a collection or a work produced under editorial direction that has a collective title (Rule 21.7)*
- *It is accepted as sacred scripture by a religious group (21.37).*

Added entries: In addition to the chief access point, other access points are assigned to names and titles that are bibliographically significant and that the user might seek (Rules 21.29-21.30).

- *Personal names: other access points are provided for*
  Collaborators (up to three; if more than three, only for the first named)
  Writers
  Editors and compilers (except, usually, for a serial)
  Translators (in some cases)
  Illustrators (in some cases)
  Some other categories of persons (for example, person honoured by a Festschrift).
- *Corporate names: an access point is assigned for prominently named corporate body, unless it is a commercial publisher, etc.*
- *Titles: an access point is assigned for title, unless it has already been selected as the chief access point, and for other titles which are significantly different from the title proper (for example cover title, running title).*
- *Series: an access point is usually assigned for series title, if not too generic in nature.*

Figure 4.2 AACR2 (2002 revision) Part II: choice of access points, Chapter 21

For these the chief access point selected is the name of the principal author (or adaptor or performer) if this is indicated prominently. If responsibility is shared between two or three persons and no principal author is indicated, then the author named first is selected; if more than three persons, the title is to be used as the chief access point, according to AACR2 (this rule is being revisited for RDA).

Works of *mixed responsibility* are works such as adaptations or revisions of previously existing works, or new works in which different persons or bodies perform different kinds of activities, for instance, a book that is the product of collaboration between a writer and an artist, or a motion picture, which normally involves a large number of people in different roles (director, producer, actors, cinematographer, etc.). The chief access point varies according to the nature of the work, for example:

- the adaptor is selected for a paraphrase, a rewriting, an adaptation for children, or a version in a different literary form;
- the writer of the text for which an artist has provided illustrations;
- the original author of an edition that has been revised, enlarged, etc. by another person, if the original author is still considered to be responsible for the work;
- the reviser of an edition, if the original author is no longer considered to be responsible for the work;
- the original author of a translation;
- the composer of a musical sound recording, if it features classical music;
- the principal performer of a musical sound recording, if it is their album; and
- the original author of a talking book (unless it has been adapted).

Some of these distinctions are not always easy to make, and the rules in Chapter 21 provide further guidance and examples to clarify difficult distinctions.

Situations of mixed responsibility are becoming increasingly common, as so many new information resources are multimedia in nature. Many people may be responsible for the contents of a CD-ROM, for example: writers, graphic artists, programmers, musicians, narrators, consultants, and so on. In such cases, it is often considered that too many people were involved for any one person to deserve main entry status – a circumstance sometimes referred to as *diffuse authorship*. In such cases, then, none of the persons' names are assigned as the chief access point; instead, the title is used. Similarly, very few films are produced by a single person, but, rather, by a team of people, performing a range of roles: director, producer, editor, scriptwriter, composer, actors, cameraman, and so on. Even though some films may be identified by their director, or perhaps by their starring actor, audiovisual cataloguers rarely assign a person's name as main entry for films or videos.

Selection of *corporate body* as chief access point is, as noted earlier in this chapter, a convention which has now become largely unnecessary in today's library information retrieval systems, but one which AACR2 still clings to. Choosing the name of a corporate body as a chief access point for an information resource is restricted to several clearly defined cases. Rule 21.1B2 specifies that to fit into this category works must meet two criteria: they must 'emanate from' (that is, be issued by or have originated in) a corporate body; *and* they must fall into one or more of the following categories:

- works of an *administrative nature* dealing with the corporate body itself or its internal policies, procedures, and/or operations; its finances; its officers and/or staff; or its resources (e.g., catalogues, membership directories);
- some specified *legal and governmental works* (e.g., laws, constitutions, court decisions);
- works that record the *collective thought of the body* (e.g., reports of commissions, committees, etc.);
- works that report the *collective activity of a conference* (e.g., conference proceedings), provided that the conference is prominently named in the item being catalogued;
- sound recordings, films, videorecordings resulting from the *collective activity of a performing group* as a whole; and
- *cartographic material* emanating from a corporate body other than the body which merely publishes or distributes it.

Selection of *title* as the chief access point is a kind of fall-back position for works whose situation does not fit into those categories that allow a personal name, or the name of a corporate body, to be the chief access point. Thus the title would usually be chosen as the chief access point in the case of videos and CD-ROMs, because they would not be put under a particular person's name, or the name of an organisation (although films are often produced by production companies, this is not covered in any of the above categories for corporate body main entry).

Rule 21.1C of AACR2 gives general directions about when to select the title as the chief access point:

- when the personal authorship is unknown and the work does not emanate from a corporate body;
- when it is the work of more than three personal authors with equal responsibility;
- when it is a collection or a work produced under editorial direction that has a collective title; or
- when it is accepted as sacred scripture by a religious group.

Added entries, or other access points, are assigned in addition to the chief access point. These other access points are assigned to names and titles that are bibliographically significant and that the user might search on, such as:

- *personal names* – for collaborators, writers, editors and compilers, translators and illustrators (in some cases), and some other categories of persons (e.g., a person honoured by a Festschrift);
- *corporate body names* – for a prominently named corporate body that is not merely a commercial type of publisher (e.g., a university awarding a thesis);

- *titles* – for title proper (i.e., main title), unless it has been used as the main entry; and for other titles which are significantly different from the title proper (e.g., cover title, running title); and
- *series titles* – if they are not judged too generic.

Examples of the choice of access points are given in figures 4.3a to 4.3h.

AACR2: deciding which version of a name to use

Part II of AACR2 is based on the principle that we should always prefer to use the form of a name which is to be found on the document in hand, *unless there is good reason to alter it*. The main reasons for altering the form of a name are:

- to be consistent with another form of the name already used in the database for the same person or corporate body, and
- to ensure that the name is not confused with another identical or very similar name for a different entity (such as another person or a corporate body).

Another reason, less common, is to add a designation that indicates the nature of the entity: for example Yothu Yindi *(Musical group)*.

Figures 4.3a to 4.3h show examples of the application of AACR2 Chapter 21.

Figure 4.3a
Title page: Henrietta Drake-Brockman *Voyage to Disaster*
Chief access point: Henrietta Drake-Brockman
Additional access point: Title

Figure 4.3 b
Title page: *Fun with Chinese Festivals*
Tan Huay Peng, illustrated by Leong Kum Chuen
Chief access point: *Tan Huay Peng*
Additional access points: *Title; Leong Kum Chuen*

Figure 4.3c
Title page: *A Field Guide to Australian Trees* Ivan
Holliday, Ron Hill
Chief access point: Ivan Holliday
Additional access points: Title; Ron Hill

Figure 4.3d
Title page: *Portraits of the South West: Essays on
Aborigines, Women and the Environment, edited by B.
K. de Garis*
Chief access point: Title (the essays are by seven
different people)
Additional access point: B.K. de Garis

Figure 4.3e
Compact disc: *Piano Concertos Nos. 2 & 4*
Composer: Ludwig van Beethoven
Pianist: Vladimir Ashkenazy
Orchestra: Vienna Philharmonic Orchestra
Conductor: Zubin Mehta
Chief access point: Ludwig van Beethoven
Additional access points: Title (and, optionally, uniform
title); Vladimir Ashkenazy, Zubin Mehta, Vienna
Philharmonic Orchestra

Figure 4.3f
Compact disc: Sgt. Pepper's Lonely Hearts Club Band, The Beatles
Chief access point: The Beatles
Additional access points: Title; also, optionally, could add for John Lennon and Paul McCartney (principal songwriters)

Figure 4.3g
Film title: The Pianist
Credits: Starring Adrien Brody, Thomas Kretschmann, Frank Finlay, Maureen Lipman, Ed Stoppard; Directed by Roman Polanski; Produced by Roman Polanski, Robert Benmussa, Alain Sarde; Written by Ronald Harwood, Wladyslaw Szpilman; Distributed by Focus Features
Chief access point: Title (or uniform title)
Additional access points: As many of the above names as the cataloguer deems necessary, at least: Roman Polanski, Adrien Brody

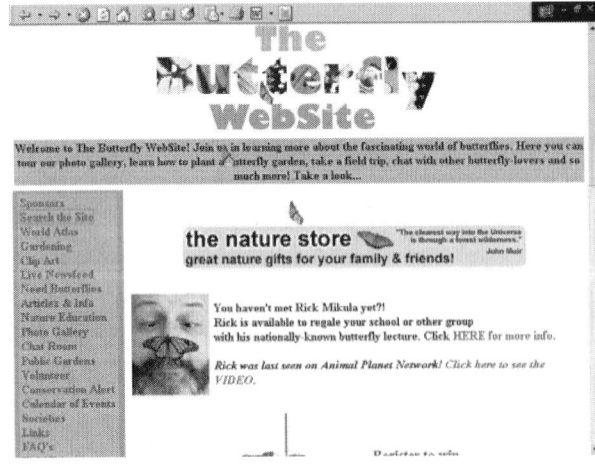

Figure 4.3h
Title on home page: The Butterfly Website
Copyright statement: © copyright 1995-2003 Family of Nature, Inc.
Chief access point: Title
Additional access points: Family of Nature, Inc.

Chapters 22-24 provide guidance in deciding on the forms of names for three types of names:

- personal names,
- geographic names, and
- corporate body names.

Personal names (Chapter 22)

Chapter 22 (Headings for Persons) is divided into three main sections: choice of name; entry element; and additions to names (see figure 4.4). These parts are followed by special rules which apply to names in Arabic, Burmese and Karen, some Chinese names, Indic languages, Indonesian, Malay and Thai (a somewhat haphazard list of languages, as Hider and Turner (2006) have pointed out). The emphasis throughout this chapter is one of least effort: the name in the form found in the information resource should be used unless there is good reason to alter the name. In applying Chapter 22 in our information retrieval systems we need to ask three basic questions, which are addressed by the three sections of the rules:

- which name, and which form of a name, should we choose? For example, on the title page the name is 'B.K. de Garis' but he signs his introduction 'Brian de Garis'.

- what should the entry element be when entering this name into our information retrieval system? For example, what is the entry element for Mr. de Garis? And for Henrietta Drake-Brockman and Tan Huay Peng?

- what additions are necessary to identify this person adequately in our information retrieval system? Do we have several Tan Huay Pengs in our database? Do we need to distinguish among them?

General rule (Rule 22.1): Choose the name by which the person is commonly known. This may be the person's real name, pseudonym, nickname, initials, religious or royal name.

Fullness of name (Rule 22.3A): If the name varies in fullness, choose the most commonly known form of the name or the form which is most predominantly used.

Choice of entry element (Rules 22.5-22.11):
- A name containing a *surname* is entered under that surname
- For persons who use their *title of nobility*, the entry element is the proper name in the title of nobility
- A name that consists of a *given name only* is entered in direct order (for example Leonardo da Vinci).

Figure 4.4 AACR2 (2002 revision) Part II, Chapter 22, Form of name for personal names

As little as possible is added to personal names, and this only to distinguish names that would be confused because they are identical or very similar. The range of possible additions to personal names, and the order of preference in which they are to be added, are indicated in Rules 22.12–22.20:

- dates, for example, dates of birth and death (Rule 22.17);
- fuller forms of the name, for example, forenames spelled out in place of initials (Rule 22.18); and
- other distinguishing terms, for example, term of address, title of position or office, academic degree (Rule 22.19).

Corporate body names (Chapter 24)

Chapter 24 provides rules for, amongst other things, the instances where corporate bodies change their names (see figure 4.5), which they do frequently. When this occurs, each name change is considered as a separate body and is represented by a different heading. These different headings need to be linked in the information retrieval system, by means of references or by other means. The name chosen for a corporate body is the name given on documents published by that body, unless it is commonly known by another name, or it is part of another body and you need the larger body's name to help identify it properly.

Form of name (Rules 24.2-24.11)
- *Variant names* (Rules 24.2-24.3): prefer the form found in the chief source of information, the predominant form, or a distinctive brief form (in that order of preference). Also, a conventional form of the name in common use is preferred to a fuller, official name.
- *Language* (Rules 24.3A, 24.3B): the form of the name in the official language of the corporate body is chosen, with a preference for an official English form of the name if there is one.
- *Additions to names* (Rules 24.4-24.11): the following elements are added to names **if necessary** to distinguish similar names or to convey the idea of a corporate body:
  a general designation, for example Yothu Yindi (*Musical group*)
  place where the body is located, e.g., Institute of Dental Health (Sydney, N.S.W.)
  name of an institution, e.g., National Crime Prevention Institute (University of London)
  year of founding of the body, or years of existence of the body.

Choice of entry element (Rules 24.12-24.14)
- The entry element is usually the *first word* in the name, with some exceptions for example initial articles, ordinal numbers.
- Names are usually *entered directly*, for example T.D. Meagher and Associates – not Meagher (T.D.) and Associates.
- A *subordinate body is entered directly under its own name, unless it falls into one of six types* (Rule 24.13). The most common of these is where a name contains a word implying subordination, for example division, department, committee, commission.

Rules for specific types of corporate bodies
- *Conferences, congresses, meetings, etc.* (Rule 24.7)
- *Government bodies and officials* (Rules 24.17-24.26)
- *Religious bodies and officials* (Rule 24.27).

Figure 4.5 AACR2 (2002 revision) Part II, Chapter 24, Form of name for corporate bodies

Geographic names (Chapter 23)

Chapter 23 provides guidance about the form of geographic names that are chosen as access points in information retrieval systems. In practice, the rules in Chapter 23 are very much related to those in Chapter 24, especially those dealing with headings for government bodies. More often than not, headings for government bodies include the name of the country, state, or municipality in which they operate, or have authority. The state government of Victoria in Australia may have a Department of Education; so may the state of New South Wales. In an information retrieval system that uses AACR2, items issued by these departments would have as access points *Victoria. Department of Education* and *New South Wales. Department of Education*. Chapter 23 also provides guidelines for distinguishing between different places with the same name, for example, *Paris (France)* and *Paris (Tex.)*. Similarly, some types of corporate body frequently need a geographic qualifier to distinguish them from others with the same name, for example the Institute of Dental Health in Sydney is quite likely to require the geographic qualifier *(Sydney, N.S.W.)* if the information retrieval system is also organising items from an Institute of Dental Health that operates elsewhere.

Chapter 23 favours the use of the English language form of a place name when there is a well-established English form – for example *New Caledonia* rather than *Nouvelle Calédonie*, *Munich* rather than *München*. It also favours the contemporary form – which does not necessarily mean the latest form, but the form used at the time of the resource's publication, if the place is no longer exactly the same territory. Constant political change causes the names of countries to change quite frequently, and this can cause confusion among the creators and users of information retrieval systems. One only needs to think of the dissolution of the Soviet Union in the late 1980s, of changes to the names of African countries in the 1960s and 1970s, and of disputed names such as Burma/Myanmar, to understand the implications of such changes upon our attempts to organise the documents of these governments.

Uniform titles (Chapter 25)

A uniform title is a convention used to collocate information resources which are variants of the same work. Classic examples are religious works. *Good News for Modern Man*; *The Transformer; The Way; Katungkatjaka Wangka; The Holy Bible;* and *Life Application Bible* are but a tiny selection of the multitude of titles used for different versions of the Bible. The organisation of music scores and sound recordings also relies on a special application of uniform titles to facilitate access.

Chapter 25 provides guidance on how to construct uniform titles and contains special rules for categories of works for which uniform titles are very important, such as music, certain religious works, and certain legal works, such as laws and treaties. It should be noted, however, that all uniform titles are *optional* according to AACR2 – they only need be used if the cataloguer thinks they would improve retrieval.

Linking related names (Chapter 26)

Throughout Chapters 22, 23, 24 and 25 phrases such as 'Refer from …', 'Make *see also* references from …' and 'Make explanatory references from …' appear. The rules in these chapters are applied in order to establish the *authoritative* form of a name. During this process various forms of a name are considered, and some are rejected. The rejected options may be the form of a name known to some users and used by them to search the information retrieval system. Chapter 26 provides guidance to ensure that those who search under the rejected form of a name are led to the heading chosen by the creator of the information retrieval system's records. This is an important function of authority control, an activity which will be examined in more detail in the next chapter of this book.

AACR2 as a standard for name/title indexing

AACR2 was not initially adopted as wholeheartedly as a standard for access points as it was as a standard for description. One of the reasons was the cost of implementing it when it was introduced: the costs of educating cataloguers and users in the new rules; the costs of providing references or other links between old and new forms of names; and the costs associated with changing cataloguing practice in local, national and international networks. These were eventually accepted as necessary because of the advantages provided by AACR2 in allowing improved cooperation among libraries, and in building library information retrieval systems which could be made more user-friendly (Gorman 1987).

The following examples illustrate the kinds of changes in forms of names from AACR1 to AACR2, and highlight the problems faced by libraries when there are significant changes to standards:

- Harvey, Douglas Ross, 1951- *to* Harvey, D.R. (if necessary, Harvey, D.R. (Douglas Ross)).
- University of Adelaide. Barr Smith Library *to* Barr Smith Library.

The number of changes required in a large library information retrieval system meant that a good deal of extra cataloguing had to be carried out – something that will not be lost on librarians as they provide feedback in the RDA development process.

Other standards for access points

Although AACR2 is the most commonly used standard for access points in information centres, it is not the only one. Other standards include the British Standard BS 1629 : 1989 *Recommendations for References to Published Materials* which covers, *inter alia*, the selection of names. For example, Section 5.1.1 indicates that 'The person or organization shown most prominently in the preferred source' is the one considered as responsible. Section 5.2 'Personal Names' deals with forms of names for people; 5.3 'Organizations of Groups' deals with forms of names for organisations.

Another important standard is *Names of Persons: National Usages for Entry in Catalogues*, compiled by IFLA. The fourth revised and enlarged edition was published in 1996. It details the preferred form of personal names for catalogue entry favoured by the national libraries and other national bodies of more than 100 countries, with respect to their own citizens and languages (International Federation of Library Associations and Institutions 1996). This survey is based on one of the Paris Principles, born out of the 1961 international conference mentioned in chapter 2:

> When the name of a personal author consists of several words, the choice of entry-word is determined as far as possible by agreed usage in the country of which the author is a citizen, or, if this is not possible, by agreed usage in the language which he generally uses (Chaplin 1966, Section 12).

The archival community has also produced a standard for access points, ISAAR(CPF): *International Standard Archival Authority Record for Corporate Bodies, Persons and Families*, now in its second edition (International Council on Archives 2004). This standard specifies data elements which can be used to create standardised access points for corporate bodies, persons and families for use in an archival description system, and also to create authority records and references from non-preferred terms.

Conclusion

Standardising forms of names in our information retrieval systems is quite possibly the single most useful of all the tasks in the cataloguing and classification process. Without standardisation, names can be effectively lost in the system, inaccessible because they do not conform to a commonly applied standard which is understood by, or is familiar to, the user. Part II of AACR2 is widely applied internationally for the purpose of standardising forms of names, particularly – but not exclusively – in library information retrieval systems.

By itself, though, the process of standardising forms of names is not enough. In addition we must ensure that the names are *controlled*, which means used in the information retrieval system in a consistent fashion, so that each document involving the same person or body is retrieved, no matter which form of the name is actually searched on. This apparently simple task is complex and time-consuming, but is vital to ensure maximum effectiveness of information retrieval systems. The task, known as *authority control*, is the subject of chapter 5.

CHAPTER 5
Authority control

In chapters 2, 3 and 4 we examined some of the standards for descriptive cataloguing in common use in libraries and information centres. This chapter looks at some more standards and tools used specifically for the purposes of authority control and examines the need for authority control in library information retrieval systems.

What is authority control?

The term _authority control_ refers to the process of ensuring that the names (of people, corporate bodies and places), titles (of documents and series) and subjects (of documents) in an information retrieval system are used in a consistent form and style. Authority control of _subject headings_ is discussed in chapter 8; we shall concentrate on control of name and title headings in this chapter, but many of the same points apply.

Authority control has three aspects – 'uniqueness, standardization, and linkages are the foundations of authority control' (Clack 1990, p.1). In practice, the process consists of three main steps:

- _distinguishing names and titles_ – the process of ensuring that the forms of the names (or titles) selected are formulated consistently and indexed in the same way, according to whatever specific standard has been selected; for example, that the name of the author _Whyte, Jean P._ is consistently indexed this way, not using other versions of her name;

- _showing relationships_ – the process of linking different versions of the same name (or title), or different names for the same person or body, to one another; for example linking _Brent of Bin Bin, Miles Franklin,_ and _Stella Marcia Miles Lampe Franklin,_ all of which are names used by the same author; and

- _documenting decisions_ – recording the decisions made in determining the first and second aspects is important because it assists later users of the headings (cataloguers, for instance) to maintain consistency more efficiently (Avram 1984, p.331).

The first and second steps were touched on in the previous chapter, particularly in relation to AACR2, and will be expanded upon below, but first we need to ask why authority control activity is needed – or at least, desired.

Why perform authority control?

When searching a database of an information retrieval system to locate information resources, or their surrogate records, by a given author, retrieval of all resources by that author cannot be assured unless the author's name is used in a consistent fashion. To take one example: Aboriginal activist and writer, Oodgeroo of the Noonuccal, for many years wrote under the name _Kath Walker,_ but in later years preferred to be known, and write, as

Oodgeroo. Let us assume that both of these names (*Kath Walker* and *Oodgeroo Noonuccal*) have been assigned as access points to metadata records in the database. If a user hopes to locate all of her writings and searches the database for only one of these names, the other name will not be found unless it is linked in some way to the name the user has searched for. The user will, therefore, only get an incomplete response to the question 'What works by Oodgeroo can this information retrieval system locate for me?' Figure 5.1 gives some more examples. The problem grows as the number of variations of a name increases. Since the databases of some information retrieval systems are very large indeed (many Australian library catalogues contain more than 1 million records), the problem can be very real, significantly reducing the effectiveness of the system.

Personal Names

variant spellings of a name: *Dante Alighieri, Dante Alleghieri, Dante Alaghieri*; *Shakespeare, Shakspeare, Shakspere*

different romanisations of non-Roman scripts: *Kaddafi, Kadhafi, Qaddafi, Qadhafi, Gadaffi*; *Chaliapine, Shaliapin, Saljapin*; *Cheng Pao-hung, Zheng Bao Hong*

different linguistic forms: *Virgil, Vergilius*; *Francesco, Francis, Francesco, Franciscus, Franz, François*

use of complete and incomplete forms: *G.M., Gaetano Melzi*; *Miles Franklin, Stella Marcia Miles Lampe Franklin*

changes of status: *Mary Anne Stewart*, who became *Lady Mary Anne Barker*, then *Lady Mary Anne Broome*; *Annie Baxter*, who became *Annie Dawbin*; *Benjamin Disraeli*, who became *Lord Beaconsfield*

change of name: *John Naumenko*, who became *John Newman*; *Jules Joubert*, who became *Francis de Sales*

use of pseudonyms and other assumed names: *Rolf Boldrewood*, pseudonym of *Thomas Alexander Browne*; *Brent of Bin Bin*, a pseudonym of *Miles Franklin*; *An emigrant mechanic*, characterising phrase used by *Alexander Harris*

use of title of another work: *Author of Waverly*, for *Walter Scott*

Corporate Names

variant spellings of a name: Central-Anstalt für Meteorologie und Erdinagnetismus; Zentralanstalt für Meteorologie und Erdinagnetismus

different linguistic forms: Canadian Library Association, Association canadienne des bibliothèques; National Library of New Zealand, Te Puna Matauranga o Aotearoa

use of shorter names or official names: RMIT, Royal Melbourne Institute of Technology; Unesco, United Nations Educational, Scientific and Cultural Organisation; Musée de Louvre; Musée national de Louvre

change of name: Telecom Australia, Telstra Corporation

Figure 5.1 Variant forms of names, based on Avram 1984, Appendix A

Authority control is, in other words, a process which assists with more efficient and effective retrieval of resources from information retrieval systems. It does this by ensuring 'that all works written by a particular author are retrievable with the same access point' and also by ensuring 'that only works by that author are entered under a particular heading'; in so doing, it saves the time and effort of the cataloguer 'having to establish the heading each time a work by the same author is cataloged' (Chan 1994, p.123). As such, it provides efficiencies in operation, such as faster searching of catalogues.

It is possible to have *no* authority control in an information retrieval system and this is in fact the case in many systems. The decision belongs to the system manager, who must balance the time and resources necessary to establish and maintain an authority file against the need to offer the best possible service to the user. It is generally agreed that authority control is necessary to provide the most precise level of retrieval, but it is also becoming apparent that keyword searching and more recent developments in information retrieval systems are improving the level of retrieval by other means. One argument often mounted for maintaining an authority file is that it ultimately reduces the amount of effort required: the cataloguer carries out the authority control procedure only once for a heading, whereas, if it is not present, the *user* must carry out authority control procedures each time a heading is accessed. 'If we shift authority control work to the users, one cataloguer's task becomes the task of many users, each one duplicating the effort over and over again' (Avram 1984, p.333). Clack observes that 'authority control is expensive; however, no control is even more so' (Clack 1990, p.9).

How is authority control carried out?

Authority files are used as the mechanism for implementing authority control. These can be established in many forms.

In a manual information retrieval system (for example, a library card catalogue) a separate sequence of cards listing headings (personal names, corporate bodies, places, series titles) can be established, on which can be recorded:

- the form of the heading decided on, according to the standard adopted;
- the AACR2 rule numbers, and any other relevant evidence, which were used to decide on the preferred form of heading; and
- the other variant forms of the heading which were not chosen as the preferred form.

In a computerised information retrieval system the same procedures are followed, but the way in which the authority file is handled is likely to be different. In one common model, a separate authority file is established in which the above decisions are entered and the headings are linked to the bibliographic records to which they apply. When a searcher enters one form of name, the computer checks the authority file, identifies the preferred name heading, and then retrieves all the bibliographic records linked to that heading. The authority file itself, with details of non-preferred forms of headings, can also be displayed if required.

How is a name linked to related names?

Once the preferred form of the name has been decided on, using Chapters 22-24 of AACR2 for instance, the next step is to show relationships, that is, to link non-preferred forms of name to the preferred form, and sometimes to link different names to each other. This raises the question of *how* this linking is done. A variety of means is used, depending on the information retrieval system. The most common way in older, manual forms of catalogue (such as the book catalogue and the card catalogue) was to provide a full bibliographic record in the catalogue, filed at the appropriate point for one form of the name, and to provide a reference which directed the user from another form of name to the preferred one, for example, *Harvey, Ross* **see** *Harvey, D.R.* Although this method of linking names was considered acceptable in older information retrieval systems, it has been superseded in online systems. The method has the obvious disadvantage of introducing an additional step into the user's search: first find one form of the name, then look up the preferred form. User studies have indicated that, if we can reduce the number of steps that we require users to make, then their rate of successful retrieval will be significantly higher.

Some modern information retrieval systems allow us to by-pass that additional step by providing access to the bibliographic record (or the resource itself) directly from both forms of name. This is carried out in various ways depending on the system's internal structure. In one scenario, the bibliographic record may be repeated at two points in the system's file, the two points being the two different forms of the name. However, in systems with authority files, what can happen is that this file links both forms of name to the metadata record, which is displayed as a result of a search on either of the forms of name.

When is a name linked to related names?

As noted in the previous chapter of this book, Chapter 26 of AACR2 gives instructions on when to link variant names and titles to each other, and also the style in which this link is displayed (if it is displayed at all). For example, if Chapter 22 has led us to choose the name *Harvey, D. R.* as the heading, Chapter 26 then requires us, based on the evidence of this book's title page, to make the reference *Harvey, Ross* **see** *Harvey, D. R.* Likewise, if our interpretation of Chapter 24 causes us to choose *CSIRO* as the heading for the Australian research organisation, Chapter 26 requires us to make the reference *Commonwealth Scientific and Research Organisation* **see** *CSIRO.* In the case of an earlier example, following Chapter 26, under *Walker, Kath* we would add a reference, **see also** *Oodgeroo Noonuccal.* Likewise, under *Oodgeroo Noonuccal* we would add a reference, **see also** *Walker, Kath.*

It is worth quoting the basic rule (26.1B1) from Chapter 26 for when to make a *see* reference, which embodies the general principle of linking names and titles whenever there is a reasonable probability that without doing so, an incomplete search would result: 'Make a *see* reference from a form of the name of a person or a corporate body or title of a work that might reasonably be sought to the form that has been chosen as a name or uniform heading, or as a title entry' (AACR 2002, p.26).

Where do authority records come from?

Twenty or thirty years ago libraries would probably have carried out all aspects of authority control themselves, doing the detective work which is sometimes required. Today's information professional is far more likely to adopt the authority control decisions made by others, to contract out the authority control service, or even to ignore the process entirely and accept the consequences of lowered retrieval effectiveness in their information retrieval systems. As noted, a considerable amount of effort is involved in the authority control process. It can often involve searching other publications, not just the document you want to catalogue – for example, to identify the official form of the name of a government department, you might need to look up current official directories of government departments, and for a personal name you might need to find the dates of birth and death of that person to distinguish them from other persons with the same name.

To save the time of cataloguers, libraries often use publications and databases which contain the authority control decisions made by other libraries. Sharing authority control data is made possible by the widespread use of standards such as AACR2 and the MARC record format for authority records (see chapter 10 for more on MARC). One of the primary sources of authority data is the *Library of Congress Authorities*, a database of name, title and subject authority records now freely available online. The Library of Congress started creating machine-readable (MARC) name authority records in 1977, and soon began to attract the attention of other libraries considering online authority files. Many libraries upload LC authority records into their library information retrieval systems, as they cover a fair amount of the mainstream material published in the Western world. Indeed, the LC authority files have significantly increased in size and coverage in recent years as other major libraries have started contributing – and not just taking – authority records through the NACO program (see later in this chapter). The LC files have thus become the authority files in many bibliographic databases, such as WorldCat, the union catalogue of OCLC (see chapter 12), the largest bibliographic database of all.

One authority control goal that has been pursued for some years is automatic checking of headings when a bibliographic record is added to a database. This goal is only now beginning to be realised with the use of more sophisticated online cataloguing systems. An example of such a system is OCLC Connexion, OCLC's new cataloguing platform, which provides a 'control heading' function that checks the headings in the bibliographic record with those on its authority file. If, after the cataloguer utilises this function, any headings in the bibliographic record fail to match, near matches may be offered as alternatives; otherwise, the cataloguer may need to investigate the name or title or subject further. If the heading is genuinely a name for a new author, then the cataloguer may still enter the bibliographic record containing the heading into the OCLC database, although it is helpful if they can create an authority record for the new name at the same time. (However, only certain member libraries are allowed to add to OCLC's authority file, namely those that are part of the NACO program.)

Authority record standards

Whether manual or online, an authority file contains *authority records*, and the format of these authority records usually follows a standard. This is certainly the case for the LC authorities. However, we should note that AACR2 itself does not currently specify a format, only the format of headings and references. Indeed, it has been proposed for authority records to be covered in the new RDA standard. Presently, libraries of the Anglo-American tradition resort to using what guidance exists in the MARC authority record documentation, and if they are members of NACO, the NACO Participants' Manual issued by the Library of Congress. MARC formats are described in more detail in chapter 10; NACO is outlined below. A more international standard that also covers this area is *Guidelines for Authority Records and References* (2001), formerly called *Guidelines for Authority References and Entries* (GARE), produced by IFLA. The second edition was influenced by FRBR (see chapter 3), and is also closely associated with the new *Functional Requirements for Authority Data* (FRAD).

Name Authority Cooperative Project (NACO)

The LC authority files are the most used in library catalogues of the Western publishing world, but they are not solely the product of the Library of Congress. In fact, the Library has found itself, due to insufficient resources, with growing gaps even in its own catalogue, with a considerable number of headings having been left uncontrolled, that is, with no corresponding authority record. It is not surprising, therefore, that they have led a cooperative authority control program called the Name Authority Cooperative Project (NACO), to encourage contributions from other major libraries. NACO currently has around 400 member institutions, representing the authority control work of various national libraries (including the British Library, and the national libraries of New Zealand, South Africa, Scotland, and Wales), major research and academic libraries in North America and beyond, and certain cataloguing networks such as SILAS (Singapore Integrated Library Automation Services) (*NACO Participants' Manual*, 2005). After receiving some training, cataloguers in the NACO member libraries contribute their authority records for new names and titles, usually directly into the LC/NACO Authority File, for the benefit not only of other NACO libraries (including the Library of Congress), but all libraries that use the file for their cataloguing (Library of Congress 2007b).

Authority control in Australia

Australian libraries, like libraries in every other part of the world, have aimed at completely 'clean' library information retrieval systems, catalogues in which all headings for names and subjects are formulated following the guidance of standards, and all variations are fully linked to the preferred form of the heading. This, however, falls into the category of unattainable goals. The authority control process takes time. Historically, authority control work was always given low priority in order to reduce cataloguing backlogs and reduce the time taken to move uncatalogued items from the library's back room to the shelves. The problem was exacerbated in the 1960s and later with the widespread use of copy cataloguing (adopting cataloguing data from other libraries and inserting it with minimum alteration into one's own catalogue). Much of the cataloguing data came from the Library of Congress's MARC records which, although generally of high quality, nonetheless reflected changes in the Library of Congress's practice regarding forms of headings. Inconsistencies were thus introduced as a result of the very tools which were reducing backlogs and introducing the economies associated with resource-sharing for Australian libraries. Typically the low priority accorded to authority control did not change with the introduction of computerised catalogues, partly because of the perceived promise that the computer could reduce, or even eliminate, the need by virtue of its keyword searching abilities. Authority control became, in Australia, 'almost a lost cause' (Gatenby 1991, p.35).

That a lack of authority control could be a major problem even in computerised information retrieval systems was soon recognised. The Australian response was to ensure that the software adopted for the national bibliographic utility, ABN, could accommodate high-level authority control work. The WLN (Washington Library Network, which became Western Library Network) software chosen allowed sophisticated authority control procedures to be carried out, albeit, from today's perspective, in a time-consuming and clumsy manner. Theoretically all participants carried out the authority control work arising from the records they added to the database, or from the records already on the database which they modified. But in practice this was rarely the case, and few libraries carried out this work. The bulk of the authority control work was done either by the ABN Office itself or by contractors working at its request.

The recent reincarnations of ABN – Kinetica and now Libraries Australia -- have seen little change in the practical application of authority control, although in the last year or two the number of authorities added to the database has been on an upward trend. While participants are still theoretically expected to carry out authority control on records that they contribute, an advisory group set up by the National Library reported a user survey had found, amongst other things, that:
- very little authority work is being carried out on the National Bibliographic Database (NBD);
- the major inhibitor to the contribution of authority data to the NBD is reluctance to use the Kinetica Cataloguing Client;
– there is a perception that authority data on the NBD is of poor quality and out of date. Conversely there seems to be a lack of perception that the NBD as a resource-sharing system requires its customers to contribute in order for all users to reap the benefits; and
- many respondents reported difficulties in maintaining a clean authority file on their local systems and felt this would be exacerbated by the import of records from other systems (NLA. EAGAD 2003).

The advisory group concluded that 'the continuing decline in contribution to the NBD and the use of local systems instead of the NBD for carrying out authority control presents a considerable threat to the NBD' (NLA. EAGAD 2002).

Libraries Australia is a special case in Australian terms because it is a *national* database, the largest in the country, and because a large number of participants contribute to it. It may be impractical to carry out effective authority control on a database of bibliographic records with these characteristics. However, there is no doubt at all that in smaller bibliographic databases such as individual library catalogues, where consistency can be better ensured because of the smaller number of personnel adding to it and modifying it, effective authority control work can be carried out. Whether they choose to, or not, is in the end a local decision: but those who make the decision must be clear about the implications of their choice on the effectiveness of the information retrieval system and, therefore, on how well their users' needs can be satisfied.

Whenever shared cataloguing or authority control work occurs, as we have already seen, it becomes particularly important that everyone uses the same standards. Thus the Library of Congress requires NACO contributors to use, in full, the Library's Z1: *Name and Series Authority Records* section of its *Descriptive Cataloging Manual*, and also the *NACO Participants' Manual* (3rd ed., 2005), in addition to the *MARC21 Format for Authority Data*, the *Library of Congress Rule Interpretations* and, of course, AACR2.

Apart from the Library of Congress (which acts as the national library for the United States), many other national libraries maintain their own authority files. However, there is also a trend towards sharing authorities at an international level. The British Library has already merged its files with the LC/NACO Authority File; Libraries Australia is moving in the same direction. Meanwhile, a Virtual International Authority File (VIAF) has been piloted by the Library of Congress, the Deutsche Nationalbibliothek, the Bibliothèque nationale de France (BnF), and OCLC. The idea here is for libraries around the world to retain their own authority files, with names established in the form of their choice, but for these to be linked to other authority records in cases where there are different established forms for the same person or organisation. In this way, libraries will be able to download a lot of authority data that they would otherwise have to create from scratch. A prototype of the system can be found on the web (http://viaf.org).

In an age of limited cataloguing resources, cooperative authority control programs such as NACO have proven invaluable. The sharing of authority records has exactly the same kind of economic benefits as the sharing of bibliographic records. However, many smaller libraries lack the resources, and in some cases expertise, to contribute *any* authority records; indeed, they often lack the resources to even link their bibliographic records to authority records, which is why automated authority control services, such as Backstage Library Works, are heavily used.

Conclusion

Three points about authority control should be noted. The first is that authority control is an expensive exercise because it takes a lot of time, and many libraries do not carry out much authority control, but live with the consequences. The second point is the need to *maintain* authority files once they have been established. New and revised authority records are continuously required due to new authors, changes of name, additional information, and so forth. Administrators need to recognise that the maintenance of authority files is an ongoing process and need to allocate resources for this purpose. This is especially important for those bibliographic databases where there are many participants inputting records, such as a cooperative cataloguing service like OCLC or Libraries Australia.

The third point is to know what we are aiming at in maintaining authority files in our information retrieval systems. One ideal is that the user does not realise that the system is making the links in the authority file. A quote from Larry Auld explains this point:

> How might authority control ideally manifest itself in a catalog? The following characteristics seem reasonable from the point of view of both the cataloger and the user. A bibliographic record, together with all variant forms of each associated heading, would be entered into the system. The computer would establish linkages

between authority records and the variant forms of headings and between the preferred forms of headings and the bibliographic record. When a user keyed in a known form of a heading, the system would follow the internal linkages and display the requested item even though the preferred form of the heading might be quite different from the form entered. Although, technically, the computer would follow one linkage to the preferred form of the heading and then a second linkage to the bibliographic record, to the user it would appear that a direct linkage existed between the form of the heading entered and the bibliographic record displayed. The authority control mechanism would be invisible so far as the user was concerned. Authority records would be displayed only on request. Cutter would have enjoyed a catalog like that! (Auld 1982, pp.326-327).

This process, regrettably, does not always occur in current library information retrieval systems.

PART III: SUBJECT ACCESS – CURRENT CHALLENGES

Introduction

Part I presented an overview of how information is organised in libraries and information centres, and Part II covered the standards that are used to provide effective non-subject description and access.

Chapters 6 to 9 constitute Part III, which is concerned with the processes and systems involved with providing access to documents through their subject content. Standard techniques using classification schemes and controlled vocabularies have been developed over many decades and are in widespread use in today's libraries and information centres. However, this area, perhaps more than most in the field of bibliographic control, is being dramatically altered by the introduction of new approaches enabled by the computer.

Chapter 6 introduces the topic and examines some of the general concepts associated with subject access. Chapter 7 looks at library classification schemes, first by examining the principles on which they are based and then by looking at specific examples. These examples include both the general bibliographic classification schemes such as Dewey, and also selected discipline-specific schemes. Chapter 8 examines in more detail the standard subject access mechanisms that are based on the development and application of a controlled vocabulary, including conventional lists of subject headings and thesauri. Chapter 9 investigates the techniques and processes through which subject access to information on the web is being provided.

CHAPTER 6
Subject access concepts

Chapter 6 introduces the mechanisms used by libraries and other information agencies to provide subject access, the processes by which we assist the user to identify information resources that contain information about a particular subject. This has traditionally involved deciding what the information resource is *about*, translating that into terms (words and phrases) or symbols which represent the subject, and providing access to these terms and symbols through the library information retrieval system. In this chapter this process is outlined, key concepts relating to subject access are defined, and some key characteristics of indexing languages are noted.

Why we need subject access

Charles Cutter's classic statement about the objectives of the catalogue is used in chapter 1, as the focus of this book, to address the question 'how do we meet user needs?' To achieve this the library information retrieval system seeks to provide access to the subject of the information resources represented in the system, and to provide guidance on what has been published or made available about a particular subject.

To Cutter's objective we can add the knowledge gained from studies of the users of catalogues (see chapter 1). We know that the majority of catalogue searches are performed either to determine whether the library owns or provides access to a particular information resource (that is, a *known item search*), or to identify information resources owned by the library (or accessible through it) that deal with a particular subject (a *subject search*).

In online catalogues, subject searching has proven particularly popular: it accounted for about 59 per cent of all catalogue enquiries in a 1983 study (Taylor 2000, p.266; Roe 1999, pp.70-71), a level that appears to have been maintained in the past two decades (Yu & Young 2004), though of course the exact proportion varies from library to library. Consequently, providing *effective* subject access to information is an essential part of offering a good catalogue. Likewise, users often want to search by subject on other kinds of bibliographic databases, such as those that cover journal and newspaper articles; indeed, subject access is even more important where documents are briefer and thus less sought after specifically. Yet, despite its significance, subject access is the part of information organisation that is the most difficult to get right. Although we have made significant progress in providing access to information resources in the digital age, 'intellectual access to the contents ... has improved very little, if at all' (Lancaster 1999, p.49). Although search engines such as Google have vastly improved subject access to the web over the past decade, even here result sets include a lot of irrelevant materials, and exclude a lot of much more relevant ones.

In the first decade of the twenty-first century, we are well and truly at a subject access crossroads, which we have been approaching for some years. From this crossroads three paths diverge. The first is the path of traditional subject access mechanisms, the *controlled vocabulary* approach represented by lists of subject headings, thesauri and bibliographic classification schemes. The second path leads in the opposite direction: it is represented by *derived* indexing, that is, the use of terms taken from the content of the information resources itself, rather than terms selected from a controlled vocabulary and assigned by the cataloguer. The third path is the middle way: it advocates the use of the traditional methods of assigning terms from controlled vocabularies augmented by natural language terms derived directly from the information resources, and also, wherever possible, by metadata provided by the sources of the resources – their authors, publishers, and so on. Each of these three paths has its strong and vocal advocates.

The process of providing subject access

Chapters 7 to 9 map in more detail the three paths that are commonly followed to provide subject access in today's multifaceted information environment. The middle path, which combines the approaches of the other two paths, can be represented as the following four-step process.

Step 1: determine what the information resource is about

This is not always as easy as one might think. *Aboutness* is not an absolute concept. It is determined in the context of the information centre and its clients, and establishing aboutness is greatly influenced by the information professional's experience, knowledge, opinions and judgment: consistency is hard to achieve. Derek Langridge devoted a whole book to the topic of subject analysis – that is, the process of determining aboutness (Langridge 1989).

Step 2: select terms from an indexing language that represent the statement of aboutness

After we have decided what the subject of an information resource is, we use an *indexing language* to express its aboutness. We can, for example, use an indexing language in which the vocabulary is made up of words in common use, or we might invent another language completely, such as the symbols in a classification scheme. This indexing language chosen is most likely to be a *controlled vocabulary*, that is, one which has some order imposed on it by indicating which terms are semantically related to which other terms. In this case we select terms from the vocabulary (usually a thesaurus or classification scheme) which best represent the information resource's aboutness. In other words we *assign* terms. Alternatively, or in addition, the indexing language used to represent aboutness may be *derived*, automatically or manually, from the words that occur in the information resource.

In selecting terms for indexing we need to be aware of *exhaustivity*, that is, the level of detail we go to in providing subject access. We can either summarise or we can be exhaustive. Exhaustive subject indexing means that the number of terms selected from the indexing language is relatively large and attempts to cover most or all of the subjects or concepts of the information resource. The extreme case is that we index *all* the words from a text. An alternative, or complementary, approach is summarising, where the main subject, or subjects, of the information resource are indicated by a limited number of terms, often selected from a controlled vocabulary. The number of terms selected is usually very small relative to the number of words in the document, often four or five terms, or even fewer. For example, for a book about four eminent Australian librarians, Metcalfe, White, Whyte and Radford, a summarising approach might indicate only that the book was about 'Australian librarians'; slightly more exhaustive indexing would also indicate that it was about Metcalfe, White, Whyte and Radford.

Step 3: assign terms, or symbols representing terms, from a controlled vocabulary

Controlled vocabularies are in common use in libraries. They are divided into two kinds: those that are presented as alphabetically-arranged list of terms, and those that are organised according to subject groupings (classification schemes). Concepts to note here are *literary warrant, pre-coordination* and *post-coordination. Literary warrant* is the concept that controlled vocabularies should accommodate only those subjects about which information resources have already been produced, rather than subjects which might theoretically exist but about which no information resources have yet been produced. However, in the web environment, it is fair to say that all sorts of subjects now have literary warrant. *Pre-coordination* and *post-coordination* refer to the ways in which we combine the terms from controlled vocabularies. The former occurs at the indexing stage, the latter at the search stage. After we decide on a number of single concepts to describe a subject (see step 2) we can do one of two things: we can index the single concepts as separate terms or we can combine several concepts into one term (pre-coordination). Where the concepts are indexed separately, in order to locate documents about complex subjects users must themselves combine various terms in their query (post-coordination). Most of the controlled vocabularies traditionally used in libraries, such as subject headings lists or classification schemes, are pre-coordinated. Take as an example the subject heading or index entry *Sharp programmable calculators*. Here there are three separate concepts (calculator, programmable, and make of calculator) that have been grouped together in one phrase – in other words, they have been pre-coordinated. The terms are grouped together *before* ('pre-') the search stage of information retrieval. Using the same example, a post-coordinated approach requires the user to ask the computer to carry out three separate searches on 'Sharp', 'calculator(s)' and 'program#', and then combine the results *after* ('post-') the searches on those terms have been completed.

The terms we select from a controlled vocabulary are represented in different ways, depending on the vocabulary. Using our *Sharp programmable calculators* example to illustrate this point, one standard controlled vocabulary – the *Library of Congress Subject Headings* (LCSH) – represents this subject by using the words as in the example (that is, *Sharp programmable calculators*). Another controlled vocabulary, the *Dewey Decimal Classification* represents the subject (though not so precisely) by the number 510.28541. This string of numbers may seem meaningless, but within the specific context of the classification scheme, it has a very definite meaning.

Step 4: determine other attributes of the information resource to search on

Subject access can also be provided by selecting words that are already present in the information resource, and then providing a means of searching these words. This approach of using words already in the information resource is known as *derived indexing* (or derivative indexing), the vocabulary being derived from the information resource as distinct from being selected (or *assigned*) from a controlled vocabulary of terms that has been especially developed to provide subject access. The indexing vocabulary is, in other words, a subset of the text of the information resource. While in theory the words used can be taken from anywhere in the information resource, in practice it is still most common for them to be derived from the title and from an abstract of the information resource.

A final question we can ask at the end of the process is: how well does the system perform in providing subject access? The key measures of the effectiveness of a subject access mechanism are *relevance*, *recall* and *precision*. These concepts are considered in more detail in the Introduction to Part IV.

Indexing languages and vocabularies

The different kinds of indexing languages have already been noted in chapter 1. To recap, we can distinguish three kinds of indexing languages:

- indexing languages which use a controlled vocabulary,
- those which are derived from the resource itself, and
- free indexing languages.

Controlled vocabulary indexing languages, then, are those in which the words and phrases – the vocabulary – are selected and authorised by a cataloguer or indexer. Their main advantage is that they provide standardisation and enable consistent use of terms to describe each subject. Their major disadvantages are that they need to be updated regularly in order to remain current and therefore effective in providing subject access, and they can be expensive to apply, requiring considerable expertise on the part of the cataloguer or indexer. Controlled vocabularies are of two types: alphabetical indexing languages, and classification schemes.

In derived indexing the vocabulary is taken from the information resource itself. The overriding advantage of derived indexing is that it requires no, or little, intellectual input on the part of the indexer: the vocabulary is already present, so subject concepts do not have to be matched with appropriate terms from a controlled vocabulary. Furthermore, derived indexing can be automated (as in KWIC and KWOC indexes). The disadvantages lie in the lack of any control over the vocabulary to minimise frustration in searching, for example by removing inappropriate or misleading words and linking related words.

The vocabulary in a free indexing language is not limited to terms found in a controlled vocabulary or in the information resource itself: they can be selected from anywhere at all. The primary advantage is that there are no constraints on the choice of vocabulary, so the words and phrases the indexer naturally thinks of can be added to the bibliographic record. The disadvantages are the same as those for derived indexing (Lancaster 1989).

Natural language or controlled vocabularies?

Derived and free indexing use natural language, that is, they are not limited to a particular controlled language. The advantages and disadvantages of providing subject access by using controlled vocabularies, or natural language, are summarised in figure 6.1.

Natural Language	Controlled Language
Strengths	*Weaknesses*
High specificity gives precision. Excels in retrieving 'individual' terms – names of persons, organisations, etc.	Lack of specificity, even in detailed systems
Exhaustivity gives potential for high recall. (Does not apply to title-only databases)	Lack of exhaustivity. Cost of indexing to level of natural language prohibitive. Terms may be omitted in error by indexers
Up-to-date. New terms immediately available	Not immediately up-to-date. Time-lag while terms are added to thesaurus
Words of author used – no misinterpretation by indexer	Words of author liable to be misconstrued. Errors in indexing terms can cause losses
Natural language words used by searcher	Artificial language has to be learned by the searcher
Low input costs	High input costs
Easier exchange of material between databases – language incompatibility removed	Incompatibility a barrier to easy exchange
Weaknesses	*Strengths*
Intellectual effort placed on searcher. Problems arise with terms having many synonyms and several species	Eases the burden of searching: • controls synonyms and near-synonyms • qualifies homographs • provides scope notes • displays broader, narrower and related terms • expresses concepts elusive in free text
Syntax problems. Danger of false drops through incorrect term association	Overcomes syntax problems with compound terms and other devices
Exhaustivity may lead to loss of precision	At normal levels of indexing, avoids precision loss through over-exhaustivity (i.e., retrieval of minor concepts of peripheral interest)
	An asset in numerical databases and multilingual systems

Figure 6.1 Comparison of natural and controlled language subject approaches. Based on Aitchison, Gilchrist & Bawden 2000, p.6

In yesterday's information retrieval systems the question was: natural language *OR* controlled vocabularies? In today's information retrieval systems the solution is 'natural language *AND* controlled vocabularies'.

Alphabetical and classification-based languages

As noted above, controlled vocabularies are of two types: alphabetical indexing languages, and classification schemes. Subject access can be provided by terms selected from alphabetical indexing languages: or, in other words, selected from a vocabulary of controlled terms. Examples include a list of subject headings, or a thesaurus. They are generally straightforward to use because the terms are usually selected from language in common use. The order in which the authorised terms are listed is conceptually arbitrary, that is, in the order of the alphabet, and the order of terms does not indicate any relationship between adjacent terms in the list. As an example, the term *puddings* is not related meaningfully to either the programming language *PUCMAT* or to *puddling,* with which it is listed. Relationships among terms are displayed in another way – by the use of a reference structure which specifies which terms are related, and the nature of the relationship (see figure 6.2).

PUCMAT (Computer program language)
  [QA76.73.P]
  BT Programming languages (Electronic
      computers)
Pucrasia macrolopha (May Subd Geog)
  [QL696.G27]
  UF Koklas pheasant
      Koklass pheasant
      Pukras pheasant
  BT Pheasants
Pudding
  USE Puddings
Puddings (May Subd Geog)
  [TX773]
  UF Pudding
  BT Desserts
  RT Cookery (Puddings)
  NT Bread puddings
      Kugels
      Plum puddings
      Rice puddings
Puddingstone
  USE Conglomerate
Puddingstone Dam (Calif.)
  BT Dams—California
Puddington family
  USE Purinton family
Puddling
  [TN725]
  BT Iron—Metallurgy
Puddling (Horticulture)
  BT Horticulture

Pueblo aged (May Subd Geog)
  UF Aged, Pueblo
      Pueblo Indians—Aged
      [Former heading]
  BT Aged—United States
Pueblo Alto Site (N.M.)
  BT New Mexico—Antiquities
Pueblo architecture (May Subd Geog)
  UF Architecture, Pueblo
      Pueblo Indians—Architecture
      [Former heading]
  BT Architecture—Southwest, New
Pueblo art (May Subd Geog)
  UF Art, Pueblo
      Pueblo Indians—Art
      [Former heading]
  BT Art, American
Pueblo artists (May Subd Geog)
  UF Artists, Pueblo [Former heading]
  BT Artists—United States
Pueblo astronomy (May Subd Geog)
  UF Astronomy, Pueblo
      Pueblo Indians—Astronomy
      [Former heading]
  BT Astronomy—Southwest, New
Pueblo Bonito Site (N.M.)
  BT New Mexico—Antiquities
Pueblo calendar (May Subd Geog)
  UF Calendar, Pueblo
      Pueblo Indians—Calendar
      [Former heading]
  BT Calendar

Figure 6.2 Relationship display in an alphabetical indexing language. Source: *Library of Congress Subject Headings*, 21st ed. (1998), p.4667

Classification schemes are another form of controlled vocabulary, but here the terms that have been selected and authorised for use are grouped together so that related subjects are juxtaposed. *Puddings* in a classification scheme is listed near *ice-cream* and other desserts. Classification schemes are therefore useful for arranging subjects so that browsing through related subjects is possible, as illustrated by figure 6.3.

Unlike an alphabetical indexing language, classification schemes require a system of notation. These notations are typically based on numbers, or on a combination of numbers and letters.

.815   Breads and bread-like foods

          Including biscuits (United States), crackers, crepes, hot cakes, pancakes, rolls, waffles

          Class here comprehensive works on baked goods

          Class main dishes based on breads and bread-like foods in 641.82; class sandwiches in 641.84

             For pastries, see 641.865

.82   Main dishes

          Including quiches, soufflés

.821   Casserole dishes

.822   Pasta dishes

.823   Stews

             Class here chili

.824   Meat and cheese pies

             Including pizza, meat loaf

             Class cooking sausage in 641.66

.83   Salads

.84   Sandwiches

             Including submarine sandwiches

.85   Preserves and candy

.852   Jams, jellies, marmalades, preserves

                Standard subdivisions are added for any or all topics in heading

.853   Candy

                Variant name: sweets (United Kingdom)

.86   Desserts

             Class here comprehensive works on candies and desserts

             For preserves and candy, see 641.85

.862   Ice cream

                Including frozen yogurt, ice milk

.863   Ices and sherbet

                Variant name: water ices

.864   Gelatins and puddings

Figure 6.3 Excerpt from a classification scheme. Source: *Dewey Decimal Classification and Relative Index*, 21st ed. (1996). Vol. 3. p.346

Subject approaches in the bibliographic record

A variety of methods of providing subject access is available, as described above. In practice several of these methods are used in combination, as indicated in figure 6.4.

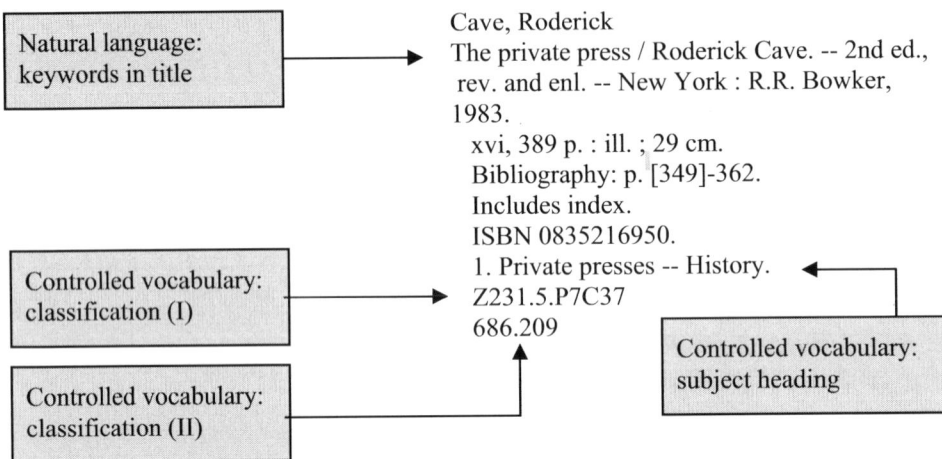

Figure 6.4 Subject approaches in a bibliographic record (AACR2)

Conclusion

Standard techniques that provide access to information resources through their subject content are in common use in today's libraries and information centres. These techniques typically use classification schemes and controlled vocabularies, although, more and more, the application of new approaches enabled by the computer is changing how subject access is provided. The following chapters look more closely at some of these methods.

CHAPTER 7
Classification

In chapter 6 we noted that the two categories of controlled vocabularies in common use to provide subject access in information centres are alphabetically arranged lists of subject terms, and classification schemes. Chapter 7 examines the second of these categories, bibliographic classification schemes: first the principles on which they are based, then specific schemes. These examples include both the general bibliographic classification schemes such as Dewey, and also selected specialist schemes. The emphasis is on the classification schemes most commonly used in libraries and information centres.

What is classification?

Classification is something that we do all of the time. Consider this list of common terms.

toothpaste	cooking oil	ice-cream	fruit juice
tea	chicken	chilli sauce	soap
clothes pegs	beans	laundry powder	instant noodles
coffee beans	dried mushrooms	curry paste	peanuts
rice	beancurd	bread	chillies
apples	flour	hair shampoo	toothbrush

If we are asked to put these into classified order, one possibility might be:

FOODSTUFFS: Will keep without special storage (such as refrigeration): tea, chilli sauce, instant noodles, coffee beans, curry paste, peanuts, rice, chillies, cooking oil, dried mushrooms, flour

FOODSTUFFS: Need special storage facilities: ice-cream, fruit juice, bread, apples, beans, beancurd, chicken

PERSONAL TOILETRIES: toothpaste, soap, hair shampoo, toothbrush

CLEANING MATERIALS: clothes pegs, laundry powder.

However, there are some problems with this classification, for example:

- there is too much in the first category: how could we subdivide this? (perhaps beverages, liquids, etc.), and

- clothes pegs are not cleaning materials: do they need their own category?

This simple example illustrates that there are many possibilities for classifying a group of entities or concepts. There is no correct way, nor any incorrect way, of classifying: there are only classifications that are best for their particular purpose. Alice experienced the difficulties of classification when in Wonderland:

'Serpent!' screamed the Pigeon.

'I'm *not* a serpent!' said Alice indignantly. 'Let me alone!'

'Serpent, I say again!' repeated the Pigeon, but in a more subdued tone, and added with a kind of sob, 'I've tried every way, and nothing seems to suit them! ... I've tried the roots of trees, and I've tried banks, and I've tried hedges,' the Pigeon went on ... 'but those serpents! There's no pleasing them!' ...

'But I'm *not* a serpent, I tell you!' said Alice. 'I'm a – I'm a –'

'Well! *What* are you?' said the Pigeon. 'I can see you're trying to invent something!'

'I – I'm a little girl,' said Alice ...

'A likely story indeed!' said the Pigeon in a tone of the deepest contempt.... . 'No, no! You're a serpent; and there's no use denying it. I suppose you'll be telling me next that you have never tasted an egg!'

'I *have* tasted eggs, certainly,' said Alice, who was a very truthful child; 'but little girls eat eggs quite as much as serpents do, you know.'

'I don't believe it,' said the Pigeon; 'but if they do, why, then they're a kind of serpent, that's all I can say' (Carroll, L. *Alice's Adventures in Wonderland*, chapter V, quoted in Langridge 1992, p.10).

Our shopping list example illustrates one end of the classification spectrum, *enumerative* schemes where subjects (in this case objects) are listed (or enumerated) under general headings. At the other end of the spectrum is another kind of approach, where subjects are broken down into smaller aspects or constituent parts (*facets*). Let us imagine that an Australian wine merchant develops a classification scheme to assist with stock control. He examines the wine they have in stock, and decides on these attributes as being important:

Colour	*Wine Style*	*Container Bottle*	*Capacity*	*Region*
White	Cabernet Sauvignon	Wine cask	375ml	Barossa Valley
Red	Chardonnay		750ml	Clare Valley
Rosé	Gewurztraminer		1 litre	Hunter Valley
	Pinot Noir		1.5 litre	Mt Barker
	Riesling		2 litre	Margaret River
	Shiraz			Rutherglen

These attributes, or *facets* in the classification context, can each be assigned a notation and then they can be combined in an appropriate order to represent the complete object. For instance, if we assign the notations W to represent White, C to represent Chardonnay, B to represent Bottle, 3 to represent 750ml, and M to indicate Margaret River, then the notation WCB3M represents a 750ml bottle of Margaret River Chardonnay.

Bibliographic classification schemes

Our examples above are not of much use in libraries and information centres. Nor are the classifications developed for scientific and academic purposes, such as taxonomies of plants or ethnomusicological classifications of musical instruments, of much use. We are primarily interested in another kind of classification, that is, *bibliographic* classification.

Bibliographic classification has the purpose of organising the knowledge in information resources so that it is accessible to those who seek it. It uses the techniques of scientific classifications and taxonomies, but is not the same as them. Rather, it is concerned with subjects as they are presented in information resources and with the information resources themselves, not with the objects and entities that are the primary interest of other kinds of classification schemes. There are important implications of this for the construction of bibliographic classification schemes. One is that there are many valid possibilities for classifying information resources, for example:

- as physical objects (books, microfilms, types of bindings, and so on);

- by their method of presentation (drawings or maps which present information pictorially, for instance); and/or

- by their intended readership (children, young adults, specialist audiences perhaps).

However, bibliographic classification schemes do not use these as their primary arrangement, although they may be used as secondary elements. Rather, the main arrangement of the subject content of information resources is based on:

- forms of knowledge (such as history, art, science, philosophy);

- categories (examples could be Space – geographical area, say; Time – decades, century; Action – engineering operation, modelling, and so on); and

- facets (such as the language facets, German, English, French, and the form facets, poetry, ballad, sonnet, of the main class of literature).

General and special schemes

Bibliographic classification schemes are usually categorised as either general schemes or special schemes. Both are usually based on *literary warrant*, which we defined in chapter 6 as the concept that controlled vocabularies (including bibliographic classification schemes) should accommodate only those subjects about which information resources have been produced, rather than subjects which may exist, but about which no information resources have yet been produced.

General schemes cover all of documented knowledge. They are usually developed and maintained for use in large libraries whose collections cover a wide range of subjects, such as academic libraries or public libraries. The examples most commonly used in libraries are the *Dewey Decimal Classification* (DDC), the *Library of Congress Classification* (LCC) and the *Universal Decimal Classification* (UDC). Some countries use general classification schemes specifically devised for that country, such as the SAB (*Sveriges Allmänna Biblioteksförening*) classification scheme used in Swedish libraries. *Special schemes* cover a more limited field of documented knowledge: examples include the *British Classification of Music*, *Moys* (for law), and *Boggs and Lewis* (for maps).

Whether general or special, bibliographic classification schemes have the same basic requirements in their components and in the manner in which they are presented:

- schedules – which list concepts arranged in order of the classification;
- an alphabetical index – which provides access to the concepts in the schedules. The index is an important part of a successful classification scheme because without it the scheme can be difficult to use; and
- *rules* – which explain how to use the scheme and assist the user (whether the information professional who applies the schemes, or the user who uses its results) to get the best from the scheme.

Specific examples of general and special bibliographic classification schemes are provided later in this chapter.

Notation

The notation is an integral part of any bibliographic classification scheme. It is the set of symbols which represent the arrangement of the scheme. Notation can be of several kinds: it can be *pure*, where only one type of symbol is used, for instance only numerals (993.1); or it can be *mixed*, where two types of symbols are present, for instance both numerals and letters of the alphabet (ML745). It can be *expressive*, reflecting the structure of the classification: for example, in *Dewey Decimal Classification* (DDC), 7 is the symbol for fine and decorative arts, 74 for drawing and decorative arts, 746 for textile arts, 746.1 for yarn preparation and weaving, and 746.13 for dyeing. A *mnemonic* notation is one that can be easily remembered, for instance where a particular notation is always used throughout the classification to represent the same concept. The Dewey system again provides an example: the sequence 94 in a DDC number often means an Australian aspect of a subject. For example, 720.9*94* represents Australian architecture.

An ideal notation in a bibliographic classification scheme has the characteristics of uniqueness, simplicity, brevity, and hospitality. *Uniqueness* refers to the requirement that no symbol or combination of symbols can be used to represent more than one concept, so that no subject or concept can be mistaken for another. *Simplicity* means that the notation should be as readily comprehensible as possible, and *brevity* that the notation be as short as possible. *Hospitality* requires that the notation should be able to accommodate new concepts or subjects by allowing their insertion into the notation. One way is to leave unfilled numbers in the scheme, to be filled when new subjects need to be incorporated. These are ideals, and the notations of bibliographic classification schemes in common use rarely achieve all of them. Brevity, for example, is particularly difficult to achieve in the notation of faceted schemes.

Enumeration, hierarchy and facets

Bibliographic classification schemes are usually described as being enumerative, hierarchical or faceted. Most of the general bibliographic classification schemes in common use are enumerative or hierarchical, although elements of faceted schemes are now present in all of them and these distinctions are becoming less clear-cut.

Enumerative schemes are those that list (or enumerate) the subjects, loosely grouping together related subjects, or aspects of a subject. Our shopping list classification scheme at the start of this chapter is an example. *Hierarchical schemes* are similar to enumerative schemes, except that they group the lists of related concepts into primary and subordinate areas, attempting to emulate the natural order of the subject as closely as possible.

Faceted schemes start from a different basis. Subjects are broken down into single concepts (or facets) and a notation is assigned to each facet. These facets can then be put together in ways appropriate to the representation of the subject of the document being classified. We noted earlier in this chapter the example of a classification scheme developed by an Australian wine merchant. As another example, some of the facets in a bibliographic classification scheme for music could be:

- type of musical instrument – clarinet (notation A), violin (C), flute (G);
- period composed – 18th century (notation 18), 19th century (19); and
- form – sonata (notation Y), symphony (Z).   YAC f/9

These facets can be *synthesised* or added together to build up notations that represent more complex concepts. Using our example, a sonata for clarinet, violin and flute composed in the 19th century could have the notation Y:ACG:19. In faceted schemes the order in which the facets are added together (the *citation order*) becomes significant. In our music example, the citation order is form, instrumentation, period of composition. Faceted schemes are typically special schemes restricted to one discipline, or a group of related disciplines, and they are typically used in special libraries. Enumerative and hierarchical schemes are used in libraries where the subjects covered in their collections are more general, such as public, school and academic libraries.

Classification schemes are sometimes thought of as being part of a spectrum. At one end of this spectrum is the faceted scheme, and at the other is the enumerative scheme. In reality there is no such thing as a purely enumerative scheme, or a purely hierarchical scheme, or a fully faceted scheme. No enumerative scheme can hope to list all possible subjects or combinations of subjects. More recent editions of DDC, essentially a hierarchical scheme but with elements of enumeration, have also made considerable use of facets. (In fact, from its inception DDC has included some aspects of facets, the most obvious example being a place always having a specific notation regardless of its location in the notation.) UDC, initially hierarchical (it was based on DDC), also has a considerable amount of faceting built into it.

Both faceted and enumerative approaches are well represented among the bibliographic classification schemes in common use, and there are reasons for this. Faceted schemes, for example, are relatively simple to compile, and there is a clearly defined process by which to develop them. The schedules of faceted schemes are relatively brief by comparison with the schedules of enumerative schemes, because they do not list complex subjects – rather, a faceted scheme lists simple single concepts that are then put together to build up a classification for complex subjects. A less useful characteristic of faceted schemes, though, is the problems caused by long notations and by citation order. Enumerative and hierarchical schemes, by comparison, have a much longer history. They have proven that they are useful and usable over a long period of time and in many different countries and cultural contexts. The most common enumerative scheme, LCC, is familiar to many library users, and the most common hierarchical scheme, DDC, even more so. Their notation is usually relatively short. They can, however, be difficult to update, sometimes requiring major structural alterations to incorporate new subjects not foreseen by the scheme's developers.

'Mark and park' or subject access?

Classification schemes have traditionally been applied in libraries for two distinct purposes:

- to provide a location for an information resource, and
- to provide access by subject to information resources.

Many have argued that the primary use of classification schemes in libraries is to provide locations for information resources so that the user can quickly find the information resource on the shelf. As Taylor states, 'Classification provides formal, orderly access to the shelves' (Taylor 2000, p.271). When this is the main purpose of classification, it is sometimes referred to as the 'mark and park' approach, with the subject access aspect of classification considered (if at all) as a secondary, albeit useful, by-product. The 'mark and park' approach has thus usually relied on alphabetical indexing languages for subject access, rather than classification schemes.

Most large libraries are much more interested in shelf location than in providing subject access through their classification. Smaller libraries, however, and especially special libraries with small collections of information resources in a clearly defined narrow subject area, are more likely to use their classification scheme as a means of subject access. The reasons for this relate to the type of material in the collection, the nature of the clientele, and whether the library is closed or open access. The UDC scheme is often used in special libraries, for instance. It has a very flexible notation with the result that it is sometimes very difficult to use UDC numbers for shelf location, because there is considerable possible variation; but for the same reasons it is very effective at providing precise access to subjects.

Some libraries have taken the 'mark and park' approach even further, and do not classify their documents at all, relying instead on specifying the location of information resources only by a general indication of category, mirroring the practice of most book stores. These *reader interest classifications* can be considered at one level as a kind of broad enumerative classification taken to extremes. They have been applied in some public libraries because of perceived inadequacies in the standard bibliographic classification schemes, such as DDC – it is assumed that most public library users are interested primarily in recreational reading and that they prefer to browse information resources (usually books) in categories such as Travel, Leisure, or Crime. The number of categories is usually between twenty and twenty-six, although as few as twelve and as many as thirty-four have been reported (Sapiie 1995). An early use of reader interest classifications was reported at the Detroit Public Library in 1945, and since then they have been used in a number of countries and in a variety of situations.

It is fair to say that most libraries consider the shelf location aspect of classification as considerably more important than the subject access function. This is especially the case now that the classified catalogue is rare in libraries, whereas it was in common use (especially in Britain) during the heyday of classification, when many new schemes were being developed. The power of (post-coordinated) keyword searching functionality provided by online catalogues has reduced the importance of bibliographic classification for subject access, although, at the same time, developers of OPACs and other online information retrieval systems are beginning to discover new uses of bibliographic classification, enabling users to browse and sort through resources via their computers, without having to walk around the library stacks.

Classification schemes: some history

The modern era of bibliographic classification began in 1876 when the *Dewey Decimal Classification* was first published. Since 1876 many other general bibliographic classification schemes have been developed and implemented – Cutter's *Expansive Classification*, Brown's *Subject Classification*, UDC, and LCC among them. Some, such as the schemes of Cutter and of Brown, have not stood the test of time. Criteria for evaluating bibliographic classification schemes are discussed in the next section. While these criteria undoubtedly play a part in determining which schemes succeed and which sink almost without trace, there can be no doubt that other factors – factors not related to the ability of the scheme to provide subject access – play a major part. For example, while a bibliographic classification scheme must undoubtedly have a notation which is hospitable (that is, it can accommodate expansion), the backing of a large organisation to provide resources for updating is perhaps much more significant in determining whether the scheme remains in use. In other words, the theoretical merit of a scheme is no guarantee that it will be used.

Another factor unrelated to theoretical merit that appears to determine the success of a bibliographic classification scheme is whether the classifications are provided on bibliographic records distributed by suppliers of centralised cataloguing. For example, DDC waned in popularity as a direct result of the small quantity of Library of Congress cataloguing copy which was supplied with Dewey classification numbers, compared with the higher amount which had LCC numbers on them; and the promoters of the second edition of the BC (Bliss Bibliographic Classification) lobbied to have BC classifications added to LC copy, recognising this to be one key to the scheme's success. They were unsuccessful.

Classification schemes developed early in the modern (post-Dewey) era are primarily enumerative. Schemes developed more recently are more likely to be faceted, largely as a result of the activities of the Classification Research Group. Formed in London in 1952, the Group has been influential in developing theory, especially that relating to synthesis and faceting, and in encouraging the development and implementation of new classification schemes. Its 1955 statement, 'The Need for a Faceted Classification as the Basis of all Methods of Information Retrieval: Memorandum of the Classification Research Group' (Gilchrist 1997, pp.1-9) firmly stated its point of view and that it would pursue research in this area – a resolution which it has amply fulfilled and continues to pursue.

Some general bibliographic classifications

The following sections describe characteristics of bibliographic classification schemes in common use, or schemes that are otherwise noteworthy. We examine briefly why each scheme, despite its problems – and they are all unsatisfactory in some way or another – is still used, and what its strengths and weaknesses are.

The basis of the following summaries of specific bibliographic classification schemes is twofold: descriptive, summarising the history and other characteristics of the schemes such as their popularity; and evaluative, based on these characteristics:

- is the scheme inclusive within its defined area, and is it comprehensive?

- is the scheme systematic – is its structure logical and understandable?

- is the scheme flexible and expandable – can it incorporate new subjects without disrupting its structure?

- does the scheme's notation meet the criteria of uniqueness, simplicity, brevity, and hospitality?

- is the scheme current and regularly updated – is there an efficient mechanism for maintaining it?

- is the terminology used in the scheme clear, unambiguous and consistently applied?

- does the scheme contain bias – can it be applied in a culturally, politically or religiously neutral way?

The bottom line for evaluating a bibliographic classification scheme is, in the end, simply: is it reliable, effective, and up-to-date? And will it be viable in the future – in particular, is there a large organisation with sufficient resources committed to its maintenance and updating (such as the Library of Congress for LCC)? History clearly indicates that a classification scheme without strong institutional support is doomed.

It should be noted that in recent years there has been cooperation and collaboration among the editors of the major general bibliographic classifications. For example, regular meetings of the editors of DDC and UDC are held and joint revision of a class is envisaged (McIlwaine 2000, p.100). It is likely that in future the differences between these schemes will become less clearly delineated as features of one scheme are adopted by others.

Dewey Decimal Classification (DDC)

DDC is here to stay, as its long history, effective administrative structure and large number of users in many countries indicate. Its popularity and capacity to endure owes less to its adherence to modern classification theory than to its ability as an efficient device for indicating shelf locations for general library collections. Its universally understood notation deserves special mention, as also does its effective administrative support. Further strengthening DDC is its ownership by OCLC, which has demonstrated its strong commitment to maintaining, updating and enhancing DDC.

DDC: summary of characteristics

The characteristics of DDC are summarised below according to the range of features identified earlier.

Nature of scheme	Hierarchical, with an increasing amount of synthesis introduced from the 18th ed.
Synthesis	Auxiliary tables, which can be used in specified situations Number-building in three ways: 1) combining classification numbers from different parts of the main schedules; 2) adding a Standard Subdivision from Table 1 to a classification number from the main schedules; 3) adding a subdivision from the auxiliary tables
Citation order	Highly specified
Notation	Pure, expressive, mnemonic, moderately hospitable Decimal notation is universally understood Decimal notation displays hierarchy
Index	Detailed index an important part of the classification
History	First ed. 1876 From 2nd ed. the 'integrity of numbers' principle ensured stability Dewey edited or oversaw all editions until 12th ed. 14th, 15th and 17th eds. poorly received 18th ed (1971) restored faith in the scheme Current ed. is 22nd, 2003
Versions	Paper (4 volumes), 22nd ed. 2003 Electronic (WebDewey): the print version will become 'a snapshot of the DDC at a point in time' and WebDewey will incorporate the continuous revision process (Mitchell 2003) Abridged (14th ed. 2004) intended for collections up to 20,000, available as part of WebDewey and in print (1 volume)
Aids	A manual is included in the scheme Online help, updates, etc in the Dewey website: http://www.oclc.org/dewey Chan, L. M & Mitchell, J.S. (2003). *Dewey Decimal Classification: Principles and Application.* 3rd ed. Dublin, Ohio: OCLC.
Use	Widespread throughout the world (200,000 libraries, 135 countries, 62 national bibliographies) Full translations available in French, Italian, Spanish, Russian, and under way in Arabic and German; abridged translations available in Arabic, French, Greek, Icelandic, Norwegian; Chinese, Hebrew, Korean and Vietnamese translations under way Used in 95% of U.S. public and school libraries, 25% of U.S. college and university libraries, and 20% of U.S. special libraries Has influenced development of other schemes
Problems	U.S. and Western, Anglo-Saxon social and cultural bias Some schedules are crowded (e.g., 600 Technology) Decimal base of 10 limits hospitality Not specific enough, e.g., in highly technical fields Notations can be long

Advantages   Most library users are familiar with DDC
Basic structure has remained unchanged since 1876
DDC numbers on most cataloguing records available on exchange
and from centralised cataloguing sources
Large central organisation (OCLC, which took over Forest Press in
1988) is responsible for updating of the scheme
Regularly revised and updated.

As noted, one of the advantages of DDC is that its basic structure has not changed since
1876. Figure 7.1 shows that basic structure.

10 main classes
000   Computer science, information & general works
100   Philosophy & psychology
200   Religion
300   Social sciences
400   Languages
500   Science
600   Technology
700   Arts & recreation
800   Literature
900   History & geography

The 600s
600 Technology
610 Medicine & health
620 Engineering
630 Agriculture
640 Home & family management
650 Management & public relations
660 Chemical engineering
670 Manufacturing
680 Manufacture for specific uses
690 Building & construction

The 630s
630 Agriculture & related technologies
631 Techniques, equipment & materials
632 Plant injuries, diseases & pests
633 Field & plantation crops
634 Orchards, fruits & forestry
635 Garden crops (Horticulture)
636 Animal husbandry
637 Processing dairy & related products
638 Insect culture
639 Hunting, fishing & conservation

Figure 7.1 Basic structure of DDC. Source: *Summaries*, DDC, Dublin, Ohio, OCLC, 2003

DDC in Australia

Melvyl Dewey was, according to John McKinlay, 'amongst the most successful colonizers of Australia' (McKinlay 1980), to the extent that Australia may have the highest proportion of DDC users of all countries in the world (Martin 2001, p.54). It is used by the National Library of Australia, all state libraries, practically all public libraries and school libraries, about three-quarters of academic libraries, and some special libraries (Martin 1997, p.62).

The first use of the *Dewey Decimal Classification* in Australia appears to have been in 1896 at the University of Sydney Library (Nelson 1986, p.25); other early adopters included the Public Library of Queensland in 1898 (*Dewey Decimal Classification* 1955), the Newcastle School of Arts, the Public Library of South Australia, and the University of Adelaide (Martin 2001, p.54). By 1899 we find H.C.L. Anderson, the influential Librarian of the Public Library of New South Wales recommending DDC to the librarian of the Wagga Wagga School of Arts (From the Desk 1994), and Edmund La Touche Armstrong, Chief Librarian at the Public Library of Victoria introduced DDC to the Lending Library (*Australian Dictionary of Biography* 1979). Armstrong's predecessor, Michael Dowden, had written to Melvyl Dewey as early as 1895 to ask whether his scheme could be used for shelving books, as well as for classifying them in a catalogue (Talbot 1985, p.12). By the turn of the century four papers about DDC had been delivered at the first two meetings of the Library Association of Australasia. Surveys in 1948, 1971 and 1973 revealed that Dewey had been fully integrated into mainstream Australian bibliographic organisation practice and indicated an increasing number of local modifications to the scheme.

The first of many modifications to the scheme to better reflect Australian practice was made in 1938 (McKinlay 1976). In 1974 the Library Association of Australia (later the Australian Library and Information Association) established a Dewey Decimal Classification Liaison Committee to represent the views of the Australian library profession to the editors of DDC. Australian input to DDC continues to this day through the Australian Committee on Cataloguing. For example, problems with the Australian historical period subdivisions in DDC21 have been addressed in DDC22, changing 994.065 – representing the period 1991-1999 – to 994.065 and 994.066 to indicate the change of Prime Minister from Paul Keating to John Howard. DDC22 includes a notation for the Australian sign language Auslan. Australian input has assisted in developing better classifications for a wide range of more general areas: one example is the creation of a specific number 792.38 for Panto (pantomime, usually performed around Christmas time, and not unknown in Australia). Minor changes have also been made in DDC to reflect Australian terminology in the index and captions. In 1993 Giles Martin was the first Australian to be appointed to the Dewey Decimal Classification Editorial Policy Committee; since 2000 the Australian representative has been Anne Robertson. This committee advises the publisher and editors of DDC about the needs of users of the scheme.

Criticisms of DDC from the Australian point of view have been aired frequently. For example, in the 1970s there was a long debate about DDC's inability to adequately represent Australian geography (McKinlay 1970, Alonso & Prescott 1977). Australian concerns were, however, not restricted to Australian matters: the treatment of mathematics and of law also came in for significant criticism (Langker 1974b, Martin 2001, p.56) and the 510 Mathematics schedule has been revised with Australian input. Despite such criticisms, there is no doubt that DDC is in Australia to stay.

DDC22, published in July 2003, indicates how DDC is updated to ensure that it reflects contemporary issues. Few major changes were introduced in this edition; rather, the changes made have been incremental and often span several editions: for example, changes to the religion schedules (200s) to reduce the emphasis on Christianity were introduced over DDC21 and DDC22. Changes reflect the input of expert groups and users from many countries and disciplines. For example, the revision of the Scandinavian literature sections in the 800s benefited from the input of Norwegian translators of DDC. In DDC22 one of the auxiliary tables, Table 7, has been removed because its role could be performed using notation already present elsewhere in the schedules and in Table 1. Captions in the schedules have been modernised and made consistent, and, in the case of the 610 schedule for medicine and health, are mapped to terms taken from MeSH (*Medical Subject Headings*), the widely used controlled vocabulary developed by the United States National Library of Medicine. The manual has been significantly overhauled to make it more consistent and user-friendly. WebDewey, the online version of DDC22, contains additional material (but the same numbers) and offers a search facility covering all the contents.

Library of Congress Classification (LCC)

LCC has been described as 'strenuously pragmatic in its outlook' (Marcella & Newton 1994, p.70). It was developed to organise the collection of the Library of Congress on the shelves, rather than with the primary aim of providing detailed subject retrieval capabilities. It is based firmly on literary warrant – the information resources added to the Library of Congress's collections – and does not aim to be comprehensive: it is, nonetheless, very detailed. It is the least international of the general schemes, with a strong United States bias resulting from its development for an American national collection. Its continuing use in large academic libraries is currently based on economic factors, rather than because it is superior to other schemes. These economic factors include its support and updating by the United States Federal Government, and the massive cost of reclassifying large collections already using LCC.

LCC in Australia

In Australia LCC is used in some academic libraries, TAFE libraries in Queensland, and a small number of specialised libraries. The scheme was selected by several of the university libraries established in the 1970s (Greig 1989, Richardson 1982). In the 1980s, other libraries, such as the University of Queensland, the Australian Defence Force Academy Library in Canberra, and the University of Tasmania Library, reclassified their collections to LCC from DDC or BC. These libraries use LCC because it is considered more suitable than DDC for large academic collections or because it provides a more detailed subject breakdown for specialised areas. For example LCC classification is suited to areas such as military, scientific and technical subjects that represent the collections of the Australian Defence Force Academy Library (Beatty 1987). It seems unlikely that LCC will be adopted more widely in Australia.

LCC: summary of characteristics

The following summary of LCC characteristics is based on the range of issues to be considered in evaluating a classification scheme.

Nature of scheme	Fundamentally enumerative
	A series of specialist classifications developed to an overall set of guidelines
Synthesis	Not well developed
Citation order	Not very highly specified
Notation	Mixed (letters and numbers)
Index	No index to the whole scheme, only to individual schedules
History	Based on Cutter's Expansive Classification, with changes in notation
	First used in LC 1899
Versions	Each schedule is revised independently
	Over 40 volumes (see figure 7.2)
	Online version (*Classification Web*) linked with Library of Congress subject headings
Aids	Library of Congress (1992) *Subject Cataloging Manual: Classification.* Washington, DC: Cataloging Distribution Service, Library of Congress
	Additions and changes available online the Library of Congress's website
Use	Academic libraries, other very large libraries
	Heavily used in U.S. but less so in other countries
	Considerable reclassification from DDC to LCC in the 1960s, especially in U.S. academic libraries – by 1971 LCC used by more than 50% of them
Problems	U.S. bias
	Designed for shelf arrangement, not subject arrangement
	Designed for one very large library, but despite this has been adopted widely, with consequent problems
	No consolidated index
	No clear theoretical basis
Advantages	LCC numbers available on many centralised cataloguing records
	Central organisation (the Library of Congress, funded by the U.S. Federal Government) responsible for updating
	Good for shelf arrangement
	Based firmly on literary warrant (that is, what is added to the Library of Congress's collection)
	Very detailed

Figure 7.2 provides a list of LCC schedules available in 2007.

A	General Works
B-BJ	Philosophy. Psychology
BL-BQ	Religion (General). Hinduism, Judaism, Islam, Buddhism.
BR-BX	Christianity, Bible
C	Auxiliary Sciences of History
D-DR	History (General) and History of Europe
DS-DX	History of Asia History of Africa, Australia, New Zealand, etc.
E-F	History: America
G	Geography. Maps. Anthropology. Recreation.
G Tables	Geographic Cutter Numbers
H	Social Sciences
J	Political Science
K	Law (General)
K Tables	Form Division Tables for Law
KB	Religious Law
KD	Law of the United Kingdom and Ireland
KDZ, KG-KH	Law of the Americas, Latin America, and the West Indies
KE	Law of Canada
KF	Law of the United States.
KJ-KKZ	Law of Europe
KJV-KJW	Law of France
KK-KKC	Law of Germany
KL-KWX	Law of Asia and Eurasia, Africa, Pacific Area and Antarctica
KZ	Law of Nations
L	Education
M	Music and Books on Music
N	Fine Arts
P-PZ	Language and Literature Tables
P-PA	Philology and Linguistics (General). Greek Language and Literature. Latin Language and Literature
PB-PH	Modern European Languages
PJ-PK	Oriental Philology and Literature, Indo-Iranian Philology & Literature
PL-PM	Languages of Eastern Asia, Africa, Oceania; Hyperborean, Indian, and Artificial Languages
PN	Literature (General)
PQ	French, Italian, Spanish, and Portuguese Literatures
PR, PS, PZ	English and American Literature. Juvenile Belles Lettres
PT	German, Dutch and Scandinavian Literatures
Q	Science
R	Medicine
S	Agriculture
T	Technology
U-V	Military Science. Naval Science
Z	Bibliography. Library Science. Information Resources.

Figure 7.2 LCC schedules available in 2007

Universal Decimal Classification (UDC)

After a long hiatus, UDC is once again thriving as a result of the establishment in 1992 of the UDC Consortium with consequent restructuring of its editing and publishing procedures, especially its updating mechanisms. Of the three general bibliographic classification schemes in common use in the English-speaking world, UDC is the only one that was developed primarily for subject retrieval. Consequently it excels at detailed subject analysis because of its many synthetic features, especially in science and technology, its areas of strength. However, when applied to the more prosaic task of indicating shelf location, its strengths for subject access prove to be its weaknesses for 'marking and parking'. UDC has been used as a navigating device for information resources on the web (Robinson 1999, p.149) and its ongoing development has the aim (not yet fulfilled) of making it the scheme of choice in web environments (McIlwaine 1998). Slavic (2006b) has conducted a worldwide survey of its use, finding that in 34 countries (including Spain, Portugal, and many Eastern European countries) it is used as the main classification system, and it is used to a lesser extent in another 90 countries.

Figure 7.3 outlines the basic structure of UDC.

0	Generalities
1	Philosophy. Psychology
2	Religion. Theology
3	Social sciences
4	Vacant
5	Natural sciences
6	Technology
7	The Arts
8	Language. Linguistics. Literature
9	Geography. Biography. History

Figure 7.3 Basic structure of UDC. Source: UDC Consortium website, http://www.udcc.org/outline/outline.htm

UDC in Australia

In Australia, UDC is used primarily in special libraries. Although there appears to be no published study of UDC use in Australia, isolated information indicates that the extent of its application is significant. In Victoria in the 1980s there were nineteen UDC sites plus several CSIRO (Commonwealth Scientific and Industrial Research Organisation) libraries. A 1988 survey of libraries in Western Australia indicated that approximately 30 per cent of special libraries used UDC, compared with 33 per cent using DDC and 20 per cent using an in-house classification scheme (Richardson & Exon 1990, p.121). The UDC Consortium's website (http://www.udcc.org/users.htm) provides a selective list of UDC users throughout the world who are willing to exchange experiences and information: four Australian users are noted.

UDC: summary of characteristics

Nature of scheme	Hierarchical with considerable faceting/synthesis, tending strongly towards a fully faceted scheme as it evolves
Synthesis	Very well developed – especially the use of ':' which allows two or more UDC classification numbers to be joined, leading to very great specificity if required Use of general auxiliary tables and symbols, e.g., '(73)' for place
Citation order	Not specified
Notation	Pure, expressive, mnemonic
Index	Yes
History	Was developed to provide detailed subject access, not for use as a shelf location device First ed. 1905 (in French), based on DDC 5th ed. Common auxiliaries for place time, language in some subject fields; and the use of ':' for adding numbers we added to DDC 5th ed. 2nd ed., French, 1927-1933, followed by abridged eds in other European languages; 3rd full ed. 1934-1948 (in German)
Versions	Produced in three versions: Full (*Master Reference File* online database – the f version of UDC, maintained as a working file by the UDC Consortium); complete (2 volumes, 2005); abridged (1 volume, 2003); the full and truncated numbers are also available in UDC Online, the web-based product.
Aids	McIlwaine, I.C. (2007). *The Universal Decimal Classification: Guide to its Us* Rev. ed. The Hague: UDC Consortium. News and updating information available on the UDC Consortium website: http://www.udcc.org
Use	Widespread throughout the world, with heavy use in Europe: 100,000 users in countries Mainly used in science/technology libraries Translated in whole or part in 23 languages
Problems	Until 1990 the updating mechanism was cumbersome and slow; major improvements have been implemented since 1990 Not good for shelf arrangement: UDC was developed primarily to provide very detailed subject access Long notation can be confusing No standard citation order, nor any guidance available until recently Lack of revision and slow rate of revision a problem until recently No overall index, though search functions available in online version Western bias
Advantages	Very flexible; Strong in science/technology areas; Enthusiasm and goodwill of users; Adoption as BS1000 Not language-dependent: e.g., used extensively in continental Europe Recent strengthening of administrative structures means that UDC is in health shape to meet future challenges

Bliss (BC) and Colon Classification

Both the *Bliss Bibliographic Classification* (BC) and the *Colon Classification* deserve mention: the *Colon Classification* because of its importance for classification theory (although it has never had a strong user base anywhere in the world); BC because it is an example of a fully faceted classification scheme once in wide use (although this is no longer the case).

BC is held in general high esteem because of its theoretical qualities – its logic, clarity, and structure in particular – but currently it has only a small user base, mainly specialist libraries, although its effectiveness as a classification scheme for small general libraries has been demonstrated at Cambridge University (Attar 2000). Previous users migrated from it to other schemes during a long period when BC was not updated, and even the steady (but slow) publication of schedules in a second edition from 1977 has not been sufficient to attract users back to it. Despite its superiority to DDC and LCC in many respects it would, Foskett notes, 'be optimistic to assume that the scheme has an assured future' (Foskett 1996, p.301). However, following agreement between the editorial bodies of UDC and BC, the BC structure has been used as the basis of revisions of UDC schedules, for example in schedules for mathematics and medicine (McIlwaine 1996).

BC: summary of characteristics

Nature of scheme	Hierarchical, with considerable use of facets and with many options
Synthesis	Comprehensive synthetic capability
Citation order	Standard citation order given but is flexible if required, with guidance provided in schedules through practical examples
Notation	Mixed: alphabetical as the base notation, supplemented by numbers (A-Z & 2-9, giving a base of 34) Flexible: e.g., can be shortened if required
Index	2nd ed. has an index for each schedule
History	First ed. 1935 (abridged); complete ed. 1940-1953 2nd ed. 1977 onwards (print only)
Aids	Guidance available on the Bliss Classification Association's website
Use	A moderate number of academic, government and special libraries in the U.K. and the British Commonwealth (notable users include some of the libraries at Cambridge University, and Senate House Library in the University of London)
Problems	Lack of updating has eroded user base
Advantages	High degree of flexibility, through alternatives to accommodate individual library needs

Figure 7.4 shows the basic structure of BC.

2	Generalia	I	Psychology
3	Multidisciplinary topics	J	Education
6	Universe of knowledge	K	Society
7	Information science	LA	Area studies
A	Philosophy and logic	LB	Geography
AM	Mathematics	LC	Travel
AY	Natural sciences	LD	History
B	Physics	P	Religion
C	Chemistry	Q	Social welfare
D	Astronomy	R	Politics
DH	Earth sciences	S	Law
E	Biological science	T	Economics and management
GY	Ecology	U/V	Technology and useful arts
H	Human sciences and studies	W	Fine arts
HA	Human biology and anthropology	X	Philology
HH	Health and medicine		

Figure 7.4 Basic structure of BC. Source: Marcella & Newton 1994, pp.105-106

BC in Australia

BC enjoyed a flurry of popularity in Australia during the 1950s. Its merits were vigorously debated in 1953-1954 in the pages of the *Australian Library Journal*, the discussion prompted by its adoption at the Australian National University, Canberra. It was considered to be the best scheme available when it was adopted at the University of Tasmania Library in 1955, in particular, because it offered better collocation of subjects than DDC (Borchardt, Marshall & Dunn 1955). However, the scheme's lack of revision caused those Australian libraries which had adopted it to reclassify to another classification scheme by the 1970s. The University of Tasmania, for instance, reclassified to the *Library of Congress Classification* (TU Goes L.C. 1973). The appearance of the second edition from the late 1970s was too late to redress the situation, even though its theoretical merits for subject retrieval are widely acknowledged. An Australian reviewer of the second edition of BC considered that 'The real challenge of the new edition of the *Bibliographic Classification* may therefore be to see whether we care sufficiently about employing effective retrieval tools to ensure that the scheme survives, eventually to replace the inadequate tools which we at present use' (Ramsden 1978, p.214). Apparently we do not; and this is especially the case in Australia, where the number of libraries using this classification has dropped to zero.

Colon Classificaton

The *Colon Classification* – 'used by a few, greatly admired by some, totally neglected by many' (Marcella & Newton 1994, p.103) – is not much used outside India, the country in which its originator, S.R. Ranganathan, was born. It is noted here because it has been influential for its theoretical contributions to classification, especially in its demonstration of the principle of facets. In this it has been pored over and its contents assimilated by the developers of other classification schemes. CC has a main class structure, then beyond that is fully faceted. Its notation is mixed and complex, using letters, numbers, some letters of the Greek alphabet, and punctuation. The first edition of CC was published in 1933; it is now up to its 7th edition (1987). Its user base is limited because, among other reasons, its compilers have not followed the integrity of numbers principle, so the frequent major changes mean that frequent reclassification is required. Its lack of institutional support, a formal editorial board, and forum for users means that its use is unlikely to increase (Satija 1997).

Figure 7.5 shows the different notations used by three classification schemes for two subject areas.

Subject Economics in the U.S.A.
DDC	330.973	(from Class 330 Economics)
UDC	338(73)	(from Class 338 Production of Wealth)
CC	X.73	(from Class X Economics)

Subject Administration of manuscript collections in British academic libraries today
DDC	025.17120941	(from Class 020 Library and Information Science)
UDC	025.171+027.7(410)	(from Class 02 Librarianship)
CC	2,3;12:8.56'N6	(from Class 2 Library Science)

Figure 7.5 Notations from three general bibliographic classification schemes. Source of CC examples: Marcella & Newton 1994, pp.100-101

National general classification schemes

National general classification schemes are devised specifically for use in one country. An example is the SAB (Sveriges allmänna biblioteksförening) classification scheme used in Swedish libraries. The *Klassifikationssystem för svenska bibliotek* (Classification system for Swedish libraries, often referred to as the SAB system (SAB-systemet)) was developed as a national classification scheme by the Sveriges allmänna biblioteksförening, a body established in 1915 to promote library activities at the national level. This classification scheme was owned and administered by SAB until 2000, when it was taken on by the Svensk biblioteksförening (Swedish Library Association). The *Klassifikationssystem för svenska bibliotek* first appeared in 1921 and is currently in its eighth edition (2006). It is basically hierarchical and has incorporated faceted principles. Its alphabetical notation has

25 main classes indicated by the letters A-V, X, Y and Ä. This scheme is used by almost all public libraries and most of the university libraries in Sweden. Like all general schemes it has limitations, for example, it is weaker in technology subjects than in the humanities and social sciences.

Another example is the *Nederlandse Basisclassificatie*, developed for use in the shared cataloguing system operated by Pica, the Dutch Centre for Library Automation (which became OCLC Pica). It is a relatively new general classification scheme, being developed in the 1980s and now in its third edition (1998). This scheme uses a numerical notation. It has 89 main categories (01 to 89) and notations are four numbers separated by a full stop after the first two numbers (for example, 06.04 history of archive science). The *Nederlandse Basisclassificatie* has been translated into German and English.

Specialised library classification schemes

General bibliographic classification schemes do not always suit some subject areas. The information professional has two options: to locate a suitable specialised classification scheme developed (and preferably also maintained) by another organisation; or to develop their own specialised classification scheme. The number of specialised classification schemes is great; the number that are regularly maintained and updated is significantly smaller.

The field of music provides one example. Problems with the music schedules in general bibliographic schemes have lead to many classification schemes being developed for music. One characteristic of the field is that it lends itself readily to a faceted approach (as we saw at the start of this chapter). Figure 7.6 illustrates an excerpt from a commonly used faceted classification scheme for music, *The British Catalogue of Music Classification*.

Physics and astronomy provides another example. *The Physics and Astronomy Classification Scheme* (PACS), prepared and published by the American Institute of Physics with input from other interested organisations, is published biennially and is available online. PACS, a hierarchical subject classification scheme, has ten broad categories subdivided into sixty-six major topics, a detailed acoustics appendix, and an alphabetical index with corresponding PACS codes. It is designed for classification of journal subject indexes, catalogs, electronic databases, and online journals in physics and astronomy. Its common use 'enables the indexes and databases from physics, astronomy and related fields to be cumulated together and searched efficiently under a single coherent scheme' (American Institute of Physics 2003).

Other notable examples of special schemes include the NLM scheme developed by the United States National Library of Medicine, the *International Patent Classification* (IPC), and the *North American Industry Classification System* (NAICS).

If a specialised classification scheme is not available, then a scheme may be created. The basic steps in creating a faceted scheme are well understood and can be readily found in the classification literature, (e.g., Marcella & Newton 1994, pp.132-138). These steps include:

- *identifying the concepts* – working from the information resources to be classified, identify the subject terms to be used;

- *analysing concepts into facets* – determine the facets from the sample of subject terms identified in the first step;

- *arranging foci within facets* – arrange the facets in a logical order;

- *establishing the facet citation order* – decide on the appropriate order in which the facets should be cited;

- *creating the schedules* – write the schedules, including the notation, index and instructions; and

- *testing and evaluating the scheme*.

A/CY   **Technique of music**

> *It is sometimes necessary to include subjects from /D, /E and /F (or any two of these) together in composite subjects, particularly when the composition or performance is qualified by nationality, place or period. /D, /E and /F are combined in schedule order, and the locality, national or period symbol (Y..), (X..) or (Y../X..) immediately follows the subject symbol which it qualifies.*
> *The stroke is omitted from /E or /F when these symbols follow immediately after (Y..), (X..) or (Y../X..) attached to the preceding subject symbol.*
> *E.g.:*
> *French opera performed in London AC/D(YH)E(YDB).*
> *Recordings of opera performed in London*
>   *AC/E(YDB)FD.*
> *Recordings of French opera performed in London 1860-1900 AC/D(YH)E(YDB/XK41)FD.*
> *British recordings of French opera performed in London*
>   *AC/D(YH)E(YDB)FD(YC).*

A/D	Composition
A/DM	Arrangement
A/E	Performance
A/EAG	Sight reading
A/EF	Conducting
A/EL	Accompaniment
A/F	Recording
A/FD	Recorded music
A/FH	Mechanical music
A/FJ	Mechanical organs
A/FK	Musical clocks

A/FY   **Musical character**

A/G	Folk music
A/GD	Street music
A/GH	Gipsy music
A/GHW	Music of various stages of life cycle
A/GJ	Childhood
A/GK	Nursery rhymes
A/GM	Music of various occupational groups
A/GMC	Seafarers
A/GND	Plantation music
A/GNF	Cowboys
A/GR	Music to accompany activities
A/GS	Music to accompany games and sports
A/GT	Hunting
A/H	Dance music

Figure 7.6 Excerpt from a specialised classification scheme. Source: Coates, E.J. (1960). *The British Catalogue of Music Classification*, p.3

Although a faceted classification scheme can be developed with relative ease, the decision to develop one's own scheme needs to be approached with considerable caution. To remain viable over a period of time the scheme must be updated regularly, so a commitment to providing the resources needed for ongoing maintenance of the scheme is essential. A better solution may be to develop a thesaurus for subject retrieval, and use a published classification scheme for shelf arrangement.

Australian use of specialised classification schemes

Examples of the many specialised classification schemes used in Australia include *Boggs and Lewis* for maps (used at the State Library of Victoria) and the *Pettee* (Union Theological Seminary, New York) classification for theology used at the Joint Theological College, Parkville, Victoria and Churches of Christ Theological College, Mulgrave, Victoria. In 1982 some Australian university libraries were using specialised classification schemes such as *Harvard-Yenching*, *Black* (Dental) and *Moys* (Law), in addition to LCC or DDC, as their primary means of classification (Richardson 1982). For music, an Australian faceted classification scheme which uses concepts from the *Colon Classification*, was described in the *Australian Library Journal* in 1954 (Olding 1954). A 1994 survey indicated that in Australia DDC (often modified), in-house schemes and the *British Catalogue of Music Classification* were most commonly used for classifying printed music, with 54, 20 and 11 per cent of the 35 responses respectively (National Library of Australia 1994).

Specialised classification schemes are sometimes developed in-house. One example of a home-grown specialised classification scheme, already noted, is the *Australian Faceted Classification Scheme for Music* developed in 1954. Another local example was a *Classification for English Literature* published in 1967 and designed especially to accommodate colonial literature (Buick 1967).

Reclassification

Reclassification usually occurs when the classification scheme in use becomes unworkable. It was particularly common in the 1960s and 1970s, largely because of dissatisfaction with the 14th, 15th and 17th editions of DDC. This disquiet resulted in many libraries reclassifying their collections to LCC or modifying DDC, modifications which in time became unwieldy, expensive to maintain, and increasingly incompatible with later editions of DDC and with DDC numbers derived from central cataloguing sources.

Reclassification of parts of collections is much more likely to occur than reclassification of the whole collection. This usually takes place when there have been considerable changes to a schedule when a new edition is published. In this situation there are two possible approaches:

1) Reclassify all of the affected range of numbers as one operation.

2) Rely on 'osmosis', as Dunkin (1969, p.112) describes it: reclassify only new additions to the collection, and perhaps also information resources on loan as they are returned. Eventually all the current information resources, and those still in use, will be reclassified to the new numbers, with the obsolete, non-reclassified items getting weeded out.

Reclassification: Australian examples

In Australia, reclassification of whole or major part of library collections from DDC to LCC has been especially common, followed in frequency by reclassification from BC to another scheme when the first edition of BC became too outdated to be workable. In the early 1970s the University of Queensland moved from DDC to LCC, one factor apparently being that more LCC classification numbers were at the time available from centralised cataloguing sources (Dobrovits 1971, McMillan & McMillan 1984). The move from DDC to LCC was made at the Australian Defence Force Academy Library in Canberra. One of the reasons given for this change was that LCC better accommodates military, scientific and technical materials (Beatty 1987).

A well-documented example of the move from BC, in this case to LCC, is that at the University of Tasmania in the 1970s. The reasons put forward for abandoning BC included the non-availability of BC numbers from centralised cataloguing services, lack of updating of the scheme and lack of any mechanism for updating it, and potential cost benefits of using standard classification. LCC was selected as the new classification for practical reasons, particularly the availability of classification numbers from other sources (TU Goes L.C. 1973; Goodram, Howard & Eaves 1974).

Classification and computers

The use of classification to provide subject access is becoming more widespread with bibliographic organisation practice now heavily computerised. The potential for computers, combined with classification, to improve subject access had been recognised for over forty years. Back in 1967 Arthur Maltby noted that 'far from abolishing the need for classifying and indexing, [the computer] gives a new meaning and impetus to new research in this field' (Sayers 1967, p.368). Early research, however, did little more than point out that the classification schemes as then structured were not consistent enough to allow progress. Research into the use of DDC in computer systems in the 1980s indicated that classification could be used effectively in three ways:

- to provide additional vocabulary terms on which to search – the terms in the index and schedules of classification schemes are a rich source of terms which indicate subject content, and searching using these terms provides improved search results

- to allow browsing by subject online – this capability could be used as a substitute for shelf browsing in the virtual library, and

- to search by class number – many OPACs allow searching on the classification notation, although surveys of users indicate that where available this option is little used.

Other uses of classification in online library information retrieval systems identified by Svenonius in the early 1980s included:

- to increase the number of relevant information resources retrieved by broadening a search;

- to improve precision by screening out unwanted information resources;
- to contextualize search terms, that is, to help to better frame the search requests and make them more precise; and
- as a switching language (Svenonius 1983).

Svenonius concluded: 'in short, not only does classification have a place in online systems of the future; it likely has such an important place that we should prepare for a resurgence of interest in both its theory and its practice' (Svenonius 1983, p.80). Two decades later, her prophecy has been fulfilled.

Marcella and Maltby provide an overview of research into classification schemes and use in computer environments (Marcella & Maltby 2000, especially chapters 4, 5 and 6). Much of it is directed towards the structure of the classification schemes. One of the main difficulties we face, if we try to make more use of classification schemes in our library information retrieval systems, is the nature of the classification schemes themselves. We have seen that the most commonly used schemes, DDC, LCC and UDC, have problems in the way in which they are structured. Their long histories of development have led to structural inconsistencies, so that both DDC and LCC are mixtures of enumeration, hierarchy and synthesis; UDC is more synthetic, but this synthesis lacks rules of application so some subjects can be cited in a wide range of ways. The DDC research agenda that its parent organisation, OCLC, is actively supporting includes research into decomposing DDC numbers to allow retrieval of facets of a topic, something that may make it more attractive as a means of subject access on the web. An example of this research-in-progress is the 'DeweyBrowser' prototype accessible on OCLC's website.

Investigation into the possibility of using classification schemes as a switching language, or as a pivot, has a fairly long history. Because classification schemes rely on a notation that is independent of language and alphabetical arrangement, they appear to be well suited to act as a pivot on which several different languages can be hinged. Such a use has potential in multilingual catalogues and between different online databases, and is of particular interest in transcending national linguistic boundaries. Joan Mitchell, the editor of the 22nd edition of DDC, envisages that Dewey, with its many translations, is well placed to play a role as a switching language (Mitchell 1997, pp.47-48). Much effort has been expended on preparing the major general bibliographic classification schemes for online use. The possibility of developing a way in which classification schemes, such as DDC, and other subject access mechanisms can work together to provide better subject access to electronic information has been investigated in the HILT (High-Level Thesaurus) project. Olson and Boll provide more detail about the application of classification in computer environments (Olson & Boll 2001, especially chapters 7 and 8).

Classification and the web

The main reason for the renewed interest in classification schemes is their potential for organising the huge amount of information that now exists on the web. The use of classification schemes for this purpose has now moved from being largely experimental to common practice. Where standard bibliographic classification schemes are found to be unsuitable, there is an increasing tendency for website designers – or information architects as they are often called – to develop their own 'taxonomies' for organising their online content. These taxonomies can be most readily seen in the menus through which website users can click through to find the information they want.

The skills required to build specialised, in-house classification schemes have thus become more useful than ever before, with just about every organisation desiring its own website. This is not to say, however, that existing schemes have been totally ignored, and an increasing number of large websites have adopted, fully or in part, established schemes such as DDC. For example, BUBL Information Service's BUBL Link uses DDC classification to organise its directory. The user can select his or her choice of arrangement: by DDC, or alphabetically by subject, country or type (the alternative arrangements are based on Dewey facets). (Figure 7.7 shows the DDC option.) Another website which offers a choice of subject approaches, in this case DDC and four alphabetical subject lists in common use (headings from the *Library of Congress Subject Headings*, *National Library of Medicine Subject Headings*, the MeSH subject headings and the CAB thesaurus), is BIOME for health and life sciences resources (http://biome.ac.uk/browse/).

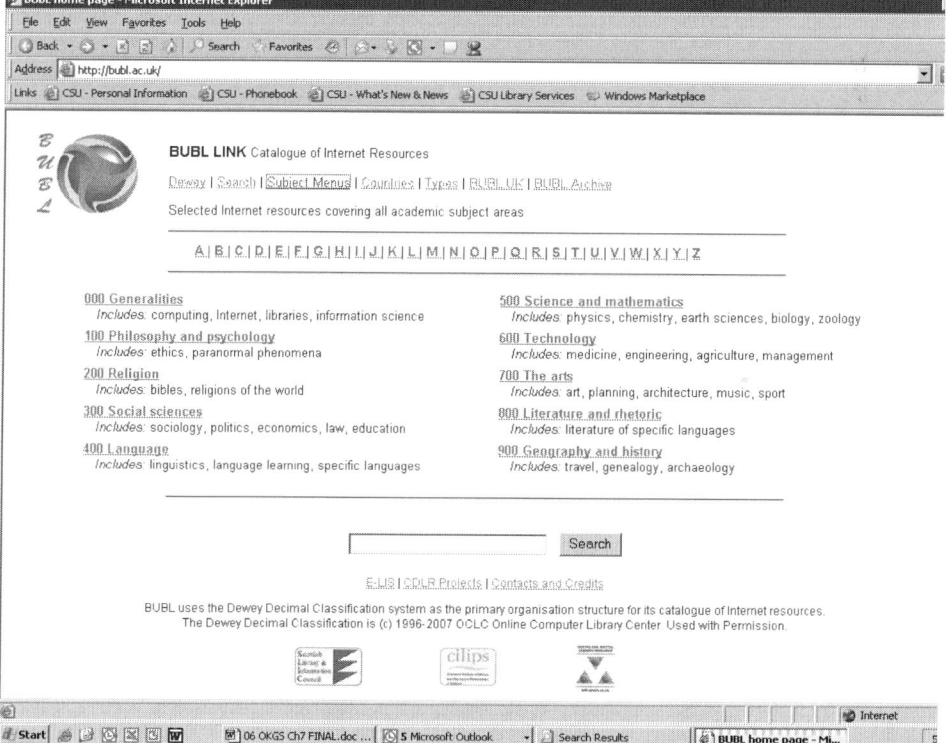

Figure 7.7 BUBL Link, internet resources arranged by DDC.
Source: http://bubl.ac.uk/link/ddc.html (accessed 1 December 2007)

LCC is also used to organise the CyberStacks website, which describes itself as 'a centralized, integrated, and unified collection of significant world wide web (WWW) and other internet resources categorized using the Library of Congress classification scheme' (*CyberStacks(sm)* 1998).

Some other experimental sites that use standard classification schemes or controlled vocabularies to organise or provide enhanced access to internet resources are listed at the Beyond Bookmarks site at http://www2.iastate.edu/~cyberstacks/CTW.htm. (The use of classification to organise web resources is discussed further in chapter 9.)

Conclusion

This chapter describes general attributes of bibliographic classification schemes and notes the schemes most commonly applied by libraries and information centres. While classification schemes remain a good way of 'marking and parking' physical collections, they are proving all the more useful in the virtual environment, providing subject access to huge numbers of internet resources, both within and across websites. Some of these schemes (or 'taxonomies') are borrowed from the traditional library world: many others are being developed for specific collections of online resources.

In addition to the use of bibliographic classification schemes, subject access is also commonly provided by applying subject access mechanisms that are based on alphabetical arrangement. The following chapter examines these, including both controlled vocabularies such as lists of subject headings and thesauri, and natural language approaches.

CHAPTER 8
Alphabetical subject access mechanisms

As noted in chapter 6, subject access to information resources in the collections of libraries and information centres is provided in two main ways: by using bibliographic classification schemes (see chapter 7); and by using subject access mechanisms that are based on alphabetical arrangement. This chapter looks at the latter, concentrating on controlled vocabularies such as lists of subject headings and thesauri, and on natural language approaches to the provision of subject access.

Orna and Pettit have described neatly the issues of using an alphabetical approach to provide subject access in the museum context. Their description also applies to information resources in libraries and other kinds of information services.

> If we want all kinds of users to be able to use collection documentation for themselves, so that they can make their own decisions about what they want and find their way to it, terminology control is an essential tool … The commonest cause [of concern] … is probably still the lack of enough 'ways in' [but] … if that particular obstacle is removed, by using technology that allows multiple ways in to the documentation – for instance by means of information-retrieval software that permits free-text search on multiple criteria – another is liable to take its place. The new difficulty arises from the sheer richness and variety of language. There are so many possible ways of describing things and of expressing concerns that, even when we have a tireless electronic slave that will find any word or phrase we ask for, what it brings us may be only a fraction of what is relevant (Orna & Pettit 1998, pp.53-54).

Types of vocabulary

The section 'The process of providing subject access' in chapter 6 indicates the steps which are taken to provide subject access to information resources. After we have decided what an information resource is about (what its subject is), we use an *indexing language* to express this subject or subjects. We can, for example, use a language that is made up of words in common use (say, in English), or we might invent another language completely. This indexing language has a *vocabulary* of words, terms or concepts. This vocabulary might be selected only from words that occur in the document, or from another source.

Three kinds of indexing languages are distinguished in chapter 6:

- indexing languages which use a controlled vocabulary (such as subject headings lists and thesauri);

- those which use a natural language vocabulary derived from the content of the resources themselves; and

- free indexing languages (words taken from any source).

The pros and cons of providing subject access by using controlled vocabularies or natural language indexing are noted in chapter 6. As a reminder, they are summarised here:

- *controlled vocabulary indexing languages*: the vocabulary is selected and authorised by a cataloguer or indexer, and an authorised list of terms (an 'authority list') is constructed and used. The primary advantage of controlled vocabularies is the consistency they provide; their main disadvantage is that they need to be updated regularly and are expensive to apply.

- *eerived indexing*: the vocabulary selected is taken from the information resource itself, often from the title or abstract. This approach has the main advantage of requiring little or no intellectual input (it can, for instance, be automated), but the disadvantage of not indicating relationships among terms.

- *free indexing languages*: the vocabulary can be selected from anywhere at all; that is, it is not restricted to terms present in the information resource or from a particular controlled vocabulary. Advantages include the lack of constraints on choice of vocabulary, allowing the user and the vocabulary to be exactly matched. The main disadvantage is, as for derived indexing, that relationships among terms cannot be indicated.

Why we still use controlled vocabularies

When computers were first applied to information retrieval, and particularly when they had developed sufficiently to provide the ability to carry out full-text searching, it was prophesied that controlled vocabularies would die out rapidly. This has proved not to be the case. Controlled vocabularies and free-text searching both have their advantages and disadvantages. The standard way of providing subject access in information centres has been through a controlled vocabulary approach. Typically two controlled vocabularies have been applied – a classification scheme, and a controlled vocabulary based on alphabetical arrangement (terms selected from a list of subject headings or from a thesaurus). But, as we noted in chapter 7, a classification scheme is used in libraries primarily to provide a shelf location. When used in this way it does not provide useful subject access, except for users who want to browse along the shelves.

Currently, as a consequence of increasing sophistication in the development and use of library information retrieval systems, we usually also provide subject access using a natural language approach, for example through keyword searching on terms present in the title, author, and subject fields of information resources. This provides two additional advantages that we can add to the benefits derived from a controlled vocabulary-based approach:

- the number of terms on which we can search is increased, and

- the terms can be combined by the searcher (post-coordinate searching).

Chan and Hodges summarise the situation, noting that 'our traditional systems for subject access … have been transported to the OPAC environment' (Chan & Hodges 1998, p.107). Consequently, our library information retrieval systems are still based on card catalogue concepts, including traditional subject access mechanisms such as DDC and LCSH. Although these traditional systems are working better than expected in providing subject access in the computer environment, they could work better still, as many user studies have indicated. It is now clear that there are ways in which improvements can be made, such as using classification online (see chapters 7 and 9), improving LCSH, and enhancing catalogue records by adding more terms that can be searched.

As we've already observed, in yesterday's library information retrieval systems the question was 'natural language OR controlled vocabularies?' In the new library information retrieval systems the solution is 'natural language AND controlled vocabularies'.

Some basic concepts

It is useful to define some key terms and concepts at this point.

Exhaustivity is about the thoroughness of subject indexing, which has a large bearing on how many subject-indicative terms are assigned. Summarising is at one end of the exhaustivity spectrum: a common example of this is the assignment of a single classification number, or only one subject heading. Somewhere near the middle is the standard practice of assigning between one and five subject headings in library cataloguing. At the other end, exhaustive subject indexing places no limit on the number of terms used: an example is the use of terms taken from the abstract of a journal article, together with many descriptors selected, perhaps from a thesaurus.

Specificity refers to how precise the terms supplied are. The terms should not refer to the genre, but to the specific example of the genre that is being described. For example, a book about possums should be assigned the heading *Possums*, not *Marsupials*.

Coextensive entry is the name for the concept that terms should be coextensive with subjects in the document. For example, a book about marsupials and mammals will require terms for both, not one or the other.

Relevance, recall and *precision* are terms used to measure the effectiveness of information retrieval systems, and are also used to evaluate the effectiveness of subject access mechanisms. They are noted in more detail in the Introduction to Part IV.

Pre-coordinate and *post-coordinate:* after we decide on a number of single concepts to describe a subject, we can use them in two ways. We can use the single concepts individually to search the system, then combine the results together at the end (*post-coordination*); or we can group together the concepts before we carry out the search (*pre-coordination*). Many Library of Congress subject headings exemplify pre-coordination. We will look at these headings next.

Subject headings lists

A subject headings list is a list of terms, arranged in alphabetical order, which have been selected for their ability to indicate subjects and have been authorised for use to provide subject access to bibliographic records. Such a list usually covers many subjects and is therefore intended for use in information centres whose collections span a wide range of subjects, such as public, academic and school libraries. (A useful analogy is with bibliographic classification schemes, where general schemes such as DDC are used in general collections, and specialised classification schemes – analogous to thesauri, described later in this chapter – are used for collections covering a smaller range of subjects.) The terms in a subject headings list tend to be broad, rather than specific, and they are often found in inverted rather than direct form, for example *Cookery, Singaporean* rather than *Singaporean cookery*. (Note in this example the pre-coordination of the two terms *Cookery* and *Singaporean*.) It is likely to have a complex, but imprecise, reference structure that links related terms. Like classification schemes, the subject headings list will be developed and maintained by large external bodies, such as the Library of Congress for LCSH, and the publisher H.W. Wilson for *Sears List of Subject Headings*.

This section examines two subject headings lists in common use in libraries throughout the English-speaking world: the *Library of Congress Subject Headings* and *Sears List of Subject Headings*. The *SCIS Subject Headings* list, widely used in school libraries in Australia and New Zealand, is also considered. It should be noted that many other subject headings lists are also widely used in libraries: another common example is MeSH (*Medical Subject Headings*) developed by the United States National Library of Medicine.

LCSH (Library of Congress Subject Headings)

Nature of scheme	A subject authority file list from the Library of Congress, initially developed by the Library of Congress for its own use; now used, and in some cases contributed to, by many thousands of other libraries with general collections. Authorised terms plus lead-in terms (references) and cross-references. Not all subject terms authorised for use by Library of Congress are part of the subject authority file – omitted (for the most part) are name headings and headings for works, which may sometimes be subjects (these are maintained in other authority files; see chapter 4). Some synthesis, principally through the use of so-called free-floating subdivisions and the addition of geographic subdivisions. Controlled vocabulary list. Basically pre-coordinate. Some post-coordination (Chan 1995, pp.34-8).
History	Developed by Library of Congress, late nineteenth century. First published 1914, followed by a continuing succession of versions and editions.
Versions	Print: now annual (30th ed. 2007). Online version: *Classification Web*, available by subscription (also includes LCC numbers); a more limited version is freely available via the LC website. Weekly revisions: available from the LC website.
Aids	LC publishes instructions: *Subject Cataloging Manual: Subject Headings*, 5th ed. (1996) with regular updates.

Use	Standard in large U.S. general libraries; widely used in other libraries throughout the English-speaking world – a de facto international standard.
	The predominant scheme used in national bibliographies and by national libraries (Heiner-Freiling 2000).
	Also used to arrange some online databases and abstracting services.
Problems	Ethnocentric.
	Rules and guides for use are complex.
	Not well understood by users.
Advantages	Library of Congress subject headings are widely available on centralised cataloguing records.
	LCSH is changing to meet demands of online use (for example, it is being made more consistent).
	Stays relatively stable: changes are slow and gradual.

Despite the wide use of LCSH, Chan notes that:

> The current Library of Congress Subject Headings system is far from ideal, but changes are being made continuously as the result of concerted efforts between the Library of Congress and the profession as a whole. In the future, we can expect this important and unique tool to continue to serve its functions in information retrieval as continuous improvements are being made (Chan 1995, p.413).

As Chan indicates, users acknowledge that LCSH is not perfect: for example, a British Library view is that it is 'a system which is in need of a lot of development' (MacEwan 1999, p.94). The major reason underlying its problems is that it was designed for the card catalogue and has not yet fully made the transition to the online environment. The most obvious example of this is the use of subject headings in inverted rather than direct word order – we used above the example *Cookery, Singaporean* rather than *Singaporean cookery*. Inverted order has considerable significance in a card catalogue, because it places the most important word at the start of the subject heading and this is the word under which the entry would be filed and would therefore be accessible. It has little relevance in an information retrieval system that is capable of searching on any word in a heading, regardless of the word order. Despite these and numerous other problems, LCSH has become a *de facto* standard for bibliographical organisation in libraries, in the same way and for the same reasons as LCC and DDC have: they are present on the many millions of LCMARC records which are available to libraries (see chapter 11). Consequently libraries will not abandon LCSH readily. They have, however, been calling for change to make this important controlled vocabulary more useful in library information retrieval systems. The most common criticisms of LCSH have been that its terminology is outdated and inconsistent, its choice of forms of headings is unpredictable (Chan & Hodges 1998, p.99), and it is U.S-centric (MacEwan 1999, p.94).

LCSH uses a variety of forms to express its authorised terms. They include single noun headings (e.g., *Laments* and *Leeches*), and a wide variety of phrase headings, including inverted phrase headings (e.g., *Love poetry, Russian*). Qualifiers may be used to resolve ambiguities and avoid semantic confusion (*Lost sheep (Parable)* is an example). Headings can be made more specific by adding further terms (called *subdivisions* in LCSH), including those that are for form (e.g., *Mexico – Juvenile literature*), chronological (e.g., *Mexico – Church history – 16th century*), topical (e.g., *Crystallography – Instruments*) and place (e.g., *Sheep – Mexico*). Some of these are 'free-floating subdivisions', so named (but a bit misleadingly) because they can be added wherever appropriate under specific categories of headings. There are a powerful device to make headings more specific, although they also provide the potential for considerable confusion and ambiguity. Examples of free-floating subdivisions are *Management* and *Research*, added wherever appropriate and as directed: hence *Libraries – Management* and *Libraries – Research*.

What to do about Australian English?

Much of the Australian writing about subject access in libraries has lamented the inability of the standard alphabetically-arranged subject headings lists to cater adequately for Australian subjects and Australian terminology. Australian English has developed its own terminology (who outside Australia has heard of *Paterson's curse*, aka *Salvation Jane*?) and variations which make it distinctive enough from American English to require alterations of LCSH for effective local use. A strong Australian emphasis on providing controlled vocabularies that work for users, combined with a certain Australian independence of spirit, have resulted in a history of modifying or replacing some of the less accessible terms in controlled vocabularies, particularly LCSH. John Metcalfe noted in 1969 that 'I have a rooted objection to consulting foreign language catalogues; my language is Australian English, I consider myself insulted by any cataloguer who expects me to look under corporations for companies' (quoted in McKinlay 1974a, p.131). Although Metcalfe was writing several decades ago, the situation has not changed markedly: a more recent manifestation of this concern related to the inadequacy of LCSH to provide adequate access to Aboriginal studies topics, making it unhelpful for Australian use in this subject area (Moorcroft 1992). The Library of Congress has recently become more responsive to suggestions from the international community (SACO – see below in this chapter – has been an important catalyst), as indicated by its adoption in 2003 of recommendations from the National Library of Australia about revision of subject headings for aboriginal Australians (previously termed 'Australian aborigines' in LCSH).

The influence of LCSH has not always been one way. A subject headings list developed by H.C.L. Anderson at the Public Library of New South Wales in 1896 was one model used for the development of LCSH (Metcalfe 1959, p.43). A descendant of Anderson's list, Sherrie and Mander Jones' *Short List of Subject Headings* (1950), developed for use in Australian public and school libraries, was still in common use in Australia in the 1970s.

A survey of Australian libraries to determine which thesauri of Australian subject terms were in use was carried out in 1994. This survey reported that terms for Aboriginal subjects (communities, language groups, clans, etc) were poorly covered. More than 75 per cent of respondents (forty-eight of sixty-three) used a published thesaurus of Australian terms. Three were most used: APAIS, LASH, and ABN Authorities. However, the lack of an acceptable common standard was indicated by the fact that twenty-eight other thesauri were also used, most with only one user (Thesaurus Usage in Australian Libraries 1996). The *SCIS Subject Headings List*, discussed later in this chapter, is another example of Australianising the controlled vocabulary.

LASH, FLASH and SLASH

The publication of the *List of Canadian Subject Headings* in 1968 provided a model for the development of a similar Australian list. (A Canadian list is still being published: Libraries and Archives Canada maintains a list of Canadian subject headings that complement LCSH, available on the web.) The Canadian example clearly indicated the feasibility of producing and using a list catering for local requirements as a supplement to LCSH, to counteract such problems as differences in terminology (for example *General practitioners* rather than *Physicians (General Practice)*; *Door-to-door selling* rather than *Canvassing*; *Hire purchase* rather than *Sales, Conditional*; and *Flats* rather than *Apartment houses*) (McKinlay 1974a). John McKinlay produced a preliminary edition of *A List of Australian Subject Headings*, published in 1978. It was designed to supplement the eighth edition of the *Library of Congress Subject Headings* and its scope was Australian synonyms, variants, additional subject headings, Australian terminology and subjects not in LCSH, and additional *see also* references (there is a very detailed review of this preliminary edition by Hine 1979). The first edition of *A List of Australian Subject Headings* (*LASH*) was published in 1981. A commentator on this first edition (nicknamed *FLASH*) echoed a similar view to that of Metcalfe: 'That a ten year old, using a touch screen terminal of an online catalogue in a public library was told to accept "Railroads" as an index heading when he wanted "Railways" is one small step away from what is Australian. He was a bit bewildered: it may not matter. It may not matter that LCSH refers from "Bushwhackers" to "Guerillas", but it does bother me and I don't believe that we should by default authorize some version of American English for our subject catalogues' (Morrison 1982, p.229).

LASH was widely adopted in Australian libraries and has been influential, even to the extent of inspiring verse:

> [it was] … a giant step for Australia,
> For this is the moment Library of Congress has been dreading,
> The Aussies have created their own subject headings …
> We had to go it alone because we couldn't exist
> With their headings outdated, racist and sexist… .
> LC often uses such an unsuitable word
> That it appears to ears to be patently absurd.
> For what they call a hen, they obviously mistook
> For our national bird, the domestic chook … (Genoni 1981).

However, a second edition of LASH (i.e., SLASH, or *Second List of Australian Subject Headings*) never got published, despite being developed by ALIA. Interest in local headings work to supplement LCSH has recently been rekindled in the form of the Australian Subject Access Project, being undertaken by Libraries Australia, which aims to continue the work of incorporating local headings, such as those produced in SLASH, into the subject authority file attached to the Australian National Bibliographic Database (ANBD). Particular attention has been paid to terms representing a new concept not hitherto covered by LCSH, for example, *Asbestos cement houses*, *Droving,* and *Mateship (Australia).* These headings are also submitted to the Library of Congress as proposed new LCSH, for its approval.

The SACO (Subject Authority Cooperative) Program

The cost and other resource implications of maintaining controlled vocabularies such as LCSH are high, and the processes are complex. Libraries, recognising that they work in 'a world of shrinking resources but expanding information' (Franks 2000, p.49), are participating in cooperative enterprises to address this issue. The SACO (Subject Authority Cooperative) Program is one example. SACO, introduced in 1992, is part of the Program for Cooperative Cataloging (PCC) administered by the Library of Congress. (PCC is noted in chapter 11.) The National Library of Australia is a member, and, indeed, suggested the idea to the Library of Congress in 1981 (Cristán 2003). SACO has grown from 18 participants in 1992 to several hundred in 2007, although many libraries only submit proposals on an occasional basis; in 1992, 678 new subject headings were contributed by SACO libraries, whereas in 2006, the figures was 3,619 (PCC 2006).

The principle on which SACO is based is simple: participants propose new subject headings to the Library of Congress so that LCSH reflect better the needs of users. However, cooperative ventures do not always run smoothly, and SACO is no exception. The guidelines for constructing LC subject headings are not easy to understand. The procedures for submitting proposals are cumbersome and need refinement to make participation more straightforward. Participants refer to the length of time it takes for submissions to be acted on, and to a United States bias in some of the decisions made. SACO shows every sign of being an effective and cost-effective mechanism for maintaining LCSH and expanding its international inclusiveness, but it is not quite there yet (Cristán 2003).

Making LCSH more useful

The debate about the suitability of LCSH for use in the online environment has been going on for many years, but its focus has changed over the last two decades. In the 1980s the discussion centred on the question 'do we need controlled vocabularies such as LCSH at all in the online environment?' It has now become 'how can we keep improving LCSH, building on it to improve its current ability to provide effective subject access?' The focus of change to LCSH has been on improving it in three ways: to make it internally consistent; to make it more current and less biased, and to allow more post-coordination (Chan & Hodges 1998, pp.102-103).

One major area where changes are being made is to the structure of the headings: adopting natural word order, consistent patterns of citation order, and direct geographic subdivision. Another area is in updating the terminology used in LCSH so that it is more current and acceptable for expressing social issues in an unbiased manner. The demand for greater post-coordination is being met by the simplification of some of the more cumbersome compound headings. Some of the more unusual examples are: *Fishes, Dressing of; Plants, Effect of prayer on; Tariff on bush roller conveyor chain; Odors in the Bible*.

Perhaps the most obvious way in which LCSH indicated its seriousness about becoming more user-oriented was in the change made in 1986 for indicating relationships among terms, from arcane and confusing symbols – x, xx, *s, s.a.*, *see, see also* – to more accessible thesaurus-like symbols – USE, UF, NT, BT, RT and so on (see figure 8.1). Some commentators insisted that this change wrongly suggested that LCSH was a thesaurus (Dykstra 1988), but users do not seem to have suffered from confusion. There are other indications, too, that LCSH is moving slowly towards the thesaurus ideal.

```
Printed circuits
    {TK7868.P7 (Electronics)}
    BT  Electric circuits
        Electronic apparatus and appliances
        Electronic circuits
        Microelectronics
        Miniature electronic equipment
    NT  Expansion boards (Microcomputers)
        Flexible printed circuits
        Motherboards (Microcomputers)
        Space card (Analog computers)
   — Testing
        NT  Boundary scan testing
Printed circuits industry  (May Subd Geog)
    {HD9696.P74-HD9696.P744}
    BT  Electronic industries
Printed ephemera  (May Subd Geog)
    UF  Ephemera, Printed
        Ephemeral printing
        Printing, Ephemeral
    RT  Street literature
    NT  Cataloging of printed ephemera
        Grey literature
        Programs
Printed fashion apparel  (May Subd Geog)
    Here are entered works on clothing and dress ac-
    cessories which are further decorated or personalized
    by screen printing after manufacture.
    UF  Fashion apparel, Printed
    BT  Clothing and dress
Printed fashion apparel industry
    (May Subd Geog)
    BT  Clothing trade
Printer ribbons  (May Subd Geog)
    BT  Office equipment and supplies
        Ribbons
Printers  (May Subd Geog)
    {Z231-Z232 (Biography)}
    NT  Child printers
        Jewish printers
        Women printers
   — Charities
        {Z243}
        BT  Charities
   — Diseases  (May Subd Geog)
        {RC965.P8}
        UF  Printers—Diseases and hygiene
            {Former heading}
   — Diseases and hygiene
        USE  Printers—Diseases
             Printers—Health and hygiene
   — Health and hygiene  (May Subd Geog)
        UF  Printers—Diseases and hygiene
            {Former heading}
   — Societies, etc.
        USE  Printing—Societies, etc.
   — Strikes and lockouts
        USE  Strikes and lockouts—Printers

Digital printing presses
Epson printers
IBM printers
Nonimpact printers
Okidata printers
Star printers
   — Upgrading  (May Subd Geog)
        UF  Upgrading of computer printers
            Upgrading of printers (Data
               processing systems)
Printers' furniture  (May Subd Geog)
    {Z249}
    BT  Furniture
        Printing machinery and supplies
Printers' imprints
    USE  Imprints (Publishers' and printers'
           statements)
Printers in literature  (Not Subd Geog)
Printers' marks  (May Subd Geog)
    {Z235-Z236}
    UF  Marks, Printers'
        Typographical devices
    BT  Printers' ornaments
        Trademarks
    RT  Devices (Heraldry)
    NT  Book industries and trade—Heraldry
Printers' marks, French  (May Subd Geog)
    UF  French printers' marks
Printers' marks, Russian  (May Subd Geog)
    UF  Russian printers' marks
Printers' ornaments  (May Subd Geog)
    BT  Book ornamentation
    RT  Type ornaments
    NT  Fists (Printing)
        Initials
        Printers' marks
Printers' rollers
    USE  Rollers (Printing)
Printice family
    USE  Prentice family
Printing  (May Subd Geog)
    {Z116-Z265}
    UF  Printing, Practical
           {Former heading}
        Typography
    BT  Graphic arts
    NT  Architectural contracts—Printing
        Architectural drawing—Printing
        Architecture—Specifications—Printing
        Book ornamentation
        Calico-printing
        Cerography
        Color printing
        Commercial art—Printing
        Documents, Printing of
        Embossing (Printing)
        Engraving—Printing
        Graphic design (Typography)
```

Figure 8.1 Page from LCSH. Source: *Library of Congress Subject Headings.* 21st ed. (1998), p.4583

Despite changes over recent years, and despite the undoubted usefulness of it as a tool for providing subject access, most users still do not understand LCSH. Research carried out in 1999 indicated an accuracy rate of only about 40 per cent for adult users of LCSH, and only 52 to 55 per cent for expert users (librarians) (Drabenstott, reported in Weiss & Carstens 2001, p.53). Studwell has argued that we need a code of clearly articulated principles on which LCSH could be based and overhauled (Studwell 1990). Although there appear to be few alternatives to LCSH, at least not for the English-speaking world, there are those who have gone further than Studwell, and consider the vocabulary's benefits to be outweighed by the considerable costs of its application. Moorcroft has argued that LCSH are 'at best, ineffective, and at worst, an indictment on the library profession. They should not continue to be used' (Moorcroft 1992, p.44). More recently, Karen Calhoun (2006) has also questioned the value of the headings even for the Library of Congress, in her report, *The Changing Nature of the Catalog and its Integration with other Discovery Tools*. Since this report was commissioned by the Library of Congress, it can be assumed that it will carry considerable weight with the Library's management. However, there have also been spirited rebuffs of the report's 'findings', particularly from Thomas Mann, a reference librarian at the Library of Congress, who argues that even in the online environment the pre-coordinated strings provide an invaluable aid to researchers wishing to perform systematic searches (Mann 2003; 2006; 2007). Whether these arguments are spirited enough to save LCSH remains to be seen. It may be that while the core of the vocabulary continued to be applied, at least to some materials, the Library may attempt to simplify its application, currently detailed in the four-volume *Subject Cataloging Manual*.

FAST

One attempt to address the issue of the shortcomings of LCSH's structure while retaining the extensiveness of the vocabulary is FAST (*Faceted Application of Subject Terminology*), developed by OCLC. It is based on LCSH, but breaks down the pre-coordinated strings making it easier to apply and easier to search on (in a post-coordinated fashion). 'The schema maintains upward compatibility with LCSH, and any valid set of LC subject headings can be converted to FAST headings', according to the FAST home page. Like any simplification, there is some loss of meaning – in this case some of the meaning embedded in the syntax of LCSH. Whether this loss is made up for by greater usability is an open question; it still requires a good deal of time and skill to apply, just like other controlled vocabularies. If FAST is going to significantly enhance subject access, new systems will need to be implemented that take full advantage of its faceted nature, employing more sophisticated search algorithms. Although it is now a few years old, its application is so far largely experimental.

Sears List of Subject Headings

Sears List of Subject Headings was developed because the Library of Congress subject headings were considered to be unsuitable for use in small and medium-sized general libraries. From its inception it has been based on LCSH, but while it is very similar in format and structure it is not an abridgement. What is written above about LCSH in general also applies to Sears. It is a vocabulary quite commonly used in school libraries around the

U.S., though LCSH also has its own set of headings specifically for children's literature. The main features of Sears are outlined overleaf, and figure 8.2 illustrates them.

Casualty insurance 368.5
    UF   Insurance, Casualty *[Former heading]*
    BT   **Insurance**
    NT   **Accident insurance**
Cat
    USE   **Cats**
CAT scan
    USE   **Tomography**
Catacombs 393; 726
    BT   **Burial**
          Cemeteries
          Christian antiquities
          Christian art and symbolism
          Tombs
    RT   **Church history—30-600, Early church**
Cataloging 025.3
    May be subdivided by topic, e.g. **Cataloging—Music**.
    UF   Cataloguing
          Libraries—Cataloging
          Library cataloging
    BT   **Bibliographic control**
          Books
          Documentation
          Library science
          Library technical processes
    NT   **Classification—Books**
          International Standard Bibliographic Description
          Machine readable bibliographic data
          Subject headings
    RT   **Bibliography**
          Indexing
          Library catalogs
Cataloging data in machine readable form
    USE   **Machine readable bibliographic data**
Cataloging—Data processing 025.3
Cataloging—Music 025.3
    UF   Music—Cataloging
Catalogs
    USE   **Booksellers' catalogs**
          Library catalogs
          Publishers' catalogs

and subjects with the subdivision *Catalogs*, e.g. **Motion pictures—Catalogs**; to be added as needed
Catalogs, Book
    USE   **Book catalogs**
Catalogs, Booksellers'
    USE   **Booksellers' catalogs**
Catalogs, Card
    USE   **Card catalogs**
Catalogs, Classified
    USE   **Classified catalogs**
Catalogs in book form
    USE   **Book catalogs**
Catalogs, Library
    USE   **Library catalogs**
Catalogs on microfilm
    USE   **Library catalogs on microfilm**
Catalogs, Online
    USE   **Online catalogs**
Catalogs, Publishers'
    USE   **Publishers' catalogs**
Catalogs, Subject
    USE   **Subject catalogs**
Catalogs, Systematic
    USE   **Classified catalogs**
Cataloguing
    USE   **Cataloging**
Catalysis 541.3
    BT   **Physical chemistry**
    RT   **Catalytic RNA**
Catalytic ribonucleic acid
    USE   **Catalytic RNA**
Catalytic RNA 574.87
    UF   Catalytic ribonucleic acid
          Ribozymes
          RNA, Catalytic
    BT   **Enzymes**
          RNA
    RT   **Catalysis**
Catamarans 797.1
    BT   **Boats and boating**
Catastrophes
    USE   **Disasters**
Catechisms 238; 268; 291.2
    BT   **Christian education**
          Theology—Study and teaching
    NT   **Bible—Catechisms, question books**
    RT   **Creeds**

Figure 8.2 Excerpt from Sears. Source: *Sears List of Subject Headings*. 15th ed. (1994), p.115

The main features of Sears are as follows:

Nature of scheme	Follows LCSH in general principles: not an abridgement of LCSH, but very similar in structure and format. Uses same reference structure (for example NT, BT, RT) as LCSH. Developed for small and medium-sized general libraries.
History	First ed. 1923; 19th ed. 2007 (872 pages). Published by H.W. Wilson.
Versions	Paper (19th ed. 2007). *Canadian Companion* (6th ed. 2001), also published by H.W. Wilson, complements Sears for Canadian subjects.
Aids	Includes section 'Principles of the Sears List' which provides introduction to principles of subject cataloguing, directions for use, and instructions for maintaining a subject authority file. Includes DDC numbers from 14th edition of Abridged DDC.
Use	Widely used in school and public libraries, especially in the United States; also used in small libraries throughout the world.
Problems	Problems of Sears similar to LCSH, for example ethnocentric.
Advantages	Advantages of Sears are similar to LCSH, for example it stays relatively stable: changes are slow and gradual.

Subject headings lists in Australia

LCSH is the major subject headings list in use in Australian libraries, mainly academic and some public libraries. It was used by more than 55 per cent of libraries in 1973 (Hine 1973) and this percentage is likely to have gone up. Its current status as a Libraries Australia standard, and formerly as an ABN/Kinetica standard, guarantees its continuing use. LCSH has its critics in Australia: as noted above, one Australian commentator has considered that the Library of Congress headings are 'at best, ineffective, and at worst, an indictment on the library profession. They should not continue to be used' (Moorcroft 1992, p.44). This critic was commenting on the way in which LCSH handles (or, rather, does not handle) Australian Aboriginal history, especially the matter of genocide (a term apparently not in LCSH at the time when the commentary was written) and the inclusion of value-laden words ('Mixed-blood') and words that have connotations of inferiority.

Sears List of Subject Headings was at one time widely used in Australian school and public libraries, being used by 40 per cent of respondents (mainly public libraries) in the 1973 survey (Hine 1973). With the advent of ASCIS, now SCIS, and the introduction of its own list of subject headings (see the following section) its use has largely ceased.

SCIS Subject Headings

The *SCIS Subject Headings* list is widely used in school libraries, its use associated with membership of SCIS which claims 85 per cent coverage of all Australian schools. SCIS (formerly ASCIS) is a service developed to provide cost-effective cataloguing data to Australian school libraries (see chapter 13). To support these activities the first edition of the *ASCIS Subject Headings* list was published in 1985. This list was based on the lists of subject headings used by various state education departments, including *Sears List* and LCSH (Foskett 1996, pp.353-357). Major features of SCIS subject headings are outlined below and are illustrated in figure 8.3.

Nature of scheme	Developed as a list of subject headings to be used in Australian school libraries in conjunction with ASCIS (now SCIS) database and cataloguing records.
	Based on terms used in Australian school library systems (every state system maintained its own subject authority list) plus Sears and LCSH.
	Aimed at reading age of 10 years.
	Uses LCSH-like features, for example model headings, geographic subdivisions
History	Pilot ed. 1983; 1st ed. 1985; 2nd ed. 1990; 3rd ed. 1994; (Melbourne: Thorpe); 4th ed. 1999, 5th ed. 2002 (Melbourne: Curriculum Corporation).
Versions	Printed and online editions available.
	File of recent subject headings available from SCIS website.
Use	Very widely used in Australian school libraries.

SCIS Subject Headings constantly develop to reflect user needs and to reflect current practice in other controlled vocabularies. The fifth edition has moved away from inverted headings to headings in direct word order (as has LCSH), has more scope notes and guidance for indexers, and all New Zealand terms have been revised. *SCIS Subject Headings* may be used to augment ScOT (the Schools Online Thesaurus) to improve subject access to online information resources (see chapter 9). Currently, it has not yet been decided whether SCISSH and ScOT, both produced by the Curriculum Corporation, will continue to coexist, or whether one or other will be dropped.

The SCIS website includes a mechanism by which users can propose new subject headings via the web. Updates and changes to the *SCIS Subject Headings* are noted in the SCIS *Connections* newsletter, also available from the SCIS website.

Amusement parks

SEN See also names of specific amusement parks*, Luna Park (Melbourne, Vic.).
UF Carnivals
Side shows
Sideshows
Theme parks
BT Circuses
Parks
NT Merry-go-rounds
Rollercoasters
RT Agricultural shows

Bali Attack, 2002
USE Bali Bombings, 2002

Bali Bombing, 2002
USE Bali Bombings, 2002

Bali Bombings, 2002

SEN Example under Bombings
UF Bali Attack, 2002
Bali Bombing, 2002
Bali Nightclub Bombing, 2002

Bali Nightclub Bombing, 2002
USE Bali Bombings, 2002

Figure 8.3 Excerpt from *SCIS Subject Headings* online. Source: New and Amended Subject Headings since publication of Fifth Edition Cumulative list May 2003, Curriculum Corporation website 2003

Thesauri

A thesaurus is another kind of controlled vocabulary, closely related to a subject headings list. The definition of a subject headings list used above in this chapter can be adopted almost wholesale for a thesaurus: it is a list of terms, arranged in alphabetical order, which have been selected for their ability to indicate subjects and have been authorised for use to provide subject access to bibliographic records. The major differences between a thesaurus and a list of subject headings are that the thesaurus is much more likely to authorise single-concept subject terms (post-coordinated) than combined ones (pre-coordinated), it will have defined closely and precisely the relationships among the subject terms it authorises for use, it will probably have been developed for a narrow subject field or discipline area, and it will probably be applied to provide subject access to documents in contexts wider than just library catalogues. Figure 8.4 summarises the differences.

THESAURI	SUBJECT HEADINGS LISTS
SIMILAR AIMS	
- used to control vocabulary used in subject searches	- used to control vocabulary used in subject searches
- more likely to be used in abstracting and indexing systems, online indexes	- more likely to be used in library catalogues
- used to display relationships among terms	- used to display relationships among terms
BUT DIFFERENT EMPHASES	
- used in defined subject fields	- cover a wide range of subjects
- specific terms	- usually terms are more general
- terms are in direct order	- order of terms can be indirect
- no subdivided headings	- Headings can be subdivided
- single terms (therefore, post-coordinate searching; terms used by searcher)	- terms can describe more than one concept (therefore, pre-coordinate searching; terms used by indexer more than by searcher)
- relationship among terms specified closely defined	- relationship not always precisely defined

Figure 8.4 Thesauri and subject headings lists compared

The thesaurus has these characteristics:

- it is usually limited in subject scope;

- although there is no 'typical' thesaurus, they have many features in common;

- the essential feature is a main display which lists descriptors (terms authorised for use) and non-descriptors (other terms which are related to the descriptor), and indicates precisely the relationships between the descriptors and non-descriptors;

- the descriptors are usually single concepts;

- the relationships between descriptor and its associated non-descriptors are displayed using standard abbreviations;

- thesauri are often developed and maintained in-house for a specific application; and

- thesauri can readily be developed for and used in multi-lingual applications.

One important characteristic of a thesaurus is the way in which the relationships between terms are displayed. After each descriptor or non-descriptor some or all of the following are given:

SN	Scope Note	indicates when to use the descriptor, defines scope
UF	Use For	indicates terms the descriptor is used in preference to
USE	Use	indicates descriptor to be used instead of the term
BT	Broader Term	indicates terms that are more general than the descriptor
RT	Related Term	indicates terms on the same hierarchical level as the descriptor
NT	Narrow Term	indicates terms that are more specific than the descriptor.

Additional terms are sometimes used: for example, TT (Top Term) to indicate the name of the broadest class to which the specific concept belongs.

Thesauri are typically used in situations where there is a need for detailed subject access to information resources and where the subject field has a defined, discrete vocabulary. They were first developed in science and technology areas in the 1960s, and in the 1960s to 1980s their most common application was to provide a controlled vocabulary for indexing and searching online databases. Thesauri were gradually adopted in non-scientific fields from the 1980s, and are now being used to organise web resources in a wide range of fields, such as public administration and business.

Thesauri can be presented in different ways. The alphabetical display, where the descriptors are presented in alphabetical order, is most commonly found. Other displays include systematic displays, where terms are hierarchically related (these have an alphabetical index), and a wide range of graphic displays (such as tree structures and arrow graphs).

Until recently most thesauri were available in print form. This is changing as the availability and use of online information resources rapidly increases, so that it is now common to access and use online thesauri. Some of these are stand-alone, such as the *APAIS (Australian Public Affairs Information Service) Thesaurus* (http://www.nla.gov.au/apais/thesaurus) and the *Canadian Thesaurus of Construction Science and Technology* (http://www.nrc.ca/irc/thesaurus/welcome.html). Others are integrated into online databases, for example, the *RILM (Répertoire International de Littérature Musicale) Thesaurus* used for searching *RILM Abstracts*. These online thesauri vary widely in the way they are presented and in their usability. One of them, the *ERIC Thesaurus*, has thirteen different websites available to search it (http://www.ericae.net/search.htm). Other notable online thesauri include: *UNESCO Thesaurus, Thesaurus for Graphic Materials* (TGM), *NASA Thesaurus, ASIS Thesaurus,* and *International Thesaurus of Refugee Terminology.*

Construct anew, or adapt?

Many thesauri are constructed by individual information centres to provide subject access to a particular subject field. Many special libraries, for example, develop their own thesaurus because standard lists of subject headings, which have been developed for use in general collections of documents, do not allow subjects to be described in enough detail in a special field of knowledge, or because these lists are not up-to-date. On occasion these thesauri developed in-house are published, and therefore become available to other information professionals, but many are not. Some examples (a very random selection) of published thesauri are:

- *Australian thesaurus of earth sciences and related terms*
- *Family thesaurus: Australian family studies indexing terms*
- *GeoRef thesaurus*
- *Musaurus: a music thesaurus*
- *Road thesaurus*

- *SPINES thesaurus: a controlled and structured vocabulary for information processing in the field of science and technology for development*
- *Thesaurus of metallurgical terms*
- *Thesaurus of psychological index terms*
- *Thesaurus of sociological indexing terms.*

Because thesauri are relatively easy to construct, information professionals are sometimes tempted to develop one even when a suitable published thesaurus is available. However, developing a thesaurus, while not especially difficult, takes much time. In addition to the initial development commitment, there is also the need to commit resources to keeping a thesaurus up-to-date. An outdated thesaurus is decidedly not useful.

For these reasons it is preferable to use someone else's thesaurus if possible. Not only is the initial expense of development saved, but another institution is likely to keep it up-to-date. If a thesaurus is needed, the first step is to see what is already available in the specific subject field. Here a thorough literature search, and asking other information professionals in the same subject field, will assist. Clearing houses that list thesauri may also be contacted: an example is the Aslib thesaurus collection in the UK.

Constructing a thesaurus

If a thesaurus does need to be constructed, the process has been well defined and described in several guides. The main steps to take are:

- identify the subject area precisely – which subjects are core terms, and which subjects are marginal?
- identify some topics (e.g., from documents you are indexing) and outline a preliminary structure of the subject area.
- refine the structure – break the topics you have identified down into individual concepts ('uniterms'). The idea of 'facets' is helpful here (see chapter 7): for example, in a paper manufacturing technology thesaurus, the facets could include:
    end-products (particular types of paper), and
    properties (for example, weight, opacity).
These can be broken down further, for example sub-facets of the facet *end-products* could be:
    acidity (alkaline, acidic),
    purpose (printing, writing, blotting, wrapping), and
    use (printer, office use, home use).
- once the structure has been decided, add terms taken from documents being indexed, other thesauri, other classification schemes, knowledge of subject specialist and so on.
- define the relationships among terms.

One information professional describes the process of constructing a thesaurus of environmental protection terms, noting that the time taken and, therefore, the resource implications are very significant indeed (Little 1993).

Published standards for constructing thesauri should be followed. These include:

- ISO 2788: 1986 *Guidelines for the Establishment and Development of Monolingual Thesauri.*

- ANSI/NISO Z39.19-2003 *Guidelines for the Construction, Format, and Management of Monolingual Thesauri.*

Thesaurus development software is now commonly used when developing a thesaurus. This software automates many of the processes, such as maintaining the consistency of USE/USE FOR, BT/NT, RT/RT relationships by checking relationships and identifying 'orphans', and providing a choice of displays (typically alphabetical and hierarchical sequences).

The renaissance of the thesaurus

The thesaurus is, suggest McIlwaine and Williamson, 'a tool in transition' (McIlwaine & Williamson 1999, p.26). The increasing, and now urgent, need to provide access to online information resources, especially those available on the web, has been one reason for an increased interest in thesauri in recent years, and it has been the subject of much research (McIlwaine & Williamson 1999, p.26-27). The thesaurus concept has been adopted in other contexts, for example, to control the vocabulary used by governments to describe their business activities or functions – these are known as *functions* thesauri. The main issues that thesauri might be able to address are providing subject access to online information resources (see chapter 9), and access to multilingual information resources. Research has also gone on into the compatibility of thesauri so that they can be combined and searched using a common interface to provide access to a wide range of information resources covering different subject areas (Aitchison, Gilchrist & Bawden 2000, Section L).

Some Australian thesauri

Many thesauri have been developed for use in Australian information centres. Two examples are outlined below.

The *Australian Pictorial Thesaurus* (APT) was developed to provide terms for indexing and searching pictorial materials and objects in Australian libraries and museums (see figure 8.5). It pays particular attention to using contemporary Australian words and phrases. APT was developed as a joint project between CASL (the Council of Australian State Libraries) and the National Library of Australia, with support from AMOL (Australian Museums Online). It was based on a thesaurus developed at the State Library of New South Wales in 1986 for indexing historic photographs, which later became the basis of a thesaurus used in that Library's PICMAN (*Pictures and Manuscripts*) database. APT was launched in 2001 (Kingscote 2003) and is maintained at the State Library of NSW. It comprises some 15,000 terms and is available online where it can be searched using either a basic or and advanced search facility. Its website provides a form for users to suggest new terms. A text file and an XML version of the thesaurus can be downloaded from the website, although it is recommended that it be used online wherever possible because this version is the most up-to-date.

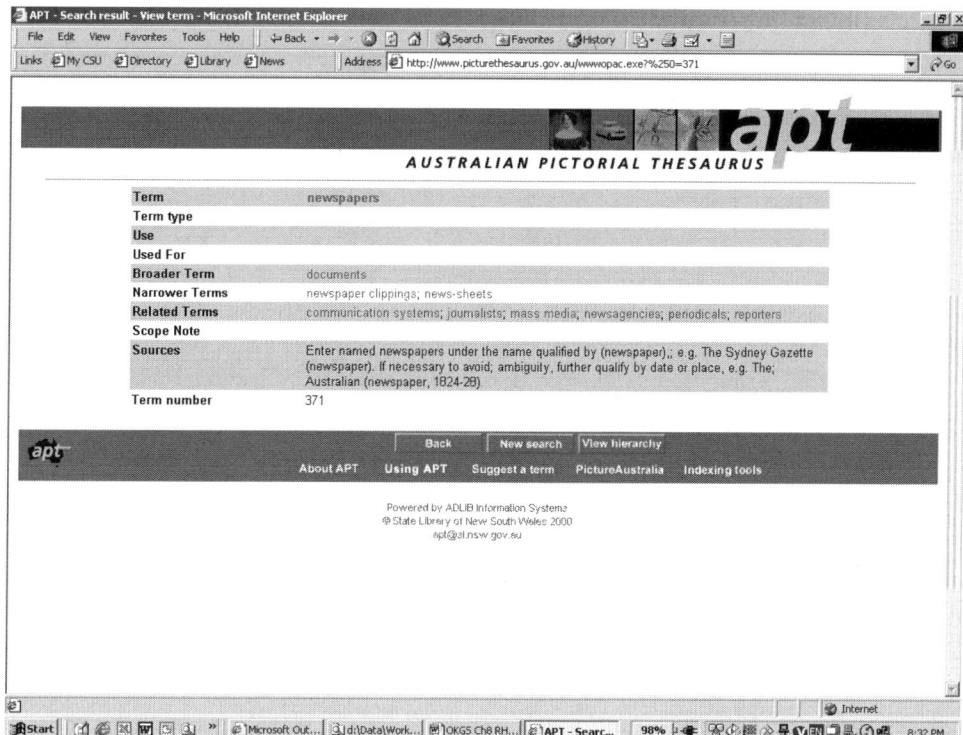

Figure 8.5 Entry in the *Australian Pictorial Thesaurus*

The ***Australian Thesaurus of Education Descriptors*** was developed by the Australian Council for Educational Research (ACER) to control subject access to Australian educational literature, in particular the Australian Education Index, prepared and published by ACER. A first printed edition appeared in 1984, a second in 1996, and a third in 2003. However, the up-to-date version is readily available online from ACER's Cunningham Library website. It was developed by identifying relevant terms from the *Thesaurus of ERIC Descriptors* (used to index documents acquired by the United States-based Educational Resources Information Center) which were then reviewed and amended by Australian subject experts to make them applicable to Australian use. For example, changes included altering American spellings to the Australian equivalent and making alterations to reflect different meanings or scope. Prefatory material explains the development of the thesaurus and describes how it is maintained, provides guidelines for indexers applying this tool, and explains the structure and format of the thesaurus. A typical entry consists of the descriptor, the date on which the descriptor was added to the thesaurus, and a reference structure which contains some or all of SN (scope note, defining the use of the descriptor), UF (used for), and NT (narrower term), BT (broader term) and RT (related term).

Multilingual thesauri are becoming more interesting to many sectors, for instance the business sector, as more people from differing cultural and language backgrounds seek information, especially on the web. Although English is still the *lingua franca* of business, scholarship, and many other areas, there are strong indications that other languages (such as Chinese and Spanish) will become equally important. Multilingual thesauri provide one tool to assist in cross-cultural communication (Jorna & Davies 2001). They have a long history, and a standard for them was published in 1985 (ISO 5964: *Guidelines for the Establishment and Development of Multilingual Thesauri*).

At a basic level, multilingual thesauri are no more than two or more monolingual thesauri whose descriptors have been cross-referenced, but they can be much more than this, depending on whether the languages represented have equivalent terms, or similar terms with differing nuances: this is referred to as degrees of equivalence (exact, inexact, partial, single-to-multiple, non-equivalence). In place of the language-specific symbols (BT, NT, UF and so on) they may use symbols that are not language-dependent:

> < in place of BT (Broader Term)
> \> in place of NT (Narrower Term)
> – in place of RT (Related Term)
> → in place of USE (Use)
> = in place of UF (Use For)

Multilingual thesauri are used in a wide range of contexts: for example, in officially bilingual countries such as Canada, and by international bodies with several official languages, such as the European Community. A good example of an online multilingual thesaurus is the *European Education Thesaurus*, which covers 17 languages.

Increased interest in using thesauri to provide subject access has been reiterated more recently in the HILT (High-Level Thesaurus) Project (2001). This project is investigating the tools required to search effectively across the full range of information resources, regardless of their subject field. The main barrier to doing this is that different controlled vocabularies (subject headings lists, thesauri and classification schemes) have been used to provide subject access and they have not always been constructed according to common standards. Rather than develop a new thesaurus, the project has conducted research into what controlled vocabularies are currently in use, the issues arising from combining them or searching them using a common search mechanism, and ways of resolving interoperability problems. Participants in the HILT Project come from archives, museums, libraries and other information sectors. The end product is likely to be a 'route map' that indicates relationships among major controlled vocabularies. This approach is valuable because, as the HILT Project Phase I report indicates, 'information resources relevant to any particular user task or problem will increasingly be distributed – across domains, regions, countries, and international and linguistic boundaries, and the importance of the subject approach is likely to be significant' (HILT Final Report 2001). Other research has been carried out into interoperability issues, for example a study to determine whether LCSH and its German and French equivalents, SWD (Schlagwortnormdatei) and RAMEAU (Répertoire d'authorité-matière encyclopédique et alphabétique unifié), could be mapped against one another to develop a multilingual thesaurus. The study indicated a high level of correspondence among terms (MacEwan 2000).

Will thesauri still be needed in the future? Most commentators think the answer is a definite yes. Marcia Bates has noted that 'We are 70 per cent there with our prototype systems … The last 30 per cent, however, is infinitely more difficult' and that 'We can do an enormous number of powerful things with computers, but effective completely automated indexing and access to textual … databases eludes us still' (Bates 1996). The issues still to be resolved before we can dispense with thesauri include different user requirements in different subject domains, and the mismatch between searchers' knowledge of the index and the index constructors' knowledge. Meanwhile, work is actively proceeding on redefining the thesaurus so that it becomes an effective tool for online subject access and is interoperable (or shareable) across many areas (Workshop on Electronic Thesauri 1999).

PRECIS and COMPASS

There have been several noteworthy attempts at enhancing subject access by building more sophisticated controlled vocabularies. A classic example was PRECIS (Preserved Context Index System), and its successor, COMPASS (Computer Aided Subject System). PRECIS was a system for providing more subject-indicative vocabulary terms to bibliographic records, developed for use in the British National Bibliography (BNB), and implemented by the British Library from 1971 until 1990. It was based on facet analysis and synthesis concepts developed by the Classification Research Group (see chapter 7), and resembled more a grammar than a vocabulary; indeed, it proved capable of being applied in more than one language. Studies indicated that PRECIS provided greater retrieval effectiveness than LCSH (Schabas 1982). Figure 8.6 shows a PRECIS string. However, PRECIS proved too expensive for BNB to continue its use, and it was replaced in 1991 by a simplified version, COMPASS (Computer Aided Subject System). Yet even COMPASS did not last long, and the British Library reverted to LCSH in the mid-1990s (Foskett 1996, p.141). A major problem was the systems' lack of adoption by other major record suppliers. PRECIS and COMPASS will probably be remembered only as an historical footnote with respect to practice; however, like the Bliss Bibliographic Classification, they are important for their theoretical contributions.

428.3'07'1094 – Schools. Curriculum subjects: spoken English language
   Activities. Teaching. *Australia.*
Study talk : a sourcebook of language study activities for the upper primary
   and lower secondary schools / the Study Talk Project Team ; Jan Boys …
   [et al.]. – Canberra : Curriculum Development Centre, 1983. – 135 p. : ill.
   25 cm.
   'Study talk was a CDC Language Development Project sponsored by the
   Queensland education authorities' – T. p. verso.
   Cover subtitle: A sourcebook of language activities.
   Includes bibliographies.
   ISBN 0 642 96281 2 : price unknown.

   1. English language – Spoken English – Study and teaching – Australia. I.
   Boys, Jan. II. Australia. Curriculum Development Centre.

PRECIS string

Figure 8.6 PRECIS in ANB records. Source: *Australian National Bibliography* (1984)

PRECIS in Australia

PRECIS enoyed significant Australian connections. A detailed research project to investigate whether PRECIS could provide subject access in an academic library was carried out at the University of Wollongong in 1976 and 1977. This study indicated that PRECIS was capable of providing good results, especially when it was used in conjunction with LCSH (Hunt 1976-77). It was adopted in Australia almost by default when the National Library of Australia purchased the BNB software to produce ANB. PRECIS strings first appeared in ANB in 1972 (see figure 8.6), and were dropped in the mid-1980s.

Improving the controlled vocabulary approach

Dissatisfaction with the traditional alphabetically-arranged controlled vocabulary approaches has been widespread, extending over many decades. It has been the focus of research to establish ways to improve library information retrieval systems. The issues are now well understood and improvements fall into four main categories:

- better authority control on subject headings and terms;
- automatic display of reference structures;
- increasing the number of subject headings and subject terms assigned per record (Smith 1991); and
- subject browsing, allowing users to browse on subject headings so that they can find the preferred term which best matches their needs.

The first of these – improving authority control – is primarily a matter of implementing provisions for making references and linking related terms. These provisions already exist in subject headings lists, but typically have not been implemented in library information retrieval systems, usually for cost reasons. Only 18 per cent of eighty-one Australian academic libraries surveyed in 1991 provided an extensive number of subject references in their OPACs (Schauder 1991, p.60). (General concepts relating to authority control are noted in chapter 5.) The second and fourth ways to improve information retrieval systems can be addressed through system design, and the current generation of library information retrieval systems often provide this facility. Much activity has been focused on the third approach: increasing the number of subject headings and subject terms that are assigned to each bibliographic record. This leads us to the second approach to providing subject access to be discussed in this chapter, namely, the use of a natural, uncontrolled vocabulary, such as that derived from the information resources themselves.

Natural language approaches

Using a natural language approach, the vocabulary (that is, the terms chosen) is often taken from the documents themselves. One of the most important consequences of this approach is that it provides access to the author's own terminology, which is often more in tune with what the users are familiar with, and often more up-to-date than thesauri or other authority lists. It is now realised that natural language searching in an information system (such as a library information retrieval system) complements controlled vocabulary searching, rather than acts as an alternative to it.

Some of the mechanisms which support natural language searching in common use include:

- *keyword searching* – source of vocabulary terms usually includes *titles* and *subtitles*;
- *records enhancement* – source of vocabulary terms also includes other *information added to the catalogue record*, such as abstracts and terms from the contents list; and
- *automatic indexing* – source of vocabulary terms is either specified parts of the information resource (for example, the title) or anywhere in the information resource.

Keyword searching

It is now commonplace for library information retrieval systems to provide keyword searching on terms already in the surrogate record. These keywords typically come from the following fields in the catalogue record:

- title,
- author,
- subject,
- a combination of these, and
- perhaps other areas too: for example, series, corporate author.

The possibilities for improving such keyword searching lie in three areas:

- providing better searching facilities, so that all parts of the bibliographic record, instead of only pre-determined fields (such as author and title) can be searched;
- adding more terms to the surrogate record – this is explained above in the section 'Enhancing bibliographic records'; and
- searching the full text of an information resource in digital form.

Improving the searching facilities of library information retrieval systems is a field where considerable research has been carried out, and many of the results have now been implemented in the systems available on the market (see chapter 14). They include:

- *Boolean operations (including word proximity and word adjacency)* – these increase the chance of getting a better match, as they allow more precise searches on the vocabulary of the database; they are now commonplace in library information retrieval systems.
- *limiting* – the ability to limit searches is useful, for example, by date of publication, languages, geographic area, format.
- *truncation of search terms* – for example, a search on *barb#* will produce records which include the word *barbecue* as well as the Australian colloquialism *barbie*. This facility provides an increased chance of the search being successful because the likelihood that the user's input term matches the indexed terms is increased.

- *automatic switching (synonym operation)* – this facility is not yet common in library information retrieval systems, despite the results of numerous user studies which have indicated that many users have difficulty in matching their input terms to subject headings.

- *automatic spell-checking* – returns suggested re-spellings when no hits result, and so on.

Enhancing bibliographic records

Enhancing bibliographic records has been standard practice in some types of information retrieval systems for many years. Commercial indexing and abstracting services, now usually accessed online, but in the past also available as printed tools, provide abstracts (brief summaries of the subject content of information resources). These can be searched on: the source of vocabulary terms is the words in the abstract, which are added to the terms in the bibliographic description (such as author; title – of article, book, or journal; publisher; volume numbering; and date of publication). Some library catalogues also include abstracts. Another common source of terms added to bibliographic records to provide additional terms for searching on is the contents list of a book.

Research over several decades, coupled with many practical implementations, has clearly established that adding more subject-indicative terms improves subject access to documents. The effectiveness of this approach relies on the ability which computerised databases give us to search rapidly on keywords, or combinations of words, so that the greater the number of different words present in the surrogate record which are searchable, the greater is the likelihood of finding information about a required topic. More precise searching by subject can be carried out than is possible with the standard library subject access tools of classification and lists of subject headings.

The average number of Library of Congress subject headings assigned has been variously calculated, one estimate being as low as 1.3 per bibliographic record. One fruitful area of research and practice has investigated the addition of terms selected from the contents pages or indexes of documents to the MARC record. This approach is known as *enhanced subject access* and has become part of mainstream subject access practice. Early experimental examples are the Subject Access Project (Cochrane 1978) and the Enriched Subject Program at the Australian Defence Force Academy Library (see below). Richard Van Orden has summarised this research and indicates the main points:

- the lack of specificity and currency in subject searches has caused users considerable difficulty in effectively searching both online and card catalogues;

- enhanced bibliographic access, such as tables of contents, abstracts, summaries, and selected index entries, can help researchers find more citations in searching online databases;

- however, controlled vocabulary searches of terms such as Library of Congress subject headings, as opposed to free-text searching of non-controlled terms, improve search precision in that the search results tend to have a higher percentage of relevant items; and

- content components, such as abstracts, that contain more words tend to result in more hits than the shorter titles for the same works. However, this increase in the number of hits is often accompanied by a lower precision or percentage of relevant records (Van Orden 1990, p.31).

The idea here is simple: one way to improve the recall for subject searches is to provide more terms for the user to search on; so for surrogate records in library systems we should add more terms – that is, we should increase the size of the vocabulary. If we take these additional vocabulary terms from the document itself, rather than from an authority list such as LCSH, then we also increase the likelihood that the vocabulary is close to the terms that the user uses – that is, we increase its currency for the user. Figure 8.7 gives an example of an enhanced catalogue record.

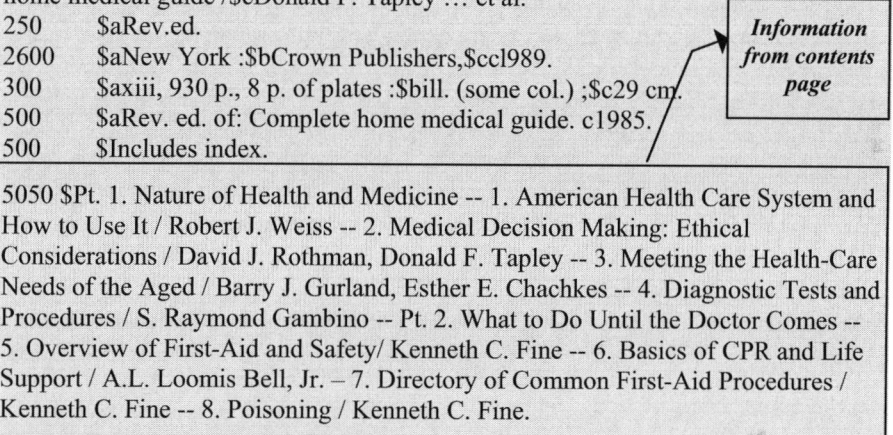

24504$aThe Columbia University College of Physicians and Surgeons complete home medical guide /$cDonald F. Tapley ... et al.
250    $aRev.ed.
2600 $aNew York :$bCrown Publishers,$cc1989.
300    $axiii, 930 p., 8 p. of plates :$bill. (some col.) ;$c29 cm.
500    $aRev. ed. of: Complete home medical guide. c1985.
500    $Includes index.

Information from contents page

5050 $Pt. 1. Nature of Health and Medicine -- 1. American Health Care System and How to Use It / Robert J. Weiss -- 2. Medical Decision Making: Ethical Considerations / David J. Rothman, Donald F. Tapley -- 3. Meeting the Health-Care Needs of the Aged / Barry J. Gurland, Esther E. Chachkes -- 4. Diagnostic Tests and Procedures / S. Raymond Gambino -- Pt. 2. What to Do Until the Doctor Comes -- 5. Overview of First-Aid and Safety/ Kenneth C. Fine -- 6. Basics of CPR and Life Support / A.L. Loomis Bell, Jr. – 7. Directory of Common First-Aid Procedures / Kenneth C. Fine -- 8. Poisoning / Kenneth C. Fine.

650 0$aMedicine, Popular.
70010$aTapley, Donald F.
71020$aColumbia University.$bCollege of Physicians and Surgeons.
74001$aComplete home medical guide.

Figure 8.7 Enhanced catalogue record (MARC format)

The addition of terms selected from contents pages of books or from other parts of the documents is now common practice, although because there is an added cost in doing so it is limited to large well-resourced libraries or to special libraries where there is a need to provide improved subject retrievability, or to library vendors that provide enhanced records as part of their service. Companies such as Blackwell's and Syndetic Solutions offer 'MARC Record Enrichment Services' in which tables of contents, descriptive summaries, and author affiliations are added to MARC records. (An example, from a catalogue record for J.K. Rowling's *Harry Potter and the Chamber of Secrets*: 'When the Chamber of Secrets is opened again at the Hogwarts School for Witchcraft and Wizardry, second-year student Harry Potter finds himself in danger from a dark power that has once more been released on the school.') Libraries use various criteria to determine which books to target for record enhancement, such as those with more diverse contents (e.g., conference proceedings), and those with vague titles.

Despite their problems – the additional cost of adding terms is the main one – enhanced records have proven their worth. They will not be used in all libraries, but will be used where the usual surrogate record is too brief and does not provide subject access detailed enough to meet users' needs. They are used quite often in special libraries with collections in fast-moving technical areas not well covered by the standard controlled vocabularies. The value of additional subject terms is also increasingly recognised by academic and research libraries.

It should be noted that adding extra terms in the bibliographic record is not to be confused with adding URLs to external information about a resource – the information needs to be indexed by the library information retrieval system if it is to be searchable. However, such links can still be a valuable addition when it comes to the selection (as against the retrieval) of material. Yeung and Tam (2003) describe the linking of bibliographic records for English-language books in the Lingnan University Library (Hong Kong) to information provided by the United States-based online bookshop Amazon.com – book reviews, tables of contents, images of book jackets and selected chapters of some books.

Assigning more subject headings per record: the Australian experience

ESP (Enriched Subject Program)
An internationally known Australian example of this procedure is the Enriched Subject Program (ESP) carried out since 1986 at the Australian Defence Force Academy Library in Canberra. By 1991 about 25 per cent of the collection (40,000 records) had been enriched. Initially the terms added were selected from the contents pages and indexes of the books, but investigation has been carried out on alternative sources of terms. The work has been extensively reported in the information studies literature (for example Beatty 1985, 1991, 1993; Byrne & Micco 1988). The ADFA Library concluded that 'the use of contents terms is a viable and cost-effective technique for dramatically increasing the number of subject access points to the contents of books' (Byrne & Micco 1988, p.442).

The SUN Trial
Another Australian experiment with adding more subject-indicative terms to enhance catalogue records was the SUN Trial carried out under the auspices of ABN. Australian contributors of cataloguing records to ABN were invited to contribute MARC records with additional terms selected from contents pages or book indexes, and a trial database was built up during 1989 and 1990. Investigation of this using a modified form of the SAP methodology was carried out at Monash University (Turner 1991).

Abstracts

A common source of additional terms that can be searched to provide subject access is the abstract – the 'brief, objective representation of the contents of a primary document or an oral presentation' (Z39.14-1997). Abstracts are commonly found in databases of information resources relating to a specific subject field, such as the online databases hosted on Dialog (see figure 8.8).

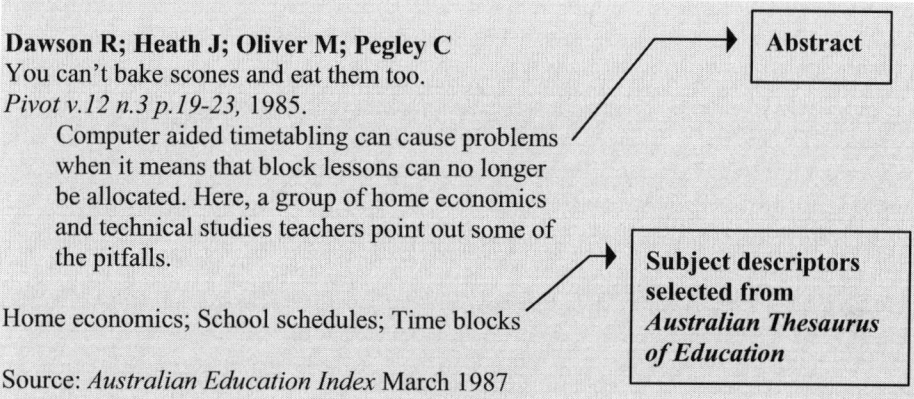

Dawson R; Heath J; Oliver M; Pegley C
You can't bake scones and eat them too.
Pivot v.12 n.3 p.19-23, 1985.
   Computer aided timetabling can cause problems when it means that block lessons can no longer be allocated. Here, a group of home economics and technical studies teachers point out some of the pitfalls.

| Abstract |

| Subject descriptors selected from *Australian Thesaurus of Education* |

Home economics; School schedules; Time blocks

Source: *Australian Education Index* March 1987

TI: The private press (History and development in Europe and America).
AU: Cave,-R
CS: Victoria University of Wellington, Wellington (New Zealand)
PB: R.R. Bowker Co. : 1983, 389p
IB: 0835216950
CP: United-States
PY: 1983
LA: English
DT: Book
AB: This book studies the history of the private press in Europe and America.
 Topics include: the origins of the private press, the quasi-official or patron's press, the scholarly press, the press as an educational toy, the aristocratic plaything, private printing and bibliomania, the author as publisher, clandestine presses--moral and immoral, printing as a middle -class hobby, printing as a fine art in the work of William Morris and the Kelmscott press, the influence of Morris in America, fine printing on the Continent, printing between the wars and after WWII, and finally the contemporary press in Europe, America, and Canada
DE: Europe-; History-; Private-sector; Publishing-
SH: Information-Generation-and-Promulgation; Publishing (3.07)
UD: 2000
AN: 2004019

Figure 8.8 Abstracts in database records (compare the second example with Figure 6.4, which shows a catalogue record for the same information resource). Source: *Information Science & Technology Abstracts Plus* (1966-2003/03)

Abstracts assist in both the retrieval and selection functions of an information retrieval system. They come in several varieties:

- *indicative* (or *descriptive*) – indicating that significant and specific information is present in the information resource (for example, 'the number of onions grown in Malaysia was determined and reported in this article'). Indicative abstracts are used for long documents, typically those that do not report experimental results.

- *informative* – summarising the data in the information resource (for example, 'According to this article, 75 million onions were grown in Malaysia'). Informative abstracts are typically used for information resources that describe experimental investigations, or other research results.

- *critical* – making a judgement about the quality of the contents of the information resource (for example, 'This article gives the number of onions grown in Malaysia, but it does not indicate which year they were grown in, so the information is not of much value'). Critical abstracts are uncommon.

Standards exist for writing abstracts, just as they do for constructing catalogue records: for example ISO 214:1976 *Documentation – Abstracts for Publications and Documentation* and Z39.14-1997 *Guidelines for Abstracts* from the National Information Standards Organisation (United States).

High quality abstracts should be concise, accurate, unambiguous, and comprehensive. They can be constructed by the authors of the information resources (this raises quality issues, such as lack of appropriate subjectivity) and professional indexers (who produce better results because they have subject expertise and are skilled at abstracting). However, abstracts often do not meet these standards, reducing their value as sources for vocabulary on which to search. Abstracts vary in quality because of errors, policy decisions (such as limited time allowed to abstract a document), or bias of the abstracter, and they are time-consuming to prepare: the abstracter must read the article (probably more than once), understand it, summarise its content, and so on. For these reasons, research into automatic indexing and abstracting actively continues.

Automatic indexing and abstracting

Automatic indexing and abstracting can be broadly defined as a process in which the computer creates the bibliographic record and abstract with little or no human intervention, using as the source of vocabulary terms either specified parts of the information resource (e.g., the title) or terms taken from anywhere in the information resource. It is an attractive idea to many information professionals, especially those who manage financial and human resources, because it has the potential to reduce the significant costs associated with employing people to construct bibliographic records and abstracts, and to reduce human error factors.

The battle continues between those who advocate an automated solution to organising knowledge and those who consider that the fully automated approach is inadequate. Advocates of the fully automated solution produce rhetoric such as this:

> Indexing … [is] a key process to facilitate information and document retrieval. Current technology provides automatic indexing based on information content *which is better than* bibliographic information which uses attributes (or defined fields) to describe the library documents (*Library 2000* 1994, p.160: italics added).

Doubts about a fully automated information retrieval future have not receded over recent years. Vocabulary issues form one group of doubts: automatic abstracting can only work on the vocabulary present in the document, as noted elsewhere in this chapter, and, if this vocabulary is inadequate, so is the resulting abstract. Authority control issues are another major concern (see chapter 5). The information resources must be in digital form, still not always the norm, although this is changing rapidly. And there are still many technical issues to be overcome.

Automatic abstracting works broadly like this. The text of the information resource is searched for words that occur frequently. Sentences in which these words occur are selected and presented in the order in which they occur in the document. A higher weighting can be given to sentences at specified locations, for instance at the start and the end of the information resources.

Automatic indexing (identifying the terms that best represent the subject of an information resource for searching purposes) works broadly like this. In *extraction indexing*, terms are extracted from the information resource for inclusion in the index on the basis of how frequently they occur in the information resource. The most frequently occurring words are included in the index. Stems (for example, think, thinking) can be recognised. In *assignment indexing*, the terms in the index are not necessarily found in the text of the information resource, but can be matched against a thesaurus. Profile terms (non-preferred terms) are matched against the thesaurus terms (descriptors) and if there is a match, then the descriptor is allocated for the purposes of determining whether a term should be included in the index on the basis of word frequency. We can use the example of a thesaurus term *childbirth* and profile terms *childbirth, labour, labor, delivery, baby* and *born*. We can develop inclusion criteria, for example, that if the term *childbirth* is found ten times in a document, we allocate the thesaurus term *childbirth*; and if *delivery* is found ten times, because it could have a different meaning (such as *mail delivery*) it must also be associated with another word from the profile term list (it should be in close proximity to that word, for example) (Browne 1996).

Although automatic indexing and abstracting techniques are not yet part of mainstream library bibliographic organisation practice, they are likely to become so. Lancaster (2003, chapter 15) can be referred to for more information about them.

Automatic indexing using title keywords

One application of automatic indexing, based on words in the titles of information resources, has been in common use in libraries and information centres for many years. Words in the title often represent the subject of that information resource – in fact there are standards in the fields of engineering and science about how to develop titles so that they are meaningful for subject searching. This does not work in all fields: for instance, documents in the humanities often do not have titles that represent the subject very well. Consider these titles:

Interior Design with Feng Shui

The Food of Malaysia

A Popular Vision

Far Flung Floyd.

Whereas *The Food of Malaysia* and *Interior Design with Feng Shui* tell us much about the contents of these books, *A Popular Vision* does not indicate that it is a study of the arts and bookselling in New Zealand in the 1930s, nor does *Far Flung Floyd* inform us that it is about South-East Asian food.

It has been standard practice for many years to produce indexes to books by using words in the titles of these books. Such indexes can provide subject access, but using them is a blunt instrument approach whose effectiveness is often low. Simple computer programs can be used to generate these *permuted title indexes*. Examples are KWIC (KeyWord In Context) and KWOC (KeyWord Out of Context) indexes (see figure 8.9).

activities in Australia, Climate
administration of the Family Court of Australia, The
Asthma services in rural and remote Australia
Australia, Asthma services in rural and remote
Australia, Banking law in
Australia, Climate activities in
Australia, Medicines in
Australia, Microeconomic reforms in
Australia, The administration of the Family Court of
Banking law in Australia
Climate activities in Australia
Court of Australia, The administration of the Family
Family Court of Australia, The administration of the
law in Australia, Banking
Medicines in Australia
Microeconomic reforms in Australia
reforms in Australia, Microeconomic
remote Australia, Asthma services in rural and
rural and remote Australia, Asthma services in
services in rural and remote Australia, Asthma

Figure 8.9 KWOC index

Permuted title indexes have many advantages: they can be constructed quickly, they are inexpensive to produce, and they can be produced by computer with little or no human intervention. Their major disadvantage is that they do not provide effective subject access, sometimes no subject access at all, if the titles from which the terms are selected do not reflect the content of the documents. Other disadvantages are that a limited number of terms in the title restricts the complete description of the subject, and that there is a lack of vocabulary control, leading to inconsistency, scattering of related topics, and so on.

Despite their problems, permuted title indexes can be useful, for instance to quickly provide limited subject access to a small collections of documents in situations where using a controlled vocabulary approach is too complex and too expensive. Special libraries sometimes use this approach for specific collections: a typical example is a collection of technical reports produced by the research and development department of a company.

Natural language processing

Automatic indexing and automatic abstracting techniques are relatively simple in computing terms, even if they don't yet produce fully effective results. Natural language processing aims to do more. It tries to:

1. interpret requests made by searchers which are expressed in free text;
2. represent all of what's expressed in the text of documents, rather than just a summary; and
3. 'understand' when a search result is a match with a user's request.

The methods of providing subject access described so far in this chapter all rely on the user who is seeking information (that is, the searcher) defining the words that are searched on. These words are checked against the words in the document, or a surrogate record representing that document, and if there is an exact match the search is considered to be successful. However, the searcher has to do a lot of work in order to achieve a successful result, such as thinking about what word or words are likely to produce a result matching what they are seeking. As an example, consider the word processing program Microsoft Word 2000. The Help button provides three possibilities for searching the Word Help database: searching a Contents list, searching an Index of words and terms, or using an Answer Wizard. The first two choices ask you to look at a list of words and identify those that match your query best. The Answer Wizard asks you specifically 'What would you like to do?' and invites you to input a question in natural language (such as 'how do I remove borders from around a table?').

Some of the issues that need to be addressed for natural language processing to be effective are illustrated in this quote from the website of a software seller, Dieselpoint:

> If you ask a shop clerk for a red pen, the clerk knows that you're probably asking for a pen with red ink, not a pen that's colored red. You'll be directed to the right section quickly. Few search engines can accomplish this simple task because they lack basic information about what's important. They do not know that 'pen' is a noun that defines a product, 'red' is an adjective that can describe ink color or body color, and that ink color is the more important attribute.

In most information retrieval tools and systems in current use, it is difficult or impossible to specify a search in natural language. This means that many of the concepts and relationships we express in natural language cannot be searched for using standard information retrieval tools. Researchers into natural language processing are working hard to change this, and there are some promising experimental systems. (See Taylor 2004, pp.284-288 for further information.)

Self-describing resources

Another way of avoiding the costs of employing an information professional to create metadata is to acquire information resources that come with metadata created at source, that is, by the author or publisher of the resource. Most academic journals insist that their authors include abstracts as part of their articles, and these are duly passed on to the indexing and abstracting databases that cover the journals. It is much less likely that libraries will be able to persuade book publishers to ensure that their authors assign LCSH to save librarians money: most authors are not at all conversant with such vocabularies. However, it may not be so hard for authors to produce short summaries, or a few key subject terms, in natural language, and it is now particularly easy for web authors to do this by embedding a few lines of metadata (metatags) into their web pages. To this end, librarians, acting with other information professionals, have recently formulated and refined the concept of metadata as the mechanism that will allow for the creation of 'self-describing' documents. In the library context this is expressed as information resources being *self-catalogued:* they are 'self-describing manifestations', the content of which includes elements of the bibliographic record contributed by the author, the distributor and publisher, libraries, and other groups, including perhaps, even users – and here we enter the world of Web 2.0 and social tagging (Tillett 1995, p.84). More discussion about such possibilities is to be found in later chapters.

Conclusion

To provide subject access to an information resource, we search on one or more of:

1) Words in the descriptive part of the bibliographic record for the information resource
   - words appearing in the title.

2) Words associated with the information resource
   - terms selected from a controlled vocabulary (a subject headings list or a thesaurus),
   - terms in an abstract we provide.

3) Words in the text of the information resource
   - words appearing anywhere in the text (full-text searching),
   - a subset of words selected from text, for example the back-of-the-book index.

When computers gave us the ability to carry out full-text searching on some resources there were many who prophesied that controlled vocabularies would rapidly die out. This has not been the case. As noted in chapter 7, controlled vocabularies based on classification schemes are enjoying renewed popularity because of their ability to provide subject access to information on the web. The situation is the same with alphabetically arranged controlled vocabularies, where considerable effort is being expended on changing them so that they are more useful for providing subject access to online information resources, and are interoperable across subject areas. General lists of subject headings such as LCSH are being implemented for this purpose, as are specialised thesauri, such as the *Art and Architecture Thesaurus*, and specialised subject headings lists, such as MeSH (*Medical Subject headings*) (McKiernan 1998). This is further examined in chapter 9.

CHAPTER 9
Subject access to web content

The internet is rapidly becoming the first port of call (and for some the only port of call) for subject searches. A new verb has entered our vocabulary: to *google*, illustrated in this quote:

> but students prefer 'Googling' to using search tools in the library's online catalogs (George 2003, p.6).

To *google* is to search the web using the Google search engine (http://www.google.com). A *google-ised* search interface is one that is simple to use and produces relevant hits. To some commentators Google may be the ideal search interface:

> In fact, when you think about it, isn't Google kind of what we always wanted in an information system? Very forgiving, user-friendly, able to take a few well-chosen keywords and produce, often, a decent set of results with something genuinely useful within the first 10 hits, containing a wide variety of documents and document types, from all over the world. Sure, it doesn't have professional-level indexing or controlled vocabulary or the niceties of systems we grew up with; but c'mon, it's not all that bad (Janes 2002, p.84).

In fact, making catalogues and other bibliographic databases more like Google has become something of an obsession – perhaps a healthy obsession – for many librarians. OCLC has recently launched its Google-like WorldCat.org interface which looks set to make a big impact on the design of library catalogues of the future (see chapter 12). A forerunner of this development was the RedLightGreen project conducted by RLG (Research Libraries Group. Aimed at improving access to the RLIN database of 120 million records for a wider range of users, rather than the librarians and researchers who have typically used it, the project attempted to 'strip away the "librariness" of the catalog so that it looks more like what students expect' (*RLG's RedLightGreen Project* 2003).

The Googlisation trend is not just affecting appearance – exemplified by a single search box – but also the functionality of catalogues, with cross-database (federated) searching, relevance ranking and split results becoming standard features. A typical example of this trend is the Search function available on the National Library of Australia's home page: a single box that searches the website, the catalogue, the whole of the Libraries Australia database, the NLA's digital collections and a database of archival finding aids. The results are divided accordingly.

Providing subject access to the internet is problematic, but Google is only part of the answer. The challenges are many, among them the sheer size and rate of growth of the internet, and the inability of any systems to provide comprehensive access to it. (There are also issues about the quality of the information available on the web, but that is not the primary interest of this book.) Many have attempted to estimate the size of the internet, and there is an industry devoted to internet statistics, based in the marketing and e-business areas. One of the many sources of these statistics available (on the web, of course!) is an internet domain survey, which attempts to do a complete search of the domain name systems and count how many domain names there are. The precise numbers are not important; the dramatic increase in the numbers is.

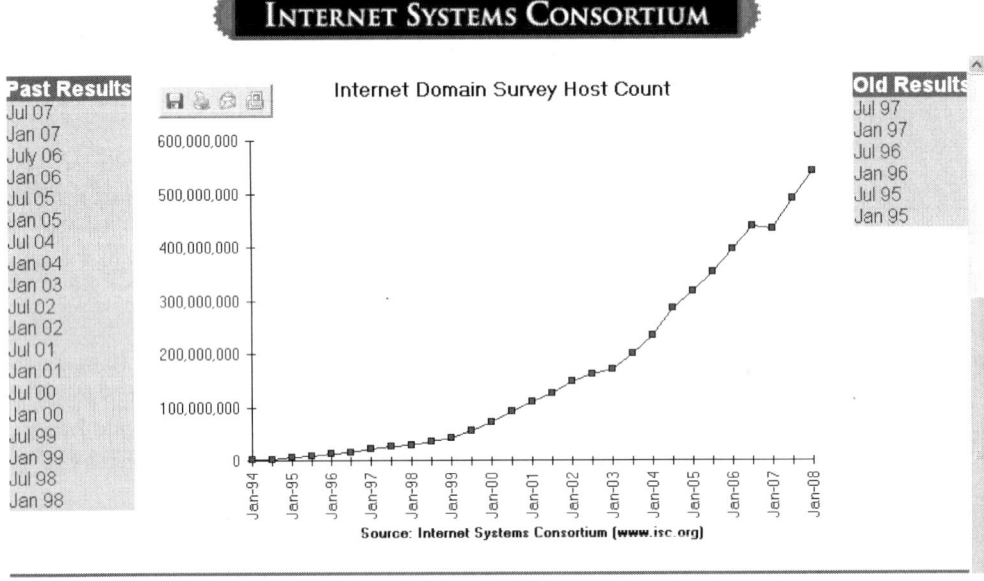

Figure 9.1 Growth of the internet. Reproduced with permission from Internet Systems Consortium website, http://www.isc.org/index.pl?/ops/ds/

No industry sector has yet been able to adequately provide access to the massive and rapidly increasing number of information resources on the web, the success of Google notwithstanding. Library bibliographic organisation standards and practices have not been able to keep up with the challenges. The library catalogue, based on a lengthy tradition of standards developed after long experience with information resources in many formats (see chapter 2), provides users with 'a known universe of possible searching behaviours and strategies limited by the nature of the catalog itself' (Weiss & Carstens 2001, p.52), but searching the internet currently has few widely accepted standards.

We can characterise the present state of providing access to information resources on the internet as embryonic and experimental. A wide range of radical alternatives to library-based methods is being explored. One resource discovery standard, Dublin Core metadata (and metadata schemes based on it), has been quite widely adopted, but this has not assisted subject searching of internet information resources. Dublin Core metadata (see chapter 10) is a data exchange format, and, as such, its primary interest is not with subject access, although it acknowledges that subject access may be provided in its *DC.Subject* element, and it recommends that 'best practice is to use a controlled vocabulary' (DCMI 2006).

There is no doubt, though, that metadata standards such as Dublin Core, and other standards such as XML and Z39.50, have been important catalysts for promoting many of the strategies on which subject access to web information resources is based, such as interoperability and the value of multiple approaches (Schwartz 2001, p.42).

What techniques for providing subject access to information resources on the internet are available to us? Current research is investigating the use of controlled vocabularies (classification schemes, thesauri, subject headings lists), ontologies and taxonomies, and subject gateways, and more besides. These are noted in this chapter. We can generalise about the range of approaches available by thinking of subject access tools as forming a spectrum (figure 9.2). At one end of the spectrum are subject access tools that rely on uncontrolled vocabularies, based on *derived indexing* (taking or deriving words from the information resource). At the other end of the spectrum are subject access tools that use highly controlled vocabularies, based on *assigned indexing* (taking words from somewhere else, such as from a list of subject headings or a thesaurus, and assigning them to the information resource).

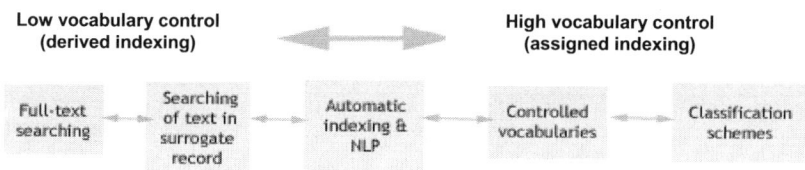

Figure 9.2 Subject access tools: a spectrum

All of the approaches in this spectrum are primarily concerned with text. Text-based information retrieval methods are by far the most dominant in past and current practice, and only recently has serious research begun into non-text-based information retrieval tools (to provide access to images and sound, for instance). So this spectrum is incomplete.

All of these approaches are valid for providing subject access to information resources on the internet, and all are being used, plus many more. This chapter provides an introduction to these approaches.

Repositioning the library catalogue

The library catalogue is increasingly providing access to a wider range of information resources than just those owned by the library or information service. State-of-the-art catalogues provide several different ways of searching (for example, basic and advanced keyword searching), link to online information resources, and include web access. Their databases include records for information resources in many different formats, definitely not limited to printed material but including maps, films, sound recordings and much more. Most recently, library catalogues include metadata for digital materials – such as online journals and full-text documents – and many of these will not be owned by the library but are available to that library's users. 'No longer are all the citations in a catalog to holdings owned by a library; pointing to materials served remotely has become commonplace'

(Thomas 2000). The library catalogue has well and truly become a pointer to information resources determined to be relevant to users of that library, regardless of whether or not the library owns these information resources, and regardless of where the information resources are located.

This reality has led to considering whether the library should also be a gateway or portal (considered later in this chapter), leading users to the wider range of information resources available on the internet. Can the library catalogue function well as 'a portal to the internet'?

> Recognizing that some patrons may prefer to connect directly with online resources without being routed through the catalog, some libraries have developed separate gateways to networked resources. These gateways facilitate access to electronic materials selected by the library by providing a single point of entry, by organizing them into categories, and using metadata, often derived from their catalog records, to assist users in locating networked resources. The gateway concept appeals strongly to those for whom speedy access to online resources is a priority, and it offers many of the desirable features of the catalog, since the bibliographic control over its contents is carefully managed by librarians. (Thomas 2000)

What lies behind this effort to develop the library catalogue as a gateway to the internet is the librarian's belief that users need a guide to resources that have been professionally selected, validated as of appropriate quality and authority, and are kept up to date. As Delsey puts it,

> important from a strategic perspective is the fact that the library catalogue functions as a guide to a collection of resources professionally searched, selected and maintained for the purpose of supporting the research and information needs of a defined community of users. With the exponential growth that characterizes the Internet, the selectivity and pre-determination of relevance that are reflected implicitly in the library catalogue take on even greater value (Delsey 2000).

Of course, the library catalogue also provides access to information resources that are not in digital form, and to historical material, so it is providing added value when compared with web search engines and similar tools, which provide access only to the web. Delsey comments that 'The fact that as an access tool the library catalogue, like the library collection itself, has an archival function is of critical importance in a networked environment so widely evanescent in nature' (Delsey 2000).

However, this approach presents some problems for libraries. Traditionally the library catalogue represents 'stability, dependability, reliability, and quality' (Thomas 2000). Information resources accessed through the library catalogue need to be available, and, in the case of internet resources, this means that they must stay mounted on the web for a significant length of time, and their URL must be stable. If not, frequent and expensive checking of URLs and updating metadata records is required.

As the library catalogue has moved to the networked environment, changes have occurred in the way access is provided to information resources. The library catalogue has shifted position. Formerly it was solely an interface between the library user and bibliographic records representing the information resources in the library's collection. It is now an interface between the library user and a wide range of information resources, not limited to those in the library's collection.

Several approaches to widening the range of digital information resources available through the library catalogue have been developed or investigated. One category of digital information resources is networked resources available through the internet. These are often linked directly to the bibliographic record, with a direct link provided through the URL. Another category is the abstracting and indexing services that provide access to the contents of journal literature, conference proceedings, compilations, and anthologies that may or may not be held in the library's collection. The catalogue can potentially link the catalogue record for a journal title to an index record for an article in that journal, and then allow the user to link directly from the index entry to the full text of that article.

Another approach is providing bibliographic records for subscriptions to aggregators' products. (An aggregator is a company that bundles or combines many electronic journals or databases and offers them as a package to a library. These have become common as many libraries seek to reduce costs, and minimise the time requirements of maintaining electronic journals and databases.) In the past, each subscriber to an aggregator's bundle of titles needed to incorporate into their catalogue references to each title in the bundle. Discussions have taken place with some vendors, such as EBSCO, ProQuest, and Gale, to encourage them to provide the bibliographic records with subscriptions to the aggregator's bundle. These records are loaded into the local library system, saving much work for cataloguers who otherwise have to create them from scratch, or search for each individual title in a large MARC record database, download records and add them to the catalogue.

The CORC (*Cooperative Online Resource Catalog*) project, undertaken by OCLC and some of its libraries, exemplifies another approach. CORC was a separate catalogue of online resources that is now part of main OCLC database, WorldCat. Cataloguers using the OCLC Connexion software can input URLs for web-based materials; Connexion will automatically generate brief bibliographic records for them, including suggested Dewey Decimal Classification numbers and subject keywords, which human cataloguers then edit and add to.

One of the trends in library catalogue development is the expansion of the catalogue so that it becomes a gateway to the web. It can never function as the *only* gateway used to all internet resources; there are simply too many resources, of varying quality. Its strength will instead lie in the librarian's ability to identify high quality, reliable web resources relevant to the library's users:

> Instead of striving for comprehensiveness, the goal of the catalog as portal must be to increase the ability of a community of users to meet their information needs by doing as much 'one-stop shopping' as possible. By including access to web resources in the catalog, libraries would be extending to some internet materials the same level of control that they have traditionally provided for analog formats ... The presence of a citation in a catalog has come to signify for the user that the source discovered is readily obtainable, that it has been chosen for its relevance to past and present foci of the community of which the searcher is a member; that the material

possesses authenticity, in that the rigor of the selection process vouches in some way for its scholarly value; and that the document consulted today will be persistently available for future examination. The wrapper of the catalog conveys respectability on its contents (Thomas 2000).

Much work has still to be done to make library catalogues more effective as gateways to information resources on the web. This includes increasing the number and range of information resources that the catalogue provides access to, and changing cataloguing practices so that access is provided to full text resources rather than only to a bibliographic record or abstract. It also includes incorporating certain features that have been loosely described as 'Web 2.0', such as user ratings and reviewers, and 'social tagging' (see later in this chapter).

A typology of web subject access approaches

Earlier in this chapter the present state of providing access to information resources on the internet was characterised as embryonic and experimental, and that a wide range of approaches are currently being used and investigated. We can understand this variety of approaches better by considering a typology of web subject access approaches.

The spectrum of subject access tools noted earlier in this chapter (figure 9.2) has, at one end, tools that rely on uncontrolled vocabularies, based on *derived indexing*, and, at the other, tools that use highly controlled vocabularies, based on *assigned indexing*. This spectrum identified full-text searching, searching of text in metadata, automatic indexing and NLP (natural language processing), controlled vocabularies, and non-text approaches. It represents a starting point only, as many other tools and approaches are being developed to provide access to web resources and are not included in it. Two typologies are suggested here, to provide a framework for this chapter (figures 9.3 and 9.4). Both are indicative only, rather than comprehensive. There is no doubt that new categories and examples will need to be added as research continues into the best ways to provide access to web-based information resources.

Search engines and subject directories

The tools of choice for most seekers of information on the internet are likely to be search engines and subject directories. However, they are not always effective and often do not provide access to relevant information resources. This is one reason why libraries have expended considerable effort on developing other ways of providing subject access to internet information resources. We need to know a little about why search engines and subject directories are not considered totally adequate searching tools: for example, we need to understand why the same web search carried out on different search engines will give different results. First, it is necessary to know about the difference between search engines and subject directories.

Subject directories of web resources are compiled from lists of sites reviewed by editors. They are usually arranged hierarchically and include brief descriptions of the various sites. Users search these descriptions by browsing them. Generally speaking, a well-designed site with extensive and original content is more likely to be listed in these directories. *Yahoo!* is

1 Tools based on uncontrolled vocabularies	2 Tools based on controlled vocabularies	3 Tools based on hierarchical lists	4 Other tools

a. Search engines:
  1. full-text
  2. extracting
  3. meta-search
	a. Classification schedules	a. Subject directories	a. Subject gateways and portals

b. Natural language processing	b. Thesauri		b. Information visualisation
	c. Subject headings lists		c. Auditory browsing
	d. Ontologies		d. Automated categorisation
	e. Taxonomies		

Explanation of terms

1a)1: Full-text search engines search on an index created automatically from the web pages gathered by web crawler software.

1a)2: Extracting search engines search on an index created automatically from the web pages gathered by web crawler software, but are more limited in the type of searches they allow.

1a)3: Meta-search engines search other search engines and combine the results (Nicholson 2000, p.22).

1b): Natural language processing is 'a range of computational techniques for analysing and representing naturally occurring texts at one or more levels of linguistic analysis for the purpose of achieving human-like language processing' (McKiernan 1999).

4d): Automated categorisation uses Intelligent Software Agents to 'traverse the web in search of products, services, or resources that match a user's interest' (McKiernan 1999, p.26).

Figure 9.3 Typology of web subject access approaches (based on McKiernan 1999)

Term lists	Classifications and categories	Relationship lists
Authority files	Subject headings	Thesauri
Glossaries	Classification schemes	Semantic networks
Dictionaries	Taxonomies	Ontologies
Gazetteers	Categorisation schemes	

Figure 9.4 Typology of web subject access approaches (based on Hodge 2000, pp.5-7)

a well-known example. Dissatisfaction with commercial subject directories has led to the Open Directory Project, 'the largest human-edited directory of the web' which uses volunteer editors (http://dmoz.org) (figure 9.5).

Search engines use software called web crawlers to gather words from sources such as web page titles and site content. These words are compiled into indexes. Thus users of search engines are searching keywords in the indexes compiled from the results located by the web crawlers. Search engine software sifts through the millions of pages recorded in the index, finding matches and ranking these matches in order of relevance. This relevance ranking is determined in several ways, including:

- *position of the words*: keywords appearing in the title of a web page, or in the first few paragraphs of text, are considered to be more relevant to the topic than words appearing in other positions on the page;
- *word frequency*: keywords appearing more frequently in a web page are considered to be more relevant than other words, and so the web pages which contain them are considered more relevant; and
- *page linking*: pages that have been linked to more external websites are given a greater weighting – this idea, similar to how articles and journals are ranked according to the number of citations they receive, was introduced by the founders of Google (Langville & Meyer 2006).

The same search carried out on different search engines will give different results. There are two important reasons for this. First, each search engine varies in the number of pages it indexes, and in the frequency with which they revisit a web page to update it: no search engine uses exactly the same collection of web pages to get its results. Second, each search engine uses a slightly different algorithm to rank results.

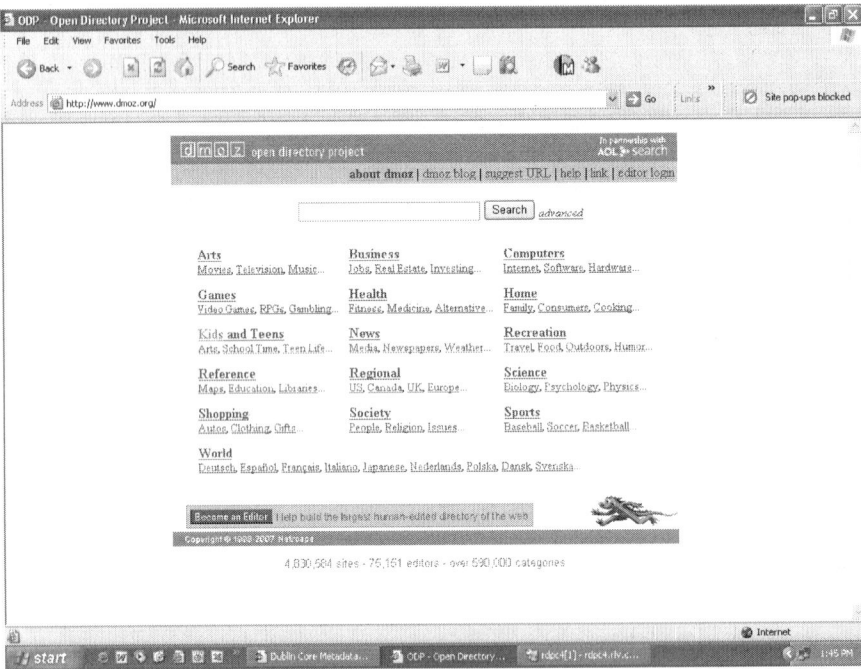

Figure 9.5 Open Directory Project (accessed 12 December 2007, http://dmoz.org)

The contents of information resources on the web are not usually created with information retrieval in mind, so the terms selected by the software to construct the indexes have the same problems we have already associated with derived language indexing (see chapters 6 and 8). Although some web authors add 'metatags' to their pages – which often give a fair indication as to content – these are not given a lot of weight by most search engines, the reason being that some unscrupulous authors include false metatags in an attempt to obtain higher rankings for their sites (a practice analogous to spam emailing). Another point to bear in mind is that search engines, unlike most library catalogues, are often commercial in nature, and rely on advertising. Thus results may sometimes be weighted in favour of 'sponsored sites'. So while modern search engines are often able to achieve quite relevant results on the first couple of screens – and most users do not look any further – this does not mean that they are providing the best resources, and it certainly does not mean that they are providing *all* the relevant ones – only a fraction of them. Indeed, the 'deep web' remains mostly untouched by most search engines, including the likes of Google and Yahoo!

Nevertheless, search engines have become very sophisticated. For example, features such as personalisation (targeting them to specific user groups, or remembering a user's previous searches and building on them), and query modification (providing tools to allow the user to narrow or expand a search) are now on offer. Notess (2007) provides a comparison of search engines which is regularly updated.

Subject gateways and portals

Many definitions of subject gateways can be found, for example:

> Subject gateways are online services and sites that provide searchable and browseable catalogues of internet based resources. Subject gateways will typically focus on a related set of academic subject areas (DESIRE 1999);

[and]

> An internet accessible collection of descriptions and location details for a range of information, generally available electronically, organised by subject or discipline, and selected for inclusion based on a published set of quality criteria (Campbell 2003).

Other definitions can be found in Campbell (2003). In this book a subject gateway is considered to be a website that provides links to online information resources (usually on the internet) which have been selected as being relevant to a particular user group, have been evaluated as being of high quality, and have been described to a high level. All of these definitions focus on three elements:

- quality control – librarians, or others, select information resources to be added on the basis of their reliability, quality, and authority;

- resource description – these are usually of high quality, being more detailed than a basic record developed by automated processes; and

- maintenance of the links to information resources – this ensures that the subject gateway is current.

Subject gateways focus on a particular subject area, and may provide both of a browseable directory and a search engine. They are very common: this very random sample illustrates the wide range available:

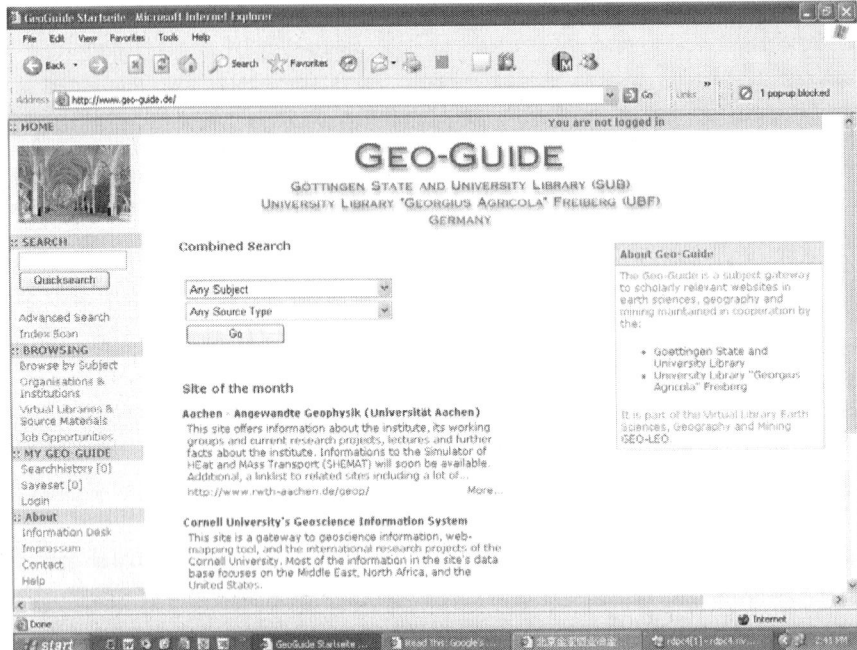

Figure 9.6 *Geo-Guide* subject gateway (accessed 12 December 2007, http://www.geo-guide.de)

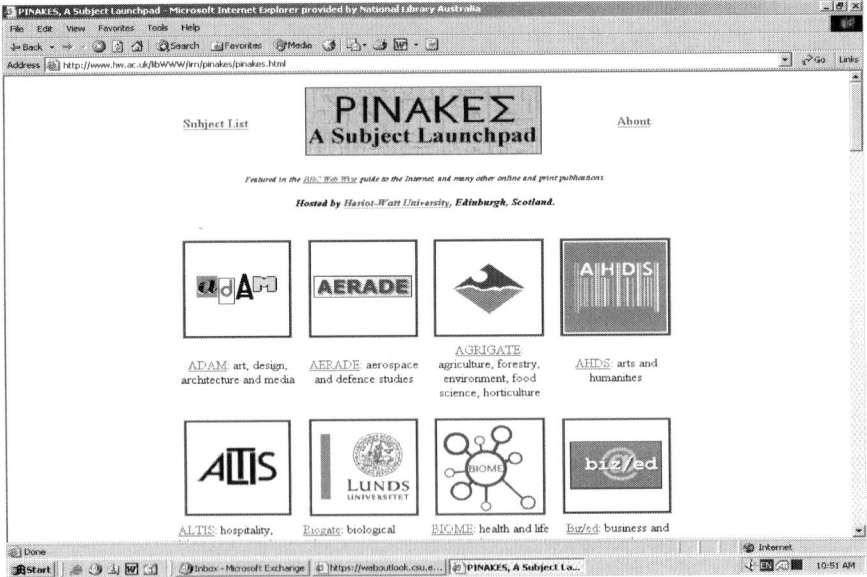

Figure 9.7 *PINAKES* catalogue of subject gateways (accessed 25 June 2003, http://www.hw.ac.uk/libWWW/irn/pinakes/pinakes.html)

- *Natural History*: 'Your guide to quality internet resources relating to the natural world': http://nature.ac.uk

- *History On-line*: http://www.history.ac.uk/search/welcome.html

- *Adventure Sports Online*: http://www.adventuresportsonline.com/

- *cultureandrecreation.gov.au*: 'Access to Australia's Culture and Recreation': http://www.cultureandrecreation.gov.au

- *Internet Library for Librarians*: 'a Portal Designed for Librarians to Locate Internet Resources Related to Their Profession': http://www.itcompany.com/inforetriever/

- *WebLaw*: internet resources for Australian legal researchers: http://www.weblaw.edu.au

- *Australia Dancing*: 'current and historical information about dancing in Australia': http://www.australiadancing.org

- *Geo-Guide*: 'an internet-based subject gateway to scholarly relevant material in earth science, geography and mining': http://www.geo-guide.de (figure 9.6)

There are also catalogues of subject gateways, such as *PINAKES* (figure 9.7).

The development of subject gateways in libraries has been guided by two imperatives: to provide access to information resources for their user groups, and to ensure that these information resources are authoritative. The remarkable increase of information resources available through the internet, combined with the difficulty of locating these resources, has lead to subject gateways being developed as an effective way of assisting users to discover high quality information on the internet quickly and effectively. Users do not always have the skills to search the internet, nor, sometimes, the ability to discern whether the information resources located are of high quality – that they are accurate, up-to-date, and unbiased. Traditionally publishers, librarians and other human intermediaries were responsible for applying quality control to the information resources they produced, purchased or provided access to through the library catalogue. This role is being extended to the internet. Subject experts identify, select and catalogue internet resources that are relevant to a specific user group, providing a description of each resource to allow the user to decide quickly if it is relevant to them.

Is a subject gateway the same thing as a portal? They are not the same, although they are closely related. A portal, especially in the business environment, is likely to include a subject gateway as well as many other tools and features, such as web-searching capability, news, reference tools, access to online shopping venues, and communication tools such as free email and chat (Thomas 2000). Portals can usually be personalised, so users can customise them to their own requirements: for example, on the *AOL* (*America Online*) portal the user can specify the day's weather and entertainment for a city of their choice. Portals can be categorised as consumer (sites such as *AOL*, *Yahoo*!), community portals developed for particular interest groups (such as *Music Australia*), vertical portals, often a unified site created by a particular service provider and organised on a special business topic (e.g., *etrade*), and enterprise portals which provide a channel for intranet and external data for a corporation or university (e.g., Charles Sturt University's *my.csu*, available to its staff and students) (Thomas 2000). A comparison between portals and subject gateways indicates many similarities, as well as significant differences (figure 9.8).

Subject gateway	Portal
Similarities	
Developed for a specific community	Developed for a specific community
Provide access to internet resources relevant to a specific community	Provide access to internet resources relevant to a specific community
Differences	
Resources assessed for quality, lack of bias, currency, etc	Strong commercial element (e.g., advertising)
Searches provide small number of specific results	Search engines provide large number of results which may be skewed by advertising
Currency of URLs is maintained	URLs may not be regularly checked
Access to a small range of information, not always highly current	Access to a large range of current information
Audio and video information less likely to be available	Audio and video information often available
	Can be customised to suit personal interests

Figure 9.8 Subject gateways and portals compared (based on Thomas 2000)

Online thesauri and subject headings lists

Chapter 8 noted that controlled vocabularies are increasingly being used to provide subject access to online information resources, and they are being redeveloped to make them more useful for this role. Some of the changes being made to LCSH, for example, are focused on making it internally consistent and allowing more post-coordination. Interest in the application of thesauri to online information retrieval is not new, but attention is again being given to it. Their effectiveness for online subject access is becoming apparent, and their ability to be a mechanism for interoperability (searching effectively across the full range of information resources, regardless of their subject field) is being recognised. (The use of classification schemes for online subject access is noted later in the chapter.) An example of research that is being carried out into making standard library-based controlled vocabularies more usable in the online environment is the *Principles Underlying Subject Headings Languages (SHLs)* (Lopes & Beall 1999), which reports the results of an IFLA investigation into identifying these principles and codifying them. The practical outcome of this research lies in its applications in allowing interoperability among different thesauri.

Chan and Hodges consider that subject access systems need to have three qualities if they are to be successfully applied in the web environment: simplicity, interoperability and scalability (Chan & Hodges 2000, p.229). Simplicity is required because in the web environment more and more people with varying levels of training are taking responsibility for providing subject data for information resources. Very few of these are trained librarians. Interoperability is required because it is now apparent that the information resources relevant to any particular user are widely distributed across countries, languages, and different kinds of institutions, and any effective system for subject access must be searchable by many different tools, and in turn needs to search many different systems. Scalability is the ability for a system to be usable in a range of situations, from a simple environment to a large-scale one.

Changes to LCSH are required if it is to meet these criteria. This task is not simple – constructing subject headings is complex and not well understood (see chapter 8); and LCSH is not interoperable – that is, it is not compatible with other kinds of controlled vocabularies such as faceted thesauri. Its advantages for use in the web environment are many: its rich vocabulary covers all subject areas, it contains links among terms, and it is widely adopted in many countries. LCSH needs to simplify its syntax and to adopt a more faceted approach. (Ellis and Vasconcelos 1999 discuss the relevance of using a facet analysis approach to search and organise the web.) These would have the effect of increasing its simplicity of use, both for the assigning of terms and the use of them for searching, and its interoperability between MARC records (which are vast in number and provide an exceptionally rich source of subject terms) and other controlled vocabularies (Chan & Hodges 2000, pp.230-232). A new role proposed for LCSH is to be a source vocabulary for the development of more specific thesauri. Its rich vocabulary – 'the largest in the English language' (Chan 2000) – makes it suitable for the role of metathesaurus, and the standardising that would occur would assist interoperability among controlled vocabularies. If this does not eventuate, then a recent offshoot of LCSH, FAST (Faceted Application of Subject Terminology), may turn out to be capable of doing the job instead (see chapter 8).

The role of thesauri and other controlled vocabularies is recognised in the metadata schema that are currently proliferating. In Dublin Core, specific thesauri or subject headings lists are not prescribed as the authority file in the DC.Subject element, but the application of a controlled vocabulary is recommended; specific vocabularies are often applied as part of particular DC implementations. An example is the AGLS (Australian Government Locator Service) metadata, whose *Guidelines for Content Creation for Subject* suggest that, if no more appropriate thesaurus exists, the Australian Public Affairs Information Service (APAIS) thesaurus (available online) should be used (National Archives of Australia 2003, 5.8.1).

ScOT (*Schools Online Thesaurus*)

Unlike LCSH, some of the newer controlled vocabularies have been developed specifically for online resources. An Australian example is ScOT (*Schools Online Thesaurus*), which has been developed by the Curriculum Corporation to describe the subject content of online curricula material in the Australasian K–12 education sector, and to enhance the discovery of these information resources (that is, to make them accessible) (figure 9.9). It was built using the MultiTes thesaurus management software and adheres to the ANSI/NISO Z39.19-1993 and ISO2788 standards for the construction of monolingual thesauri.

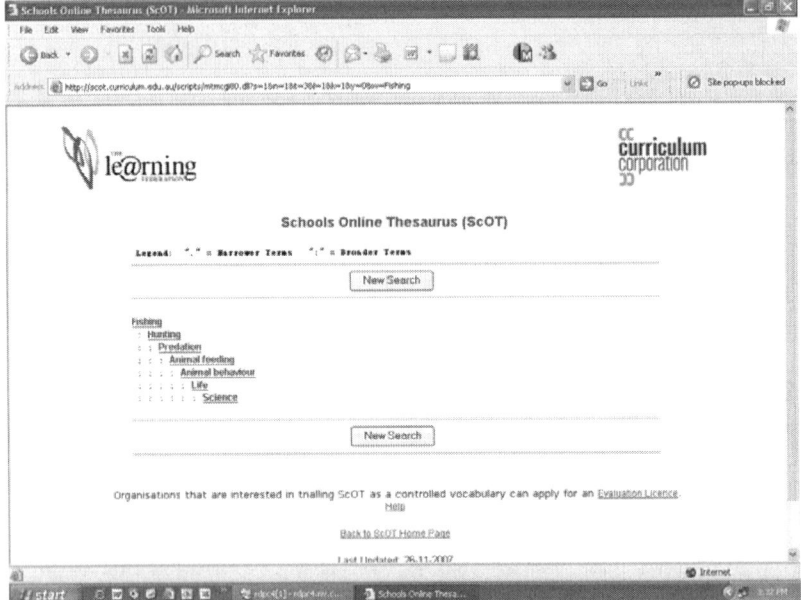

Figure 9.9 Entry in ScOT (accessed 12 December 2007, http://scot.curriculum.edu.au)

An awareness of who is responsible for the ScOT initiative helps us to understand it better. The three partners are The Le@rning Federation, education.au limited, and Curriculum Corporation (who is also the project manager). All three are owned by the education ministers of the federal and state governments in Australia, plus the New Zealand government. ScOT's primary purpose is to provide subject access to online curricula material produced by these bodies. Thus ScOT is being used to index resources in EdNA Online, a national online service for the education sector, developed by education.au limited. It is also being used to catalogue items on the SCIS bibliographic database (see chapter 13 for more about SCIS).

ScOT is still not quite a finished product, but its latest version, 7.1, covers the broad range of curriculum content (Arts, Business and industry, Education, Technology, Science, Mathematics, Literacy, Languages, and Literature, Studies of society and environment), totaling 10,486 subject terms, including 7,266 preferred (i.e., authorised) terms.

ScOT has been developed separately from the *SCIS Subject Headings* (see chapter 8). This is because of the differences between the online learning objects that ScOT is being applied to, and the information resources to which *SCIS Subject Headings* are applied in school libraries. The *SCIS Subject Headings* contain many pre-coordinated and inverted headings, and these are difficult to apply in a computerised environment, as noted elsewhere in this chapter. They are based on literary warrant, that is, on information resources already in the SCIS database, whereas ScOT has been developed to provide systematic coverage of the curricula (*Schools Online Thesaurus* 2007). It is not yet clear whether ScOT will become the primary controlled vocabulary for school library catalogues.

Classification and the web

Chapter 7 suggested that the renewed interest in classification schemes stems in part from their potential for organising material on the web. The examples of BUBL (using DDC) and CyberStacks (using LCC) were noted. Classification schemes are increasingly being used for organising and providing access to information resources on the web, separately from, or in conjunction with, thesauri or other controlled vocabularies.

The advantages of using a classification scheme to provide subject access to information resources on the web are many:

- users are already familiar with classification schemes which they have used in libraries;
- library staff are familiar with classification schemes and have been trained in their application and use;
- the cost of creating a new classification scheme is high;
- classification schemes assist in browsing and navigation, especially useful in a subject area new to the searcher;
- the hierarchies in some classification schemes provide a way to limit or expand searches; and
- classification schemes have the potential to act as a switching language between different vocabularies (for example, several thesauri on the same topic, or in different languages) (Schwartz 2001, pp.48, 75-76).

Most general classification schemes are hierarchical and enumerative, although faceting is increasingly being incorporated (see chapter 7). While hierarchical schemes are helpful for organising web information resources, as indicated by some of the examples provided below, further advantages are offered by faceted classification schemes. As Schwartz (2001, p.51) explains: 'The notational string contains the complete notational "bit" for each topic and can be deconstructed for purposes of rearrangement (and retrieval)'. The standard general library classification schemes such as DDC and LCC cannot be totally effective for providing access to digital information resources without some modification. Such changes are needed to make classification schemes:

- up-to-date and hospitable to new terminology and concepts being added;
- flexible and expandable ('including possibilities for decomposing faceted notation for retrieval purposes' (Schwartz 2001, p.77);
- easy to understand and intuitive to use; and
- universally applicable (Schwartz 2001, pp.77-78).

The established schemes are well aware of the need to change and are working towards it, for example by improving internal consistency. Where once there were calls for a new 'universal' classification scheme to be developed, the emphasis of current research into classification is on deconstructing (that is, increasing the faceting of) the major bibliographic classification schemes such as LCC, DDC, UDC so that they can be better applied to providing subject access to online information resources (McIlwaine & Williamson 1999, p.26).

Applications of existing schemes

DDC has in recent editions been working towards improving internal consistency with an eye to online use in both web and OPAC environments. For example, citation order and faceting have been standardised. Significant research into the application of DDC in the online environment has been carried out, most notably at OCLC. Early research by Vizine-Goetz (1996; updated in Vizine-Goetz 2002) indicated that DCC and LCC have an advantage for supporting topic browsing over web subject directories (she used the example of *Yahoo!*). The potential for DDC to act as a switching language has been understood for some years, based on its availability in translations into many languages (see chapter 7), and this promise is being developed in some projects (Vizine-Goetz 2002). DDC can be combined with other controlled vocabularies to provide improved subject access to online information resources (Saeed & Chaudhry 2002). The work required to turn DDC into a fully effective tool for providing subject access to web resources is now well on the way. Joan Mitchell, the editor-in-chief of DDC, argues that 'in a world where information flows freely in all formats across national and linguistic boundaries, it is important to have a standard knowledge organisation system that can represent concepts in a language-independent fashion' (Mitchell 2003) and DDC, with its many translations and its international audience, is well positioned to become this standard system.

Many examples can be found of the application of Dewey to providing subject access to web resources. CyberDewey (figure 9.10), developed as a proof-of-concept site, is a good example of the validity and robustness of DDC for organising a large collection of web resources. Blue Web'n ('a library of Blue Ribbon learning sites on the web') (figure 9.11) provides a facility where DDC categories can be used to narrow searches.

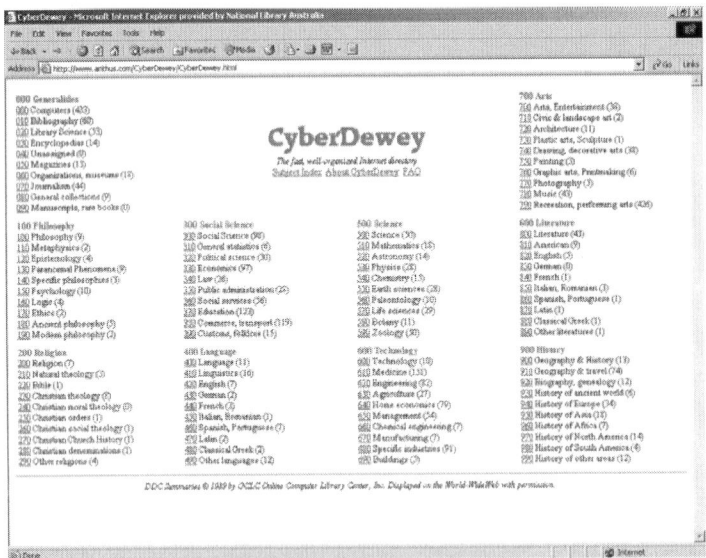

Figure 9.10 CyberDewey (accessed 25 June 2003, http://www.anthus.com/CyberDewey/CyberDewey.html)

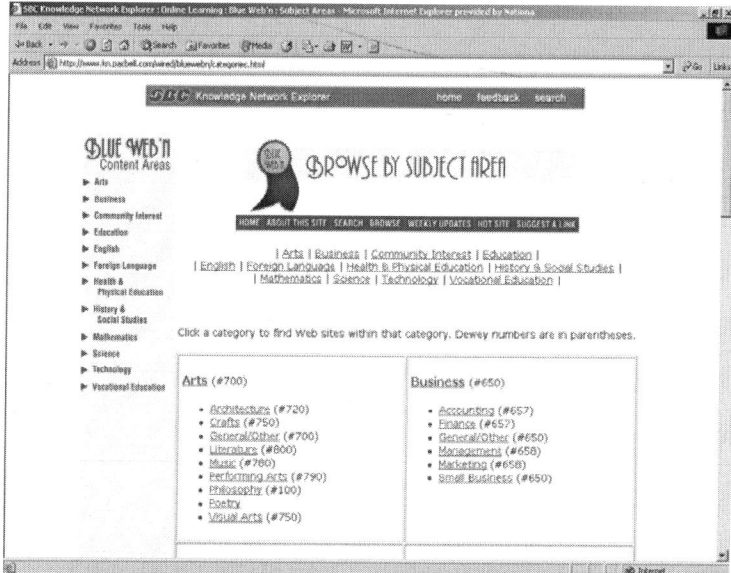

Figure 9.11 Blue Web'n (accessed 25 June 2003, http://www.kn.pacbell.com/ wired/bluewebn/categories.html)

A site developed by La Trobe University in Australia, called Claygate, allows users to search for subject gateways by DDC number. A subject gateway to web resources about Canada, Canadian Information By Subject, is also organised by DDC. However, probably the best application of the Dewey scheme is BUBL Link, referred to in chapter 7.

LCC is at the hierarchical/enumerative end of the classification spectrum. It therefore 'does not lend it so well to hypertext browsing as Dewey' (Schwartz 2001, p.65) and is not used as often for organising and accessing web resources. UDC, although the most faceted of the three main library classification schemes, has also not been applied a great deal, probably because it is less well known in those countries (Slavic 2006a).

Ontologies and taxonomies

There is confusion about the precise distinctions between ontologies, taxonomies and other terms when they are used by the information industry in relation to resource discovery on the web. Hodge (2000, p.6) suggests that the terms 'classification schemes', 'taxonomies', and 'categorisation schemes' are effectively interchangeable, all referring to 'ways to separate entities into 'buckets' or broad topic levels' (Hodge 2000, p.6). Gilchrist takes some care to distinguish between thesauri, taxonomies and ontologies (Gilchrist 2002). They all, he considers, deal with natural language. The thesaurus has already been defined and described in chapter 8. Compared with thesauri, taxonomies typically define relationships more precisely. Ontologies go even further: they add more information about the context in which the relationships operate (Gilchrist 2002, pp.15-16), and express the relationships and contexts in a computer understandable language (Qin & Paling 2001). 'The fundamental difference between an ontology and a conventional representational vocabulary is the level of abstraction and relationships among concept' (Qin & Paling 2001).

One characteristic that currently distinguishes taxonomies and ontologies from thesauri is the context for which they have been developed and in which they are used. Thesauri have a long history, based primarily in the library and information science sectors of the information industry. Taxonomies and ontologies have been developed (in ignorance of the large body of information science research and practice, some claim) by new players, including those from corporate sectors as part of the developing knowledge management community. Hodge notes, for instance, that taxonomies 'are increasingly being used in … knowledge management systems to indicate any grouping of objects based on a particular characteristic' and that ontologies 'are often connected with systems for data mining and knowledge management' (Hodge 2000, pp.6-7). Taxonomies are already widely used. The term can apply to something as simple as web subject directories (noted above in this chapter) and as complex as a corporate taxonomy providing access to information about the organisation (its business processes, standards, guidelines, people) and also about the information that business deals with (Gilchrist 2002, pp.12-13).

A useful definition of ontology for our purposes is this:

> Within the environment of the web … an ontology is not simply a conceptual framework but a concrete, syntactic structure that models the semantics of a domain – the conceptual framework – in a machine-understandable form (Jacob 2003, p.19).

Ontologies are still in the experimental stage and have not yet become part of the standard tools libraries use to provide subject access to web resources. However, the significant interest in them, for example in the role they will play in the Semantic Web (described in chapter 15) suggests that they soon will.

On the surface this may not appear to have much to do with practice in libraries and information centres. Taxonomies and ontologies, it is claimed, provide the means to organise and provide access to complex digital information resources better than traditional library practice can. However, the fact that they do have much in common with the longstanding classification processes that are part of standard library practice means that library and information professionals are increasingly engaged in experiments with ontologies and taxonomies.

Perhaps the most important characteristic of taxonomies and ontologies is that they are usually developed for very specific contexts, often a particular website or intranet, and are not usually applicable to other collections of resources across space and time – unlike a lot of bibliographic classification schemes.

Information architecture

The effective retrieval and navigation of online content – on websites and on intranets – is now widely recognised as critical for many successful functioning of many organisations, both in terms of their internal operations and their customer service. With so many organisations having large amounts of electronic information that is, or should be, available online, the design of websites and intranets so that this information can be readily accessed has become a full-time job for a new segment of the information profession, who are often referred to as *information architects*. These people are commonly consultants who combine project management and information organisation skills with expert knowledge of web applications and usability issues. The information organisation component involves structuring the site's network of pages and files, constructing effective taxonomies for menus, utilising other forms of metadata for search systems, and so forth. Since many of these activities are akin to those traditionally undertaken by cataloguers and other librarians, it is not surprising that many information architects (though not all) have library and information science backgrounds. Standard guides on organising websites and intranets, such as Morville and Rosenfeld's *Information Architecture for the World Wide Web* (2006), are now well established.

Designing an effective site, however, is only half the battle. It is also vital that the usability of a site is continuously reviewed and that a site is able to evolve as new users emerge and new content is added. An extremely well developed website is of little value if the information on the site is out of date and irrelevant. To ensure that their sites remain current, many large organisations now have a member or team of staff permanently assigned to this activity of *content management* (sometimes it comes under the responsibilities of a 'knowledge manager'). Content management systems, which help to collect and process digital information from across the organisation and its systems, are now widely used to assist with this task.

Social tagging and folksonomies

Although information architects may be able to create controlled vocabularies, such as taxonomies, on a small scale for particular websites, it is clear that there are many collections of digital resources for which it would be quite impossible to apply any kind of controlled vocabulary – there are just too many resources that would need to be classified and indexed. We have already noted that an alternative to controlled vocabularies are those based on natural language – either found within the document or assigned separately by the author/publisher. Some online services are thus actively encouraging contributors of resources to do their own tagging – examples include Flickr (the popular database of digital images), YouTube (for video clips) and Technorati (for blog postings). This may be regarded as a form of *social tagging*, that is, the vocabulary is based on the language of society at large. However, it is also possible for tags to be created by users, as well as contributors. This is also a form of social tagging, and is sometimes referred to as *collaborative tagging*. Examples of sites that allow users to add metadata tags (metatags), and not just their comments (as on, for example, Amazon.com), include del.icio.us and MyWeb, which both collect website bookmarks. Some content management systems are also building in this capacity, as are some digital libraries. There are even experiments to supplement controlled vocabularies with collaborative tagging in library catalogues. Where tagging is restricted to categorisation, the word *folksonomies* is often been used to describe social (i.e., folk) classifications (i.e., taxonomies).

A good deal of discussion and research about the value of social tagging has been carried out in the last two or three years, and there is likely to be a lot more to come. Clearly, where professional indexing is too expensive, and automated indexing proves too unreliable, an uncontrolled vocabulary based on the views of contributors and users is better than none. Equally clear is that this vocabulary will have serious shortcomings: recall will be hampered by the lack of treatment of synonyms and inconsistent word forms, and precision will be reduced by the problem of homonyms. However, recall may be increased through greater exhaustivity (more representation of component parts of a resource) and multiple view points (in the case of collaborative tagging). It has also been pointed out that users may feel more engaged with a collection if they are contributing to its metadata (Bearman & Trant 2005). There are issues, among many others, of scalability and trust. Golder and Huberman (2006) have observed (in the case of del.icio.us) that 'a significant amount of tagging, if not all, is done for personal use rather than for public benefit'. However, they also point out that 'even information tagged for personal use can benefit other users', and that the apparent stability of folksonomies, at least in some contexts, suggest scalability and reliability may not be quite such a problem as might be imagined.

There does appear to be some middle ground between the controlled and social tagging camps: allowing users to tag resources, but restricting the choice of tags to a particular (controlled) vocabulary. This compromise approach does not altogether avoid the relativism of collaborative tagging, but may alleviate some of the problems associated with the 'pure' approach (which have been summarised by Peterson, 2006). Furthermore, if professional indexers benefit from the provision of scope notes and references, to guide them in their choice of terms, it is very likely that amateur metadata creators would also benefit from similar – though perhaps simpler – assistance.

Providing access to non-text data

Traditional information retrieval tools were developed to search text. Until recently, any retrieval of information from databases or information resources containing images or sound was carried out by searching the textual metadata for these resources. The techniques developed for providing access to text through its description and analysis do not readily transfer to non-text resources. Few standards exist for non-text indexing, which is still largely experimental. However, with the web now hosting large quantities of non-text resources, efforts are being made to develop more effective means of providing access to images and sound resources.

Indexing images has traditionally been carried out using text-processing techniques, where the text searched is that in a caption (such as title, or name of the painter or photographer) or text supplied by an indexer (for example, a description of a photograph). This is the technique applied in Picture Australia, a gateway that provides access to online image collections available on the web (figure 9.12).

Alternative techniques for indexing and retrieving images are based on providing access to their internal characteristics, such as colour percentages, colour layout, and textures in the images. These content-based approaches may be combined with searches on text and keywords. IBM's QBIC (Query By Image Content) web page (http://wwwqbic.almaden.ibm.com) provides an explanation of how QBIC works and provides links to some demonstrations, including artworks in the Hermitage Museum. (A good starting point for more information on this topic is Chen and Rasmussen 1999).

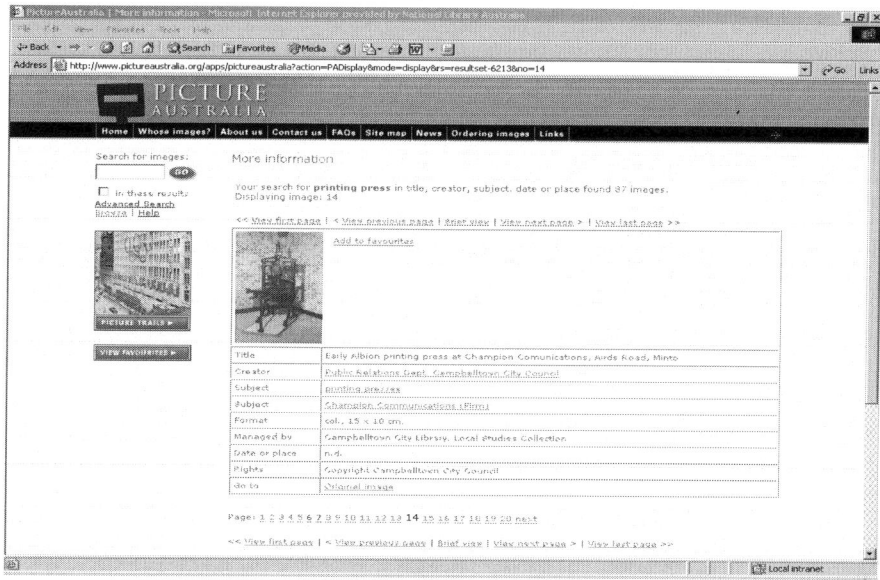

Figure 9.12 Picture Australia (accessed 26 June 2003, http://www.pictureaustralia.org)

For sound resources, a distinction is usually made between spoken word (for example, spoken word in television and film sound tracks, or radio broadcasts) and music. Spoken word does not present major problems for indexing and information retrieval. One standard way of doing this is to use speech recognition software that converts the spoken word to text, then use standard text-searching software to search that text. Providing access to music is much more complex, and is an area where much research is being carried out (ISMIR 2007).

Indexing and providing access to the information content of video and film is also complex, but research is providing some possible solutions. Audiovisual material, such as video and film, contain audio content and visual content, and may have textual content associated with them (for example, synopses or stock shot lists). For the textual content, traditional textual indexing and information retrieval techniques and systems are used. Other techniques, such as speech recognition for spoken word and image recognition on individual frames, are being investigated and applied.

Conclusion

This chapter has not provided a comprehensive overview of all of the processes that are being applied, or experimented with, to provide better subject access to information resources on the web. There is, for example, no mention of the Semantic Web, a development that has the potential to bring together many of the approaches described in this chapter. (Instead, the Semantic Web is discussed in chapter 15.) Even so, one of the conclusions that can be drawn from this overview is that librarians have more to learn, and apply, from the web-search industry, which tends to dominated by computer scientists.

Conversely, library-based practice still has a lot to offer the web. Bates, for example, strongly emphasises that library and information science practice and research has much to offer to those concerned with improving web retrieval. She suggests that the web industry considers and applies some of the lessons learned, including:

- use faceted classifications, not 'old-fashioned hierarchical classifications';
- don't use 'ontologies' – label it what it really is, that is thesaurus, or classification;
- use thesauri developed for information retrieval, not general dictionaries or thesauri developed by linguists for other purposes;
- take note of the Bradford Distribution – understand and work with the 'underlying statistical characteristics of information in designing information retrieval';
- design for scalability from the start – IR systems are size-sensitive;
- pay attention to the design of the indexing system, keeping human users in mind; and
- don't ignore information expertise – hire it! (Bates 2002).

This lack of take-up of the lessons learned by the information sciences over many decades is also noted by Vizine-Goetz: 'The web community does not understand library subject systems, has little knowledge of them and what is known, is often based on misinformation. Library schemes are perceived to be outmoded, out-of-date, and only useful for print and older material' (Vizine-Goetz 2000). She suggests that 'we will need to reengineer and re-conceive our schemes for new uses, including

- [Automatic] indexing/categorization,
- Surfing vs. searching,
- Navigation,
- Providing alternate views,
- Presenting research results (Vizine-Goetz 2000).

There is another lesson that should be kept in mind: we may sometimes be pursuing the wrong goal. We have, perhaps, tacitly assumed that we want to provide subject access for *all* internet information resources, and so we are working on mass responses, 'solutions' such as self-indexing documents. But a better question to ask is 'not whether we can organize the web, but whether we can organize those parts of it which are important to our communities. This is, after all, what we have been doing in libraries for centuries' (Schwartz 2001, p.145). We should be doing what libraries have always done – being very selective about the information resources we wish to provide access to, evaluating them on the basis of quality (their authority, lack of bias, currency, and so on), and then devoting our bibliographic organisation resources to providing high-level access to those. The future is likely to be one where standard library tools for subject access are developed to enhance their use for web resources, and are combined (for example, classification schemes with thesauri, and controlled vocabularies with social tagging), and one where interoperability will feature more prominently.

PART IV: BIBLIOGRAPHIC DATA EXCHANGE AND MANAGEMENT

Introduction

Parts II and III discussed standards and methods used in describing information resources for the purposes of their retrieval in, or via, information retrieval systems. The creation of standardised metadata is by no means, however, the end of the story. Metadata needs to be used effectively.

Additional standards need to be employed if the metadata is to be used in more than one system, that is, if it is to be *exchanged*. The first four chapters of Part IV examine standards for bibliographic data exchange and organisations that facilitate the sharing of metadata. Even if bibliographic data is not exchanged, it still needs to be *managed*, that is, it needs to be stored and manipulated in a system. How metadata is managed in a system and how it is utilised by a system for the benefit of users varies considerably. The last chapter of Part IV looks at what some of the modern library information retrieval systems can do with metadata.

This introduction to Part IV examines some general requirements of information retrieval systems, such as what an effective system is, and how we know if a system is effective. Chapter 10 describes some of the technical standards applied by the latest systems. Chapter 11 relates some important organisational agreements which have facilitated bibliographic data exchange, while chapter 12 discusses the importance of bibliographic utilities – organisations, and their systems, specifically set up for the exchange of metadata and cooperative cataloguing. Chapter 13 presents examples of metadata sharing from Australia. Chapter 14 examines computer systems used at the local level, including integrated library systems.

What makes an effective information retrieval system?

To identify characteristics required for an effective information retrieval system we can look again at the objectives of a library information retrieval system developed in chapter 1:

- to enable a person to find a document in any format of which the author, the title, the subject, or other specified characteristics are known;
- to show what documents by a given author, on a given subject (and related subjects), or in a given kind (or form) of literature, can be delivered to the user, by whatever delivery mechanism is appropriate;
- to assist in the choice of a document which meets the information needs of the user; and
- to deliver a copy of a required document to the user.

Chapter 1 also noted three primary tasks required to achieve the aims of library information retrieval systems:

- to uniquely identify a document so that it cannot be confused with other similar documents;

- to provide the user with access to documents, if they know the name or names of a person or organisation associated with these documents; and

- to provide the user with details of the subjects of documents.

In this context we should also remember what studies have told us about the requirements of library information retrieval system users: that most searches are either known item searches or subject searches, with the latter being particularly popular in online library catalogues.

From this it is possible to identify four principal characteristics required for an effective library information retrieval system in today's networked environment. We can deduce that the system:

- must provide information that is as accurate as possible to its users;

- must use commonly agreed-upon standards for organising information;

- must be as easy as possible to use, consistent with delivering accurate information and maximum effectiveness; and

- must be linked to networks and utilities that enable the maximum benefit from exchanging bibliographic information.

Because today's economic environment requires pragmatism, we can add a fifth characteristic:

- the system must achieve its capabilities in a cost-effective way.

How do we know if an information retrieval system is effective?

To be completely effective an information retrieval system must match the results of a search exactly with what the user requested. This is an impossible aim, except in very small databases. While a document retrieval system is likely to hold a number of records relevant to what the user is seeking, the rest will not be of interest. Of the relevant items, some will be very relevant, but others will be less relevant. To use the example of a subject search, relevance is determined by the topic, as well as by factors such as what language the item is in, and when it was published. A search by a user on a given topic may result in documents being retrieved which match the criteria of the search but are not relevant to the search: for example, a search for a document about the game of *cricket* may also retrieve documents about the insect.

More precise measures have been developed to help us ascertain the effectiveness of an information retrieval system. Using these measures, we are in a better position to determine what kinds of changes are needed to improve the system, and the effect of such changes; the end result is improved systems for everyday use. The key measures are *relevance, recall* and *precision:*

- *relevance* – having direct bearing on the subject requested;

- *recall* – the number of relevant documents retrieved from a search; hence

- *precision* – the number of documents which are relevant in the results of a search.

Useful measures of system effectiveness have been derived from these concepts, such as:

- *recall ratio* – number of relevant documents retrieved/total number of relevant documents in the system; and

- *precision ratio* – number of relevant documents retrieved/total number of documents retrieved.

The ideal is that we recall all relevant documents in the database, that is, a recall ratio of 100 per cent, but this is very unlikely to be achieved in practice. Similarly, system designers aim for a 100 per cent precision ratio – that all the documents retrieved are relevant – but this is equally unlikely in most cases.

Note that recall and precision rates are inversely proportional. In other words, as one goes up the other tends to go down. As the aim is to achieve 100 per cent recall *and* 100 per cent precision, the result is that compromises are always necessary in designing an effective information retrieval system (Hunter & Bakewell 1991, chapter 20; Foskett 1996, chapter 2).

Requirements for system effectiveness

System effectiveness can usefully be measured at three stages:

- the input stage – what is entered into the information retrieval system;

- the processing/user stage – what happens in the system; and

- the output stage – what is retrieved from the system.

Input requirements – We can include here such factors as:

- the system can accept data which adheres to accepted standards, so that the results are accurate and can be widely and readily comprehended;

- minimum effort is required to input data: for example the system can accept data in a variety of ways – scanning in, keyboarding, downloading from other systems;

- the data which is input must be consistent and accurate;

- the data can be input at minimum cost;

- the data can be input readily and speedily; and

- the system has features which reduce the amount of human effort and provide high levels of consistency, for example automatic checking and matching procedures for data input.

Processing/user requirements – Included are:

- system maintenance procedures are easy to carry out;

- the system is not costly to maintain;

- easy-to-use help facilities are available to assist maintenance personnel;

- the system has room for expansion;

- the system is user-friendly and easy to learn and use;

- online help and online tutorials are provided;

- the system is neutral and objective, for example, it is not ethnocentric, and does not propound or enforce a specific biased set of ideas;
- the system's response time is as short as possible; and
- the system is capable of being used by as many users at the same time as possible.

Output requirements – These include:

- the data output is understandable to the user;
- the system must provide its users with results which achieve a high degree of precision (that is, there is an appropriate balance between recall and relevance); and
- the system must produce some result regardless of approach.

These requirements should be kept in mind when reading the following chapters.

CHAPTER 10
Technical standards

This chapter is concerned with what can be loosely described as technical standards in bibliographic organisation. The term *technical standards* as used in this book includes the following:

- conventions and agreements about data communications standards, including protocols (e.g., OSI, LSP, Z39.50, OAI, OpenURL), and format standards/frameworks (e.g., MARC, Dublin Core, RDF/XML);

- computer hardware standards, such as those which promote equipment connectivity; and

- other technical standards used in the field of organising information, such as standard sizes for catalogue cards.

These technical standards are essential for efficient, economical networking, which is the basis of effective practice in library information retrieval systems. The last two sets of standards, those for telecommunications infrastructure and for other technical standards, receive only a brief mention.

It is worthwhile to remind the reader of the benefits of standardised metadata. Standardisation allows considerable economic savings, and is helpful to users who, when transferring from one system to another, do not have to learn new practices and conventions. It is common practice for libraries to obtain bibliographic records from other sources and insert these records into their own information retrieval systems, preferably without modification. This widespread exchange of metadata takes place on a daily basis and on a massive scale internationally. How this exchange happens is the topic of this and the following chapter.

Data communication standards

OSI (Open Systems Interconnection)

Information centres have long sought the goal of networking their information retrieval systems (regardless of who developed, implemented and sold the system) so that the benefits which accrue from ready sharing of bibliographic data can be realised. For this to occur there needs to be agreement on standards for communication of messages and data. The standards for message content (such as AACR2) are noted in earlier chapters. The standards which enable data to be communicated from one system to another are based on the OSI (Open Systems Interconnection) Reference Model.

The OSI Reference Model is a series of protocols which enable systems to communicate easily with other systems, regardless of who supplied the system: it is vendor-independent.

While the full technical details are of interest primarily to system developers, what is significant to us here is what OSI allows to happen. OSI has allowed major steps to be taken in the development of interconnection of library information retrieval systems, so that it is now commonplace for bibliographic data to be sent from one system to another in any part of the world, and for a user of one system to search the bibliographic data in another system which may be – literally – anywhere else in the world.

The first library implementation of the OSI model was LSP (the Linked Systems Project), which is noted in more detail below. The Linked Systems Project led directly to the development of the Z39.50 standard by the American National Standards Institute. Its significance for exchanging bibliographic data should not be underestimated (Webb 1993, pp.10-11).

OSI in Australia

The potential of OSI was realised in Australia early in its development. The Sydney-based cooperative CLANN (College Libraries Activity Network of NSW – see chapter 13) tendered for a computer system which was OSI-capable, and its choice of system, GEAC, met this requirement (O'Mara & Peake 1985, p.2). In June 1986 the National Library of Australia issued a 'For Information' sheet which noted:

> The National Library of Australia accepts that it has a role in identifying standards which will be suitable for the interconnection of library systems and in encouraging the use of such standards within Australia ... The Library also recognises that the emergence of OSI standards will have an impact on its own services, particularly those provided through the Australian Bibliographic Network (ABN). NLA will establish a Working Party on OSI (Open Systems Interconnection 1986, p.10).

The Library established a Working Group on Library Systems Interconnection which in early 1988 decided to focus its activities on developing an OSI-based interlibrary loan system for Australia, to be implemented by establishing an interface between the interlibrary loan subsystem of ABN (now Libraries Australia) and local email systems such as the State Library of New South Wales' ILANET (Wade 1988). The scope of this Group's considerations broadened to encompass all communications facilities, especially the internet, and in 1995 it changed its name to Electronic Libraries Forum (ELF). ELF has ceased to function, but its legacy lives on, particularly in the Libraries Australia ILL (interlibrary loan) system.

LSP (Linked Systems Project)

The OSI model was used as the basis for LSP. This aimed to link the computer systems of the Library of Congress and two of the major United States-based bibliographic utilities, WLN and RLIN, so that each member of the project could have access to the bibliographic resources of the other members. These three partners were later joined by a fourth utility, OCLC. The first procedure to be implemented was the sharing of the Library of Congress's Name Authority File. RLIN was first to receive the authority file in 1985, and OCLC in 1987.

A copy of the file was maintained by RLIN and OCLC and updated on a daily basis (Gredley & Hopkinson 1990, pp.247-249). In 1983 LSP participants submitted their Record Transfer and Information Retrieval protocols to ANSI (American National Standards Institute). The Record Transfer protocol was set aside in preference for the development of what became FTP. The Information Retrieval protocol was not accepted immediately, but after further refinement was approved by ANSI in 1988 as Z39.50.

Z39.50

Z39.50 is arguably the most significant of the developments based on experience gained from OSI and LSP. ANSI/NISO Z39.50, entitled *Information Retrieval: Application Service Definition and Protocol Specification*, is a set of rules which allows data communication and is applied to bibliographic data to enable search and retrieval from remote bibliographic databases. The protocol is vendor-independent, though it has been developed with input from many of the leading system vendors. It operates by defining a standard format for a search which is understood by both the *client* (for example, the local OPAC) and the *server* (for example, a remote database which is part of an information retrieval system in another city or country).

> The client takes its own local search format, translates it to the standard Z39.50 search format, and sends it to the server. The server takes the standard search format, translates it to the local search format, and performs the search ... Once the client receives records from the server, it can construct how the records are displayed. The Z39.50-compliant client makes it transparent to the user that the information has come from a completely different system (Ward 1994, p.640).

An important characteristic of Z39.50 is that it can be implemented over the internet and other TCP/IP (Transmission Control Protocol/Internet Protocol) networks. More specifically, it allows library users in, say, Brisbane to use their familiar local OPAC to search OPACs in, say, North America, without having to be aware that the distant OPACs require different commands to access their contents. The Z39.50 protocol translates one set of commands to the other, and back again (see figure 10.1).

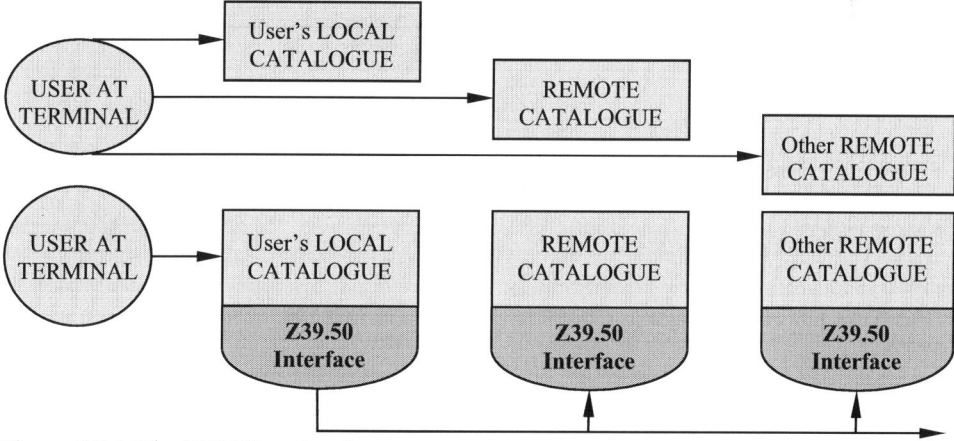

Figure 10.1 The Z39.50 protocol

The implementation of Z39.50 has proceeded with startling rapidity, so that the aim of the protocol – 'the transparent expansion of accessibility' (Ward 1994, p.641) – has become a reality. Many libraries, including the Library of Congress, offer Z39.50 access to their catalogues, while most current library systems now offer Z39.50 clients as a standard feature. The Library of Congress maintains the Z39.50 website, which includes a Z39.50 gateway to a long list of libraries' catalogues. The standard was last revised in 2003.

However, it should be added that there have been far fewer implementations of version 3 of Z39.50, which is the one that accommodates holdings status information and thus optimises the power of the Z39.50 distributed union catalogue for interlibrary loan process: users can search simultaneously on all the catalogues for their item and find the library at which it is currently available for loan, without having to perform the additional steps of logging on to individual library OPACs.

Beyond Z39.50

While cataloguers have found Z39.50 to be an extremely useful protocol in recent years, it has, like MARC, not yet been put fully implemented by all library systems. Few libraries have version 3 servers, for instance. There is also the question of standardising the *search profile*. Searching is a complex affair, even in an ordinary OPAC, which has to decide exactly what functionality it is offering the user: for example, which fields does a keyword search retrieve on? do the keywords have to match the field or subfield exactly? does it allow for truncation? what kind of truncation? and so on. The point here is that the Z39.50 protocol must specify exactly how the client wants to search the server – this is called the client's profile. Unfortunately, indexing is done differently in different systems, and so Z39.50 servers cannot support every possible profile. Thus the client must be set to a particular profile that their targeted servers *can* support. Several profiles have been established that serve as benchmarks as to what a client may expect a server to be able to support, perhaps most famously the Bath Profile (so-called because it was established in Bath, England, home of UKOLN, the United Kingdom Office for Library and Information Networking). If both Z39.50 client and Z39.50 server work on the basis of the Bath Profile, then searchers are in business. However, this does yet not offer very sophisticated searching, and commonly users are not able to search through Z39.50 as effectively as they can in their host retrieval systems.

Z39.50 has been around for quite some time by computing standards – like MARC, it predates the internet. Also like MARC, it has not been embraced by too many institutions or system developers outside of the library community. Some programmers complain about the standard's inflexible and conservative nature. As a result, there have been moves to make it more dynamic and more generic. One such move has been the development of ZING, which stands for Z39.50-International: Next Generation, and which metamorphosed in early 2006 into the SRU standard – *Search/Retrieval for URL*. Unlike Z39.50, this is based on the web standards of HTTP and XML, so in effect it is a new standard, but aims to perform essentially the same function of standardising search and retrieval across online databases. SRU and Z39.50 share the same official website, which states that the former 'is a standard XML-focused search protocol for internet search queries, utilising CQL (Contextual Query Language), a standard syntax for representing queries.' The fact that it is based on XML and CQL suggests that it may indeed prove popular with the wider information profession, and not just librarians.

Open Archives Initiative (OAI)

Another project which aims to appeal to the broader information community is the Open Archives Initiative (OAI). This project has already proven highly successful, in fact, having been used by many information agencies (and not just libraries) as a means of sharing their digital resources, and the metadata that goes with these resources. It was begun in 1999, and produced the first Open Archives Initiative Protocol for Metadata Harvesting (OPA-PMH) in 2001, and a new version the following year. This standard performs a similar function to that of Z39.50 and SRU, but at a more basic level. At the last count, there were 738 repositories (data providers) registered as OAI-compliant, as well as several service providers (clients, in Z39.50 language) which enable the harvesting of these repositories based on specified metadata. The project has involved a variety of participants, including some notable digital libraries and the Library of Congress; it has certainly been quite a success story, even though it is not used on anything like the same scale as Z39.50. Useful overviews of the standard are given by Breeding (2002) and Rusch-Feja (2002).

OpenURL

OpenURL was developed in 2000 following research carried out by Herbert Van de Sompel and Patrick Hochstenbach at Ghent University, Belgium. The fruits of this research were commercialised by the library system vendor, exLibris, and turned into its SFX product; other vendors have followed suit with similar 'linking' products. Subsequently a new ANSI/NISO standard, *The OpenURL Framework for Context-Sensitive Services* (2004), was established.

Like Z39.50, OpenURL is a protocol which establishes a particular search request format for a server, in this case an OpenURL server, to act upon, but unlike Z39.50 the server is under the control of the user's own information centre. The primary aim of the OpenURL framework is to link the metadata to resources in other databases, in the same interface.

If they are to compete with the likes of Google, today's library information systems need to provide not only bibliographic access, but also *direct* access to the information. Z39.50 clients retrieve only MARC records, and, at best, holdings information; if the MARC record contains a URL, this may or may not point to the resource itself – it might only be for a related resource, or the web resource may not be accessible to another user through that URL, since it has not been subscribed to by the user's own library through that URL, or perhaps the URL is broken. The user may still have access to the full-text of the resource, but it may take him or her a long time to find the right database which leads to such access.

OpenURL offers a potential solution to the problem of 'the wrong link'. It can also offer more 'right links'. It works like this: the information retrieval system that the user is searching in retrieves metadata for a journal article, say, that the user is interested in following up on. A link to the full-text may or may not be provided, but even if it is, it might not work – perhaps the library has not subscribed to full-text in this particular database. However, if the information retrieval system is OpenURL-aware, it would have identified the user's library as one in which it should forward OpenURLs to the library's OpenURL server (or service component). The OpenURL server receives the OpenURL, which is, as its name suggests, a URL. To be more precise it is an actionable URL, which means it tells the server to do something, that is, to search in all the systems it is linked to for the metadata represented in the URL.

It is not so difficult for the external information retrieval system to get the library's OpenURL server to search for the metadata the user is interested in, because it is based on the link it is already providing: if this link is in a standard OpenURL format, it will work. The OpenURL format includes a 'hook' before which is substituted the name of the OpenURL server's particular IP address; after it, the metadata is set out in a standard way that all OpenURL servers can understand.

The library's OpenURL server receives the OpenURL and starts interrogating the other OpenURL-compliant information retrieval systems the library owns or subscribes to. If it finds other OpenURLs in other systems with some or all of the same metadata, then it sends them to the user as a pop-up window on their PC. All the hard work of following up on a citation has thus been done for the user: if the library has any access to the full-text, through any of its OpenURL-compliant systems, it will appear in front of the user as a link ready for them to click on (that is the theory, anyway!).

There is a very good reason why the OpenURL format is not based on MARC: most articles whose full text can be accessed remotely are not catalogued using MARC; they are much more likely to be abstracted and/or indexed in some other format. This is not, however, to say that MARC databases cannot be OpenURL-compliant. The format is not complex and can be mapped from MARC and other schemas reasonably easily.

MARC (Machine-Readable Cataloguing)

What is MARC?

MARC (Machine-Readable Cataloguing) is the main data communication standard in use in libraries today. It is a format – more correctly, a group of formats – for the exchange of bibliographic and other data among computerised library systems. Its status as an international standard was assured very rapidly after its development by the Library of Congress in the mid-1960s. MARC is one of the two essential sets of standards (along with ISBD/AACR2) which enable the exchange of bibliographic records to take place internationally on a massive scale. Fundamentally it is nothing more than a standardised format for bibliographic information; in practice it is a very detailed system of coding for formatting library cataloguing data so that it can be read and manipulated by computers. The bibliographic data needs to have first been constructed according to AACR2, or the first edition of AACR, or another cataloguing code. It works best with AACR2 and is updated to conform, more or less, to this code. Figure 10.2 illustrates a bibliographic record in MARC format.

Although MARC is often referred to in the singular – as *the* MARC format – there are in fact more than 20 MARC formats for bibliographic data, but they are similar and share one important characteristic: they all adhere to an international standard, ISO 2709:1996

Format for Information Exchange. Also, most hold official status in the country in which they were developed, that is, most are national formats used by national bibliographic agencies (Gredley & Hopkinson 1990, p.70).

MARC format
LEADER 01067nam 2200289 a 4500
001	abn89008249
008	s1988 tmaach 00010 eng d
020	0909739277
035	L895009013
040	TSL$cTSL
043	u-at-tm
082 0	027.4/094/61$219
100 10	Levett, John,$d1933-
245 14	The origins of the State Library of Tasmania /$c[by] John Levett.
260	Hobart, Tas. :$bTasmanian State Committee of the Australian Library Promotion Council with the assistance of the State Library and Archives Trust,$c1988.
300	[19] p. :$bill., facsims., ports. ;$c25 cm.
504	Includes bibliographical references.
610 20	Tasmanian Public Library$xHistory.
650 0	Public libraries$zTasmania$zHobart$xHistory.
710 2	Australian Library Promotion Council.$bTasmanian State Committee.
984	2014$c027.49461 L663o

One output style
a m
Levett, John, 1933-
The origins of the State Library of Tasmania / {by} John Levett. Hobart, Tas. : Tasmanian State Committee of the Australian Library Promotion Council with the assistance of the State Library and Archives Trust, 1988.
[19] p. : ill., facsims., ports. ; 25 cm.
Includes bibliographical references.
ISBN 0909739277
1. Tasmanian Public Library–History. 2. Public libraries–Tasmania–Hobart–History.
I. Australian Library Promotion Council. Tasmanian State Committee. II. Title
027.4/094/61 9
TSL abn89-008249

Another output style
AUTHOR/S	Levett, John, 1933-
	Australian Library Promotion Council. Tasmanian State Committee.
TITLE	The origins of the State Library of Tasmania / {by} John Levett.
PUBLISHER	Hobart, Tas. : Tasmanian State Committee of the Australian Library Promotion Council with the assistance of the State Library and Archives Trust, 1988.
COLLATION	[19] p. : ill., facsims., ports. ; 25 cm.
SUBJECT/S	Tasmanian Public Library–History.
	Public libraries–Tasmania–Hobart–History.
NOTES	Includes bibliographical references.
ISBN	# 0909739277
ABN RID	abn89008249

Figure 10.2 A bibliographic record in MARC format

What does MARC allow to happen?

Before the development of MARC by the Library of Congress, many libraries had to perform most of the cataloguing for the items they acquired themselves. The Library of Congress and other national bibliographic agencies (such as the British Library) did offer catalogue cards for some materials (the materials that they acquired), but having these cards printed to order was a costly and time-consuming business; also, the cards did not necessarily conform to the styles of catalogue records created in-house.

> The redundancy and duplication of effort, if measured by modern industrial standards, was staggering. It was not uncommon for ten or more individual (acquisitions, cataloging, filing, and preparation) staff members to be involved in getting a book to the library shelf (Culkin 1992, p.84).

One consequence of this duplication of effort by many tens of thousands of libraries throughout the world was inconsistency. Despite the best efforts of cataloguers (and they have been considerable), cataloguing rules could not be interpreted uniformly. MARC was thus developed with the following objectives in mind:

- reduction in labour and production costs by cataloguing a document once and once only,
- standardising of the cataloguing process to ensure consistency of cataloguing, and
- standardising of data communication and transfer (Culkin 1992, p.83).

Once standardised, and with widespread agreement about the standards, the catalogue record can be created once, then widely and rapidly disseminated to multiple users. Even if there were some local variations in cataloguing policy, these could be accommodated much more readily with an electronic record, which can be edited more tidily than can a typed card.

In addition to rapid, widespread transfer and communication of bibliographic data, the MARC record also allows different outputs. The same cataloguing information, once it has been coded into MARC format, may be manipulated to produce several products:

- bibliographic records with full MARC tags, for import/export of bibliographic data to another computer database;
- display of as much (or as little) of the bibliographic record as is wanted, in a local system; and
- display of the bibliographic record in whatever format is required – for example in printed form (as an entry in a book catalogue, or as a catalogue card), or in a local library information retrieval system such as an OPAC.

As a data exchange format, MARC allows libraries to share resources and develop cooperative networks. This has two major effects:

- using MARC, bibliographic records can be readily exchanged, union catalogues can be easily maintained, and costs of cataloguing can be minimised; and
- service to the user can be improved: the benefits include better resource discovery through comprehensive union catalogues.

In short, MARC allows flexibility in library information retrieval systems.

A brief history of MARC

In the late 1950s the Library of Congress started to consider automating its procedures. In the early 1960s the Council of Library Resources financially supported a study to determine the feasibility of automating some of its procedures, culminating in the influential King report published in 1963 (King 1963). Other studies were also carried out, for example, investigations into the feasibility of converting Library of Congress cataloguing records on cards to machine-readable format so that they could be printed using a computer. Such projects led to a pilot MARC project, initiated in January 1966, which aimed to establish whether distributing LC machine-readable cataloguing data to user libraries was feasible. Distribution on a trial basis began in October 1966 and by June 1968 about 50,000 cataloguing records for books in the English language were available in machine-readable form and had been distributed to the participating libraries (Gredley & Hopkinson 1990, chapter 3; Chan 1994).

The success of the first MARC trial encouraged the Library to proceed with distributing cataloguing data in machine-readable form on a larger scale. The original data exchange format which had been devised for the limited trial was revised in 1968 to become the MARC II format for monographs – 'the archetype of all subsequent MARC formats' (Gredley & Hopkinson 1990, p.77). The Library of Congress's MARC Distribution Service was established in March 1969 with the aim of disseminating bibliographic records in MARC format to subscribers. Initially the records in MARC format, distributed on magnetic tape, were only for recently catalogued English-language monographs, but this was gradually expanded to include other languages and other formats. In 1970 the Library of Congress set up the MARC Development Office to oversee and coordinate the development of this important new library standard.

The success of these experiments by the Library of Congress encouraged other national bibliographic agencies to try their hand. The BNB began work in 1967 on developing a MARC format suited to its requirements, and tapes containing BNB records were being distributed to libraries by 1969. Other countries also developed their own formats. By 1972 there were fifty-four subscribers to LCMARC, and by 1973, twenty-two institutions subscribed to BNBMARC (Gredley & Hopkinson 1990, p.82). The MARC structure was established as a United States standard by ANSI in 1971 (ANSI Z39.2) and as an international standard by the ISO in 1973 (ISO 2709). As they became used increasingly outside the Library of Congress, the LCMARC formats became known as USMARC.

As well as a proliferation of MARC formats developed for use by different countries, the Library of Congress was expanding the number of formats for different document types. MARC II, developed initially only for monographs, reached a fifth edition in 1972. Additional USMARC formats for serials, maps, films, manuscripts and music followed, and a preliminary edition of a USMARC format for authority data appeared in 1976. A draft edition of a format for machine-readable files was completed in 1979. The quantity of bibliographic records available in USMARC format steadily increased during the 1970s, assisted by several large cooperative projects in the United States, such as the RECON

(REtrospective CONversion) and CONSER (CONversion of SERials, now called Cooperative ONline SERials) projects.

By the 1980s the number of USMARC formats for different information-bearing media was causing problems by encouraging variations from the standard, for example variant tagging for the same bibliographic data elements in different formats. Separate formats for different media meant that cataloguers needed to be conversant with the differences between each format, and to decide which format to use where bibliographic items had characteristics of more than one medium. For example, for a serial issued on CD-ROM, should the MARC format for serials or the MARC format for computer files be used?

The Library of Congress therefore began the process of *format integration* – of rationalising these differences – by initiating a consultative process in 1985, and by revising many of the separate MARC formats so that the differences were minimised. This resulted in the USMARC format for bibliographic data being issued as a unified standard, applicable to all media, with consequent improvements in its ease of use. Format integration made for 'a single USMARC bibliographic format that provides the complete range of content designation for all types of materials and in which all information of the same type is identified by the same content designation' (Patton & Weiss 1993, p.11). Following this integration exercise, the USMARC format became easier and more economical to maintain, as did the systems which implemented USMARC.

The 1980s also saw a move from the use of the MARC format as a tool to produce catalogue cards and printed lists of catalogue records, to one which was used primarily to produce machine-readable records. Although using MARC records to produce catalogue cards already represented a substantial saving of effort, as local computerised library information retrieval systems were adopted in the 1980s, the MARC format's full potential started to be realised. It became possible, and then rapidly became the norm, for the local library information retrieval system to directly load the machine-readable records in MARC format and then manipulate, edit, or expand them to suit the requirements of the institution. The bibliographic utilities, national cataloguing agencies and some of the largest libraries became more distributors of MARC records in machine-readable format, than suppliers of catalogue cards and printed lists of catalogue records.

Dialects of MARC

The early history of MARC, with two variants developed only two years after its introduction, presaged future developments. This trend can be likened to the development of dialects of a language – in a reversal of linguistic history, American English was the base language, from which a colonial offshoot developed in the United Kingdom.

BNBMARC was developed in 1967 to suit the production requirements of the printed *British National Bibliography* using a computer. It was a single format, unlike its United States equivalent with several different formats. Its increasing use nationally was reflected in its change of name from BNBMARC to UKMARC, formalised in the first edition of the *UKMARC Manual*, published in 1975. By 1975 the UKMARC and LCMARC formats were showing substantial differences which resulted from the differing roles of the Library of Congress and the British Library, and from the distinctions between library catalogue (in the case of the Library of Congress) and national bibliography (as with BNB). 1980 saw the publication of the second edition of the *UKMARC Manual*, 'an integrated, unitary format, with some material-specific fields' (Gredley & Hopkinson 1990, p.103). By 1990 the British Library was distributing MARC records to 'some 200 United Kingdom libraries and other institutions ... for local cataloguing and housekeeping purposes' (Hunter & Bakewell 1991, p.193).

In the 1970s and 1980s, many other countries developed their own MARC formats following the success of LCMARC and BNBMARC. For example, there was CAN/MARC in Canada, AUSMARC in Australia and INTERMARC in France. Countries both large and small felt the need to develop their own national version. Reasons for developing a national MARC format owed less to the actual use of a format and more to reasons such as national pride. 'A national [MARC] format became as mandatory as a national airline', Janifer Gatenby noted (Gatenby 1987, p.5).

The proliferation of dialects of the MARC format meant that even by the mid-1970s their coordination was perceived as desirable. One of the primary aims of the MARC format, facilitating the international exchange of bibliographic records, was becoming more difficult as the divergence from a single standard increased. Concern about this led to the selection of the USMARC II format as the basis for ANSI Z39.2 in 1971, and as the basis for ISO 2709 in 1973. This concern to standardise and make the MARC format more effective as an international communications format also led to UNIMARC (the UNIversal MARC format) which first appeared in 1977 and CCF (Common Communication Format), also based on ISO 2709, published in 1984 (Gredley & Hopkinson 1990, pp.92-93). Alas, neither of these standards had much effect on the proliferation, and it was not until the 1990s that the trend started to be reversed.

In the end, economics forced this reversal. With publishing becoming increasingly international, libraries outside of the United States found the USMARC databases increasingly attractive: there were USMARC records created by American libraries for the items they were acquiring. Eventually they would abandon their own MARC dialect and purchase and/or migrate to a USMARC-based system. This avoided the need to maintain conversion programs and also avoided data loss. A national MARC dialect might be nice to have, but too much of a luxury in the face of the drive to cut libraries' processing costs. Thus in the 1990s the MARC dialects began conforming more and more to the base version of the MARC format – again an analogy with English, where American television programs have had a globalising influence on the language – culminating in full compatibility (that is, surrender). Both AUSMARC and SAMARC (from South Africa) gave way to USMARC in 1997, in the same year that the Library of Congress and the National Library of Canada reached agreement on full harmonisation of USMARC and CAN/MARC, giving birth to MARC 21 – a MARC for the twenty-first century. MARC 21 continues, in effect, the evolution of USMARC, and as such supersedes it. It is already the world's dominant MARC format, and looks set to become a genuinely international standard, especially with the demise of UKMARC, capitulating to its 'older brother' in 2002. MARC 21 is used in many Latin American, Asian and Middle Eastern countries, including Mexico, Brazil, Venezuela, Peru, Chile, and Argentina, Thailand, Malaysia, and China, Egypt, Saudi Arabia, and Kuwait (Radebaugh 2003) (see figure 10.3).

Standard	Country
USMARC	United States
UKMARC	United Kingdom
NORMARC	Norway
AUSMARC	Australia
MAB	Germany
CAN/MARC	Canada
INTERMARC	France
DANMARC	Denmark
IBERMARC	Spain
LIBRISMARC	Sweden
UNIMARC	IFLA
FINMARC	Finland
MARCAL	Latin America
MALMARC	Malaysia
PHILMARC	Philippines
CATMARC	Catalonia
Japan/MARC	Japan
KORMARC	South Korea
Chinese MARC	Taiwan
SAMARC	South Africa
SINGMARC	Singapore
New Zealand MARC	New Zealand
SBN/ANNAMARC	Italy
Indian MARC	India
MEKOF	USSR
PUL MARC	PR China
INDOMARC	Indonesia
China MARC	PR China
HUNMARC	Hungary
RUSMARC	Russia

Figure 10.3 MARC family members (in rough chronological order of establishment)

UNIMARC

The proliferation of different MARC dialects in the 1970s led to the search for a lingua franca, and UNIMARC was developed by IFLA to this end. As the dialects developed and matured, the differences among them widened. This meant that an institution which wanted to use the MARC tapes of an institution which used a different dialect of MARC needed to write a conversion program; moreover, this program had to be revised each time either of the dialects was revised (which happened fairly frequently in most cases). For organisations which received MARC tapes from several sources, multiple conversion programs were required. UNIMARC was thus developed as a translation format to allow MARC formats to be converted to other formats. Using UNIMARC, the institution only needs to maintain two conversion programs – one from its own MARC format to UNIMARC, and the other from UNIMARC to its own MARC format. The first edition was published in 1977 and a second edition in 1980. Also in 1980 UNIMARC was given a boost when several national libraries agreed to exchange records in UNIMARC format. The introduction to the second edition of UNIMARC noted:

> A number of national libraries including those of Australia, Canada, Japan, Hungary, South Africa, the United Kingdom and the United States have already agreed to use UNIMARC as their exchange format with implementation to take place early in the 1980s (quoted in Gredley & Hopkinson 1990, p.178).

A test of the potential effectiveness of UNIMARC in 1981 established, however, that more development of the format was necessary. This led to the publication of the *UNIMARC Handbook* in 1983 (Hopkinson 1983) which assisted in interpreting the format for use; this became the *UNIMARC Manual* in 1987, at which point the format embraced other media apart from books and serials. Since 1991, the Permanent UNIMARC Committee has regularly updated the format. A UNIMARC format for authority records dates from the same year.

However, UNIMARC's adoption was slow and has had relatively little impact. In 1986 only five countries offered UNIMARC output for their MARC records. ABN for instance, offered records to overseas subscribers either in the national format (AUSMARC) or in USMARC; it felt there was little incentive to implement UNIMARC because the records it wished to obtain were readily available in USMARC format, on which its system was based (Cathro 1988). UNIMARC's slow development and adoption has been attributed to the length of time required to write complex conversion programs; the fact that many libraries already had conversion programs for the sources they used; and that at the same time as UNIMARC was being developed another exchange format, the UNISIST (noted below), was also being developed. Another reason for the waning of enthusiasm 'must surely lie in economics ... Exchange of bibliographic data was only one of many activities that had to adapt to financial constraints' (Gredley & Hopkinson 1990, p.196). As one commentator has observed, UNIMARC 'could have been an international standard like ... ISBD ... or ... AACR2 but its potential has so far not been realised and, like the international language Esperanto, its practical adoption has been disappointing' (Gatenby 1987, p.5).

MARC 21

MARC 21 is currently the major version of MARC in use internationally, so we need to know more about it. There are, in fact, five MARC 21 formats, each one for a particular kind of data: bibliographic data, authorities data, holdings data, classification data and community information.

- *bibliographic data format* – Separate formats were initially developed for different types of material (books, archival and manuscript materials, computer files, maps, music, visual materials, serials) to accommodate the differences. However, this proliferation of different MARC formats had the opposite effect to what was intended, resulting in confusion rather than clarification because the cataloguer needed to know the details of several different formats. As already noted, the difficulties of applying a variety of increasingly detailed formats lead to the development of a unified (or integrated) format;

- *authority data format* – This format is used in the creation and maintenance of authority records, for name headings, uniform titles, subject headings and references to headings;

- *holdings data format* – This format is for data about holdings for serials and non-serials, including copy-specific data. Alternatively, fields in the bibliographic MARC record can be used instead of it;

- *classification data format* – This format is used in the construction and maintenance of classification records, which define classification numbers; and

- *community information format* – This format is used to share records that describe non-bibliographic resources that can be used to serve a community's information needs.

Structure of the MARC record

What is contained in a bibliographic record in MARC format? It is 'a sequential string of characters … with each character having a number or 'address' within the string' (Chan 1994, p.407). The MARC format consists of three main elements:

- *leader* – this element contains information needed for the computer to process the data in the rest of the record, for example the total length of the record, its status (whether it is a new or a corrected record), what type of material is represented (e.g., book, map, or sound recording), its encoding level (whether the bibliographic data is for a full, medium or brief record), and so on;

- *record directory* – this is a computer-generated index to the location of data in the MARC record (it is not supplied by the cataloguer); and

- *data fields* – the fields which contain the specific data relating to the document being catalogued. A few of these fields are control fields of fixed length with only coded information, but most of the fields are of variable length. Each field has a numeric tag which identifies the bibliographic data element (e.g., 245 indicates title, 260 is for the publication details, 300 for physical details, etc.). The tags are necessary because of the variable length format, so they indicate to the computer when one set of data elements has ended and another set is beginning. For further delineation, MARC uses subfield codes, consisting of a 'delimiter' character, and a letter or number – these tell the computer when one subfield has ended and another is about to begin.

Figure 10.4 illustrates the MARC fields in common use.

008	Fixed fields
020	International Standard Book Number (ISBN)
050	Library of Congress Classification number
082	Dewey Decimal Classification number
100	Personal name main entry
110	Corporate name main entry
111	Conference or meeting name main entry
130	Uniform title main entry
240	Uniform title
245	Title
246	Variant title
250	Edition
260	Imprint
300	Physical description
440	Title of series
600	Personal name subject heading
610	Corporate name subject heading
650	Topical subject heading
651	Geographic subject heading
655	Genre or form subject heading
700	Personal name added entry
710	Corporate name added entry
856	URL

Figure 10.4 Major MARC fields

A bibliographic record in MARC format contains more than the bibliographic data in the old card catalogue record (that is, the data as prescribed by AACR2 or other cataloguing standards). There is also, as mentioned above, control data which is used to enable the bibliographic record to function properly in the information retrieval system, as well as a great deal of coded information which provides additional retrieval mechanisms and also indicates how an information system should manipulate the records, for example, whether it should index a particular piece of data or not.

MARC records are structured in a fairly complicated way and need to be handled using specialised applications. Standard library management systems have such applications built in to them, but some are also available as stand-alone tools. A list of these is available in the MARC website, which in turn is part of the Library of Congress website (Library of Congress 2007a). They include editors, validators (checking to see whether the MARC coding is valid), converters (e.g., converting metadata in on MARC format to another), and so on. Figure 10.5 illustrates the relationships between a resource, AACR2 and MARC.

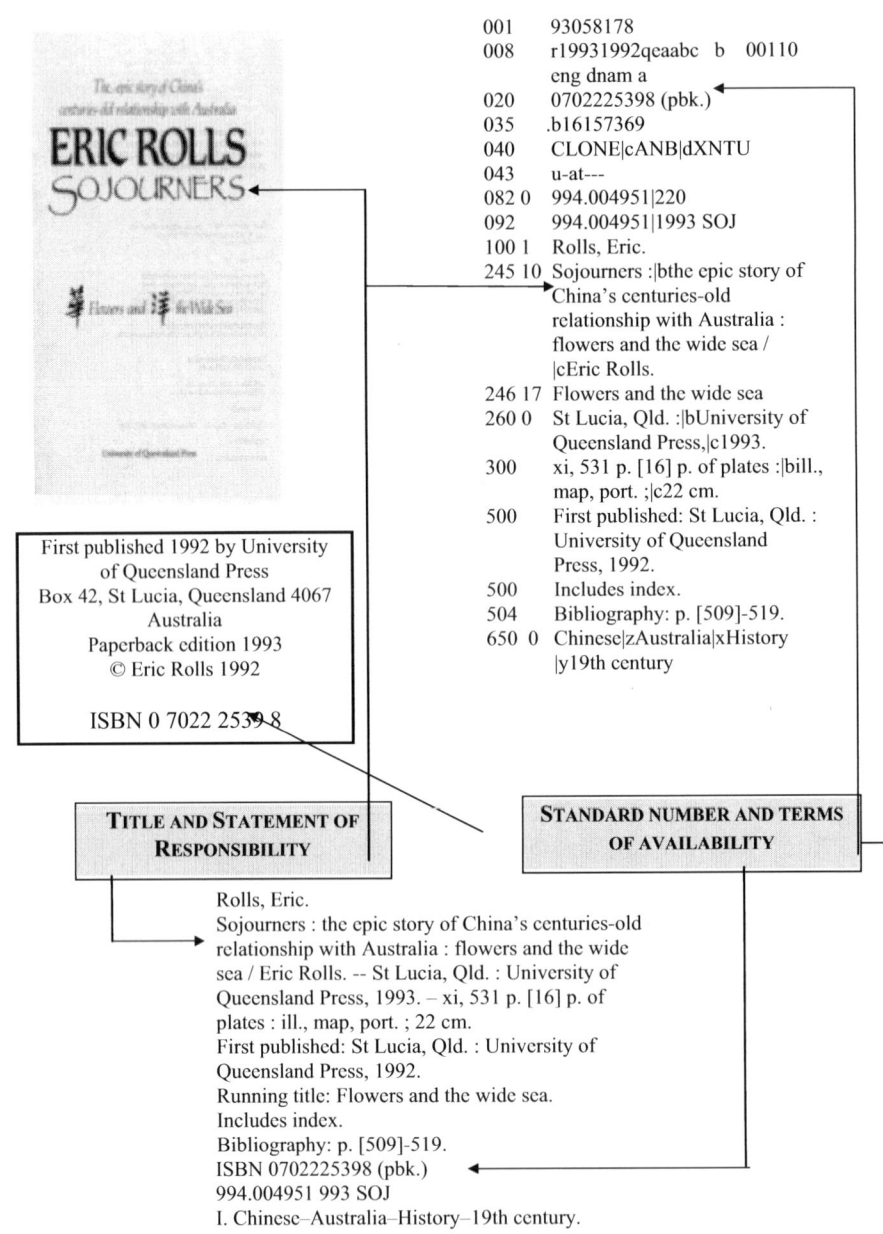

```
001    93058178
008    r19931992qeaabc  b    00110
       eng dnam a
020    0702225398 (pbk.)
035    .b16157369
040    CLONE|cANB|dXNTU
043    u-at---
082 0  994.004951|220
092    994.004951|1993 SOJ
100 1  Rolls, Eric.
245 10 Sojourners :|bthe epic story of
       China's centuries-old
       relationship with Australia :
       flowers and the wide sea /
       |cEric Rolls.
246 17 Flowers and the wide sea
260 0  St Lucia, Qld. :|bUniversity of
       Queensland Press,|c1993.
300    xi, 531 p. [16] p. of plates :|bill.,
       map, port. ;|c22 cm.
500    First published: St Lucia, Qld. :
       University of Queensland
       Press, 1992.
500    Includes index.
504    Bibliography: p. [509]-519.
650 0  Chinese|zAustralia|xHistory
       |y19th century
```

First published 1992 by University
of Queensland Press
Box 42, St Lucia, Queensland 4067
Australia
Paperback edition 1993
© Eric Rolls 1992

ISBN 0 7022 2539 8

**TITLE AND STATEMENT OF
RESPONSIBILITY**

**STANDARD NUMBER AND TERMS
OF AVAILABILITY**

Rolls, Eric.
Sojourners : the epic story of China's centuries-old
relationship with Australia : flowers and the wide
sea / Eric Rolls. -- St Lucia, Qld. : University of
Queensland Press, 1993. – xi, 531 p. [16] p. of
plates : ill., map, port. ; 22 cm.
First published: St Lucia, Qld. : University of
Queensland Press, 1992.
Running title: Flowers and the wide sea.
Includes index.
Bibliography: p. [509]-519.
ISBN 0702225398 (pbk.)
994.004951 993 SOJ
I. Chinese–Australia–History–19th century.

Figure 10.5 Relationships between resource, AACR2 and MARC

AUSMARC

AUSMARC, the Australian MARC format, was first published by the National Library of Australia in 1973. Its format was initially very close to UKMARC, but adopted features of USMARC with the publication of the AUSMARC authorities format in preliminary draft versions in 1983 and 1986, and a final version in 1988. The move towards complete integration with USMARC took a major step in 1991 with the National Library's announcement that AUSMARC would be completely phased out in the system that would replace the ABN. This announcement was followed in 1998 with confirmation that AMICUS, the software behind Kinetica, would not output records in AUSMARC.

AUSMARC resulted from a decision in 1970 to automate the production of the *Australian National Bibliography* and to generate and disseminate MARC records as a by-product of this process. It was because the National Library was to use BNB computer programs for this purpose that the initial draft version of AUSMARC, circulated in October 1970, was very close to UKMARC. Production of the ANB using a computer system began in September 1972. The first edition of AUSMARC appeared in 1973, and a second edition, incorporating minor changes, was published in 1975. A draft revision of AUSMARC which incorporated the provisions of AACR2 (published in 1978) and provisions for serials and non-book materials formats was released in July 1978 for comment by the user community. AUSMARC3, incorporating this feedback, was published in late 1979 (Cathro 1980). A strong element of nationalistic pride is present in a statement about this process:

> In Australia, the National Library has boldly led the world with the publication of a new edition of the AUSMARC books format, the AUSMARC Projected Media format in 1980, and drafts of Serials, Cartographic Materials and Sound Recordings and Music in 1981. All of these adhere to the principles of the new *Anglo-American Cataloguing Rules*, 2nd ed. The new books format was published before corresponding changes were made to the UK and LC formats.... . Therefore we, in Australia, have implemented these changes and new formats into existing systems and have done so without the benefit of overseas experience (Gatenby 1981, p.2).

How different was AUSMARC from USMARC? – for this is the key question in relation to AUSMARC's acceptance and widespread use, particularly in the 1990s. One reviewer of AUSMARC's first edition noted in 1974 the essential major problem with AUSMARC – that it differed from USMARC and BNBMARC:

> Each new format, while ostensibly MARC-compatible, differs in some way from its predecessors. Programs for processing LCMARC must be modified to handle BNB, and further modified to process ANB ... It is difficult to accept that all of these variations are justified either because they represent 'improvements' or because each country is so unique that its publications require significant variations to formats already in use (Jacob 1974, pp.196-197).

In this she was pointing the way to the eventual rationalisation of AUSMARC with USMARC/MARC 21 some two decades later.

The arguments for maintaining a separate Australian MARC format were identified in 1980 as:

- 'some national differences in record formats due to the purely national scope of some of the data' (Cathro 1980, p.56), for example, the United States copyright number found in LCMARC;

- PRECIS data in AUSMARC (this data was present because AUSMARC was initially based on BNBMARC, which accommodates PRECIS) – 'Australia could not use the LCMARC format without some modification' (Cathro 1980, p.56);

- historical reasons – AUSMARC is based closely on UKMARC;

- there is no place for consulting Australian libraries in the process of developing and maintaining LCMARC, which is firmly based at the American Library Association;

- UNIMARC's role will grow and lessen problems with data exchange, thereby lessening the problems which different formats cause; and

- the declining costs of processing MARC records will lessen the interest in and need to standardise formats (Cathro 1980).

At the same time as arguing for a separate Australian MARC format, the National Library was conscious that it could not afford to deviate too massively from USMARC, as this statement in 1983 indicated:

> very reasonable attempt has been made to prevent the gap between [AUSMARC] and USMARC from widening further, except where this would have violated AUSMARC's existing structure (Cathro 1983, p.10).

By 1987, there were a number of editions of AUSMARC:

- *Australian MARC Specification: Books.* 3rd ed. (Canberra: National Library of Australia, 1979)

- *Australian MARC Specification: Sound Recordings & Music Scores.* Draft. (Canberra: National Library of Australia, 1982 and 1986)

- *Australian MARC Specification: Projected Media* (Canberra: National Library of Australia, 1980)

- *Australian MARC Specification: Cartographic Materials* (Canberra: National Library of Australia, 1983)

- *Australian MARC Specification: Serials* (Canberra: National Library of Australia, 1983)

- *Australian MARC Specification: Authorities* (draft only, issued 1982 and 1986) (Gatenby 1987, p.12).

This may appear to be similar to USMARC before format integration, with its multiple formats, but unlike USMARC, 'the meaning of specific coding is consistent among the formats' (Gatenby 1987, p.7). In 1987 some of the major differences from USMARC were noted as:

- punctuation – AUSMARC does not require ISBD punctuation. The coding of some bibliographic data fields, for example series and uniform titles, is more like the coding used in UKMARC than in USMARC;

- the subfield coding of many fields is quite different from both USMARC and UKMARC; and

- the format is not as comprehensive as LCMARC – for example, it does not cover technical reports, machine-readable data files, two-dimensional representations (such as pictures), three-dimensional representations (such as realia and kits) (Gatenby 1987).

International trends in relation to MARC were having their effect on AUSMARC by the end of the 1980s. AUSMARC had been steadily growing towards USMARC but there were still sufficient reasons to maintain it as a separate format, although the attractions for the National Library to abandon its time-consuming maintenance must have been strong. These reasons included its structural strength (unlike USMARC there was no conflict in coding between different types of formats) and, more pragmatically, that most library information retrieval systems sold and used in Australia stored their bibliographic data in AUSMARC or were based on AUSMARC. However, by 1989 these reasons were not sufficient and the *AUSMARC Bibliographic Format* draft, which was widely circulated for comment, moved much closer to USMARC. Its two major moves in this direction were a single consolidated format and format integration. One consolidated format was given in place of the formerly separate publications for books, serials, cartographic material, projected media, and music and sound recordings, necessitating changes 'mainly to resolve ambiguities, inconsistencies and redundancies resulting from the integration of the formats into one' (*AUSMARC Bibliographic Format* 1989, p.1). The USMARC format integration process also necessitated some changes. AUSMARC needed to be compatible with USMARC so that data conversion in ABN, which received and distributed USMARC and AUSMARC records, was cost-effective.

In 1990 the National Library consulted widely through a survey asking whether USMARC should be adopted as the Australian standard in place of AUSMARC. This resulted in the decision to phase out AUSMARC3, to implement a fourth edition of AUSMARC and to make AUSMARC4 records available from the National Bibliographic Database (NBD) through ABN from January 1992 until implementation of a new software base. As noted earlier, AMICUS, the software behind Kinetica, does not output records in AUSMARC, leaving MARC 21 (formerly USMARC) as the only output option for bibliographic records procured from the ANBD. Australian libraries are now fully aboard the MARC 21 bandwagon.

Is MARC perfect?

It is generally acknowledged that MARC is not perfect. One of the most articulate of its critics is Michael Gorman, who has described the MARC format as something to be marvelled at, 'one of the Seven Wonders of the modern library world' (Gorman 1990b, p.v); but he cautions that we should not consider that 'everything about MARC is, and always has been, perfect. In fact, the MARC format … has many serious flaws that lie deep in its history and development' (Gorman 1990b, p.v). The brief outline of its history above has indicated some of the reasons why these problems have arisen. Other reasons commonly ascribed are:

- it is complex – for example, it contains much more detail than most libraries need;
- consequently it takes a long time to learn thoroughly;
- its structure is inflexible;
- it exists in different dialects;
- it is old-fashioned, being in effect an automated version of a manual catalogue entry; and
- it has not fully realised its early promise of cost savings.

Let us look in more detail at two of these criticisms. Probably the chief objection is that it does not take advantage of the new ways of manipulating bibliographic data which the computer allows: '[it] remains an automated version of a manual catalogue entry … Because of this, the question of whether MARC is the most suitable format for machine-based systems must be asked …' (Hunter & Bakewell 1991, p.137).

Its origin lay in moves by the Library of Congress to automate the production of their catalogue cards, and despite three decades of development it has not moved far from that basis. According to Gorman:

> [this is its] fatal flaw … The MARC format is not and never was a rethinking of the nature of bibliographic data…. . The order, nature and analysis of bibliographic data in MARC II (the first operational manifestation of MARC) sedulously followed the order, nature, and analysis of bibliographic data current in the Library of Congress in the mid-1960s (Gorman 1990a, pp.70-71).

The new formats for online metadata that have been developed in recent years seriously challenge MARC because of its relative inflexibility. This issue is discussed further below.

Another frequently voiced objection is that adopting MARC has not resulted in cost savings in the cataloguing process to the extent initially envisaged. Culkin, after presenting the results of a 1989 comparison of costs of cataloguing in the United States, concludes that 'the bottom line is that the primary and most obvious benefit that the invention of a standardized communications format was supposed to address has not been realized' (Culkin 1992, p.88). Reasons for this relate to its complexity, so that it takes considerable time to learn and to maintain, and also to its inflexible structure, resulting in time being spent to bend items catalogued to fit.

Despite these and other objections, many believe that MARC (and AACR2, to which it is closely related) is not beyond redemption, although some have called for a major overhaul (Heaney 1995). There have been several serious attempts to do just this, including those that led to standards such as XOBIS (XML Organic Bibliographic Information Schema), developed by Lane Medical Library, and MODS (see later in the chapter), developed by the Library of Congress. Meanwhile, there are still plenty of practitioners who do not see the problem with the MARC format itself, only its lack of application in the new online world, and that this can be solved simply by wrapping it up in XML – hence the Library of Congress also offers a MARCXML standard. Whether this turns out to be sufficient remains to be seen.

Other MARC-like formats

MARC is by no means the only bibliographic data exchange format that complies with ISO 2709: there are other MARC-like formats developed at the same time as MARC was being developed. This category of formats is largely made up of those developed by commercial indexing and abstracting services, such as the one developed by Chemical Abstracts (CAS). The two non-MARC exchange formats briefly noted below are both based on ISO 2709.

UNISIST

UNISIST (World Science Information System), a Unesco-sponsored project, developed a standard for the recording and exchange of abstracting and indexing data in machine-readable form. The outcome was the *UNISIST Reference Manual for Machine-Readable Bibliographic Descriptions*, first published in 1973 with a second edition in 1981 and a third in 1986. Also developed as part of the UNISIST initiative, and used more widely, was the *ISDS (International Serials Data System) Format* which bears a close relationship to the MARC format for serials.

CCF (Common Communication Format)

Another Unesco-sponsored initiative is CCF. Work began on it in 1978 and a manual was published in 1984 (a second edition was published in 1988). It was developed from existing international exchange formats with the intention of being able to handle bibliographic records from both libraries and commercial indexing and abstracting services, something which at the time of its development other exchange formats could not accommodate. It was adopted rapidly by several institutions, most notably the Dag Hammerskjöld Library at the United Nations headquarters in New York (Hopkinson 1991, p.173). Two offshoots of CCF were developed in the early 1990s: CCF/B for bibliographic information and CCF/F for factual information. CCF remains a standard implemented across a range of systems, especially in developing countries such as India (Chandrakar 2001).

Newer metadata formats

MARC remained the format standard of choice for most libraries until the late 1990s. It was then that some librarians went further than criticising the shortcomings of MARC: they advocated abandoning the standard in favour of emerging ones such as Dublin Core.

It is important at this point to remind ourselves of what MARC is and what it is not. It is an exchange format standard, but it does not specify how the content should be compiled within its record structure. Content standards such as AACR and LCSH have already been discussed in Parts II and III of this book. MARC, however, has been developed largely on the back of particular content standards, such as AACR and LCSH. Indeed, as we noted earlier, MARC has been updated in line with AACR revisions. As such, MARC is designed for librarians and library catalogues; it is much less designed for other information professionals and their particular files of metadata, which are often built according to other standards.

In the 1990s, museums, archives, records centres and other non-library institutions started moving their own metadata into online retrieval systems. However, for the most part, they did not see MARC as an appropriate standard for their systems, and developed their own instead. Apart from being seen as essentially a library standard, it was also, by this time, a rather old-fashioned one – in computing terms. Therefore, in 1993 the museum community established CIMI (Computer Interchange of Museum Information); in 1994 the American government officers created GILS (Government Information Locator Service); in 1998 the archival community established EAD to exchange information based on ISAD, instead of ISBD; and so on.

It was not long before a new trend began to emerge. Just as different MARC variants had proliferated in the 1970s and 1980s, so different non-MARC formats started to proliferate. In this case, the cause was not so much nationalism, as it had been with MARC development, but what one might still consider a kind of parochialism. That is, different information communities developed different exchange formats according to their own, existing content standards.

There is nothing necessarily wrong with this trend, however. While it may always be questioned whether a certain element of a specialist metadata format is absolutely necessary, it is still the case, even today, that information providers work with different users and different products. The functions of libraries have not yet merged with those of archives, museums, colleges, research institutions, government departments, business information centres, and so on. Correspondingly, their respective resources also need to be described and represented slightly differently, whether they are archival materials, museum objects, art works, music files in online databases, websites, learning resources, research papers, government documents, email communications and attachments, data in KM databases, business reports, and so on.

This trend has become something of an explosion over the past decade, with numerous variant format standards (often referred to as *schemas*) having being established for a myriad of purposes and contexts. Those who develop new metadata schemas are doing so *for* the online environment, and thus do so *in* this environment. There are many directories and discussion forums on the web covering these new standards (for example SchemaWeb), along with their official websites, and other websites featuring implementations, and so on. It is fast becoming an almost impossible task for the information professional to keep up!

There are two solutions to the problem of standards proliferation: one can translate or one can unify (Hider 2004). The main attempt at unification has been Dublin Core, and we will discuss this later. First, we should mention that the trend of proliferation has, fortunately, been matched by an intense interest in translation, that is, converting metadata from one format into another. Conversion programs, based on mappings known as *crosswalks*, are now in abundance; they have become much easier to create with the introduction of more flexible mark-up languages such as XML. For example, there are well-established crosswalks and converters between MARC 21 and Dublin Core (DC), MARC 21 and ONIX, DC and EAD, DC and UNIMARC, and so on, (DC, ONIX and EAD are mentioned below).

It has thus become critical for information retrieval systems to cope with all these possible formats by means of accurate conversion programs and thus secure *interoperability*, that is, the ability to work with other systems even if their metadata is formatted differently. The sharing of information resources between the different information communities has become not only possible but almost a matter of course in the past few years, and if they are sharing resources, then it also makes a good deal of economic sense to share the metadata for those resources.

It is not necessary to detail each new metadata schema here – it would take a whole book to do so and would in any case be out-of-date within days – but it is worth noting a few more of those most likely to last. We should bear in mind that some of the new standards are likely to be superseded before they impact in a serious way upon the metadata world. For example, IAFA templates were established in 1995, the same year as was Dublin Core, for the exchange of internet file descriptions; in contrast to DC, they are now almost forgotten (although they evolved into a format used in one particular project, called ROADS).

Dublin Core

After three decades as the primary exchange format for bibliographic data, MARC now has a challenger, Dublin Core (DC). This format does the same thing as MARC: it provides a format, or schema, into which a resource's metadata can be recorded. If two systems are both familiar with the format, then the metadata can be exchanged. In theory, Dublin Core could be used in a manual system, but its main function is to enable the exchange of metadata between different online systems. Moreover, it has been designed to function not only in automated library systems, but in other kinds of information system being developed by information professionals outside of the library community. Indeed, its main purpose is for use across the various information domains. In this respect, it stands out from the rest of the schema pack.

Dublin Core was established as a standard in 1995, at a workshop hosted by OCLC, which is based in Dublin, Ohio. It is called 'Core' because it attempts to cover the core metadata required by the various information professions for their respective resources. The format comprises of fifteen elements, which may be likened to the fields that are used in MARC – only that there are far fewer DC elements. These elements are listed in figure 10.6. Any metadata that cannot be defined in terms of the fifteen elements would have to be dealt with outside of the standard. For example, if the archivists required additional elements for their specialised purposes, then they could add on other elements to the fifteen core elements and produce an extended DC format.

Title	Creator
Subject	Description
Publisher	Contributor
Date	Type
Format	Identifier
Source	Language
Relation	Coverage
Rights	

Figure 10.6 The fifteen DC elements

Dublin Core is both favoured and disliked for the same reason. That is, it is designed as the lowest common denominator, a format that is community-neutral, but by being so, it does not structure metadata in the detailed ways which some of the specialists in the various information communities consider necessary. Indeed, it was not too long before qualifiers were added to accommodate refinements of some of the elements, as desired by the specialists. For example, the Description element was qualified by 'Table Of Contents' or by 'Abstract'. Similarly, the Subject element was qualified by particular controlled vocabularies, including LCSH and DDC (see chapter 6).

It is no accident that those working with Dublin Core choose to use the term metadata instead of bibliographic data. There are two reasons for this. First, they may wish to use a more community-neutral term: bibliographic data is seen as data which comes from libraries. Second, they may perceive the new form of metadata as significantly different from that which appears in old library catalogues. This is because the new metadata relates to digital objects, and what is more, can be *part* of these objects, embedded in their mark-up language (see below for a discussion of mark-up languages). Although Dublin Core can readily be used for metadata that is not attached to the resources they describe, it is especially suitable for embedded metadata. Indeed, some of its elements function at the administrative level, that is, they inform the computer how to manage the digital object itself.

Dublin Core has been implemented, either fully or partly, in a wide variety of projects, some of which are listed on its official website. Examples of extended DC formats include AGLS (Australian Government Locator Service), with 19 elements, and EdNA (Education Network Australia), with 23 elements, and the NLM Metadata Standard with 50 elements (if one counts qualified elements). DC is relatively simple to use, but it can accommodate sophisticated metadata such as controlled vocabularies, if desired. The standard has perhaps been most successful in two areas: as the basis for digital library projects, particularly for some of those involving non-library institutions, such as museums; and in efforts to organise the web, such the 'Librarians' Internet Index' (formerly 'Librarians' Index to the Internet') website. Indeed, DC enthusiasts have been developing software that makes it easy for ordinary webmasters to describe their own resources in DC format.

DC has thus established itself as a successful universalist metadata format. It was formally ratified by the International Organization for Standardization in 2003, as ISO 15836, and by NISO in 2007, as Z39.85. A range of application profiles and other related standards are being developed to support DC, which has close links with the W3C group, the nearest the internet has to a governing body. Much more detail about the Dublin Core Metadata Initiative (DCMI) can be found on its official website.

TEI headers

TEI stands for Text Encoding Initiative, a consortium of universities and other institutions set up to encourage the standardisation of digital texts to facilitate the sharing of such documents. The TEI standard is designed for scholarly texts, and as such has proved popular in the humanities and social sciences. Metadata is added to the digital text in the form of a header, the standard for which was influenced by ISBD and AACR2. It was established in 1994 (the initiative itself was launched in 1987), and has been employed in well over 100 digital library projects. There is a simplified version called TEI Lite. The standard has enthusiasts in both North America and Europe. An example of a TEI header is shown in figure 10.7.

```
<teiHeader>
<fileDesc>
<titleStmt>
<title>Assessing Information on the Internet: Toward Providing Library Services for
Computer Mediated Communication</title>
<author>Martin Dillon</author>
<author>Erik Jul</author>
<author>Mark Burge</author>
<author>Carol Hickey</author>
</titleStmt>
<editionStmt>NA</editionStmt>
<extent>NA</extent>
<publicationStmt>
<publisher>OCLC Online Computer Library Center, Inc., Office of Research</publisher>
<address>6565 Frantz Road Dublin, Ohio 43017-3395</address>
<date>1994</date>
</publicationStmt>
<seriesStmt>NA</seriesStmt>
<notesStmt>
<note> 856 7 $u http://www.oclc.org/oclc/menu/reschdoc.htm
$z For an introductory page to an electronic version of: Assessing information on the
Internet $2 http</note>
<note> 856 1 $a ftp. rsch.oclc.org $d ftp/pub/internet_resources_project /report
```

Figure 10.7 From the TEI header for Martin Dillon's 'Assessing information on the Internet'. Source: Pouchard 1998, Appendix A

EAD

Encoded Archival Description (EAD) is now an established standard in the archives community. Like MARC 21, it is managed by the Library of Congress, on whose website can be found its official home page. The format has a similar structure to the TEI header, comprising some 145 elements. It is most likely to be used in conjunction with ISAD (see chapter 3), the new standard for archival description.

CIMI

The CIMI Standards Framework included one of the most important schemas for the museum community. Although the Computer Interchange of Museum Information (CIMI) has ceased to function, its standard, which is, in fact, a customisation of the TEI header, lives on.

IEEE LOM

This schema, IEEE 1484 Learning Objects Metadata (IEEE LOM), has been applied to many repositories of online learning objects, and is thus an important standard in the education field. IEEE stands for the Institute of Electrical and Electronics Engineers, Inc.. A related, earlier standard is IMS (originating from the Instructional Management Systems project), which is also still widely applied.

GILS

Government Information Locator Service (GILS) is a standard applied by United States government agencies for organising government documents. It includes 88 elements and is used with the Z39.50 protocol. It maps to MARC quite well. Christian (2001) provides a good overview. The British equivalent is e-GEMS, while Australia has AGLS.

CSDGM

CSDGM (Content Standard for Digital Geospatial Metadata) is a highly specialised format, designed for the metadata of geospatial information resources, for example, digital maps. It was established by the United States Federal Geographic Data Committee. It comprises some 340 elements. Less heavyweight versions exist, for example, Australia's ANZLIC, with 41 elements.

ONIX

Online Information eXchange (ONIX) was finally established in 2000, as a product of a European project. It is now managed by EDItEUR, which is 'the international group coordinating development of the standards infrastructure for electronic commerce in the book and serials industries'. The standard may become the most important in the publishing industry since the ISBN, the foremost driver being the revolution of internet bookselling (Holdsworth 2002). Several of the leading publishers (e.g., Cambridge University Press, McGraw-Hill, Penguin, Random House, University of California Press) are already making their ONIX-based metadata available to libraries, including the Library of Congress (specifically in its CIP program, see Medeiros 2004).

MODS

Metadata Object Description Schema (MODS) was developed by the Library of Congress in response to those who considered MARC too cumbersome and detailed. It is based on XML, and is designed for use in systems that may also need to handle the MARC format, as it is based on a subset of MARC fields and thus maps very well across the standards. It is proving quite popular among librarians who would like to use a library-oriented schema, but do not see the need (and perhaps who do not understand) the complexity of MARC. It has also been used successfully as a switching format between MARC and non-MARC schemas (for example, by Libraries Australia in their harvesting of online Australian government documents for incorporation into the Australian National Bibliographic Database, see Missingham 2004). MODS now has an authority data equivalent, namely MADS – Metadata Authority Description Schema – based on the MARC 21 format for authority data.

METS

Yet another schema recently developed by the Library of Congress is METS (Metadata Encoding and Transmission Standard). This has been designed specifically for metadata about electronic publications in digital libraries. Additional elements of administrative metadata, detailing the structure of the electronic content, are stored in this format. Such administrative metadata is necessary for the management of these digital resources.

VRA Core

This set of 19 elements, together with various sub-elements, has been developed by the Visual Resources Association, based in North America, which represents art librarians and curators, and in particular those working in the cultural heritage sector. The standard is used in some digital library projects, and is designed to connect metadata for collections, individual works, and images of those works.

Which format to choose?

Given the large number of new exchange formats for metadata, only a fraction of which have been listed above, the question facing a new information retrieval system implementer is, of course, which one, or ones, to select. More specifically for librarians, the question has been expressed as 'Is MARC dead?' (the title of a panel discussion at ALA Meeting, July, 2000). Are those who advocate MARC's demise, such as Tennant (2002), correct?

If they are, it does not, in any case, appear to be a very swift death. MARC records continue to be created in numbers that continue to exceed records based on Dublin Core and other schemas. First, then, we need to consider the reasons why MARC still has many supporters, despite its cumbersome structure. Indeed, some librarians might argue that the MARC format is like the automobile powered by an internal combustion engine – although we may object to some of its characteristics (it causes air pollution, for instance) we find it very difficult to do without. We have to acknowledge that:

- there are hundreds of millions of bibliographic records in MARC format;
- these records are readily available (often at no cost); and
- almost all library computer systems currently on the market are still based, at least partially, on MARC.

There are, in other words, huge amounts of 'legacy' data, the value of which would be dramatically affected by a change to another format. As Michael Gorman comments:

> The irony is that we have a vehicle that has allowed an unprecedented level of international and national exchange of bibliographic data ... but that vehicle bears the same relationship to a true computer-based bibliographic format as a Model T does to a Concorde. Moreover, the very success of MARC has created an inert mass [of MARC records] that becomes daily more resistant to change (Gorman 1990a, pp.70-71).

Despite its old-fashioned Model T characteristics, we should be wary of abandoning MARC while many of the alternatives are considerably less well-established than MARC, with correspondingly less metadata and systems behind them. Most commentators (e.g., Johnson 2001) consider that, for this reason alone, MARC will remain relevant well into the future.

Neither is it the case that MARC cannot be improved, that it is a lost cause. It continues to have a large community of users on hand to aid its development. USMARC was simplified by its format integration in the 1980s; it became connectable to the internet with the introduction of the 856 field for the location (e.g., URL) of electronic resources in the 1990s; and has now been made more programmer-friendly through its MARCXML expression.

Another new feature that the Library of Congress and other libraries have taken advantage of recently is the introduction of subfield *u* to several other fields, apart from the 856 field. This is the subfield for the Uniform Resource Locator (URL), and allows cataloguers to embed hypertext links of tables of contents, bibliographies, and other bibliographic information into MARC records and thus provide improved OPAC displays for them. As Radebaugh explains, 'subfield $u in field 505 (formatted contents note), for instance, allows library users to double-click on a link displayed in an OPAC and be taken directly to an online table of contents. The catalog of the future is here' (Radebaugh 2003, p.44).

We should not exaggerate MARC's shortcomings and throw out the baby with the bathwater. Some librarians have jumped on the bandwagon and denounced MARC as far too complex and difficult to catalogue with (such librarians are normally not cataloguers themselves). However, what they sometimes confuse is the complexity of AACR and other content standards with the complexities of MARC. There are not *that* many MARC codes to master; MARC is not especially more detailed than many other coding systems.

Some MARC critics also consider the format unsuitable for non-traditional materials. To refute the idea, a collection of essays was published as long ago as 1990, demonstrating that the format could be successfully applied to a much wider range of materials than those formats for which it had been developed. Furthermore, it could accommodate mechanisms for subject access more sophisticated and more effective than the controlled vocabularies (such as the Library of Congress Subject Headings (LCSH)) traditionally used in libraries (Petersen & Molholt 1990). More recently, the MARC format has proved perfectly usable for organising electronic files on the internet, as shown by OCLC's CORC project, the database of which has now been integrated into WorldCat, OCLC's union catalogue.

Some of the critics of MARC may have failed to grasp fully the fact that MARC is a *format* standard, and as such a container for all sorts of metadata. It is not, in fact, a difficult exercise for a skilled cataloguer to fit anything into this container reasonably well, including metadata for the motorcycle once owned by Bob Hawke on the Libraries Australia database, referred to in chapter 3. Whether or not the metadata is the most effective for some materials is not so much a problem of MARC, as it is a problem of, say, AACR or LCSH.

With the crosswalks in place between MARC, Dublin Core, EAD, and others, perhaps we are, in fact, asking the wrong question: perhaps we do not need to choose MARC and DC, or champion another particular standard, but work on accommodating several of these standards. This means accommodation at the system level – ensuring that future systems are interoperable – and also at the human level – ensuring that metadata specialists are familiar with a range of standards and prepared to apply different standards in different situations – MARC may not be dead, but it does not need to be god.

In fact, this multi-standard approach is already a reality in many of the larger libraries and information centres. To make full use of these systems, it is not enough to be an expert in MARC. Metadata specialists are being hired on the basis of their breadth of standards knowledge, not just their depth of knowledge. In some cases, multiple standards are not only accommodated, but are actually mixed: digital libraries and resource access projects are now being built using customised schemas that borrow elements from several of the established formats.

Mark-up languages

Both digital resources and their metadata need to be read by the computers that download them. In the web-based environment, files are read and displayed with the help of mark-up languages. These are systems of codes that *mark up* the documents so that a computer's web browser can display them in the way that was intended, with various fonts, colours, and other layout features. The mark-up language that has made the world wide web what it is today is HTML, or Hypertext Markup Language.

However, the codes, or labels, used in HTML can also be used to identify and describe different elements of the digital objects. In this way, it performs a similar role to MARC: it codes elements for both identification and manipulation purposes. HTML includes meta tags; in other words, labels for metadata. They are available if webmasters wish to use them – though they do not have to be used.

Dublin Core was first introduced in the mid-1990s, when HTML was in its heyday. It played an active part in developing HTML further, so that its own format could be expressed through HTML. Figure 10.8, which shows the metadata part of an HTML document, expressed in DC format, indicates how this is done.

```
<link rel = "schema.DC" href = "http://purl.org/DC/elements/1.0/">
<meta name = "DC.Title" content = "A Dirge">
<meta name = "DC.Creator" content = "Shelley, Percy Bysshe">
<meta name = "DC.Type" content = "poem">
<meta name = "DC.Date" content = "1820">
<meta name = "DC.Format" content = "text/html">
<meta name = "DC.Language" content = "en">
```

Figure 10.8 DC metadata coded in HTML

This was not, however, the end of the story. The problem with HTML was that it did not allow for local definitions to be added, that is, one could not extend the meanings of its labels. As the web grew up, this became more of an issue, and SGML (Standard Generalised Markup Language) was seen by some as the answer. This standard actually predates HTML (it was established in 1986 as ISO 8879), but is much more complex. Nevertheless, for those who wished to develop their own metadata schema, it was much more convenient to work with than was HTML. It still forms the basis of standards such as CIMI and it was originally the basis for the TEI header and EAD.

Given the difficulties in implementing SGML, a streamlined version was published as the Extensible Markup Language (XML) as a W3C Recommendation in 1998. W3C is the consortium of computing experts that acts as the standards body for the world wide web, and has been responsible for the development of all the mark-up languages used on the web, as well as its protocols and other standards such as HTTP, URL, SOAP (an exchange protocol based on XML).

XML now underpins most of the important web developments, even though most of the web is still based on HTML, and most metadata schemas now have standard expressions in XML. Compare the Dublin Core metadata format encoded in HTML, in figure 10.8, with another set of DC metadata encoded in XML, in figure 10.9.

```
<?xml version="1.0" ?>
<rdf:RDF xmlns:rdf="http://www.w3.org/1999/02/22-rdf-syntax
ns#"xmlns:dc="http://purl.org/dc/elements/1.1/"> <rdf:Description
about="http://purl.org/DC/documents/notes-cox-816.htm">
<dc:title>Recording qualified Dublin Core metadata in HTML</dc:title>
<dc:description> We describe a notation for recording qualified Dublin Core metadata in
HTML meta elements. </dc:description>
<dc:date>1999-08-18</dc:date>
<dc:format>text/html</dc:format>
<dc:language>en</dc:language>
<dc:publisher>Dublin Core Metadata Initiative</dc:publisher>
</rdf:Description></rdf:RDF>
```

Figure 10.9 DC metadata coded in XML

Both SGML and XML have established several standard ways in which metadata schemas such as Dublin Core can be expressed; one way is through a subset of standards called Document Type Definitions (DTDs). Thus Dublin Core, and many other schemas (including MARC 21), have registered DTDs, allowing web documents to be encoded with metadata, as defined by these schemas, in a way that can be easily read by external applications.

Some Dublin Core advocates cite its compatibility with XML as a good reason for adopting it in favour of MARC. They should bear in mind, however, that MARC 21 can now be encoded in XML as per its MARCXML schema, developed by the Library of Congress. An example of how a MARC field can be written up in XML is given in figure 10.10. According to Scharf, the 'archaic communications and storage format of existing library catalogs currently keeps them segregated from other information resources on the web. Putting these catalogs in a more universally accepted format [that is, XML] should keep libraries relevant and accessible in the future' (Scharf 2002, p.23).

```
700 10 $aRutherston, Albert Daniel,$d1881-1953.
```

becomes

```
<data-field tag="700" ind1="1" ind2="0">
<subfield code="a">Rutherston, Albert Daniel,</subfield>
<subfield code="d">1881-1953.</subfield>
</data-field>
```

Figure 10.10 A MARC field in XML

RDF

All the metadata schemas expressed in XML should conform to the Resource Description Framework (RDF), if they are going to be favoured by XML developers. RDF is a standard framework for structuring metadata in XML. It does not favour one particular schema over another, just as ISO 2709 allows for various MARC and non-MARC formats. Developed by the W3C group, RDF is in effect the metadata part of the XML standard. It has influenced the work on the Semantic Web (discussed in chapter 15), and is said to be a key component of it (Berners-Lee 1998). The standard allows for relationships between web documents to be identified by computer, although it does not go as far, in this respect, as *topic maps*, which describe more complex relationships (Fitch 2002).

Namescapes

XML allows elements from different metadata schemas to be combined in the same digital object by means of another innovation, namescapes. A namescape is a qualifier that indicates how the metadata term is to be defined – according to which schema. In this way, customised schemas that mix appropriate elements from several established formats can be developed. This mix-and-match approach has been adopted by some of the newer digital library projects.

Other data communication standards

We should remember that many data communication standards have an impact on the exchange and management of metadata. For example, modern software is based on a whole host of such standards, including the mark-up languages noted above. In this book we are not interested in all of these, but we do need to note the set of standards for character sets and their codes. This has become a critical issue for those who work with non-roman scripts.

Chinese readers, for instance, wish to access documents in Chinese characters, instead of in a romanisation that does not express all of the information in these documents. The need for vernacular scripts to be part of modern information retrieval systems is even more pronounced in the case of other languages, such as Tamil and Thai, where romanisations are barely known. Of course, it is now perfectly possible to both display and index non-roman characters electronically, and some integrated library systems have been accommodating certain non-roman scripts, particularly CJK (Chinese, Japanese Korean), for quite a number of years. However, for bibliographic data containing these non-roman characters to be exchanged with other systems, each system needs to be based on the same system of character encodings. Again, a standard is required. The primary standard in this area is Unicode, which is what ISO 10646 is based on. Unicode is a very large character set that aims to be the universal character set for computer applications in general, not just for information retrieval systems. It also aims to cover just about all the language scripts of the world, even hieroglyphics. Its official website puts it this way:

> Unicode provides a unique number for every character, no matter what the platform, no matter what the program, no matter what the language. The Unicode Standard has been adopted by such industry leaders as Apple, HP, IBM, JustSystem, Microsoft, Oracle, SAP, Sun, Sybase, Unisys and many others. Unicode is required by modern standards such as XML, Java, ECMAScript (JavaScript), LDAP, CORBA 3.0, WML, etc., and is the official way to implement ISO/IEC 10646. It is supported in many operating systems, all modern browsers, and many other products. The emergence of the Unicode Standard, and the availability of tools supporting it, are among the most significant recent global software technology trends (Unicode, Inc. 2003).

However, some information retrieval systems are still not fully Unicode compliant. Some are still based on other character set encodings such as EACC (East Asian Character Code for Bibliographic Use) and GB (*Guojia Biaozhun,* the People's Republic of China national standard for character encodings), and a good deal of work remains to be done to allow metadata in non-roman scripts to become as usable as that which is available in the roman alphabet.

Before we leave the area of data communication standards, there is one other standard that looks set to play an important role in information organisation practice, namely RSS, or Really Simple Syndication (formerly RDF Site Summary). This is in fact a family of formats based on XML/RDF, that are not quite metadata formats in the same way as Dublin Core and MARC, but instead allow computers to identify and collect new pieces of information available from websites – in other words, they are designed to contain information about changes and updates to online information resources. RSS thus facilitates automatic syndication of web content: news sites, blogs, databases, and so on offer a RSS-based 'alert service' (feed); those interested point their RSS-based client software in the direction of these feeds and receive regular updates without having to manually access the sites. There are several ways in which this new standard may affect information organisation practice. First, it potentially allows catalogues and other bibliographic databases to *disseminate* their new metadata, rather than wait for users to log on to their systems and (possibly) find the metadata. Second, it makes it easier for cataloguers to keep track of changing information resources (what AACR calls continuing resources), which may require corresponding changes in their metadata. Third, it looks set to have a significant impact on the way information professionals – and a lot of other people for that matter – keep up to date with changes in their profession.

Computer hardware and other technical standards

Other standards greatly affect the ability of libraries and information centres to exchange metadata, but receive only brief mention in this book. Chief among them are the multiplicity of computer hardware and software standards which have been developed over the past decades to produce the networked world of information we have today. For example, at the basic level, standards which prescribe how plugs and cables connect to each other are essential.

Many technical standards not related to computers have been developed for library use. One common example, and an early example of a data exchange format, is the standard size of the catalogue card, established in the early twentieth century at five inches by three inches. Filing rules is another example.

Conclusion

This chapter considers some of the technical requirements which we need to have in place before we can exchange metadata between information retrieval systems and thus gain the economies (in terms of reduced costs and increased efficiency) which this provides. Alternatives have recently been developed which are threatening to replace MARC, CCF and other metadata exchange formats, such as Dublin Core and RDF/XML. However, the jury is still out. It is likely that no single decision will be made, but that several solutions combining different standards will become popular. It is also likely that all standards will continue to evolve and adapt to new technology, if they are to survive. Apart from adaptation, the key to a successful standard is that it is implemented on a large scale, as MARC has been for the past three decades.

CHAPTER 11
Arrangements for bibliographic data exchange

Previous chapters have examined many of the questions relating to content and format standards for metadata, in particular, what the standards are and why they are required. In chapter 10, technical standards such as MARC were examined. These standards allow for electronic exchange of metadata. However, in order for this exchange to be successful, those parties involved in metadata exchange need to establish a comprehensive agreement about how and what metadata is to be shared through bibliographic networking.

Hagler notes that the goals of bibliographic record exchange are:

- to gather and format bibliographic data elements for each document as soon as it is published, or even before it is announced; and
- to store the result in such a place and manner that any bibliographer, library cataloguer, or indexer can retrieve, select from, adjust, and use the data in any local file, for any type of administrative or information-retrieval purpose, in any form of output (Hagler 1997, p.171).

But the ideal is difficult to attain. As Hagler indicates, numerous barriers stand in its way:

- who should create the model record?
- who should be responsible for transmitting it to different categories of potential users?
- what is the most effective communication path from the agency which creates the record to the one using it?
- how should the cost of each resulting bibliographic service or product be apportioned (to indicate omission)?
- how can quality control be administered if responsibility for record creation is dispersed among different agencies?
- what priority should be assigned to pursuing standardisation where it conflicts with local service and administrative considerations? (Hagler 1997, p.172).

It is all very well to have standards for bibliographic description and other aspects of bibliographic organisation, and technical standards in place, but more is needed – widespread agreement in the library community to apply those standards and agreement on the mechanisms to exchange standardised records. For many decades libraries have agreed to participate in networking and resource-sharing arrangements. These arrangements usually involve compromise, especially to resolve conflicts between local requirements (such as institutional objectives) and the requirements of the network and its members. For example, the individual library often needs to accept cataloguing data which does not meet its own needs or standards completely, but which follow standards agreed to by all other participants in the network. Even more of a compromise, it may be obligated to create original records according to content standards it does not wholly favour.

Exchanging bibliographic data

The goal of exchanging bibliographic data has long been present in the library community. If every record were constructed according to the same standards, and if there were some way in which these standardised records could be shared throughout the library community, then every information resource in the world would only have to be catalogued once: everyone else who wanted a copy of that record could get it. If this system could be made to work, then the outcome would be greatly increased efficiencies in organising information, for cataloguing can be a time-consuming, skilled and therefore expensive process. But cooperation, even in these days of knowledge economies, is an unnatural act (Martin 1987, p.27), most especially because it is often perceived to compromise the integrity and independence of the individual library or information centre. As Paul Dunkin (quoting A. E. Housman) notes about the Library of Congress in relation to cataloguing in the United States:

The grizzly bear is huge and wild;
He has devoured the infant child.
The infant child is not aware
It has been eaten by the bear (Dunkin 1969, p.142).

Nevertheless, cooperation has been promoted and encouraged energetically and effectively. According to the Library of Congress, resource sharing is based on a number of fundamental premises which include:

- sharing of resources among libraries is necessary to meet library users' needs;
- the ability to share resources to meet library users' needs depends on the continued participation and willingness of libraries to cooperate;
- it is neither efficient nor economical for every library to duplicate the effort involved in certain functions, such as original cataloging;
- technology has facilitated rapid and efficient delivery of information, including bibliographic data about the location and availability of library resources; and
- networking promotes the most efficient and effective use of rapidly developing technology (*Towards a common vision* 1985, p.91).

These premises, although formulated for the American context, are no less valid for libraries in many other countries.

Bibliographic data exchange has a long history. Charles Jewett, librarian of the Smithsonian Institution in Washington, is usually cited as the progenitor of cooperation because he developed a union catalogue of all books in public libraries in the United States in the 1850s. One essential step in this task was the development of a stereotyped catalogue entry which could be reused (Piggott 1988, p.11; Dunkin 1969, pp.143-149). Others who have promoted the concept include Paul Otlet and Henri La Fontaine who in the 1890s initiated a comprehensive subject index to published knowledge.

A more long-lasting scheme, still running today, is the Cataloging Distribution Service provided by the Library of Congress. In 1901 it offered copies of its printed catalogue cards for sale, and only discontinued this product in 1997. Nowadays, instead, the service provides MARC files available via FTP, as well as various other related products, such as print and online versions of the Library of Congress Subject Headings, the Library of Congress Classification Schedules, and the Library of Congress Rule Interpretations. It is a service that has kept up with technology and offers the libraries a very important bibliographic resource – not only are its products of high quality and large quantity, they are nowadays mostly available through the internet, guaranteeing currency. Furthermore, LC's catalogues and authority files are now available free-of-charge to those libraries with Z39.50 clients, via LC's Z39.50 server. Indeed, it is now almost unthinkable that the cataloguing operation of a modern library in the English-speaking world could be administered economically without using at least some catalogue records which originate from the Library of Congress.

Other national libraries have also been serving the bibliographic needs of their countries' libraries, and of those beyond, for a long time. The Bibliographic Services division of the British Library has provided a similar service to that of the Library of Congress, most notably in the form of its product the British National Bibliography (BNB), since the 1950s (Piggott 1988, pp.14-18). In 1967 the National Library of Australia began a service which provided catalogue cards derived from the Australian National Bibliography (ANB). A pilot scheme for cards for overseas publications was implemented in 1969, and a full overseas card service, based on catalogue cards from the Library of Congress, started in 1970 (Catalogue Card Service 1967; 1969). Like libraries in the United States, most British and Australian libraries today acquire their catalogue records in MARC format through online and CD-ROM sources. BNB is no longer distributed on cards, while ANB is no longer published as an entity, although MARC records for BNB and ANB materials can still be obtained.

Cataloguing in Publication (CIP)

With respect to large-scale cataloguing distribution services, particular note should be made of the CIP (Cataloguing in Publication) programs. CIP refers to cataloguing produced *before* an item (most commonly a book) has been published. Often, the provisional catalogue record is printed on the item itself, so that libraries get both the item and the CIP record at the same time. The mechanism works like this: a publisher sends a proof copy to the national cataloguing agency or its agent, who catalogues it rapidly and sends the CIP data back to the publisher, so that it can be included on the book when it is published. Because the national cataloguing agency works from proof copies of the book, rather than the book itself as finally published, there are often discrepancies between CIP data and correct cataloguing, but the CIP record is nevertheless a useful basis for the full, updated record. The publisher benefits from the free advertising generated by early inclusion of their publications in the country's national bibliography, which is often used as a selection tool by libraries. An example of a CIP record from the National Library of Australia is shown in figure 11.1.

The Library of Congress started a CIP program in 1959 (Piggott 1988, pp.18-20); its comprehensive program started in 1971 and has since produced more than a million records, saving the library community considerable cataloguing resources (Library of Congress 2001). Although the National Library of Australia did not start its full CIP program until 1974, it is worth noting that, from 1946 to 1952, the NLA (then known as the Commonwealth National Library) collaborated with the publisher Angus and Robertson to produce cataloguing records from proof copies of books supplied by that publisher, and that these were then printed and distributed as catalogue cards to libraries (*Australian Cataloguing-in-Publication Program* 1976); furthermore, in 1953 Axel Lodewycks, at the University of Melbourne's Baillieu Library, described the 'self-cataloguing book', and in the same year Australian publisher F.W. Cheshire demonstrated that the idea was feasible (Lodewycks 1953; Lodewycks 1961; Lodewycks 1990).

National Library of Australia
Cataloguing-in-Publication data

Alexander, Stephanie, 1940-
Stephanie Alexander: the cook's companion.

     Bibliography.
     Index.
     ISBN 0 670 86373 4.

     1. Cookery, Australian - Dictionaries. 2. Food - Dictionaries.
     3. Nutrition - Dictionaries. I Title.

641.300994

Figure 11.1 CIP record from the National Library of Australia

Requirements for successful exchange

In order for the exchange of bibliographic records to be successful, certain requirements need to be met. These fall into two main categories:

- agreement on standards, and
- agreement on who takes responsibility for the various procedures which need to be regularly carried out.

In addition, there needs to be an effective mechanism for delivering the bibliographic records to where they are required.

Agreements about standards

Standards for exchanging records need to be agreed upon and adhered to by all participants in any scheme for exchanging metadata. Two kinds of standards are required:

- *content* standards for creating the bibliographic records (e.g., AACR2 and ISBD), and
- *format* standards for exchanging records (e.g., MARC).

Agreements about responsibilities

Bodies concerned with resource sharing and networking in the context of bibliographic control need to agree in considerable detail on their responsibilities in order to make the resource-sharing mechanisms work smoothly. These organisational agreements need to decide:

- which agency (or agencies) in each country takes responsibility for cataloguing that country's imprints, and
- which agency (or agencies) takes responsibility for disseminating bibliographic records from other countries.

The agreements fall into two categories:

- those needed at the international level, and
- those needed at the national and local levels.

International agreements: Universal Bibliographic Control (UBC)

The mechanism that has enabled the international exchange of bibliographic data among libraries on a massive scale over the past thirty years was the UBCIM Core Programme of IFLA. It was organised through a series of international agreements which ensured that an agency in each country (usually the national library) accepted responsibility for preparing the bibliographic records for that country's publications, and then sent copies of these bibliographic records to the relevant agencies in other countries. Those agencies then ensured that libraries in their own country had access to the records.

Although the programme closed in 2003, the principles behind it continue to be implemented by libraries around the world, with a new alliance having been established between IFLA and national libraries, namely, the IFLA-CDNL Alliance for Bibliographic Standards (ICABS).

The UBC concept is based on several tenets:

- that all documents should have an original bibliographic record made for them only once
- that this original record is available to anyone else in the world who wants it
- that this original record is based on internationally accepted standards, and
- that the people best able to catalogue the publications of a particular country are the cataloguers of that country.

The UBC Programme was formally established in 1974, but its origins go back to 1969, to a resolution made at the International Meeting of Cataloging Experts in Copenhagen. The programme's major achievements include the development of the ISBD standards and the development and promotion of UNIMARC, referred to in chapter 10 (Anderson 1974; Anderson 1982).

Requirements for UBC at the international level are:

a) universal recognition and acceptance that each national bibliographic agency is the organisation responsible for creating the authoritative bibliographic record of the publications of its own country; and

b) universal recognition and acceptance of standards in creating the bibliographic record, for the contents of the record and also for its physical form (Anderson 1974, p.12).

International agreements: Program for Cooperative Cataloging (PCC)

The Program for Cooperative Cataloging (PCC) was established by the Library of Congress in 1995, following the success of collaborative projects such as CONSER and NACO. PCC was initially envisaged as a North American program, but has expanded its vision to the rest of the world. While it is firmly rooted in the standards used by the Library of Congress, there is increasingly a recognition that these standards need to be negotiated with the other PCC libraries, including those outside the United States. The mission statement of the program is as follows:

The Program for Cooperative Cataloging supports access to information resources, with a focus on the changing needs and expectations of the end user. The Program achieves its goals through cooperative efforts to increase cost-effective creation, sharing, and timely availability and use of authoritative records. These records are created using cataloging standards (currently AACR/MARC based) or derived from other bibliographic files and resources according to accepted standards. The Program assists with the promulgation of standards, develops education and training opportunities for catalogers, and influences the development of cataloging and resource discovery tools in its support of record creation activity (Library of Congress 2007b).

As the Library of Congress is committed to the UBC concept (described above), the PCC might be considered as an implementation of UBC. PCC members agree to follow the standards set out by the PCC, which are much more detailed than those developed by the UBC Core Programme; indeed, they are appropriate for what might be termed 'elite cataloguing', performed by national and large academic and research libraries. PCC cataloguers are required to follow not only ISBD and AACR, but also LCRI and additional documentation such as the participants' manuals.

There are four PCC branches: BIBCO, CONSER, NACO and SACO. SACO is open to everyone who assigns Library of Congress Subject Headings and/or Library of Congress Classification numbers. Cataloguers can submit a proposal for a new subject heading or LCC number using a form available on the SACO website. NACO is the name authorities program, whereby participants enter their new authority records onto the LC/NACO Authority File, usually through OCLC (a major bibliographic utility – see chapter 12). NACO libraries can apply to join CONSER and BIBCO. CONSER is for serials cataloguing, while BIBCO is for the cataloguing of all other materials. Again, CONSER and BIBCO participants usually enter their bibliographic records onto the OCLC database, thus giving many thousands of other libraries immediate access to the records. NACO, CONSER and BIBCO require records of a high standard, and a library must first have its staff undergo a period of training and review before it can become a full member of any of these programs.

The PCC has a Policy Committee and a Steering Committee, each made up of representatives from major PCC libraries; there are various other committees and subcommittees (PCC 2006). However, the Program itself is run by the Library of Congress, with a small dedicated team coordinating training and carrying out quality control. On the other hand, this team is very much dependent on the assistance of experienced PCC cataloguers based in other libraries. Moreover, the Library of Congress is itself struggling to maintain its level of contribution, as cataloguing staff retire without being replaced. In June 2006, the Library ceased its series control efforts, despite this being a PCC activity (Library of Congress 2007c): the result is that other PCC libraries are now attempting to make up for the shortfall! It is clear that all libraries, even the Library of Congress, are now very much dependent on each other, and that cooperative programs such as the PCC are crucial to the long-term survival of detailed library cataloguing.

National and local agreements

Requirements for UBC at the national level are:

a) the means of ensuring that it is possible to make the bibliographic record of each new publication as it is issued (that is, by legal deposit or similar government regulation, or by voluntary agreement); and
b) the machinery by which that bibliographic record can be made, that is, the establishment of the national bibliographic agency which will:
i. establish the authoritative bibliographic record for each new publication issued in the country,
ii. publish those records with the shortest possible delay in a national bibliography which appears regularly,
iii. produce and distribute the records in a standard form (cards, machine-readable tapes, or acceptable alternatives),
iv. receive and distribute within its own country similar records produced by other national bibliographic agencies, and
v. create a retrospective national bibliography of the country's published output (Anderson 1974, p.11).

Other agreements may also be needed at the national level and at local (state or smaller) levels. Such agreements are accepted and adhered to by agencies whose primary function is to make available bibliographic records to individual libraries, or sometimes to groups of libraries. (Examples of such groups are noted in chapters 12 and 13.) Successful resource-sharing networks of this kind have in place agreements about:

- ownership of the records,
- legal and contractual arrangements among members,

- costs and charges to be made for services,
- sanctions against members who offend against the rules of the network,
- responsibility for providing technical (hardware and software) support, and
- responsibility for providing technical (cataloguing) support.

In addition to these agreements, successful resource-sharing networks have mechanisms in place to hear and act on the views expressed by their members. Examples of the kinds of mechanisms for this include:

- forums at which users can voice their complaints and needs to the network management, and
- committees which are responsible for monitoring standards and setting new standards.

Delivery mechanisms: sources of bibliographic data

As already noted, successful exchange of metadata depends on agreements on standards and on who takes responsibility for various procedures. It also needs an effective mechanism for delivering the bibliographic records to where they are required.

Copy cataloguing refers to the process of locating a bibliographic record created by another institution for the information resource being catalogued, then making a copy of that record, preferably and usually by electronically downloading that record into the local library information retrieval system (Bliel & Renner 1990). This process is made possible by the enabling mechanisms of UBC and by adherence to standards such as AACR2, ISBD and MARC. The bibliographic records can come from a wide range of sources, including:

- international and local bibliographic utilities,
- local vendors such as book suppliers, and
- the catalogues of other libraries.

The most common sources of bibliographic records for many libraries and information centres are the bibliographic utilities. The largest utility, by a long way, is OCLC, based in the United States. The key feature of most of the services offered by bibliographic utilities is that they are based on a large database of records, normally in MARC format. More detail about bibliographic utilities is given in chapter 12.

Some information centres also subscribe to databases of MARC records, either online or on CD-ROM. These sources can be especially useful for retrospective cataloguing projects (cataloguing or re-cataloguing materials previously collected). Examples include OCLC's *CatCD* and The Library Corporation's *ITS.forWindows* CD-ROMs.

It is of course possible that a library will not use bibliographic records created by others, at least not in every case. *Original cataloguing* is the process of creating a catalogue record from scratch. Because this process is time-consuming and expensive it is usually carried out only where a record cannot be located for an information resource, for instance when the item is of a specialised or very localised nature. For instance, the semi-published newsletter of the Hydroponics Society of Kalgoorlie-Boulder may not be distributed beyond that region, and so the Kalgoorlie-Boulder Public Library may be forced to create its own record for the resource.

Conclusion

This chapter covered some of the questions relating to organisational arrangements which are needed to allow effective metadata sharing and bibliographic networking. It examined the prerequisites for successful cooperative ventures in the field of bibliographic control. While we have noted some large-scale *distribution* services of bibliographic data, the most successful cooperative ventures are, of course, *two-way*. That is, not only do libraries download records from the Library of Congress and elsewhere, but they also have the opportunity to *contribute* records for the benefit of other libraries. The provision of this opportunity by many bibliographic utilities is, indeed, often the key to their success. These utilities are the subject of the next chapter.

CHAPTER 12
Bibliographic utilities

This chapter describes bibliographic utilities, which represent the largest of the library information retrieval systems. Bibliographic utilities are a particular category of information retrieval system, initially established to supply bibliographic data in MARC format, but now offering a much wider range of services. Many of the services they offer are based on their very large bibliographic databases; typically these databases are tens of millions of records in size. The largest ones are international in scope, although mostly based in North America, and have been an important model for many of the smaller-scale ones. In fact, the largest utilities, and in particular OCLC, have become very influential in the development of bibliographic organisation practice and standards. Throughout this chapter the five principal characteristics of effective information retrieval systems which were noted in the introduction to Part IV should be kept in mind, for they form the focus of this discussion of bibliographic utilities.

Chapter 11 noted the library community's long-standing goal of exchanging bibliographic data, and the long history of achieving this goal. Bibliographic utilities were introduced as one of the primary means through which MARC records could be obtained; that is, as a delivery mechanism for MARC records. However, they offer much more than this.

One definition of *bibliographic utility* is:

> a non-profit organization serving as a source of bibliographic data stored in machine-readable form, which data are available to those affiliated with the utility (usually library members) for such purposes as online cataloguing and interlibrary loan through a telecommunications network (*World Encyclopedia of Library and Information Services* 1993, pp.119-120).

This definition embraces the central features of a utility:

- it is a source of metadata,
- records are in electronic form (more specifically, in MARC format),
- the data is available for local library information retrieval systems, and
- the records are delivered to members using telecommunications networks.

Utilities also provide many other services, not all of which are based on the MARC record database. Examples include equipment purchasing services and preservation services. This chapter details some of the most influential and largest of the bibliographic utilities.

Bibliographic utilities: some history

Bibliographic utilities were set up initially in the early to mid-1970s to assist cataloguing operations by centralising the tasks and making them less expensive. The main feature of these utilities was a large MARC record database which was used to produce cataloguing products, typically catalogue cards. Later the output was in electronic form, such as magnetic tapes or diskettes with MARC records on them, to be loaded into local library information retrieval systems.

At first the utilities offered only cataloguing functions. Later, as their operators and their clients became more familiar with the new tool and its potential, other activities were offered from the MARC database. The most important of these were:

- enquiry functions – for example, using the database to answer reference queries;
- location information – for example, determining which library holds a copy of a sought document; and
- readers' advisory work – such as assisting the reader in the choice of a relevant work.

Later still, other services were offered, such as access to other databases, circulation control, and equipment purchase. However, the key characteristic of most of the services offered by bibliographic utilities remains that they are based on a large database of records in MARC format. A timeline of the development of bibliographic utilities up until 1999 is given in figure 12.1.

OCLC

OCLC, as the first bibliographic utility, made many mistakes from which its successors learned. However, OCLC itself has also learned from its problems and now occupies an extremely influential place internationally in the provision of MARC records and in many other areas of networked library services. OCLC was founded, as the Ohio College Library Center, by Frederick Kilgour in 1967. In 1971 its online union catalogue became available at Ohio University, which was the first of its member libraries to catalogue material online. Membership was expanded to non-academic libraries in Ohio in 1973. By 1976 the two millionth record had been input to the OCLC database and the number of members outside Ohio was increasing rapidly, reflected in 1977 in a name change to Online Computer Library Center. OCLC's database grew rapidly: 7 million records were reached in 1980, 13 million in 1984, 23 million in 1990, 50 million in 2003, and more than 95 million in 2007 (*The WorldCat database* 2007). These records have been produced by more than 9,000 institutions and are linked to one billion holdings statements! The figures speak for themselves.

OCLC has expanded considerably from offering only cataloguing services to United States-based libraries and currently offers a wide range of services to an international clientele. Its website includes sections for OCLC Asia Pacific, OCLC Canada, OCLC Latin America and the Caribbean, OCLC Middle East and North Africa, and OCLC Pica (which covers Europe and Southern Africa) – the regional offices are in the process of dropping their regional nomenclature, in favour of the straightforward 'OCLC', signalling how interconnected their operations have become, and the degree to which the library business is now a global activity. Altogether, OCLC claims that more than 60,000 libraries were using OCLC services and products, located in 112 countries and territories around the world.

Bibliographic utilities: some important developments since 1966

1966	MARC Pilot Project begins
1967	Ohio College Library Center formed as regional processing centre for Ohio academic libraries
1968	Library of Congress begins distribution of machine-readable cataloguing records
1970	Ohio College Library Center implements offline system for catalogue card production
1971	Ohio College Library Center introduces online cataloguing system
1971	University of Toronto Library Automation System (UTLAS) formed to extend automation initiatives begin by library's systems department
1972	Ohio College Library Center extends cataloguing service to non-academic libraries in Ohio
1972	BALLOTS system becomes operational at Stanford
1973	Ohio College Library Center expands cataloguing service to libraries outside Ohio
1973	UTLAS introduces CATSS online cataloguing system
1974	RLG formed
1974	MARC Applied Research founded; introduces MARCFICHE cataloguing service
1976	BALLOTS cataloguing service introduced to California libraries
1977	Ohio College Library Center changes name to OCLC Incorporated
1977	Washington Library Network (WLN) initiates online cataloguing service for libraries in Pacific Northwest
1977	UTLAS becomes an ancillary enterprise of University of Toronto, separate from the library
1978	RLIN cataloguing service initiated by RLG as outgrowth of BALLOTS
1979	OCLC signs first participating library outside of United States
1980	Informatics introduces MINI MARC turnkey cataloguing system
1981	OCLC Incorporated changes name to Online Computer Library Center, but retains abbreviation
1981	OCLC Europe office established
1981	Auto-Graphics Interactive Library Exchange (AGILE II) system introduced
1982	Brodart introduces Interactive Access System
1983	Library of Congress replaces printed National Union Catalog with microfiche edition
1983	UTLAS incorporated as private company owned by University of Toronto
1983	OCLC establishes Enhance program as quality control initiative for contributed cataloguing
1985	The Library Corporation introduces BiblioFile, first CD-ROM cataloguing product
1985	UTLAS acquired by International Thomson Organization
1985	WLN becomes Western Library Network
1985	LSSI introduces videodisk implementation of MINI MARC turnkey cataloguing system
1986	OCLC Asia-Pacific Services Office formed
1987	UTLAS introduces Japan CATSS implementation
1987	WLN introduces LaserCat CD-ROM cataloguing product
1987	GRC International introduces LaserQuest CD-ROM cataloguing product
1987	Gaylord introduces SuperCat CD-ROM cataloging product
1988	OCLC introduces CatCD cataloguing product
1989	UTLAS introduces Chinese CATSS implementation
1990	WLN becomes private, not-for-profit corporation
1992	UTLAS introduces Korean CATSS implementation
1992	UTLAS acquired by ISM Information Systems Management Corporation
1992	Open DRA Net introduced on internet
1995	OCLC Latin American and Caribbean Office established
1997	CATSS bibliographic utility acquired by Auto-Graphics; Impact/MARCit web-based cataloguing service introduced by A-G Canada
1997	The Library Corporation introduces ITS.MARC web-based cataloguing service
1999	OCLC acquires WLN

Figure 12.1 Timeline of bibliographic utility development, 1966-1999 (after Saffady 2002)

OCLC offers many products and services based on the needs of its vast library clientele. At the time of writing, its website outlined these products and services as follows:

- *cataloging and metadata*: 'We offer full-service online cataloging, simple copy cataloging, MARC record collections, offline cataloging, customised OCLC cataloging from your materials vendor, automated copy cataloging for materials purchased and custom cataloging services. We also administer the Dewey Decimal Classification system, the most widely used library classification system in the world.'

- *collection management*: 'Use our collection development services to meet your collection goals. Assess the strengths and gaps of your collection with our targeted analysis tools. Streamline your selection and ordering process with our automated materials selection service. Serve your culturally diverse community with easy-to-order, shelf-ready collections of non-English materials.'

- *digitisation and preservation*: 'Our digitisation, microfilm and archival services are designed to protect and share your collections. Manage your special collections, or turn to the skilled staff at our preservation centers.'

- *econtent*: 'Enhance your collections with eContent from NetLibrary (eBooks, eAudiobooks, eJournals and databases), plus full-text electronic journals and a variety of online reference databases.'

- *reference*: 'Through FirstSearch, we offer online access to full-text documents, abstracts, indices and WorldCat, the world's most powerful bibliographic database. We also partner with the Library of Congress to provide a comprehensive virtual reference service.'

- *Resource sharing*: 'Create, send and track interlibrary loan requests with WorldCat Resource Sharing. Take users from an article citation in WorldCat to the full-text version with WorldCat Link Manager, an OpenURL linkng and listing service. And our ILL management system ILLiad helps high-productivity libraries streamline their processes.'

Many, though not all, of the services and products mentioned above are based on OCLC's primary asset – it's bibliographic database and union catalogue, called WorldCat. Not only is it massively popular as a source of records for cataloguers, but it also forms the basis of a hugely successful interlibrary loan (ILL) and document delivery service. Between July 2001 and June 2002, a staggering 8.9 million interlibrary loans were arranged through OCLC's ILL system, ILLiad. It is by far the most successful ILL system in the world.

These services rely on a positive, collaborative culture among its member libraries that OCLC has been at pains to promote over the past three decades. Those libraries which contribute records and resources – and there are many thousands of them – are rewarded through discounts and special privileges.

The WorldCat database now contains not only bibliographic and holdings data, but also links to a rich source of digital resources. More than 400 languages are represented on WorldCat, and the full range of resource formats: books, serials, sound recordings, audiovisual media, scores, maps, manuscripts, electronic resources. The database includes records loaded from many of the major cataloguing agencies, including the Library of Congress, the United States National Library of Medicine, the United States National Agricultural Library, the United States Government Printing Office, the British Library, the National Library of Canada, Casalini Libri (Italy), and the national libraries of Australia and New Zealand.

MARC records can be downloaded from WorldCat in a number of ways. The circumstances of the libraries using (or potentially using) OCLC's services vary enormously, so it is important for OCLC to offer such flexibility. WorldCat records can be downloaded from its CD-ROM product, CatCD, or via its Z39.50 server, or received as files via FTP, or by using its own cataloguing software, Connexion, which can connect to the OCLC server through the internet or through a dedicated line. The Connexion application can be downloaded onto a local PC and used as a client, or it can be used through a standard web browser. The software has been developed in tandem with WorldCat's migration to a new platform, which is based on Unicode, thus allowing cataloguers to input roman and non-roman scripts in the same interface (previously OCLC offered a special application for CJK cataloguing). It also allows metadata to be input in Dublin Core format, as well as MARC, and has other features that facilitate the description of online resources. Furthermore, the client version offers a 'batch cataloguing' facility, so that multiple records can be searched for and downloaded in one go. For those with compliant library systems, records can be downloaded in real time through TCP/IP. The software continues to be enhanced, according to the wish lists of its many users.

Given the importance of WorldCat to OCLC's business, it is not surprising that OCLC has been in the forefront of heading off the challenge from Google and other search engines to the traditional library catalogue. OCLC's solution can be summed up as, 'if you can't beat them, join them.' In other words, the aim is to make WorldCat part of the web. Thus OCLC has a vision of WorldCat becoming a digital library in its own right, and not just a bibliographic database. To this end, it is doing all it can to increase the number of records in WorldCat that represent, and link to, online resources (Dean 2002). It has also taken a great leap forward by opening up WorldCat to *all* web users, not just librarians: the database is now freely accessible through the web at the WorldCat.org home page (figure 12.2). Furthermore, it has formed an alliance with Google, whereby subscribed users can search (some of) WorldCat as part of their Google search. The object of this 'Open WorldCat' program is clear: to make the database as accessible as possible. In fact, WorldCat contents are now harvested by several prominent web services, including Amazon.com, Ask.com, ERIC, Google, Google Scholar, Google Books, and Yahoo! Search.

Perhaps the most innovative service that OCLC has recently launched is WorldCat.org. As noted, this is the web's gateway to the whole WorldCat database, but it is even more than this. The service allows libraries to insert a search box into their own website, which provides the same access to WorldCat and also highlights those resources listed in results sets available in the local library. WorldCat.org thus looks set to bring library collections to web users in a revolutionary new way. Users can even add their own reviews of items through a mechanism similar to that offered by Amazon.com.

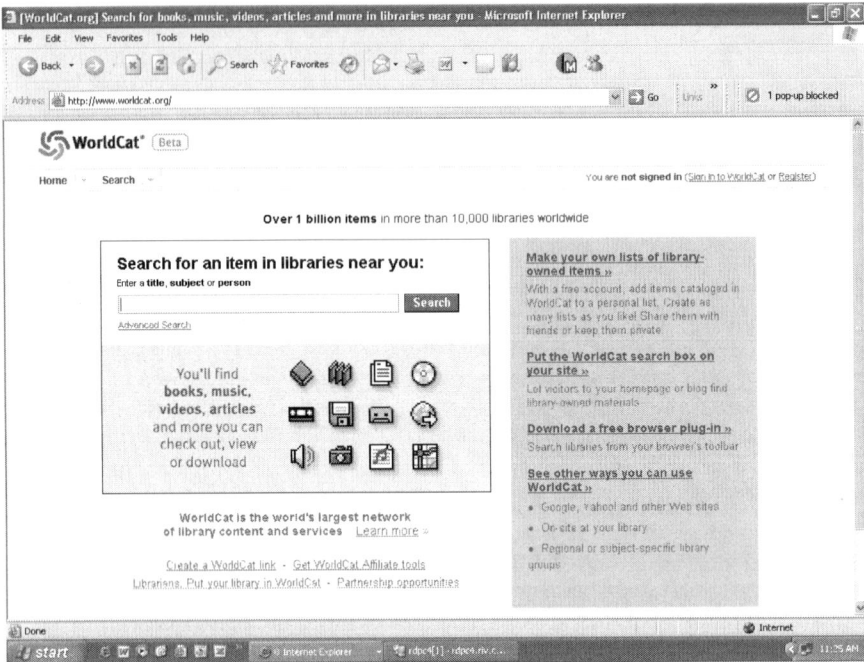

Figure 12.2 OCLC's WorldCat.org home page (accessed 12 December 2007)

This is not the place to detail all of OCLC's products and services, but it is worth highlighting a few others to demonstrate that the utility is not simply about bibliographic records. Another major area of library activity, namely reference work, has benefited from OCLC's FirstSearch service, which provides access through a single search interface to a wide range of quality reference databases. It is easy for library patrons, as well as professionals, to use, offering three levels of interface (basic, advanced and expert) – another example of OCLC's commitment to accommodating the needs of all its users. Also in the reference area, OCLC's virtual reference service, QuestionPoint, is gradually building up a 'knowledge base' of answers to users' questions that can be utilised by (subscribing) reference librarians around the world. In other words, to use traditional library parlance, it allows for the sharing of *vertical files*. It shall be interesting to see whether this service will develop a database as significant as WorldCat. Two factors might make this 'reference utility' less successful than OCLC's bibliographic utility. First, libraries probably experience less overlap in their reference questions than they do in their acquisitions, making the economic value of cooperation more dubious. Second, while a fact-retrieval system may be a practical tool for many reference situations, facts are often best put into their documentary (that is, bibliographic) context, which means that the patron might like actual documents to further explore his or her question, and not merely a direct answer.

Despite the many success stories that OCLC has been able to proclaim, it is not without its critics. One of the charges levelled against OCLC since its earlier years has been that it had a 'dirty' database; that is, there were many duplicate records of doubtful quality. This can cause problems because the user of the cataloguing service is faced with a choice of several different records for the same bibliographic item. OCLC has carried out regular programs aimed at reducing the number of duplicates, such as checking all headings in the bibliographic file against the authority file; participating in the CONSER (Cooperative Online Serials) project which aims to improve the quality of cataloguing records for serials; and developing the Enhance program which allows selected participants to correct or improve records directly rather than requesting OCLC to make the changes (Bliel & Renner 1990). Nevertheless, complaints about records are still a regular feature of the OCLC users' listservs. In this respect, OCLC might be regarded as a victim of its own success. As the contingent of contributing libraries becomes ever larger, so too does the amount of substandard cataloguing. It is the nature of cataloguing that not all of it can be corrected by machine (otherwise it would be done by machine in the first place, and not by cataloguers), yet OCLC's resources for manual quality control efforts are relatively small.

OCLC in Australia

Australian librarians were interested in OCLC almost from its inception and in 1974 the feasibility of an Australian link to OCLC was investigated. A rough cost estimate was presented at a 1974 seminar on OCLC attended by its founder and director, Frederick Kilgour: if 360,000 books were catalogued using OCLC, the annual cost of the system online would be $720,000 'plus the cost of printed cards'. It would initially be available only in state capitals (*OCLC Link Proposal* 1974). The seminar was the occasion of 'the first link from Australia to … Columbus' (Columbus, Ohio, the base of OCLC) (Peake 1996, p.5). A 1975 visit to OCLC by Dorothy Peake resulted in a detailed report which paid special attention to factors she believed to be of significance to Australian libraries. It concluded that the Australian link to OCLC is technically feasible, and that: 'Australian systems staff could, however, gain invaluable experience … [from OCLC]. Australia needs expertise in this area if satisfactory network developments are to take place. This … is perhaps the best contribution that OCLC can make to Australian network developments' (Peake 1976, pp.40-41).

Cost, rather than technical feasibility, appears to have been the main concern about using OCLC in Australia. A detailed study published in 1976 examined the hypothetical cost for the La Trobe University Library. It concluded that reducing costs by using OCLC would be unlikely, but that increasing the productivity of cataloguing staff was probable (Stecher 1976).

The introduction of the MIDAS service offered by the Australian national telecommunications provider offered the prospect of cheaper communications costs and a 1978 study investigated the feasibility of using MIDAS for online access to OCLC. The problem until then was the cost of a leased line ($200,000 per year) and an unhelpful time difference between Australia and the United States which resulted in only four to five hours daily when OCLC was accessible during Australian business hours. Dial-up access through MIDAS proved more economical, and hit rates were found to be high. Further detailed investigation was recommended (Gatenby, Rogerson & Peake 1978).

In 1979 MIDAS was again used to connect to OCLC to supplement AMRS records, this time searching for older material including serials and audiovisual titles. The small sample size allowed limited conclusions to be drawn: ' At best one can say that it would be worth our while exploring OCLC deeper because on the basis of this preliminary search there is every indication that searches would be successful at least fifty per cent of the time regardless of the age, languages, subject matter or place of publication of the item' (Dobrovits & O'Mara 1979, p.6).

Interest continued at a high level during the late 1970s and early 1980s, as indicated by reports such as Marta Chiba's on visits to OCLC, RLIN and WLN in 1980 (Chiba 1982). In the late 1980s reports started to appear of OCLC use as a normal part of cataloguing procedures, or for special projects. OCLC's CJK service was in use at the Australian National University Library in 1988 (OCLC/CJK 1990). Also in 1988 OCLC announced that it had: 'entered into a record exchange agreement with National Library of Australia in September, 1988. In addition, by this agreement, National Library of Australia and users of Australian Bibliographic Network (ABN) can use the OCLC database for retrospective conversion' (Wang 1992).

Other users of OCLC services have also written of their experiences. Dial-up access to OCLC for music cataloguing was investigated by CAVAL in 1988 (Bourke 1992, p.24). Three libraries (Sydney Conservatorium, State Library of Queensland, and University of Western Australia Library) were using the CAT CD450 *Music Cataloging Collection* in 1991. All reported a much higher hit rate for music than with UNILINC or ABN – 30 per cent compared with 75–95 per cent for music on CAT CD (OCLC CAT CD450 1992). Another specialist offering from OCLC, its CJK service, was investigated in detail and adopted by the University of Melbourne Library (Hu 1990).

OCLC's services are important for Australian libraries for several reasons:

- OCLC's huge database is a great source of MARC records – hit rates as high as 98–99 per cent for mainstream English language monographs were reported in 1993, although only 20 per cent for Eastern European titles (Martin 1996a, p.167); similar rates can still be expected today;
- it is strong in CJK records, of increasing importance to Australian libraries;
- it has other subject strengths, for example music; and
- it is now available 24 hours per day, with only a small amount of regular scheduled downtime (at the weekend).

With the arrival of the internet, telecommunication costs have become a minor consideration for Australian libraries, and OCLC services are now used by many cataloguing departments on a routine basis, either directly, or through Libraries Australia.

How does OCLC measure up to the five characteristics of effectiveness noted at the start of this chapter? The system must:

- provide information to its user of the highest possible accuracy – although OCLC has had a reputation for a 'dirty' database in earlier years, large-scale clean-up programs have mitigated against this;

- be as easy as possible to use, consistent with being as accurate as possible – again, recent implementations of user-friendly front-ends such as Connexion and FirstSearch have gone a long way to address criticisms in this area;

- use standards for organising information – the OCLC databases are constructed based on an array of current international standards, in whose development OCLC often plays a major role; and

- be cost-effective – high hit rates compensate for relatively high charges set by OCLC.

It is a fairly safe bet that OCLC is here to stay, not just as the dominant bibliographic utility, but as a key player in the world of information organisation and provision.

RLIN

RLIN, the utility owned by the Research Libraries Group (RLG), was a major rival of OCLC until they merged in 2006. The millions of records in the RLG Union Catalog have now mostly been migrated over to OCLC's WorldCat database (which explains the recent surge in WorldCat numbers). It might be said that this event cements OCLC's domination of the bibliographic record supply market. Nevertheless, it is worth examining the contributions made by RLIN and other ex-utilities, for along with OCLC they have shaped the bibliographic organisation practice of today.

RLIN was founded in 1978 as the Research Libraries Information Network by the Research Libraries Group (RLG) in Stanford, California. It was based on the BALLOTS (Bibliographic Automation of Large Library Operation using a Times Sharing System) library information retrieval system, developed by Stanford University from 1967 and was acquired by RLG in 1977. RLIN's genesis as a research library-oriented information retrieval system means that its strength lied in its MARC records for specialised materials. This was enhanced by its structure, which allowed each member to maintain its own local data within the larger total database, and for this data to be displayed with other versions of the same record. Many records for the same item might be considered a disadvantage for low-level copy cataloguing, but is a definite boon for specialised materials because cataloguers can select the record which most closely meets their requirements.

The name 'RLIN' came to refer to a particular interface and system for viewing and working with the RLG databases, consisting of the *RLG Union Catalog*, and other important database such as ESTC (the *English Short Title Catalogue*), the *Hand Press Book Database* and *SCIPIO: Art and Rare Book Sales Catalogs*. RLIN also provided a direct link (through Z39.50) to the *CURL Union Catalogue*, the *Deutsche Bibliothek Database* and the National Library of Australia.

The main RLG bibliographic database consisted of eight files: Books, Serials, Maps, Computer Files, Visual materials, Recordings (sound), Scores and Archival and Mixed Collections. By 2006, there were altogether around 50 million unique records – a number surpassed only by OCLC WorldCat. In terms of absolute records, it was actually larger than WorldCat, as it included local, variant (i.e., non-unique) records for different libraries. RLG's academic orientation meant that its database had many more records for items in non-English languages and non-book formats than WorldCat: it had two million records for microforms, for instance. It also had three million records for items published before 1900. Nevertheless, there was substantial overlap between the RLIN and OCLC databases, which is not surprising, since many of their largest contributors have been the same institutions, including the Library of Congress, the National Library of Medicine, the United States Government Printing Office, CONSER, and the British Library.

Several of the RLIN system's capabilities were developed in response to the specialised needs of RLG's owner-members. For example, one of RLIN's strengths was its multi-script capabilities. In the mid-1990s RLG claimed that 'RLIN is the only online catalog to support all the scripts used in the LC-designated JACKPHY languages (Japanese, Arabic, Chinese, Korean, Persian, Hebrew, and Yiddish) – where romanisation fails to provide adequate bibliographic identification and access – plus Cyrillic' (*RLG Services for Information* 1994). Unlike OCLC, RLIN also offered subject searching from an early date; indeed its strong search capabilities were considered, from inception, to be a major advantage.

Subsequent RLG services indicated a move towards greater client focus, for example the introduction of Eureka as a user-friendly web-based interface to the RLG databases. An automated copy cataloguing service (Marcadia) based on users' brief records was also introduced. Like OCLC, RLG branched out into other library markets, developing software for ILL and document delivery, for example. It offered a digital preservation service, and had a notable image database called the AMICO [Art Museum Image Consortium] Library, containing more than 100,000 representations of works of art, along with metadata, from leading art museums.

Although RLG had considerably fewer members than OCLC, different membership requirements makes direct comparison unhelpful. Both shared a strong growth rate, as did their databases. RLG began in 1979 with four owner-members. By 1982 it had grown to twenty-nine owner-members, and in 1988 there were thirty-six owner-members. In 2003 RLG had more than 160 member institutions, covering many of the major research libraries in the United States (including the Library of Congress), and also some key research institutions around the world, such as the British Library, the national libraries of France, New Zealand, Scotland, Spain, Switzerland and Wales, the Direction des Archives de France, the national archives of Australia and the Netherlands, Imperial College, Kings College and the London School of Economics, the International Institute of Social History in the Netherlands, the National Gallery of Art in London, the National Gallery of Canada, and the Wellcome Library for the History and Understanding of Medicine, London. However, the number of contributors to and users of the RLG databases was very much greater.

RLG had strong ties with the archives and museums communities, and developed online services that catered specifically for the needs of archivists and curators. Its Archival Resources service was built on the EAD standard (see chapter 10), which RLG helped to develop.

RLIN in Australia

Until 1995 RLIN use in Australia was limited to occasional low-volume use as a source for specialised bibliographic records. The Australian National Gallery in Canberra reported that it had used RLIN since 1985, not only to verify references, but also as a source of catalogue records and to verify name headings (Bruce 1989). The Australia's Book Heritage Resources Project, which recorded bibliographic records for books printed before 1801 held in Australian libraries, regularly searched RLIN for cataloguing records on which to base the records it contributed to ABN (Morrison 1993). The University of Melbourne Library also explored RLIN as a possible source for CJK records, and compared RLIN's CJK services with those available from OCLC. However, it decided in favour of OCLC (Hu 1990).

RLIN considerably raised its profile in Australia in 1995 when it provided access via Eureka to the RLIN bibliographic database, plus eight specialist files. Thirty-eight Australian university libraries contracted for access, through CAUL, for a six-month trial. In 1996 the State Library of New South Wales assessed RLIN's suitability as a source of catalogue records to supplement the records available from ABN, and to determine the value of importing records for books, music CDs and videos from RLIN to ABN. Access to RLIN was using the internet via telnet. One major issue identified in the trial was the time it took for a record selected from the RLIN database to appear on the ABN database. The report concluded that it was a feasible procedure, with some provisos, particularly the need to streamline some ABN procedures (Turner & Crowe 1996).

Access to the *RLG Union Catalog* increased markedly when Kinetica (formerly ABN and now Libraries Australia) made the database available through a Z39.50 link (conversely, the National Library of Australia offered its catalogue to RLG members via Z39.50). A 2000 report from Kinetica put the proportion of transactions involving the RLG database at five per cent of total Kinetica cataloguing (National Library of Australia 2000). Used as a second or third source of bibliographic records, RLIN was considered worthwhile and affordable – in some cases, more so than OCLC. It remained, however, more attractive to those libraries with special collections.

Auto-Graphics (A-G)

ISM Library Information Services, formerly UTLAS (University of Toronto Library Automated System), was acquired by the company, Auto-Graphics, in 1997. The contents of its MARC databases continue to be sold together with its cataloguing software, but there is no longer any cataloguing membership.

This bibliographic utility has its origins, as UTLAS, in a library automation system developed at the University of Toronto, an early pioneer in library automation, in 1963. In 1971 the university privatised UTLAS as a non-profit corporation. From 1973 it became more widely available, first in Ontario and then in the rest of Canada, and it moved into the United States and Japanese markets through the Japanese publisher and library supplier Maruzen Company in the early 1980s. In 1985 it was purchased by International Thomson Organization, and in 1992 by Information Systems Management (ISM) Corporation of Winnipeg. It was reported in 1990 as having more than 2,500 users, including over 70 per cent of all Canadian university and research libraries (Hunter & Bakewell 1991, pp.206-207). In the mid-1990s, Grosch commented that 'while Utlas has widened its international impact … it certainly is not a threat to OCLC's dominance as the world's leading bibliographic utility' (Grosch 1995, p.147).

UTLAS was usually reckoned to be one of the four major utilities, along with OCLC, RLIN, and WLN (see below), but dropped away somewhat in the 1990s. Auto-Graphics has focused on developing library software products; it is not really any longer in the record supply business.

WLN

WLN was acquired by OCLC in 1999, marking the end of a utility that had been as influential for its software as for its MARC database. It began life as the Washington Library Network based at the Washington State Library, changing its name to Western Library Network in 1985. In 1989, WLN changed its status from a division of the Washington State Library to become a private non-profit corporation. While its membership remained limited to one hundred or so libraries mostly located in the western United States, it was able to establish itself through its cataloguing software, which it licensed to some major libraries, such as the British Library, National Library of China, and University of Chicago at Illinois, and also to the national libraries of Australia, New Zealand and Singapore as the basis for their own national bibliographic utilities. The software was sometimes sold with the records from its database, which, although smaller than those of OCLC, RLIN and ISM, was a very helpful start for retrospective conversion projects. The database had reached the three million record mark by the mid-1980s, and stood at 11 million in 1998.

While the WLN software was not very user-friendly by today's standards, it proved to be a robust system, serving cataloguing networks particularly well. Three of the services offered by WLN are worthy of note. In 1987 it offered LaserCat, a subset of its bibliographic database, on CD-ROM – the first bibliographic utility to do so; WLN's automated collection analysis tool, Conspectus, has been further developed by OCLC; and its advanced authority control mechanisms assisted greatly in keeping its database 'clean' (especially when compared with OCLC) – they have also been utilised by OCLC post-takeover.

Other bibliographic networks

As well as these major bibliographic utilities, many smaller bibliographic networks have been developed over the last thirty years or so for the primary purposes of maintaining a bibliographic database and exchanging bibliographic data. Some of these networks are (or were) based on library type, some on a particular integrated library system, and most are regional or national in nature. In recent years, many of these networks have started to develop new products and services, and have upgraded their existing ones, such as their cataloguing software, in a bid to stay relevant to their members, who are finding a direct internet connection to OCLC and other major record suppliers an increasingly attractive, and affordable, alternative. Many of the older networks have already lost their battles, and it is, at present, unclear if new local networks will grow up to replace them.

The major distinction between these networks and the larger bibliographic utilities lies in their constituency. Although the utilities began by offering services on a local basis (Washington State for WLN, members of the Research Libraries Group for RLIN, and college libraries in Ohio for OCLC), their memberships rapidly expanded to comprise libraries and information services throughout the world. In contrast, the regional and national bibliographic networks offer services to a more clearly defined membership, and often the advantages of membership are based on the way the networks can respond quickly to local needs and issues. Many regional networks in the United States, such as NELINET (New England Library Information Network) and OHIONET, in fact began as buffers between individual libraries and OCLC. These *broker* networks function as OCLC service centres, and, in addition, often host regional union catalogues and act as a focal point for local activities. Others, such as PALINET which serves Pennsylvania and much of the mid-Atlantic region, pre-date OCLC but adopted their services to further regional aims and to automate existing operations (Wright 1996).

Many countries have a national bibliographic network of some sort or another. For example, there is Libraries Australia in Australia, *Te Puna* (formerly NZBN) in New Zealand, SILAS in Singapore, SABINET in South Africa and LIBRIS in Sweden. These networks usually host one or more national databases, some of which are considered to be national union catalogues or national union lists of serials, and so on (see below for more discussion on union catalogues). Some of these national networks are limited to a particular kind of library, most commonly university libraries: the CURL network mentioned below is an example.

It is worth noting that the United States does not have a national bibliographic database as such, although of course OCLC WorldCat represents a very large number of U.S. library catalogues. Instead, regional networks abound. Many of their names end in 'NET', as do the three mentioned above, as well as, for example, ILLINET (Illinois), and SOLINET (Southeastern United States). An exception is AMIGOS (Southwestern United States). The United Kingdom does not have a national union catalogue yet either (though it has recently launched a serials union catalogue). The more libraries with different library systems and belonging to different networks that a country has, the more difficult it is for it to construct one, as their construction requires considerable cooperation and coordination.

Some networks are limited to a particular type of library, which are considered to have similar interests, such as university, school or public libraries. A significant academic library network in the United Kingdom is CURL (Consortium of University Research Libraries), representing many of the major university libraries there. Its union catalogue (Copac) comprises some 30 million records and can be accessed online by the public for free. There have been several other significant cooperatives in the United Kingdom, such as LASER, and similar networks continue to exist in other European countries and elsewhere.

Some networks have evolved into library system vendors, expanding on their original cataloguing software and throwing in their database as part of the package (ISM/Auto-Graphics is a larger-scale instance of this). Often, users of the software are former members of the network. BLCMP started life as the Birmingham Libraries Cooperative Mechanisation

Project, and is now a system vendor by the name of Talis, backed up by a MARC database of 29 million records. Also in the United Kingdom, SWALCAP (South West Academic Libraries Co-operative Automation Project) became SLS, Ltd. and successfully sold a system called Libertas; the company was acquired by Innovative, another system vendor, in the mid-1990s.

Recently the distinctions between the local networks and the major bibliographic utilities have begun to blur. Given the rapid spread of internet use, improvements in telecommunications generally, and the increased telecommunications experience of librarians, libraries can now much more easily bypass the local providers and engage directly with the utilities. Indeed, it is not difficult now for libraries to link up with several utilities and other external databases simultaneously. For example, a large Australian library may use Libraries Australia as its primary source of catalogue records, but may also access the catalogues of other library catalogues both in Australia and overseas through a Z39.50 client to obtain additional MARC records.

Databases and union catalogues

OCLC and most of the smaller bibliographic networks host databases that are used not only as a source of records, but also as union catalogues. A union catalogue is, literally, the *union* of the catalogues of a group of libraries, such as a catalogue of all parliamentary libraries, or of all libraries in one state, or of all libraries in a country. Union catalogues are essential for any sharing of library collections, particularly through interlibrary loan (ILL) arrangements. Thus the bibliographic utilities and networks have been able to offer ILL services on the back of these union catalogues, as well as the considerable economies produced by the sharing of bibliographic records. Members contribute not only bibliographic records, but also their holdings information, for the benefit of other members. Since resource sharing is often carried out on a local scale, some of the regional networks have been able to develop union catalogues of more relevance to their members than those of OCLC and RLIN. For example, the CURL network's union catalogue, mentioned above, is offered to the public for free on the Copac interface, and is an important bibliographic tool for academics and research students based in the United Kingdom, comprising the merged online catalogues of the 28 CURL libraries, including the British Library, National Library of Scotland, the National Library of Wales, and 23 of the largest university libraries in the United Kingdom and Ireland (*Copac* 2007).

In fact, the Copac catalogue goes further. By utilising the Z39.50 protocol, it is able to provide the current status (availability) of a resource in any of the featured libraries by sending a request to the relevant local library system and pulling back the required information. Some union catalogues are based entirely on Z39.50. In such cases, there is no central database at all, only a Z39.50 client which asks each of the libraries' Z39.50 servers for both bibliographic and holdings data (see figure 10.1). These are sometimes referred to as *distributed* union catalogues, and can be readily assembled providing each library involved agrees to a standard Z39.50 profile for consistent retrieval. We have already noted that some of the regional bibliographic networks no longer perform such an important role as record suppliers; likewise, as telecommunications become easier, quicker and cheaper, the possibility of distributed union catalogues may make their central databases less relevant as resource-sharing tools.

The shelf-ready market

We noted earlier how the bibliographic utilities were developing new services and products, and not relying on the size of their databases to maintain their dominant positions in the new computing environment in which they now find themselves. They are linking resources to metadata in more direct ways, so that, for instance, a customer can download the e-book along with the MARC record. Selling both the resource and the record has been a practice developed by many library vendors in recent years. They sell their (physical and virtual) copies to the library together with a file of MARC records representing these items, or perhaps even catalogue them directly into the local system's database on the library's behalf. In a fiercely competitive market, providing shelf-ready books is a major selling point. Shelf-ready may mean just that: all the technical processing has been taken care of by the vendor, including the accessioning, cataloguing, labeling, and so on – items are ready to be placed on the library shelf. The trouble is that if a library purchases most of its materials from vendors offering such an added-value service there may be much less need for it to join and/or contribute to a bibliographic utility or network. The vendors may in some cases contribute records and holdings on the library's behalf, but if they have no contractual obligation to do so, they may well choose not to. The quality of the bibliographic records the vendors supply is also a concern, even when they do end up in the utilities' databases. Kellsey (2002), for instance, has found that a significant proportion of records for European language monographs in OCLC and RLIN were created by vendors to minimal standards and have never been upgraded. One must bear in mind that library vendors are commercial organisations with a different outlook from that of most libraries.

Shelf-ready books are attractive to many libraries with shrinking technical services departments. Libraries may need to be reminded by the bibliographic utilities and networks of the benefits that their membership brings. Some utilities have tried to tackle the problem head on. For example, OCLC has teamed up with several leading vendors to offer the PromptCat service, which upgrades a library's order records as soon as the full records become available. The utilities will need to continue to work not only with the libraries, but also with the key vendors if they are to remain the force they have become.

Conclusion

> The trend is quite clear that by the end of the twentieth century a library of virtually any size will have an online system through which it will perform its daily operational tasks. Moreover, this system will be part of a vast international communications network, which will bring worldwide resources to even small libraries (Grosch 1995, pp.150-151).

With the rise of the internet in the latter half of the 1990s, Grosch's prophecy came true for the developed world. No longer does a library need to belong to one particular network. Through the internet, libraries are connected to a network of networks, and not just to bibliographic networks offering MARC records. Libraries and other information centres are now able to access a range of digital objects in a range of formats, as well as descriptions of them in a range of metadata formats. In order for bibliographic utilities and networks to remain relevant in this new information world, they must recognise that simple MARC records are no longer enough. They need to provide services and products that add value to the basic metadata: for example, software that can do more with the metadata; metadata of better quality, of greater coverage, or of greater versatility; and databases that provide access to data as well as metadata. End-users are no longer content with just a reference, so information professionals cannot afford to be either. Those utilities and networks that are able to build on their bibliographic expertise and provide even better quality access to information resources, no matter where in the world the customer may be based, are the ones that will thrive in the coming years.

CHAPTER 13
Bibliographic data exchange: an Australian case study

> One way into a book is to look up the National Library of Australia cataloguing data, which is printed on the reverse of the title page. Although it tells you nothing about the writing, it at least gives you a swift fix on what's in the book (Campion 1999, p.23)

How did this cataloguing data get onto the book? What does its presence there indicate?

This chapter presents an extended case study that illustrates how bibliographic records are exchanged in the Australian library community. Although the case study focuses on Australia, the structures and practices it describes are also relevant to other countries, jurisdictions and regions. These structures and practices are international in large part, with changes to accommodate specific local concerns. For example, in Singapore, libraries use bibliographic records constructed to internationally-agreed standards by libraries all over the world, which they get from the SILAS database. This is similar to the processes described in this chapter for Australia.

The exchange of bibliographic records works like this. The bibliographic records for information resources are constructed to internationally-agreed standards by cataloguers working for a national cataloguing agency, or by cataloguers based in other libraries. These bibliographic records are added to shared databases that are accessible to anyone who subscribes to them, or who meets other requirements for participation. The national cataloguing agency takes responsibility for adding to a national database the bibliographic records for information resources produced in that country, which they have usually obtained through legal deposit legislation. Bibliographic records from national cataloguing agencies in other countries may also be added to the national database. These shared databases, therefore, contain bibliographic records for information resources from a wide range of sources, not limited to one country. When a library receives a copy of an information resource, it first checks the shared database to see if the information resource has already been catalogued. If there is a bibliographic record for it on the shared database, the library downloads a copy to its own database of bibliographic records and may add additional information to it, such as location information within that library. If there is not a catalogue record for it on the database(s), the library constructs one according to internationally-agreed standards for its own database, and also adds it to the shared database. (This paragraph is, of course, a summary. The actual situation is much more complex: for example, the library may search more than one database to locate bibliographic records, and may add its records to a regional database it shares with other libraries, rather than to its own database.)

Let's rewrite the preceding paragraph more specifically for the Australian context.

Bibliographic records for information resources are constructed to internationally-agreed standards (AACR2, the latest editions of DDC and LCSH, the MARC format) by cataloguers working for the National Library of Australia, or by cataloguers based in Australian libraries. The National Library of Australia produces the bibliographic records for information resources produced in Australia, which they have obtained under legal deposit legislation. These bibliographic records are added to the Australian National Bibliographic Database (ANBD), which is available through Libraries Australia, a national bibliographic network providing access to a range of other databases, as well as ANBD. Individual libraries that are members of the network also add some bibliographic records to Libraries Australia. Bibliographic records from national cataloguing agencies in other countries (in the case of Australia, the main sources are the United States, Britain, New Zealand and Singapore) are also uploaded into the ANBD on a regular basis. When an Australian library receives a copy of an information resource, it first checks Libraries Australia to see if the information resource has already been catalogued. If there is a bibliographic record for it on the ANBD or one of the other Libraries Australia databases (which now includes OCLC WorldCat), the library downloads a copy to its own database of bibliographic records (i.e., catalogue) and adds some additional local information to it, such as a call number (the location of the copy within that library). The download is usually triggered by the addition of a holding statement (which indicates that the library owns a copy) to Libraries Australia. If there is no catalogue record for it in the Libraries Australia databases, the library constructs one according to internationally-agreed standards for its own database, and also adds it to Libraries Australia. (Libraries in Australian schools are a significant exception to the practice just described. They search the SCIS database of MARC records, rather than Libraries Australia, and download bibliographic records from it to their school's database. Most do not, however, contribute bibliographic records to the SCIS database.)

This chapter first notes some background material: the availability of MARC records in Australia and the ANBD, union catalogues in Australia, and the broader context of UBC which provides a framework for bibliographic data exchange. It then examines the influence on Australian bibliographic organisation practice of the ANBD and Libraries Australia, which describes itself as 'Australia's library network'. Libraries Australia is described here principally as a tool to assist libraries to be more efficient in their bibliographic organisation practices, although its other services will also be noted. The chapter then considers other examples of library networks that are (or have been) influential in Australia: the focus of this section is, as it was with Libraries Australia, on the services that assist libraries to be more efficient in their bibliographic organisation activities. These include national networks such as SCIS and state-based examples such as CAVAL and Technilib (in Victoria) and UNILINC (in New South Wales).

Readers should note that chapters 9 and 10 of Harvey (1999) provide more detailed historical information than does this chapter.

MARC records in Australia and the ANBD

Bibliographic organisation in libraries is inextricably linked with the MARC record, and Australian practice is no exception. It is, therefore, important to know more about the introduction and use of MARC records in Australian library practice. Australian librarians observed the development of the MARC format in the United States and the United Kingdom during the 1960s with considerable interest. By 1971 the National Library of Australia expressed its interest in MARC in three ways: as a creator of Australian MARC records, as a distributor of MARC records for Australian libraries, and as a user of MARC records in its own existing operations, such as the production of the national bibliography and the maintenance of the national union catalogue (Ellis 1973, p.30).

In March 1974, AMRS (the Australian MARC Record Service) was launched by the National Library of Australia. The AMRS database initially consisted of MARC records for monographs from the Library of Congress, the BNB (British National Bibliography) and some Australian MARC records; Canadian MARC records were added later. AMRS products were provided in machine-readable form, with cards also available. AMRS appears to be an Australian first: Ketley notes that though other overseas national bibliographic agencies were at the time also providing MARC services, Australia was the first to provide a selective service from a multinational database (Ketley 1988). Initial reactions to AMRS were enthusiastic and it was influential in stimulating Australian interest in automated library automated systems (Cations 1978, p.81). AMRS was heavily used, peaking at about 280 customers and 220,000 requests in 1979-80 (Ketley 1988, p.85).

Current bibliographic organisation practice in Australia is based on the ANBD. The name 'National Bibliographic Database' was first applied in 1981 to the MARC record database that formed the basis of the Australian Bibliographic Network (ABN). The database originated from a file of 1.5 million records from the Library of Congress, plus original cataloguing contributed by participants to the WLN database (ABN also used the WLN software). Added to these were records from the Australian National Bibliography (ANB), records from the member libraries of ABN, and MARC records from the United Kingdom, Canada, the United States, New Zealand, Vietnam, and other countries.

In May 1988, by which time ABN had become firmly established, AMRS records were also incorporated into the ANBD. ABN participants continued to add large numbers of records, together with their holdings information, so that the ANBD could also act as a union catalogue of Australian libraries. Indeed, the National Library actively pursued the development of the ANBD as a national union catalogue, for example, by adding holdings data from libraries that did not contribute data directly to ABN (Cathro 1991, p.42). It continues to identify relevant libraries and to encourage and assist them in adding their holdings data to the database.

The ANBD, currently accessed through Libraries Australia, is the primary source of MARC records for Australian libraries. The ANB (which records Australia's published output) is also derived from the ANBD (Haddad 2000). Libraries Australia continues to add MARC records to the ANBD from national and international sources, such as the national bibliographies of Britain, New Zealand, and Singapore, and the MARC files produced by the Library of Congress. Australian libraries also continue to contribute significant numbers of records as members of the Libraries Australia network (figure 13.1 indicates its growth).

In 2007 it contained about 17.5 million records for bibliographic items and 42 million holdings statements.

The ANBD is of crucial importance to the way in which most Australian libraries carry out their day-to-day activities: not just bibliographic organisation, but also document delivery, interlibrary lending, resource discovery, and collection development. It is an essential tool for resource sharing among Australian libraries.

Union catalogues in Australia

Australian libraries have long recognised that, because of the nation's isolation and its limited library collections, sharing of collections is vital to offering comprehensive library services. Union catalogues in their current Australian implementation are, like bibliographic control, inextricably linked with the MARC record, and with UBC and its associated delivery mechanisms. Although it is not their primary role, they have provided, especially in the past, a source of bibliographic records, particularly for small libraries (Stockdale 1981, p.138).

Union catalogues in Australia are now based on shared databases of MARC records, but they have a long history that pre-dates the ANBD and similar databases. An early example was the 1889 union catalogue of scientific literature in Sydney libraries; more influential was the Commonwealth Council for Scientific and Industrial Research's *Catalogue of Scientific and Technical Periodicals in Australian Libraries* (1930), the predecessor of *SSAL* (*Scientific Serials in Australian Libraries*). Another important union catalogue was *SALSSAH* (*Serials in Australian Libraries: Social Sciences and Humanities*), begun in 1944 in card form and published in book form in 1963. National union catalogues of monographs date from 1960: these, too, were initially in card form and were later issued on microfiche. These, and similar developments, led to the establishment of a single online national union catalogue, the ANBD, containing location information for all formats held in libraries in Australia and accessible through ABN (now Libraries Australia) (Biskup 1994, pp.161-164, 453-454). Union catalogues add value to libraries' collections of information resources and act as an indicator of a nation's intellectual wealth; Australia is well served through the ANBD and Libraries Australia (Hider 2002).

UBC in Australia

As noted in chapter 11, UBC (Universal Bibliographic Control) agreements provide the context in which international exchange of bibliographic records occurs. UBC can be characterised as a way of ensuring that libraries carry out cataloguing of information resources in the most efficient way possible. It is based on simple concepts: all information resources should be catalogued only once, the bibliographic record of an information resource should be freely available to any library that wants it, and national libraries are the best places for the cataloguing of the information resources of a particular nation. UBC depends on all participants using the same sets of standards, the most important being the MARC record format and ISBD/AACR2.

UBC, to be successful, requires an efficient database that is accessible to all libraries in a country. In Australia this is the ANBD, available through Libraries Australia. SCIS (the

Schools Catalogue Information Service) also performs this role for Australian school libraries. Australia is, of course, not the only country in the world that is a keen participant in UBC. Just how important UBC is to other countries can be easily verified. Even libraries as large and heavily resourced as the British Library benefit significantly from the availability of bibliographic records because of UBC: they 'simply do not have the money' to go it alone (Oddy 1999, p.38).

ABN and its successors

The prominent position of Libraries Australia in the Australian information services arena cannot be fully understood without some knowledge of the origins and development of its predecessors, ABN and Kinetica.

ABN's significance extended beyond its existence as a national shared cataloguing network. It was also the focal point for cooperation among Australian libraries, being described as 'a source of technical and political strength for Australian libraries' (Groenewegen 1992, p.21). Only six years after its inception, ABN was described as 'the outstanding success story of Australian librarianship in the last decade, and a very positive example of the nation's libraries harnessing their resources to develop the most cost-effective and equitable mechanism for library operations and resource sharing' (Horton 1987, p.9). Participation of Australian libraries in ABN was high, with 54 per cent of Australian libraries who responded to a 1992 survey contributing to ABN, increasing to 71 per cent if the number of libraries who intended to contribute in future is added (*Library networks in Australia* 1992, p.1).

ABN's genesis

OCLC's success (described in chapter 12) prompted the National Library of Australia to examine the possibility of establishing a similar national online cataloguing system for Australia. A feasibility study in 1976 proposed that an online national bibliographic support system be created. It would 'reduce the rate of increase in the cost of cataloguing and increase the ability of libraries to respond to needs of users', and 'provide the means for the development of efficient resource sharing by Australian libraries' (*BIBDATA Network* 1976, pp.3-4). Initial concerns about the high cost of a network and the lack of suitable software were resolved when WLN software, developed for resource sharing among public libraries in Washington State in the United States, became available. The National Library implemented the WLN software in 1980 for its in-house system and in 1980 actively promoted a nationwide network based on WLN software. Although the proposal was not enthusiastically received, partly because it cut across regional activities such as CLANN in New South Wales and CAVAL in Victoria (see later in this chapter), and partly because its selection would be a *fait accompli*, without users having had significant input into its design (Cathro 1991, p.38), the National Library proceeded.

The National Library's *Draft Proposal for the Development of an Australian Bibliographic Network* (1981) indicated five aims for ABN:

1. To develop a comprehensive national data base of machine-readable records for all types of library materials, providing:
   i) a pool of bibliographic records, and

ii) related location information reflecting the holdings in Australian libraries of particular items described in the pool of records.

2. To implement an enquiry system which permitted the widest possible access to the national data base in the most effective and efficient manner.
3. To provide a range of products and services based on the national data base.
4. To accommodate a range of decentralised services with a view to promoting the fullest possible use of the national data base.
5. To develop an Australian authorities system (*Draft proposal* 1981, p.25).

Establishment and growth of ABN

ABN can be said to have truly begun on 2 November 1981. It had six clients: the National Library of Australia, one public library service, two university libraries, one state library and a government special library (Cathro 1991, p.40). To achieve its two main aims – to provide online shared cataloguing facilities to participating libraries, and to maintain a national union catalogue with participants' holdings available online – early efforts were directed towards increasing the number of users and the size of the database. Over the years ABN offered encouragement and financial incentives to libraries to convert their existing catalogue records and add them to the NBD. The number of users received a boost in 1982 when most members of CAVAL (a Victorian consortium of academic libraries established in 1979) joined ABN. Figure 13.1 illustrates ABN's success in achieving its aims. By 1991 it could be claimed that 'virtually every Australian library of significant size' was an ABN member, although not necessarily a heavy user, and that 'every state and territory is well represented amongst ABN clients, and there are a handful of overseas clients' (Cathro 1991, p.40).

Indicator	1981 Nov	1983	1985	1989	1993	1995	1997	1999	2001	2003	2005	2007
Members	6	88	323	763	1250	1300	>1400	1400	1150	1030	1006	1258
Biblio file (000,000)	2.1	2.6	3.7	6.3	9.8	11.1	12.7	10	11.5	12.5	14	17.5
Holdings file (000,000)	0.2	1.2	3.1	8.9	17.7	21.9	26	31.5	33.2	36.4	39.1	42

Figure 13.1 The growth of ABN/Kinetica/Libraries Australia. Based on *ABN handbook Part I* (1986); *ABN News*; *National Library of Australia Gateways*; and information from Kinetica/Libraries Australia staff (some figures are estimations)

Services offered by ABN

When it was established in 1981, ABN offered only a limited range of services, all concerned with cataloguing processes. These included bibliographical services (e.g., copy cataloguing, original cataloguing, review of cataloguing), enquiry services (e.g., online reference services, holdings information), user support (e.g., training, Help Desk), documentation (e.g., data preparation manuals, training manuals, reference manuals), and products (e.g., catalogue cards, COM catalogues, printed catalogues, accessions lists, printed bibliographies, machine-readable records). The next few years saw ABN move from offering only cataloguing-support functions to adding services to reflect widening interests, improving the system's user-friendliness, and responding to Australia's multicultural heritage.

Initially all members of ABN were expected to be Full Service members who contributed their cataloguing records to the ABN database, but other categories of user were rapidly introduced to provide users with more flexible options. Value-added services were offered, one of the most significant examples being the interlibrary loan subsystem, implemented in September 1989, allowing online transmission of interlibrary loan requests (although not of text of the requested documents) and electronic payment. Other significant developments provided new software, Supersearch in 1990 and SOFI (Supersearch Ozline Friendly Interface) in 1993, for searching the NBD, as alternative interfaces to the WLN-based search which was not user-friendly. The products offered from the NBD continued to be extended, for example a CD-ROM product was announced in late 1998. Figure 13.2 lists the milestones in ABN's services and products.

Over the years, access to ABN's databases and services varied as technology changed. Initially access was through a leased line, the most expensive option used primarily by larger libraries, or by dial-up access using a modem, implemented in 1983 to offer access to low-volume users. Gateway access allowing full-service facilities was also available through other computer systems. In 1997, the National Library strongly encouraged users to access via the internet and the leased line access option was phased out. By 1998, 78 per cent of all networked traffic was via the internet (*Kinetica implementation project* 1998).

ABN: organisation and structure

Some indication of how ABN was organised helps us understand its place in Australia's library services. A central office based at the National Library of Australia in Canberra was responsible for the day-to-day running of the whole operation, for database maintenance, and for training and assistance to users. ABN's governing body was the ABN Network Committee, which developed policy and carried out forward planning. Most of this Committee's members were elected by users of the Network.

Probably the most important ABN body for the library user was the ABN Standards Committee, whose role was to oversee the development and quality of the ABN database. Its decisions about standards affected the cataloguing actions of all contributors to the NBD, and, as a consequence, the ability of all users to locate information on the database.

Users had input into ABN through users' meetings held annually, and state-based user groups. The ABN Office was also in regular contact with users in other ways. It operated a Help Desk which was an invaluable source of assistance for new users and for the inevitable need to trouble-shoot network and communications problems. It issued a regular newsletter (formerly *ABN News*, now *National Library of Australia Gateways*, which has now moved online and has a broader, NLA-wide scope) and provided generous quantities of technical documentation to its users.

1978 March	WLN software installed in National Library
1980 October	ANB (*Australian National Bibliography*) records added
1980 November	BNB records added to the database
1981 March	ANB Pilot Project started
1981 May	First meeting of ABN Standards Committee
1981 September	Bibliographic file reaches 2 million records
1981 November	ABN operations begin
1981 December	First meeting of Network Committee
1982 August	First ABN User Meeting held in Adelaide
1983 January	Dial-up access available
1983 May	1 millionth holdings statement added
1983 June	Ability to input non-book records implemented
1984 February	Bibliographic file reaches 3 million records
1984 May	2 millionth holdings statement added
1985 September	Number of full participants reaches one hundred
1986 January	4 millionth holdings statement added
1986 March	Charging changed to encourage addition of holdings to NBD
1987 March	Bibliographic file reaches 5 million records
1988 April	Downloading facility implemented
1988 May	AMRS and ACS phased out and operated fully from ABN
1988 September	OCLC and ABN agreement for OCLC records to be added
1989 September	Interlibrary loan subsystem implemented
1990 March	10 millionth holdings statement added
1990 May	ABN and Technilib establish links between systems
1990 September	Supersearch launched
1991 September	RFI for new ABN/Ozline system issued
1991	$105,000 allocated for improving quality of authority and bibliographic files
1992 May	Two-hundredth Full Service user
1993 March	SOFI (Supersearch-Ozline Friendly Interface) launched
1993 May	CJK Project starts
1993 July	NLA and New Zealand sign an MOI to jointly develop NDIS
1993 September	Bibliographic file reaches 10 million records
1996 December	Records for recent Australian publications available by FTP
1996 December	World1 development terminated
1997 January	NSP announced
1998 January	AMICUS software (IBM) selected for NSP
1998 March	OLIB VDX software selected for interlibrary loan utility
1998 September	Ozline decommissioned, transferred to Informit Online
1999 first quarter	Kinetica implementation

Figure 13.2 Milestones of ABN. Based on *ABN Handbook Part I* (1986); *ABN News*; National Library of Australia Gateways

The ABN Office also had responsibility under UBC (see chapter 11) for providing bibliographic records in MARC format for Australian-published records to the international community, and for making the MARC records from other countries available to libraries in Australia.

ABN at the local level

ABN was used at the local level primarily for cataloguing operations. It was also used for reference enquiry work and for location enquiries, document requests and document delivery, but these are not noted further here.

For cataloguers in Australian libraries, ABN was the major source of MARC records for downloading to their local information retrieval systems. Its main role was the supply of bibliographic data, which was downloaded to the local system and processed there to service local needs (see chapter 14). ABN's significance lies particularly in the fact that it was especially tailored to Australian requirements, most particularly in its coverage of Australian imprints. To illustrate this point, in October 1996 nearly 2,400 bibliographic records were added to the NBD by ABN participants, a valuable source of cataloguing data not obtainable from any other source (Martin 1996b).

Libraries used ABN for cataloguing purposes in two main ways. *Original cataloguing* (where there is no bibliographic record available because the document has not been catalogued before) could be done by entering a new record directly onto ABN, then loading the MARC record created on ABN back onto the local information retrieval system from tape or diskette ordered from ABN, or by direct downloading. *Copy cataloguing* was carried out by adding a holdings statement (an indication that the library has a copy of the document) to a record already on ABN. The catalogue record was then loaded back onto the local information retrieval system.

The 1986 *ABN Handbook* suggested that the 'substantial' benefits of joining ABN for the individual library included reduction in the rate of increase in cataloguing costs, streamlining of cataloguing procedures, reduction in 'duplicative cataloguing effort' which allows staff to be redeployed to 'more productive activities', and improved services to readers, for example through better knowledge of what has been published and what is held in the collections of other libraries (*ABN Handbook* 1986, pp.9-10).

Published case studies about the effects of participating in ABN are plentiful and tend to confirm that the official ABN view of the benefits of joining was valid. A detailed and thoughtful early viewpoint is that of a medium-sized academic library at the Queensland Institute of Technology (now Queensland University of Technology). It reported that the benefits of joining ABN included a reduction in the cost of cataloguing and greatly improved hit rates. The university's view was not uncritical, but 'the benefits outweigh the drawbacks' (Cochrane 1988, p.3).

Resolving issues

Five issues characterise ABN's history: charging policy, maintaining database quality, responsiveness to users, catering for a multicultural Australia, and software issues. From

ABN's outset, the issue of charges was contentious. Federal Government approval for the National Library of Australia to proceed with ABN was given only on the condition that its services be charged for on a cost-recovery, user-pay basis. An early debate in the Australian library profession was about the extent to which the National Library was itself a user of ABN and the extent to which it should therefore contribute to ABN's costs. Charges have been adjusted over time to provide various incentives: for example, the charge per holdings record added to ABN, which was levied in the first few years, was transformed in 1986 to a credit given to libraries who added holdings, so that the location data was built up. In preparation for Kinetica a new charging regime, based on a subscription fee that provides unlimited use of a number of services, was introduced (*Simpler Charging* 1998).

Maintaining database quality was a constant concern for ABN. Quality issues were caused by the way in which MARC records from overseas sources were added to the database in bulk loads, and by the addition of many MARC records by participants who inevitably had varying levels of cataloguing skills and who used local variations to international standards. Many duplicate records appeared on the database. The ABN Office implemented a reviewing process in which samples of MARC records added to the database were examined to ensure they satisfied specified minimum standards. Standards are an important, indeed essential, part of the ANBD and its operations. For example ABN required adherence to specified minimum levels of cataloguing standards, which include AACR2 level one for original cataloguing, although some maintained that these minimum standards were unnecessarily high and counterproductive for many Australian libraries (Down 1982). Authority control was another ongoing issue for ABN. One of the reasons given for the selection of the WLN software was that it allowed participants to maintain a high level of authority control, which is essential for a high-quality database (see chapter 5). Unfortunately, the ability of the software was not matched by the willingness and ability of participants to carry out the sometimes complex tasks involved (Cathro 1991).

From its inception ABN actively sought to be responsive to users and, wherever possible, incorporated their views into its operation and management. Annual meetings of users were held from 1982 and several states had active local user groups. The ABN Annual Users' Meeting acted as a forum where issues causing friction could be aired. Other forums for user input, such as ad hoc expert practitioner groups to help the National Library of Australia to evaluate user requirements for software development, and to advise on ABN's subject authority file, were convened.

A long-standing issue for ABN was the question of how to deal with records for documents in scripts other than roman script. Vernacular scripts, especially Chinese, Japanese and Korean (CJK), have particular significance for Australia. An initiative to provide Australian libraries with a national shared cataloguing system that could handle and display CJK scripts began in 1993. The National CJK Project started as a consortium of seven university libraries and the National Library of Australia. This CJK system 'would be the Australian national union catalogue for CJK items, will provide copy cataloguing, and will serve as an OPAC for libraries that do not have CJK script capability in their local systems' (*INNOPAC Chosen* 1994; Groom 1995). The National CJK System's database became operational in June 1996. By June 1997 it contained more than 807,500 bibliographic records and more than 250,000 holdings statements and had about eighteen full service members. The National Library's commitment to this service continued as ABN became Kinetica, culminating at the end of 2005 in the merging of the CJK and ANBD databases through their mutual migration to the new OCLC Pica system, the basis of the transition to Libraries Australia. At that time, the CJK database contained in the region of 866,102 bibliographic records and 622,704 holdings statements.

Software needs to be modified and upgraded over time to meet the demands of its users. The ABN software, written between 1975 and 1977, was developed at a time when catalogue cards were the major output product. For ABN some software development was shared with WLN and the national libraries of New Zealand and Singapore, which also used the software. Although changes were made to the WLN software during its lifetime, ultimately ABN was relying on old software which was became less and less responsive, was cumbersome to modify, and expensive to maintain because it was written in an archaic programming language, PL1 (Cathro 1991, pp.48-49). In 1994 the National Library announced that it would jointly develop, with the National Library of New Zealand, completely rewritten software running on an up-to-date hardware platform. The Australian end, named World1, was heavily promoted throughout Australia in a series of roadshows during 1996, but in late 1996 the National Library of Australia and the National Library of New Zealand terminated the contract with the software developer for reasons never made public. In January 1998, the National Library announced that a new system would become operational in early 1999, based on IBM's AMICUS integrated library system (*New National System* 1998), named Kinetica (suggesting energy, speed and motion), and encompassing a group of services to be known as the Kinetica Search Service, the Kinetica Cataloguing Service and the Kinetica Document Delivery Service.

Kinetica

Kinetica represents another key chapter in Australian bibliographic practice: the transition from the pre-internet days of ABN cataloguing to a much more flexible and multifaceted service based on modern computing and interfaces. Kinetica was more than a cataloguing service, billing itself as 'Australia's Library Network'. Its 2003 publicity brochure, *What is Kinetica?,* described it as:

> a modern internet-based service for Australian libraries and users. This service can be used for interlibrary lending, reference, collection development and cataloguing. The core of Kinetica is the National Bibliographic Database (NBD), which records the location details of over 35 million items in most Australian libraries. Through Kinetica, libraries have access to many major international databases ... The Kinetica service is managed by the National Library of Australia and uses international library standards and protocols for its content, data exchange and to search other similar systems.

Kinetica was implemented in the first quarter of 1999, taking over from ABN, although implementation issues resulted in some users continuing to use ABN until late in that year. Since 1999 constant attention was paid to improving Kinetica's services to users and to providing easier access to a wider range of resources for a wider range of users. One example is the Web Input Interface, implemented in 2001, to make it easier for infrequent users to input new records to the ANBD, thereby encouraging the development of the database. Other examples include: a trial to offer access through Kinetica to OCLC WorldCat; upgrading of KineticaWeb search screens, to provide for differing levels of user expertise (simple, advanced, expert); and making available to customer libraries Blackwell's Table of Contents data.

Libraries Australia

Despite the modernising efforts of Kinetica, complaints about some aspects of its service, most notably its software, led to a 'redevelopment project', the result of which included the acquisition of new web-based cataloguing software from OCLC Pica, originating from the Dutch national network (Pica), and used for several union catalogues in Europe. This meant a migration of the ANBD to a Unicode-based platform which allowed to the CJK and ANBD databases to be merged.

The project also resulted in a new strategic direction for the network, with the emphasis on a service for everyone, not just cataloguers. The reference interface, KineticaWeb, was made more user-friendly and responsive, so that it could be easily used by individuals who had not received specific training. Moreover, the interface was developed into a much wider gateway, allowing access not only to ANBD, but to a wide variety of other databases, such as Picture Australia, and simultaneously, through a federated search facility. With this new emphasis, came a new name – Libraries Australia – to indicate that the service was for libraries in general, not just their cataloguers, and that it was also about libraries – serving as a gateway to the nation's collections, be they in traditional or digital format.

The network has always been keen to promote the ANBD as a national resource for the widest possible utility, and the logical conclusion was for it to be made *freely* available to the general public. This happened with the birth of Libraries Australia. Anyone with an internet connection can search on both the ANBD and the Picture Australia database through the Libraries Australia basic interface; individuals and libraries have to join the network (i.e., pay) to use the advanced search facility.

In reality, the name change to Libraries Australia did not signify a radical shift of focus, but rather an evolution that started during the network's Kinetica days, when it began calling itself 'Australia's Library Network'. Its document delivery services, and other non-cataloguing products and services (e.g., the Australian Libraries Gateway and Picture Australia) were well established before it became Libraries Australia; these services look set to expand as Libraries Australia continues to look for new resource sharing opportunities.

Databases of Libraries Australia

Libraries Australia offers its member libraries many more databases, besides ANBD and Picture Australia, providing access to the following databases through the Z39.50 standard. They can be searched individually or simultaneously. In addition, the OCLC WorldCat Authorities database can be searched separately.

- Australian National Bibliographic Database

- Picture Australia (Pictures from Australian cultural agencies)

- ARROW (Australian academic research)

- British Library Catalogue

- Canada Institute for Scientific and Technical Information (CISTI)

- Chinese University of Hong Kong

- Consortium of [British] University Research Libraries

- E-Library

- Hong Kong University of Science and Technology

- Library of Congress Catalogue

- OCLC WorldCat

- Powerhouse Museum OpenSearch

- National Film And Sound Archive OpenSearch

- Singapore National Union Catalogue

- Te Puna (New Zealand National Bibliographic Database)

- University of Hong Kong

The most important of the above database from a cataloguing perspective is OCLC WorldCat. We noted earlier that Kinetica had provided access to WorldCat on a trial basis; not surprisingly, this access was very popular with libraries, who were thus able to avoid subscribing to OCLC directly, which is by no means cheap. A break-through agreement between Libraries Australia and OCLC in 2007 allowed the network full access to the many millions of MARC records in WorldCat on an ongoing basis.

Libraries Australia and cataloguing

Libraries Australia provides a number of ways to download MARC records from its databases, and to upload records contributed by its member libraries. MARC records can be downloaded directly through Libraries Australia Search service, or they can be downloaded via FTP as batch files (i.e., sets of records) through the Record Export Service. Specific sets of records can also be ordered on request. Even more flexibility is offered to contributors of records:

- online addition and amendment of bibliographic records and holdings statements via the Libraries Australia Search or Libraries Australia Client interfaces,

- offline batch contribution of new or changed bibliographic records and holdings statements using Libraries Australia's Record Import Service, and

- third-party contributions.

To encourage contributions from libraries with limited cataloguing expertise, the Libraries Australia Search interface includes a 'Web Cataloguing form', which 'can be used for adding minimal level MARC records and holdings. As the name suggests, the user fills in a form and no knowledge of MARC is required. A minimum level entry must include title (including the filing indicator), publication date, country of publication, bibliographic level and type of material. Libraries Australia Web Cataloguing can be used to create new records, and add, edit and delete library holdings' (Libraries Australia 2007).

Because the ANBD remains central to Libraries Australia Cataloguing services, its coverage and quality control continues to be of major interest to Libraries Australia users. Libraries Australia therefore continues to perform quality control and 'clean up' operations on the database, and to make it as easy and affordable to contribute to the database as possible.

How users influence Libraries Australia

The formal organisation and structure of Libraries Australia retains many features of ABN and Kinetica, including its well-developed user advisory mechanisms. Users have direct input to Libraries Australia through a range of committees and meetings of users. The existence of many active forums is a strength of the network and contributes to its continuing relevance to Australian libraries.

The Libraries Australia Advisory Committee advises on strategic and policy issues, and on changes in the library community that may affect Libraries Australia services. Its membership represents key stakeholder groups, with representatives from the National Library of Australia, CASL (Council of Australian State Libraries), CAUL (Council of Australian University Librarians), representatives from special libraries, public libraries, and members elected by the library membership of Libraries Australia.

Small expert advisory groups provide advice to Libraries Australia on specific topics, as required. Currently, there is one such group, looking at 'Institution Specific Data' – what kind of local data may be needed in libraries' catalogue records that is not input at the network level (i.e., not found in the ANBD records). The idea is to provide 'a new service which will allow libraries to use a localised version of Libraries Australia as a public access catalogue for their collections' (Libraries Australia 2007). Previous expert advisory groups have provided advice on a wide range of topics:

- ABN Network Committee
- ABN Standards Committee Documentation
- Access to Electronic Resources
- Authority Record Delivery
- Bibliographic Standards
- Cataloguing of Electronic Resources
- Cataloguing Workflows

- Document Delivery Service

- Enhancements

- Electronic Resource Cataloguing

- Reference and End User Services

- Subject Headings

All users of Libraries Australia are eligible to send representatives to participate in the network's annual forum (i.e., user group meeting), where stakeholders and Libraries Australia staff are able to share views and discuss future directions. Reading the reports of these meetings (available on the Libraries Australia website) provides an insight into the network's current issues and thinking.

Autonomous local Libraries Australia User Groups have been established in all states (and the ACT) to offer feedback and advice. The National Library of Australia also operates a moderated email discussion list, librariesaustralia-l, as a forum for announcements and discussion of day-to-day matters of interest to Libraries Australia users.

Libraries Australia into the future

Some of the issues that apply to Libraries Australia are the same issues that its predecessors had to deal with – charging policy, maintaining database quality, responsiveness to users, catering for a multicultural Australia, and software issues. These need to be seen in a wider context as Libraries Australia expands its role beyond services primarily aimed at supporting cooperative cataloguing and interlibrary lending. In relation to the cataloguing services it offers, the future of Libraries Australia is closely linked to its ability to provide a source of relevant MARC records to Australian users. As Australian library collections, both physical and digital, become increasingly international (that is, many resources are now acquired from sources outside Australia), so the importance of tapping into international sources of bibliographic records becomes critical. In this respect, Libraries Australia's recent agreement with OCLC may well turn out to be key to the network's survival over the short to medium term.

Other Australian networks

Libraries Australia is only one gateway or network that is used by Australian libraries for bibliographic organisation purposes. The rest of this chapter considers other examples of library networks that are influential in Australia. These include national networks such as SCIS and state-based examples such CAVAL (in Victoria) and UNILINC (in New South Wales).

Australia is a country of library networks. This should not be surprising, as few libraries in other countries have the brief of providing services to clients who are as geographically widespread as in Australia with its immense distances and sparse population. A 1992 survey of library networks sought to 'develop a national picture of the operation and interrelationship of local, regional and national networks for the sharing of bibliographic information, including the relationship of libraries and networks to ABN, and to the "NBD".' This survey indicated a high level of ABN membership and also noted that, of the 742 respondents, 'a significant proportion (42 per cent) were involved with other networks – in all, 28 networks were mentioned by two or more respondents' (*Library networks in Australia* 1992, p.1).

Many of those networks were subject-specific, for instance medical, financial or theological; this chapter is concerned with networks of a more general nature, and in particular networks such as SCIS, UNILINC and CAVAL, whose activities and services are based on large databases of bibliographic records in MARC format.

The 'heroic age' of networking

The idea of a national shared catalogue system, debated by the Australian library profession for some years and culminating in the BIBDATA proposal in 1976, had been preceded by some activity in developing regional networks. The most notable examples were a cataloguing service for South Australian school libraries and, in Victoria, a technical services centre for public libraries and a scheme involving cooperative cataloguing for academic libraries. The frustrations and thrills of these early days of library computer networking in Australia, the 'heroic age of Australian library automation', are vividly recalled by one of the pioneers, Dorothy Peake (Peake 1996). The proposed introduction of a national system, it was thought, would not reduce the need for regional networks. The consensus at a 1977 meeting was that regional interests were best served by regional networks *in conjunction with* a central database, the primary function of which was the supply of MARC records (Dobrovits 1978, Fielding 1978, Schmidmaier 1978, Undy 1978).

What had brought about this consensus? The concept of a centralised database to supply MARC records had been firmly established by 1975 through the ANB/MARC service and AMRS. By 1976 the regional activity was flourishing with the founding of CAVAL, CLANN and Technilib. The strong and continuing local role for regional systems was fully recognised by the time ABN became a reality in the early 1980s. By that time the preferred terminology had changed, to *library networks, library cooperatives* and *consortia*. These regional consortia were of different types: state-based, such as the Western Australian Library Board; cooperatives such as Technilib, developed to provide a common library technical processing facility to member libraries; cooperative groups organised on a geographic or common interest basis, such as SAERIS in South Australia; and not-for-profit companies, such as CAVAL and CLANN, where a range of services was provided to members (*Draft Proposal* 1981, p.43). The National Library of Australia proposed an active partnership between the consortia and ABN, with the consortia acting as channels or service points for ABN products and services. The consortia's role would be 'as resource users under ABN for the provision of bibliographic processing, and as resource providers for other types of service within the network ' (Llewellyn 1982, p.17). This model envisaged a simple one-way flow, as shown in figure 13.3. The reality was not to be so simple and various approaches were taken in the following years.

A summary of the 1992 activities of three Australian consortia (Wade 1993) indicates how the 1982 model had been interpreted in practice. Technilib was the closest to the 1982 model, providing its members with cataloguing data as well as undertaking a wide range of services, primarily directed at allowing member libraries to place an order with Technilib and have the fully-processed shelf-ready book delivered. ABN was used as one source of cataloguing data, but definitely not the only one. CAVAL did not supply cataloguing data to its members. It provided ABN training and downloaded records from ABN of the holdings of member libraries, using these as the basis of its regional OPAC, COOL-CAT. Its other services were not based on the use of ABN. UNILINC concentrated much more on providing its members with services needed for day-to-day operation (an integrated library system, providing acquisitions, cataloguing, authority control, and circulation functions, for instance – and running a union catalogue of its members' holdings, available online and on CD-ROM). Initially, it made minimal use of ABN. Probably the consortium closest to the 1982 model was one established after ABN had been running for several years. SCIS, formerly ASCIS, provided cataloguing products to its school library members, and, in order to do this, maintained a database of MARC records, which come, in large part, from ABN. Much has changed since 1992.

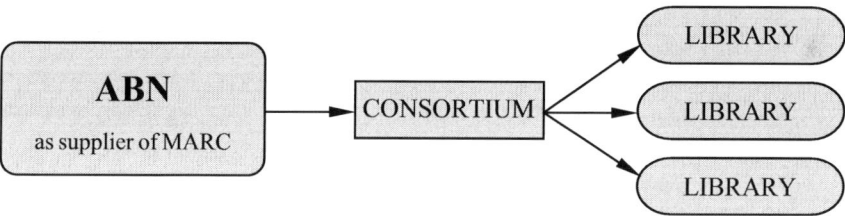

Figure 13.3 Model of consortia activities. Based on Llewellyn 1982

SCIS: the (inter)national school network

SCIS, a cooperative venture of state government education systems, coalitions of Catholic and independent schools, and the federal government, was established to 'provide a service with the aim of reducing the cost and duplication of effort required by teacher librarians in cataloguing resources in schools' (Curriculum Corporation 2007). It is a division of the Curriculum Corporation, which is owned by the Australian ministers for education. A school library information system, if it uses the SCIS database of MARC records, 'can contain the most up-to-date cataloguing records that have been approved by the education systems of Australia' (*Schools Catalogue Information Service* 1998). Teacher librarians, thus relieved of many of the tasks associated with bibliographic control, can concentrate on promoting information literacy and supporting teachers and students in curriculum delivery. SCIS does this by providing services from a database of bibliographic records of information resources of interest to schools (video recordings, CD-ROMs, kits, poster and pictures, games, charts, websites, slides, and maps as well as books and, increasingly, websites). A large number of Australian school libraries, about 85 per cent in fact, are SCIS users (SCIS 2007). Those which are not include libraries in large independent schools and joint-use school-community libraries – some of these use Libraries Australia instead. A significant number of international schools and New Zealand schools also use SCIS, so it can claim to be an international system, although it remains primarily Australian in outlook and management.

SCIS provides its cataloguing services from a database of MARC 21 records (prior to 1996 in ASCIS80 format, a simplified version of AUSMARC). These records have SCIS Subject Headings rather than LCSH, and both full and abridged DDC classification numbers. Recently, descriptors from the Schools Online Thesaurus (ScOT), have also been made available on new SCIS records (see chapter 9). In 1998 the database contained approximately 600,000 records in total, with about 3,000 new records being added each month and SCIS had more than 6,000 members. By 2007 the numbers had grown to about 970,000 records, with about 3,500 new records being added each month (SCIS 2007).

SCIS began life as ASCIS (Australian Schools Catalogue Information Service) but changed its name to SCIS in 1992 to acknowledge New Zealand users. This brief history outlines its achievements; a fuller history is available on the SCIS website (SCIS 2007). It had been recognised in Australia for many years that school libraries had different cataloguing needs from other kinds of libraries. Discussions in 1971 addressed the possibility of extending the National Library's card service to schools. This was trialled in 1973, but was unsuccessful, partly because LCSH was not considered appropriate for Australian school libraries, and partly because of the costs for individual schools.

Douglas Down and Wesley Young were commissioned to report on the viability of establishing a cataloguing service network for Australian school libraries. They produced a first report in 1974, and a second report, *Australian schools cataloguing service*, in 1977, which served as the catalyst for the Commonwealth Schools Commission to fund a pilot scheme to examine the viability of a national service. This was based on SAERIS (South Australian Education Resources Information System), which had been implemented in 1977 and used a database of MARC records developed from the National Library's MARC record service. ASCIS, based in Melbourne, appointed an Executive Director in 1983 and by 1985 was solidly up and running. It used DOBIS/LIBIS software to produce catalogue cards, microfiche and magnetic tapes. Initially 4,000 schools received products from a database consisting of 200,000 records. This database was established using records from SAERIS, the Western Australian Department of Education and the ACT Schools Authority. The first edition of the *ASCIS subject headings list,* the need for which had been clearly pointed out during initial planning stages of ASCIS, was published in 1985.

Throughout its history, the network has added new services to meet user needs as the following examples illustrate. Cataloguing records were made available on floppy disk in 1986, and in the following year ASCIS introduced dial-up services, including email and online ordering of products. In 1989, mechanisms to encourage user input into the revision of the ASCIS subject headings list were introduced: a second edition was published in 1990, a third in 1994, a fourth in 1999 and a fifth edition in 2002. Additions and changes to subject headings in the latest edition are now available from the SCIS website. Other services have included a retrospective conversion service, SCISRECON, which offered an inexpensive source of MARC records for school libraries automating their card catalogues, and a search-only CD-ROM version of the SCIS database, SCIS On DISC. In 1997 DOBIS/LIBIS software was replaced by Voyager software, which provided the opportunity to introduce new procedures and services, such as a web OPAC interface and downloading of records to local systems. Two major new services, SCISCD and SCISWeb, were introduced in 1998. SCISCD, available on a subscription basis was a CD-ROM version of the SCIS database from which records could be downloaded to a local system. It proved useful to schools for copy cataloguing, especially to those without an internet connection who could not access SCISWeb. Access to the SCIS database via the internet was implemented through SCISWeb, which has developed into a highly successful platform. Also in the late 1990s, the charging basis was changed from a per record basis to an annual subscription based on the number of students in the school.

The introduction of SCISWeb resulted in a significant increase in use because of factors such as the ability to download records directly into the local system, instead of waiting for them to be delivered on diskette. SCIS also offers SCIS Authority Files, containing authorised names and subjects, for libraries to download; subscribers can also look up the SCIS Subject Headings and Schools Online Thesaurus online.

The operation of SCIS is likely to change in the future. One factor is the extent to which its MARC record database is changing. Formerly, records were contributed to the SCIS database from all states, by cataloguing agencies based in the departments of education. However, a reduction in the number of centralised school library operations has resulted in a decrease in the number of centralised agencies contributing cataloguing records. In 2007 records were contributed by cataloguers based in the education departments of New South Wales, Queensland and Western Australia, further records being contributed by contract cataloguers in Victoria, South Australia and New Zealand (SCIS 2007). This may result in a database which is less representative of all Australian school libraries. SCIS may need to widen its range of accredited contributors of MARC records, perhaps following a model more like Libraries Australia.

SCIS users are a satisfied lot, according to a survey of more than 1000 users in 2002. The SCIS database provides a hit rate of almost 85 per cent, and SCISWeb was considered to be easy to use (Curriculum Corporation 2003). The high level of satisfaction suggests that SCIS's strategy of providing cataloguing services carefully tailored to the needs of school libraries and the skill levels of staff employed in school libraries is working effectively.

Technilib: innovation but not success

In 1996, Technilib, the oldest of the networks in Australia, closed. Technilib was established in 1975 to provide 'a range of cost-effective services of professional standard through efficient and innovative technical services and inter-library networking' to public libraries in Victoria (Technilib brochure 1993). It achieved this by providing and supporting library technical services at costs lower than individual libraries could achieve, providing a telecommunications network linking libraries, and maintaining comprehensive databases of bibliographic records to support Technilib network participants. Technilib's ownership by Victorian public libraries lead to its offering pioneering multicultural services, such as a completely online Greek script catalogue not relying on transliterated script (*Cataloguing: It's All Greek* 1990). Its membership grew from five in 1975, to more than fifty members in the 1990s. They could choose from a wide range of technical services and products, including cataloguing services in a large number of languages. Technilib's central database in 1993 consisted of about 410,000 bibliographic records and more than 1 million holdings statements. Despite its many innovative services, Technilib was unable to sustain its activities as the political climate forced a major restructuring of its members, in effect reducing their number dramatically. After the demise of Technilib in late 1995, CAVAL took over some of its activities, such as the foreign language cataloguing service, and the approximately 500,000 MARC records and 900,000 holdings statements in its database were sent to the National Library of Australia for adding to the ANBD (Cathro 1997, p.9).

CAVAL: Victoria's academic library network

The key to CAVAL's activities, past and present, is found in its name: Cooperative Action by Victorian Academic Libraries. It is owned by nine Victorian universities, but its activities extend a long way beyond the libraries of these universities. CAVAL's services are closely linked to the requirements of academic and research libraries in general, and its current core areas of operation – professional development and training, multilingual solutions, information management and access, and preservation and storage – reflect this.

CAVAL was established in 1978 after a consultant's report recommended the creation of a machine-readable database as the basis of a shared cataloguing system. It initially had six members – the four Victorian university libraries, one college of advanced education, and the State Library of Victoria as an affiliate member. By 1979 CAVAL's database contained 45,000 records, from which was operated a shared cataloguing system using batch computing facilities supplied by the Libramatics computer bureau. The products available were a microfiche union catalogue and microfiche catalogues for member libraries. Other services in line with CAVAL's goals of library resource sharing and cooperation, such as a reciprocal borrowing scheme, were developed and promoted.

The introduction of ABN was a powerful catalyst for CAVAL to reassess its shared cataloguing role. In 1981 it participated in the ABN pilot project and in 1983 CAVAL's directors decided to support ABN in preference to maintaining its own shared cataloguing system database. However, the desirability of eventually operating a regional database for CAVAL members was still recognised. CAVAL's database, by now 360,000 records, was transferred to ABN. CAVAL established and coordinated a Victorian ABN Users Group, carried out training for ABN, acted as a coordinating body between ABN and its Victorian users, and carried out activities such as authority control work on ABN on behalf of some of its members. CAVAL also offered specialist contract cataloguing services, for instance supplying skilled personnel to assist member libraries with cataloguing backlogs.

In addition to its ABN activities, CAVAL continued to develop a regional database of bibliographic records, functioning as a union catalogue of the holdings of its members. After trials of suitable software in 1984 and 1985, COOL-CAT (CAVAL Operated On-line Catalogue) was introduced in 1986, reaching 400,000 records by 1988 and 600,000 records by 1989. An enhanced COOL-CAT system was launched in 1992 and the database was issued on CD-ROM in 1993. The number of records in its database by then stood at 1.5 million records. The regional database, CAVAL suggested, offered significant advantages to its members: for example, the COOL-CAT software was considerably more user-friendly than ABN and could be used by naïve users; and a fixed subscription cost could be offered, of considerable interest to library managers for budgeting purposes. COOL-CAT contained more than 2.3 million records by 1997. A web interface was implemented in 1998. In 2002 COOL-CAT moved from a centralised database of records extracted from the ANBD to a web-accessible distributed catalogue, based on Z39.50 communications protocols, that searches the catalogues of member libraries. However, as ABN/Kinetica became more affordable and its cataloguing interface more user-friendly, so the competitive advantage of COOL-CAT diminished; the service was closed in the mid-2000s. Nevertheless, COOL-CAT played a key role in the development of the CARM (CAVAL Archival and Research Materials) Centre, a joint storage facility for low-use material opened in 1997 and now holding about one million volumes, and the legacy of the database lives on as the CARM catalogue – an inventory of the material stored at the Centre.

One characteristic of CAVAL's activities not shared by the other Australian networks established in the mid to late 1970s was its decision to support ABN in preference to maintaining its own database of cataloguing records. The significance of this for the fledgling ABN was significant, for it provided both a source of cataloguing records with local holdings (as distinct from the United States-oriented database it had inherited from WLN) and also a boost in the number of libraries (even if all were academic libraries located in Victoria) which used the services of ABN.

CAVAL is currently the leading provider of cataloguing training in Australia, offering short courses and customised training in various aspects of information organisation, as well as extensive contract cataloguing services, specialising in foreign language materials.

UNILINC

UNILINC Limited began life as CLANN in 1978. CLANN was planned and established in the mid to late 1970s 'to reduce the rate of rise in per unit cataloguing costs' (CLANN *Annual report* 1979–80, p.5). At this time many CAE (college of advanced education) libraries in New South Wales were newly established and sought to have their cataloguing processes automated from the outset. Federal funding for libraries during the 1970s resulted in greatly increased acquisitions and large cataloguing backlogs grew fast. There was, therefore, a real and demonstrable need to share the cataloguing effort. Against this background, an investigation into the feasibility of centralised cataloguing services for colleges of advanced education in New South Wales was carried out during 1975 and 1976 by Carmel Maguire and Dorothy Peake, resulting in the incorporation of CLANN as a non-profit venture in 1978.

Initially CLANN had five members, all of them colleges in New South Wales, and operated using computer services provided by Libramatics, based on a database containing 85,000 records. Its membership grew rapidly, with its online services offered to fifty-seven libraries, including school and special libraries, in 1987. Its database also increased: to 322,000 records in 1984; 833,000 bibliographic records and 2.7 million holdings statements in 1990; and 2.9 million bibliographic records at the end of 1996. Membership of UNILINC at the end of 2007 stood at 22 institutions, with clients numbering in the hundreds (UNILIC 2007).

In its early years CLANN, in common with its sister consortia CAVAL and Technilib, relied on the computing services of Libramatics, which it continued to use for cataloguing until

1987. In 1984 it received approval to operate its own computer system and in 1986 a GEAC library system was implemented, initially offering an OPAC and circulation modules and, from 1987, cataloguing and acquisitions modules.

From its inception in 1980, the CLANN database offered a respectable 80 to 90 per cent hit rate for current cataloguing. In 1989 CLANN issued its CD-CAT CD-ROM, the first MARC database to be developed and issued on CD-ROM by an Australian organisation. The reason for producing the CD-ROM version of the OPAC at the time was to overcome the data communications costs of offering online services in remote locations, coupled with the slow response time on 2400 baud links at the time.

In addition to offering systems, CLANN began in 1981 to offer consortium buying services for products such as Dialog and Ausinet (the first such initiative in Australia), as well as other services such as contract cataloguing for members and training in cataloguing and other aspects of library work. In 1991 CLANN reviewed its Articles of Association to take account of changes in higher education in Australia and also took the opportunity to adopt the more inclusive name of UNILINC. That year also saw the implementation of Liblink, developed by UNILINC and an Australian company, CPS, to link the OPACs of nine universities in New South Wales and offering searching using a common set of commands.

By 1992, the list of services offered by UNILINC included database development, access and retrieval; acquisitions and electronic ordering; patron cards, barcodes and labels; cataloguing; authority control; advice on hardware and software; the 3M patron self-check system; ABN dial-up; and access to other networks such as Medianet. It also offered retrospective conversion services, contract cataloguing services, and the CD-CAT CD-ROM. In 1996 the list of services offered by UNILINC was similar. UNILINC's core business was still 'the provision of the one shared integrated library management system', the 'Shared System' (UNILINC Limited Annual Report 1996) which had moved from a GEAC system to DRA software. Work was continuing on maintaining the quality of the database, and the UNILINC Authorities Librarian continued to maintain authority records. The database was accessible through the web using the WEBCAT interface. The CD-CAT database continued to be available on CD-ROM, as did services such as contract cataloguing, database subscriptions and training.

UNILINC's role has continued to evolve. Its core business is still the provision of the Shared System (which in 2002 began to use the Aleph software developed by Ex Libris) to meet member libraries' needs for a library management system and to support reciprocal borrowing and interlibrary lending. It provides other cataloguing services such as contract cataloguing services to libraries and book suppliers across Australia, and training on the Libraries Australia system. It also provides a wide range of other services. These include facilities management, consultancy services, managing the UNILINC Reciprocal Borrowing Scheme, and negotiating database deals for members.

Other networks and consortia

There are other networks and consortia in Australia, and preliminary feasibility studies for several more have been carried out. They have usually been developed to represent either regional interests or sector interests, and sometimes both.

Networks based on regional interests include LINNet (Libraries in the Northern Territory Network), established in 1982. This is a Territory-wide library network, available to all public, community, secondary school and college libraries in the Northern Territory and operated by the Northern Territory Library Service. The centralised LINNet database provides access to the combined holdings of its over 50 member libraries. In 1993 it contained 416,000 bibliographic records and 1.6 million holdings statements; in May 2003, 473,000 bibliographic records and 1.08 million holdings statements. In Western Australia, discussions to establish WALN (Western Australian Library Network) commenced, but planning was discontinued when ABN proved its viability by 1983.

Sectoral networks have included SAENET, set up in 1978 to cater for the computing needs of the South Australian advanced education sector and to operate a shared cataloguing system for college libraries. It was eventually phased out in favour of ABN. OLC (the Office of Library Cooperation) was established in Sydney in 1980 by university libraries in New South Wales but did not establish its own shared cataloguing system, preferring instead to act as an ABN service point for its members.

Some smaller consortia also exist, usually based on sharing a single library information retrieval system in order to spread the costs of networking and to make accessible the resources of a typically small number of members. An example is LIBNET, a consortium of college libraries in Victoria established in 1985 to share a library computer system, based at the then Footscray Institute of Technology. AWA's URICA system was installed and modified to enable it to be used on a networked basis. Cataloguing was done on ABN then downloaded onto LIBNET (Parker 1987). Another example of a small consortium is LibLink, a group of public libraries in Victoria, joined in 1997 by Royal Melbourne Institute of Technology Libraries (LibLink Launches Access 1997).

Conclusion

It is now difficult to imagine how bibliographic organisation practice in Australian libraries could occur without Libraries Australia. Networks such as SCIS, CAVAL and Unilinc are also now firmly entrenched in Australian bibliographic organisation practice. Hand-in-hand with Libraries Australia, they have contributed to the development and maintenance of bibliographic organisation standards since the early 1980s. Although there have been casualties along the way, most notably the demise of Technilib, the large networks and many smaller ones are definitely here to stay, and it is likely that new networks will arise as new commonalities among libraries and other information agencies emerge.

One of the keys to the success of networks such as Libraries Australia, SCIS, CAVAL and UNILINC is the extent to which they are able to integrate with the information retrieval systems used in libraries and information centres. These systems, commonly known as integrated library systems, are noted in the next chapter.

CHAPTER 14
Local systems and OPACs

In the introduction to Part IV we considered the range of factors which make an effective document retrieval system. Chapters 12 and 13 examined bibliographic utilities, large-scale systems shared by many member libraries, in some cases across the world. This chapter notes some general requirements and characteristics of information retrieval systems used in *individual* libraries and information centres. Those that contain the library catalogue are commonly known as integrated library systems (ILS) or library management systems (LMS). The discussion focuses on three aspects of these smaller-scale library information retrieval systems:

- the bibliographic database and its relationship to other functions of the integrated library system,

- the bibliographic maintenance module (or cataloguing module) of the integrated library system, and

- the OPAC module of the integrated library system.

Definitions

Nearly every definition of the integrated library system makes these two points:

- An integrated library system relies on the same data in a single database to provide four basic functions (acquisitions, cataloguing, circulation, and the online public access catalogue).

- The database comprises bibliographic data (e.g., cataloguing records) as well as other data necessary to carry out library-related functions (e.g., borrower files for circulation purposes) (*Integrated Library Information Systems* 1983; Prytherch 1995; Tedd 1993, p.121).

The key point here is that there is one common database of bibliographic records which supports most, if not all, of the functions performed by the integrated library system. We have already become familiar with many of the characteristics of a bibliographic database: for example, it is likely to be in MARC format, constructed according to AACR2 and other standard codes for providing bibliographic access, and it will use authority control concepts to ensure its consistency and quality. The implications of having a common database for all functions of an integrated library system are significant: the effectiveness of all of the modules will stand or fall on factors such as the quality of the records in it and its ease of use.

This book is not concerned with the hardware aspects of the integrated library system. They can be PC-based or Macintosh-based, they may run on larger computers, or they may be installed on large mainframes, they can be stand-alone or networked – they exist with all sorts of capabilities, for a very wide range of installations. Many hundreds of commercial systems are available in the marketplace, and there are also several free, open source products available for smaller-scale solutions. This chapter does not note specific examples of integrated library systems and the reader will need to look elsewhere for that information. What it does do is present some of the requirements to ensure that cataloguing and OPAC operations of the integrated library system function effectively and efficiently.

Some history

Because integrated library systems are now commonplace, we sometimes forget how rapidly, and how recently, they were adopted in libraries. Automation of the cataloguing process was initially based on the large-scale cataloguing support systems (that is, the bibliographic utilities) which offered bibliographic records in a standard format as their major product. From the 1970s came the development of other areas of library automation, initially circulation systems or serial title listing systems, as stand-alone modules. Those systems used the services of a computer processing bureau, such as Libramatics, to batch process transactions. In batch processing, bibliographic records altered during the day were processed at night as one batch, hence the main database (the bibliographic file) was updated only once per day. Unfortunately, stand-alone modules all too frequently 'relied largely on the precariously supported initiatives of local programmers' (Henty & Steele 1988, p.100).

From the late 1970s onwards, turnkey systems were introduced into the market and soon became popular. Turnkey systems were so called because they could be purchased, installed and then turned on with a key, like a car – that was the theory, at least, although the practice often differed considerably. However, as the market grew for these systems, so did their quality: there was money to be made in library automation. In the 1980s, for a library system to compete in the market place, it needed not only to be turnkey, it also needed to be *integrated*. This meant that the basic modules had to be connected and work together. On top of the bibliographic database, circulation systems were rapidly developed, followed by the addition of other modules such as an OPAC and, later, an acquisitions subsystem.

From about the mid-1980s dramatic changes in computing capabilities – increases in processing power, and decreases in data storage costs and the price of hardware – meant that even small libraries could afford in-house automation: for example, by 1996 almost 70 per cent of Australian school libraries were automated (Dillon 1997, p.6). By 1992 the number of integrated library systems outnumbered in-house systems in Australian university libraries by four to one (Maguire 1993, p.57). Audrey Grosch, one of the pioneers of library automation in the United States, puts it thus:

> Most early systems grew out of the circulation application, were enhanced to use a MARC-compatible bibliographic database and were then revised to provide a direct interactive search access. Then, some other functions such as acquisitions were offered, but many of these systems of the early eighties did not actually offer a total

cataloging support environment and did not have authority-based databases. Their databases were loaded by libraries performing and maintaining their cataloguing on one or another bibliographic utility – usually OCLC. The resultant utility magnetic tapes records were preprocessed and loaded into the local system ... With ever powerful and low cost computing, it was inevitable that the functions of cataloging itself also would not need to be done on a large central host system but would most desirably be done on the local library system with links to the bibliographic utility for resource bibliographic record sharing and authority information. In other words, through the decade [the 1980s] it became apparent that the networks' major role would become their union catalog, and locational and switching capability to facilitate actual document delivery via interlibrary loan and secondarily as a raw MARC record supplier (Grosch 1995, p.67)

The benefits gained from the integration of the discrete modules into an integrated library system were in at least four areas. One was economies in equipment: the additional CPU memory and disk storage needed when modules were added to the base unit were relatively small compared to the total cost. Economies in resources expended in writing and maintaining in-house software, which was usually of lower quality than the best of the commercial integrated library systems, were also possible. There were further economies by avoiding the labour-intensive and error-prone activity of re-keying what was essentially the same bibliographic data into separate databases. Perhaps most important, though, were the opportunities for offering improved service and new kinds of services. These benefits were made possible largely because of the structure of integrated library systems, particularly their development around a central database of bibliographic records. Rather than requiring a number of stand-alone systems the integrated library system offered a single system which did everything – or, more likely in the early stages of their development, promised to do everything, but was considerably better at some functions than at others.

The first integrated library systems typically used a database of bibliographic records in which records could be updated, new records added and unwanted records deleted interactively, rather than in batch mode. Immediately we can see that there is a significant benefit in providing more up-to-date information to users, such as the circulation status of a document (whether out on loan, for instance). In many cases, all library functions including acquisitions, serials management, and circulation, as well as the cataloguing and authority maintenance functions with which this chapter is concerned, were performed using the constantly updated database. The online catalogue was probably the most significant aspect of library computer systems from the users' point of view. As Grosch puts it, the online catalogue is 'a directly patron searchable system, one that would act as the library's catalog itself, instead of producing serial magnetic tape output to create a catalog in microfilm or microfiche form' (Grosch 1995, p.66). In the early 1980s, no library system available on the market could support all of these functions, although many could offer excellent versions of some of them; by the late 1980s, libraries with adequate budgets could choose from a range of them, or at least they could if they wished to use a system based on the roman alphabet.

Development of library systems in Australia

A survey of computer-based systems in Australian libraries in 1968 listed twenty-one institutions with a total of thirty-eight 'operational' systems; by 1975 a 50 per cent increase in both the number of libraries and systems listed was noted (Schmidmaier 1975, p.8). In 1979 the Royal Melbourne Institute of Technology Library was the first in Australia to install a turnkey system, LIBS 100. Other turnkey systems appeared shortly afterwards, including CLSI and GEAC (from the United States) and URICA (from Australia). For some time, these systems co-existed with systems developed in-house. Peake notes that 'these first [turnkey] systems did not always prove easy to implement but they were a significant advance on what had gone before' (Peake 1996, p.13).

Regular surveys of Australian library automation developments were published for some years in *Australian Academic and Research Libraries* and elsewhere. They indicate that Australian library managers were not altogether ruled by logic when making decisions about which integrated library system to purchase: they also followed fashions. In 1988, Henty and Steele noted, 'Nearly every head librarian or head systems librarian wants to be different and to buy the automated "flavour of the month"' (Henty & Steele 1988, p.103). The consequences have been serious, as this quote notes:

> The University of Tasmania was the first Australian library to install the URICA system. Not long afterwards, the State Library of Tasmania became the first Australian library to install Adlib … It is a brutal economic fact that neither library is large enough to have had the funds to use its chosen system to the best advantage, nor to have developed it as it would have liked (VALA 1991, p.280).

Australia's distance from the rest of the world has been a significant factor in integrated library system selection, with choices influenced by the availability, or otherwise, of local support services for maintaining a given system. Several Australian developers and vendors, such as AWA with URICA and Stowe with Book, were initially successful in attracting sales, but typically did not sustain their success in the face of strong opposition from much larger companies based overseas. Stowe was acquired in 1998 by GEAC, a major systems vendor from North America. AWA is still Australian-owned, having become part of the Sanderson Group, now called Civica – its system is called Spydus. Some other home-grown systems that are still used in a significant number of Australian libraries, particularly smaller libraries, include: Oliver and Alice, sold by Softlink, and used particularly by school libraries; the Bookmark system, developed by the Education Department of South Australia, also used in many school libraries; InfoVision Technology's Amlib; and Insight Informatics' Libero. Although some Australian systems are sold overseas, particularly in the Asia-Pacific region, none has had a large impact on the main North American and European markets.

In 1993 the benefits of computerised local catalogues were considered to be:

- the ability to produce multiple copies of the catalogue,

- an increased number of access points for both staff and users for searching,
- elimination of card filing,
- potential use of catalogue records obtained from elsewhere,
- the ability to produce subset catalogues,
- the ability to exchange catalogue data with other libraries, and
- an opportunity for the catalogue to interface with other housekeeping modules (Tedd 1993, p.124).

Some of these benefits already seem irrelevant. To give only three examples: the low cost of CD-ROMs makes the ability to produce multiple copies of their catalogues readily available to even the smallest libraries; access to the internet enables greater interconnectivity of library systems; and MARC records are now downloaded from all kinds of online sources as a matter of course. Probably only a few hundred information professionals have filed catalogue cards in Europe and North America in the last few years!

Over the past decade, advances in computing have made automation a possibility for even the smallest libraries; and in many cases, a reality. There are now several bibliographic database systems designed for small-scale use which are freely available on the web. Some of these are open source, some run on the web itself, some support MARC, others do not.

Modules in the integrated library system

The modern integrated library system usually offers these functions as its basis:

- acquisitions,
- circulation control,
- serials control,
- bibliographic maintenance (including authority control),
- OPAC, and
- interface to a bibliographic utility.

Other functions are also available in many integrated library systems. These are often optional and can be purchased as add-on modules if required. They include:

- housekeeping functions: archives management, booking facility (e.g., for videos or equipment), and housebound borrowers;
- bibliographic functions: thesaurus construction and maintenance;
- external links: interlibrary loan, community information, email, remote access to the OPAC, and online connection to a book or serials vendor; and
- management functions: statistics keeping and reporting, transaction logging, and finance.

The master bibliographic database serves as the basis from which these functions are offered. Figure 14.1 illustrates the relationships among these functions in one integrated library system. Although taken from a brochure for a (leading) system over a decade ago, the basic architecture that it shows remains standard.

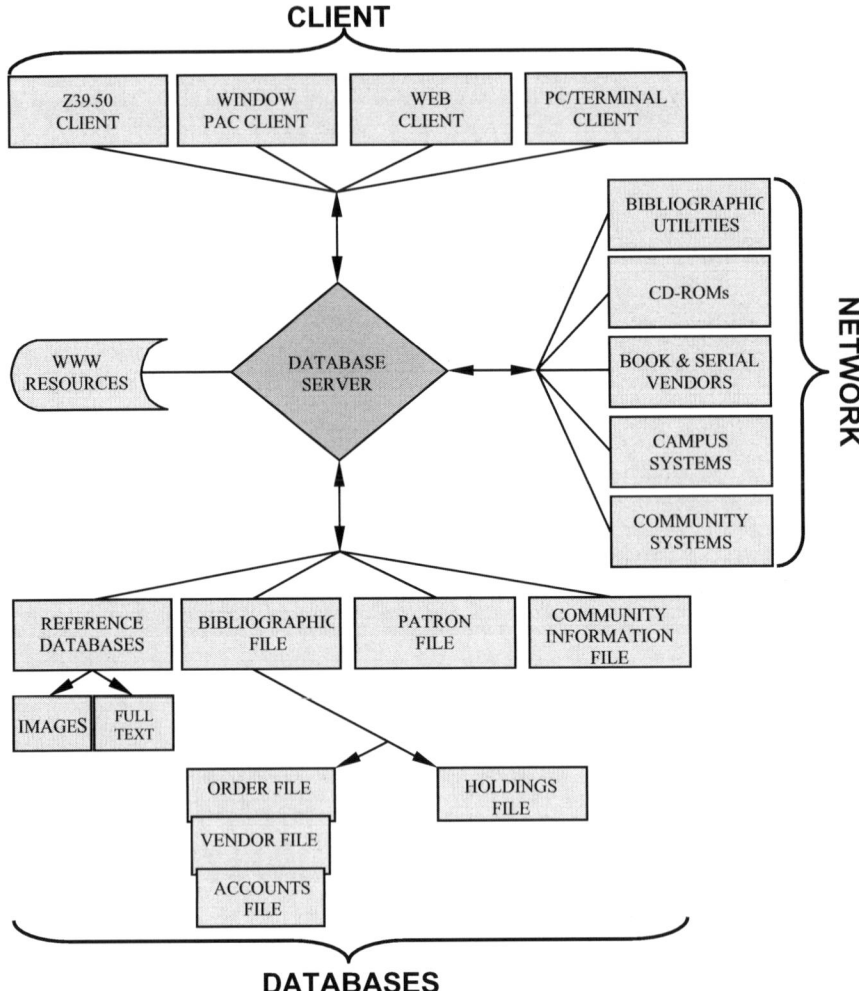

Figure 14.1 Typical integrated library system architecture. Based on INNOPAC
Brochure 1995

The master bibliographic database

We have already noted that the same master database of bibliographic records is used by the
core modules which make up an integrated library system, and the quality and efficient
functioning of it is central to effective integration. There are two particular concerns when we
consider the master bibliographic database:

- quality of the contents of the database, and
- how effectively the linking functions among different modules are performed.

Database quality and record structure

Parts II and III addressed the importance of the quality of database content. The fact that the database in an integrated library system supports many functions does not reduce, but rather increases, the need for database quality to be maintained. One question that is frequently raised in the context of integrated library systems, which by definition are localised, is whether the MARC record structure is the most appropriate. Of most significance here is whether anything needs to be added to the MARC record to enable it to function in an integrated library system. In practice the answer has, until recently, been no. The MARC record structure has proven itself to be full enough to accommodate localised data (perhaps too complex in the eyes of some, as we have already seen in chapter 10). Some systems use a separate record for holdings data based on a separate MARC format, but it is still MARC. In such cases, the bibliographic record and holdings record are linked; otherwise, the holdings data is embedded in the bibliographic record, in a prescribed MARC field (e.g., the 852 field).

However, there have recently been calls for systems to convert from MARC-based databases to those based on other formats, such as Dublin Core, or at least for the MARC records to be 'wrapped up' in more flexible and programmer-friendly coding, such as XML. Although few systems in the current market are genuinely XML-based, there is certainly a movement towards greater interoperability. This will mean the development of systems that can work outside of the MARC environment, accepting, for example, metadata in Dublin Core format. This important trend is discussed later in this chapter.

Retrospective conversion

Retrospective conversion (often called *retrocon* for short) refers to the process of converting bibliographic records which have been manually produced – usually on cards – into machine-readable versions. Although most libraries have completed this conversion by now, there are still some smaller libraries with work to do, and some large libraries with special collections that have not yet been dealt with. The goal of retrospective conversion is to improve access to a collection by creating a single online file of bibliographic records for the library's *whole* collection, which is a significant aspect of database quality.

Retrospective conversion became an issue for libraries after the first flush of enthusiasm for applying computers to the cataloguing process had faded. As the technical challenges were met, the realisation grew that to offer a fully effective computer-based service, the library must have all of the contents of its catalogue in machine-readable form. This contrasted with the typical situation where the OPAC only provided access to material catalogued from a particular date, usually the date from which the library started entering bibliographic records for its new acquisitions into the computer database. Closed card catalogues coexisted with computer terminals, and as users became more familiar with the OPAC and grew to appreciate its advantages, their reluctance to search more than one catalogue also grew. Users typically would not carry out a search in more than one catalogue, and the card and microfiche catalogues came to be ignored. (We have already noted how users often do not perform more than one or two searches for the same subject, author or item, and that the fewer steps required on the part of the user to meet a particular search goal, the more likely they will be performed.)

The cost of retrospective conversion, particularly for large libraries, has been high and often proved to be a major stumbling block to more rapid progress. Only in recent years could the largest libraries claim that all of the bibliographic records for resources in their collections were accessible through the OPAC. It should be noted that computing costs were much higher in the 1980s than they are today, and that major budget allocations were necessary to undertake comprehensive retrocon projects twenty years ago. Today, those smaller libraries that are still in the process of automating can do it relatively cheaply, particularly with the large databases of MARC records now available – although, of course, some of these smaller libraries operate on very limited budgets and resources, and still find it a major challenge.

Retrospective conversion usually follows these steps:

- a search code is selected for the records which are to be converted: for example, ISBN, or author plus first words of the title;
- the search code is matched against a large database of bibliographic records such as OCLC, either online or on CD-ROM;
- the records which result from the matching process are edited to conform to the library's cataloguing practices and standards;
- original cataloguing records are created for items not found on the large databases available to the library;
- the new records are merged into the existing catalogue; and
- editing and authority control of the merged catalogue is carried out.

It is very likely that records resulting from the retrospective conversion process will, in some way, be inconsistent with records in the existing bibliographic file. Key questions in quality control are, therefore: to what extent should it be carried out, and how much time and money can be allocated to the quality control process. Retrospective conversion can be outsourced or carried out in-house, or a combination of the two. OCLC still offers a popular retrocon service; it is worth noting that many libraries joined, and continue to join, bibliographic utilities, in the first instance, for retrocon purposes.

Effectiveness of integration

The second concern relating to the master bibliographic database is how effectively the linking functions among different modules are performed. The most obvious example is that of the circulation module, where a borrower's record is linked to the records in the bibliographic database to indicate which resources are on loan to that borrower. This is standard in every integrated library system available today. The efficiency achievable through effective linking of the modules is the main advantage offered by the integrated library system – resulting in improvements in service, reduction in time spent in system-related activities, and reduced error rates.

Improvement in service to the end-users of the system can be seen in almost every facet of the operation of the integrated library system. As already noted, one example is the linking of circulation records to catalogue records so that the catalogue record display indicates that an item is on loan, when it is due back in the library, whether anyone else has reserved the document, and so on. 'Save the time of the reader', said Ranganathan.

Integrated library systems also reduce the time required to perform system-related activities. For example, compared with the situation when libraries operated several unintegrated systems, one now deals with only one system vendor (the supplier of the integrated library system) and there is a reduction in staff training time. (The implication here is that the time saved can be devoted to improving the service aspects of the information centre.)

There is also less chance of error in the bibliographic record when the same record is used for all functions. Furthermore, end-users may benefit from a more comprehensive, one-stop picture of the library collection and acquisitions. For example, entering a brief or interim record into the database at the time an information resource is ordered serves as the basis for a full catalogue record when it arrives, and also serves as an aid to the end-user by indicating that the resource is on order. The OPAC would then invite the user to reserve the item.

The bibliographic maintenance module

The bibliographic maintenance module (or cataloguing subsystem) of an integrated library system usually allows the following:

- original bibliographic records can be created (original cataloguing);
- bibliographic records can be imported from external databases, for example, through a connection to OCLC or RLIN, or from a MARC-record database on CD-ROM (copy cataloguing);
- bibliographic records can be edited and deleted;
- authority control can be performed; and
- output products such as catalogue cards, printouts and spine labels can be produced (Ferguson & Hebels 1998, p.92).

Many issues relating to effective operation of the bibliographic maintenance module need to be considered when assessing an integrated library system for purchase. They include:

- ease with which MARC records can be imported into the system;
- ability of the database to accommodate records in formats other than MARC;
- ability of the database to accommodate additional fields in the MARC format;
- ease with which quality can be maintained in the database; and
- availability of online help, documentation and training provided by the system's vendor on an ongoing basis.

Creating original bibliographic records

Many tasks associated with creating and editing bibliographic records are made easier through the use of formatted screens (see figure 14.2) which help to ensure quality of bibliographic records by providing prompts to the cataloguer, reminding them of what information is required (e.g., mandatory fields such as title). Facilities for automatic verification of data, input in the original cataloguing process, are also available in bibliographic maintenance modules. Common examples are verifications that the MARC coding is valid and that headings in the record match those on the authority file.

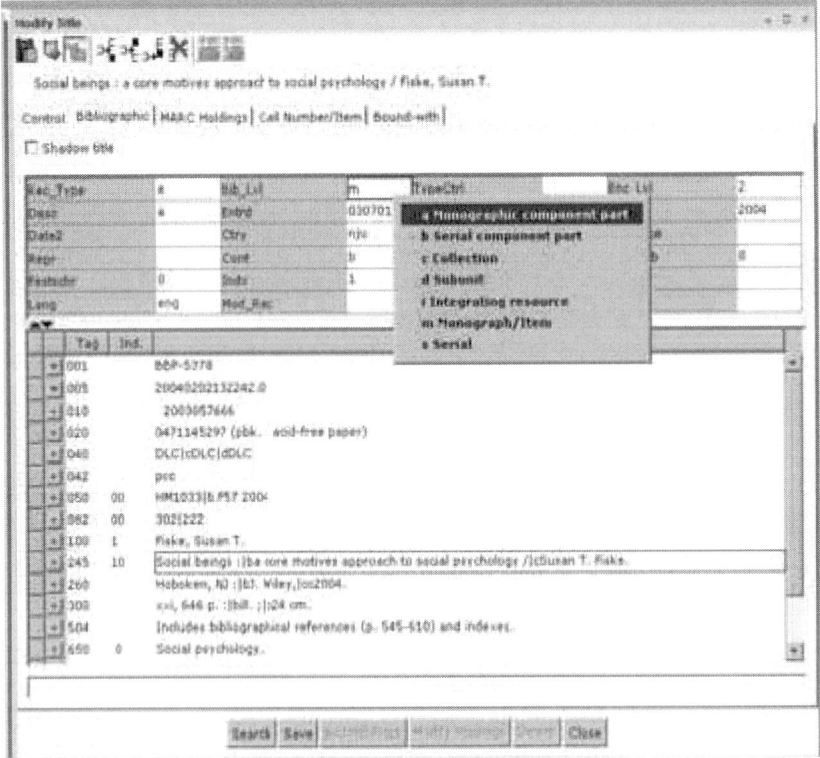

Figure 14.2 Entry type definition display on the Symphony platform (SirsiDynix). Source: http://www.sirsidynix.com

Importing bibliographic records

Bibliographic maintenance modules need to provide for importing MARC records from databases external to the integrated library system. It should be possible to import records in quantities ranging from one record to bulk loads of many thousands of records. The module should also allow importing records from a variety of sources through a variety of devices. Some systems allow for records to be downloaded directly from an outside source into the catalogue, without any intervention required by the system support staff. Some systems allow for downloading of records through the Z39.50 protocol (i.e., they have a Z39.50 client), so that cataloguers can search for records using their own system's interface. There are many large catalogues, including that of the Library of Congress, which now accommodate the downloading of their MARC records through their Z39.50 server – in many cases, free-of-charge, with no restrictions.

In the past it was desirable for the system to handle more than one MARC variant, such as AUSMARC and USMARC. If a database was in AUSMARC, for example, USMARC records would be converted into AUSMARC during the import process. Now that there are fewer MARC variants, with MARC21 having become the standard in many countries, this is no longer so much of an issue. However, those libraries with non-MARC21 databases should consider whether a MARC21 converter is available, given the enormous numbers of records that would be available to them if it were.

There is a similar consideration for those libraries that have an OPAC that can display non-roman script. If they wish to import records which include, say, Chinese characters, they can do so straightforwardly if their system uses the same character set and its corresponding codes as those on the imported records, but if not then the system will need a converter that maps the two sets of codes. For Chinese characters, there are at least five sets of codes in common use: Big5, EACC, GB, HZ and Unicode.

Another desirable attribute of the bibliographic maintenance module is the ability to define a variety of record formats, not just MARC. As the OPAC takes on a new role as the gateway to a range of information resources, regardless of their location, instead of being simply the access point to the catalogue of one collection, the ability of the integrated library system to store and handle records in non-MARC formats, such as those produced by an in-house indexing project or a collaborative digital library project, becomes more important.

Editing bibliographic records

Once the records have been added to the master bibliographic database, it should be possible to edit any part of them. The editing facility needs to be available for individual records, for instance to correct an error in a record imported from another source. It should also be possible to edit globally: an example of this is to strip all holdings statements from downloaded records, if they are inappropriate for the (local) library.

Authority control

The bibliographic maintenance module must allow authority files to be developed and maintained. The authority file should be accessible while data is being entered during the original cataloguing process and the record editing process, so that headings can be selected and checked. Adding new headings to the authority file, either automatically or following review, should be straightforward. The bibliographic maintenance module should provide for creating *see* and *see also* references, and for global changes of headings (i.e., a simultaneous change of a particular heading in whichever bibliographic records it occurs) such as those which result from changes in names of government departments or countries. It should be possible for new headings to be added to the authority file as the result of downloading of authority records, in the same way that bibliographic records can be downloaded. The system should automatically create an authority file entry when a new heading in a bibliographic record is added or imported, and should automatically delete headings when the last bibliographic record in which they are included is deleted. Unfortunately, the emphasis here is on *should* – few systems fully offer all of the above features; indeed, there are still systems which do not even offer a MARC-based authority file.

Output products

The bibliographic maintenance module should be capable of providing output in a range of formats, apart from that of the OPAC itself. Commonly required output formats include:

- catalogues: catalogue cards, catalogues on COM (Computer Output on Microfiche) or COLD (Computer Output on Laserdisk), and printed catalogues; these may be required for backup purposes and also for distributing copies of the database to other sites;

- stationery: spine labels and barcode labels; and

- printed reports: for instance for all new catalogue records added to the database during a specified period, or all authority file headings altered.

Alternative cataloguing platforms

While many libraries use their own systems for their cataloguing, there are many more which use another platform for at least some of it. This is not because these libraries do not have a cataloguing module in their local systems, but because they are participants in a cooperative cataloguing network, such as OCLC, and as such elect to use the network's common software for their cataloguing. Some libraries, however, despite being members of a network, might prefer to upload their original cataloguing from their own database to the union catalogue, and so use their own system's cataloguing module. Their staff may find their own cataloguing module more user-friendly, for instance. There are several possible workflows that might interface between a library and a bibliographic utility, but the aim is normally to have the library's cataloguing – both copy and original – represented on the common bibliographic database as well as in the library's own catalogue.

OCLC's cataloguing application is called Connexion, and can be used through a web browser or as a client that sits on the cataloguer's desktop. It is, of course, in OCLC's interests to make the software as user-friendly as possible, and they have been responding to cataloguers' needs for a very long time; Connexion may not possess all the functionality that every cataloguer desires, but it is supported by a large team of developers and is continuously being improved on. Again, users benefit from sharing – when things go wrong, there are plenty of users to ensure OCLC's response is swift; there are also plenty of users to suggest new features to make cataloguing that bit easier.

Libraries that use external software such as Connexion will enter records into the common database first, and then download them into their own system. Although many libraries still download records as batch files – usually on a periodic basis, such as every week – it is now possible for such records to be downloaded directly into their local database through the internet. For those libraries which require very up-to-date catalogues, a facility that allows for this downloading of records into their live database is a major boon.

The OPAC module

OPACs are typically referred to in terms of generations. The distinction between three generations of OPACs was first made by Charles Hildreth and his typology is now commonly accepted, and has been recently extended as a fourth generation begins to emerge. The first generation appeared in the early 1980s. They were derived from traditional catalogue systems, so that the access points they offered were similar to those of the card catalogue: author, title as phrase, call number or classification, and perhaps subject headings. These early OPACs worked on the principle of exact matching, and were intolerant of any input errors. They are sometimes referred to as phrase-indexed or pre-coordinated OPACs.

OPACs belonging to the second generation provided better search facilities based on keyword searching and post-coordination of keywords. They are usually operated by a simple command language (for example: *AU = Salmond J*). The choice of access points is expanded to include keyword searching on words from titles, subject headings, authors or other names, and searches using Boolean operators. Second-generation OPACs usually offered at least two levels of user interaction (simple/novice and advanced/experienced).

Third-generation OPACs started being sold commercially (as part of new integrated library systems) in the 1990s. They built on the basic features which made the second-generation OPACs so much more popular and powerful than the card catalogues. Before we move on to the revolutionary new features of the third generation, we need to note the basic features of a successful second-generation OPAC.

Basic OPAC features

Because the OPAC is a component of an integrated library system, it offers much more than the retrieval of bibliographic records, although that was initially its primary function. Most OPACs allow users to:

- find out whether resources in a collection are on loan or are available to consult or borrow, and
- check their own borrower information and make reservations.

Comparisons and evaluations of OPACs abound in the cataloguing literature. A 1994 example indicated that of the OPACs surveyed, there was a distinct lack of uniformity in the features offered (Zumer & Zeng 1994, p.96), though common features found in all of them included:

- searching on a range of access points (e.g., personal author, corporate author, title, subject, call number, series),
- controlled term searching,
- choice of predefined output formats,
- choice of full display or brief citation, and
- display of index or thesaurus to assist the user.

Most of the OPACs provided:

- menu selection (88 per cent),

- context-sensitive help (82 per cent, compared with only 6 per cent which offered a tutorial online), and

- free-text searching on default field (65 per cent).

A comprehensive checklist developed in 1994 to evaluate OPACs listed 170 features grouped into ten categories:

- *database characteristics* – for example what information is displayed (call number, author, title, subject heading(s), location, loan status, and so on).

- *operational control* – for instance whether it offers: a menu-driven or command-driven interface, the ability to place holds or reserves, viewing of items on loan to a user, downloading of records to own PC, and emailing of results.

- *searching facilities offered* – for example does the system provide: keyword searching and of what fields, Boolean operations, adjacency operator, word proximity operator, weighted term search, limiting of search by dates and other characteristics, hypertext links from one record to a related record, and saving of search results.

- *subject search aids* – that is what is available: browsing of classification, subject headings, and display of cross-references.

- *access points* – for example via which fields (author, title, subject etc.) can a user access data.

- *screen display options* – for example which of the following are available: labelling of fields, choice of brief and full record display, and circulation status displayed with call number.

- *output control options* – examples include user selection of specific fields to display, ability to display the results of several searches, user-specified sort keys, and display of retrieved records in decreasing order of probable relevance.

- *commands options* – questions to pose include are they consistent? do they perform the same role in different contexts? is there a standardised syntax? and is the number of keystrokes kept to a minimum?

- *user assistance functions* – which of the following are available: online tutorial, general help messages, contextual help messages, error messages (are there enough? are they clear?), and spell checking software.

- *OPAC usability via remote access* – questions include are there adequate logon and logoff instructions, and are there restrictions in terms of times of day access is available (Cherry 1994, pp.192-195).

This 1994 checklist is still applicable today, although many more desirable features resulting from networking developments can now be added. Indeed, the list continues to be extended. One which is fast becoming possible with recent technological innovations is speech synthesis of both the input and the output. Another checklist to evaluate world wide web displays of bibliographic records is also available and can be used profitably in conjunction with the 1994 checklist (Cherry & Cox 1996).

These checklists and other writings articulate principles of good design to ensure that OPACs are as user-friendly as possible. Such principles include:

- *navigational features* – the user should know where they are, where they came from, and where they can go next, and this should be displayed on every screen;
- *familiar vocabulary* – no jargon and codes; laymous terms.
- *system messages* – should be clear and neutral;
- *hel*p – assistance should be available online from every screen; and
- *response time* – fast response is fundamental.

The third generation: WebPACs

In 1993, Tedd noted that most operational systems were still second-generation OPACs. However, most libraries have since then upgraded their library systems and now provide their users with a third-generation OPAC. Indeed, anything less would appear very out-of-date in the face of the pervasiveness of the modern search engines available on the world wide web.

The third-generation OPAC differs from its predecessors in two major areas: its human-computer interface, and the search capabilities it offers. It is likely to have a GUI based on *graphic user interface* Windows, and support a natural language interface which accepts search expressions in ordinary language, with facilities for using a dictionary to provide for abbreviations, synonyms or spelling variants. Its searching capabilities include non-Boolean retrieval techniques (based on best match rather than exact match), searching of enhanced records by including additional controlled and uncontrolled access points (such as chapter titles in books), and using terms selected from relevant records retrieved to enhance the search strategy. It will display the most relevant records retrieved first, and provides context-dependent help (Tedd 1993, pp.141-142). Some of the important new features are summarised below:

- *interoperability*: direct and transparent access to databases other than the main bibliographic database, so that the OPAC acts as a *gateway* to resources such as online databases, including other OPACs; ability to search many databases at one time; Z39.50 capability, which is one mechanism that allows for this and also for users to search other OPACs through the internet while still using their base OPAC's search interface; ability to handle MARC and non-MARC data formats.
- *functionality*: full multimedia capability (e.g., ability to handle sound clips, video clips and still images); support for non-Roman scripts; searching capabilities which go beyond the usual highly-structured, field-based text-string-based searches (e.g., relevance ranking, full-text retrieval); support for enhanced records.
- *user-friendliness*: mouseable, graphical user interface (such as Windows); choice of GUI (e.g., one designed for children); context-dependent help; online reference works such as dictionaries and encyclopedias; downloading of search results to diskette or by emailing; creation of personal lists ('shopping carts' in web parlance); query expansion.

Perhaps the most important development in OPACs, however, has been their recent transformation into WebPACs. While some second-generation OPACs could be accessed through the internet via, for example, the TELNET protocol, the WebPAC is more than simply *online*, for it is able to provide the same type of interface as that of other web-based search engines. It provides access to remote users in the same way as it does to those in the physical library, and as such has become one of key components of many new hybrid and digital libraries. The WebPAC not only provides bibliographic access, that is, access to the surrogate records, but can also offer access to (online) information resources themselves. If MARC-based, the WebPAC offers links to the resources through the 856 field, which contains the URL. The digital resource, which may be mounted on the library's own server, or located on an external site subscribed to by the library, can then be downloaded onto the user's PC (the user may sometimes need to enter a password first). The WebPAC can also offer links to related, virtual resources (e.g., biographic information about an author, or a review of the resource).

In this way, WebPACs can offer *instant* access to digital resources as well as traditional bibliographic access to resources located in a library's physical collections. As such, they represent the hybrid nature of most contemporary libraries, comprising of both physical and virtual information resources. These OPACs facilitate the end-user's search for information more efficiently and effectively than did their predecessors: instead of the regular visit to the library, the library now comes to the patron. Even for resources in the library's physical collections, the remote-access OPAC allows users the convenience of selecting and reserving items whenever they are logged on to the internet, without having to be at the library, and saves them from wasted journeys in cases where the resources they are looking for are not there.

As well as the more convenient access to information resources, OPAC users are now able to find a greater range of resources. They can search multiple databases containing, or linked to, both data and metadata, and that data could be in the form of images, video and sound, as well as text. We should not forget that OPACs are not only used by library patrons. The new OPACs enable library staff and other information workers to perform many of their tasks more efficiently and effectively. For example, remote access to numerous libraries' OPACs greatly facilitates resource sharing and interlibrary loan.

OPAC issues: towards the next generation

Despite more than two decades of research and experimentation, OPACs continue to frustrate many users just as they did a decade ago: 'Online catalogs still seem to be highly imperfect systems. If the user matches a request with the database, the result will be some sort of success' (O'Brien 1994, p.236). It is well established that typically the process of searching for information is iterative, in that the search query is slowly refined as the results of previous searches are fed back into it. Despite this the design of most WebPACs still assumes that users can specify a search query at the start of the process, a search query that is capable of being satisfied with a result from a single search session. Subject searching provides an example. The use of controlled vocabularies in library databases (see chapter 6) often leads to failure, a null result, because the search process requires a precise match to succeed. User interfaces are another area of concern to users. While there has been some research into alternative interfaces, commercial OPACs have rarely implemented this research.

In the mid-1990s, Christine Borgman observed that the large amount of research into user search behaviour has not, by and large, influenced OPAC design except in some experimental systems (Borgman 1996). This has begun to change, but only in the last few years, as librarians have come to realise the importance of the OPAC as key to the use, and value, of their physical and virtual collections. It is imperative that the next generation of OPACs are not simply available on the web, but that they are attractive and rewarding. As we mentioned in earlier chapters, many librarians are now very concerned that their libraries' OPACs and other databases are increasingly being sidelined as Google and the other major search engines on the web take over the information world – users try the library catalogue only as a last resort, if the web search engines fail them. Although the main issues here are the legacy of physical collections yet to be digitised and the quantity and quality, or otherwise, of internet resources, it cannot be denied that search engines such as Google offer a far more sophisticated functionality and interface than does the average library OPAC, and that this matters. Librarians appear to be losing their lead role as the field of bibliographic organisation is transformed by the world wide web, and they need to fight back. As Joseph Janes points out, 'It seems inevitable that Google, and its successors, will profoundly affect search practice, and, in a smaller way, librarianship. Perhaps the more important question is how we might be able to affect them' (Janes 2002, p.84).

Discussion about how to make WebPACs both look and act like the Googles of the virtual world has thus become quite urgent, as demonstrated by the popularity of lists such as NGC4Lib (Next Generation Catalogs for Libraries), and many papers at recent conferences and seminars (for example, the Australian Committee on Cataloguing devoted its 2006 annual seminar to the topic (*Beyond the OPAC* 2006)). We have seen that the trend is towards user-centred OPACs: catalogues no longer sit in murky rooms awaiting their users' patronage. But this can, and no doubt will, be taken further – by the next generation of OPACs. The goal is to make users want to go to the OPAC first, and then to Google. We saw in chapter 12 how OCLC has been leading the way towards achieving this goal with its WorldCat.org service.

With some of the commercial library systems still not quite up to the task, some librarians are taking matters into their own hands, by building their own WebPACs on top of their basic systems – these WebPACs are, in effect, 'plug-ins'. This requires a good deal of computing nous, but is no longer as difficult as it might have been a decade or so ago. Some open source 'shells' are now available to assist development teams. It is worth having a look at some of these efforts (accessible through the web, of course), such as the 'Bradford OPAC 2' (BOPAC2) and the new OPAC at the State Library of Tasmania.

There are several ways in which these 'next generation' OPACs are more user-friendly. In terms of navigation, they present what are known as *faceted* displays. That is, the various metadata elements in citations are separated out so that the user may follow up by browsing or searching for other resources through one or more of these elements. This is, in fact, an extension of the 'related resource' hyperlinks that have been available on OPAC interfaces for several years, but goes further by making more facets available, and by making it easier for users to explore arrays within facets more readily. Rather than working out exactly what they they want at the beginning of a search, users can 'forage' for resources by clicking on different attributes in lists and by switching between facets. Figure 14.3 shows how the new OPAC at the State Library of Tasmania allows for exploration of a range of metadata facets –

as listed on the left-hand side of the screen. Users can refine their search by author, finction/non-fiction, format, genre, topic, audience, availability, and so on.

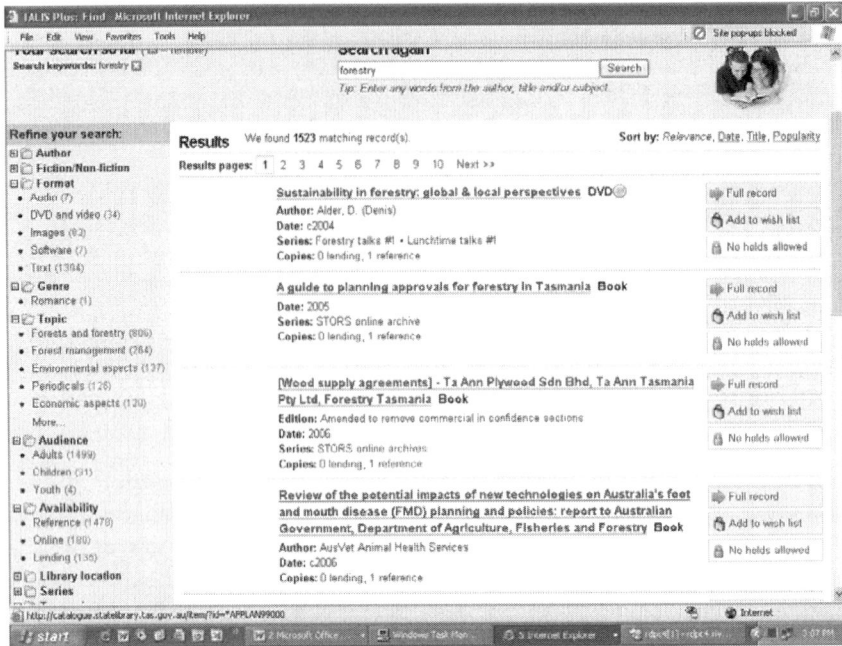

Figure 14.3 Results display on State Library of Tasmania OPAC (TalisPlus)

In similar vein, the emerging generation of OPACs are often 'FRBRised' – that is, they present results at the work, expression, manifestation and item levels, so that all the resources representing a particular work are grouped together and users can 'drill down' through the various expressions (editions, translations, etc.) to find particular copies. An example of a FRBRised catalogue is shown in figures 14.4 and 14.5, featuring the Virtua OPAC from VTLS, a system vendor which pioneered FRBRisation.

The new OPACs also offer a more personal service. For example, they may allow users to customise the interface and functionality according to their own preferences. They may also be able to build up user profiles based on previous searches, and alert individual users to new resources that might be of particular interest to them (perhaps through RSS feeds). Furthermore, the new OPACs are attempting to better integrate themselves into users' wider information seeking and use. For instance, they may offer a facility for downloading citations into a personal bibliographic manager such as EndNote. And it can work the other way too, with tools allowing users on external sites to automatically look up their library's OPAC. For instance, there are now 'plug ins' that can be added to web browsers so that users can automatically search their specified catalogues using bibliographic information found on external sites (e.g., Amazon.com), or just by typing in a search box on the tool bar. Other innovative features have been recently explored in the Melvyl Recommender Project by members for the California Digital Library team (see the project's website for the reports).

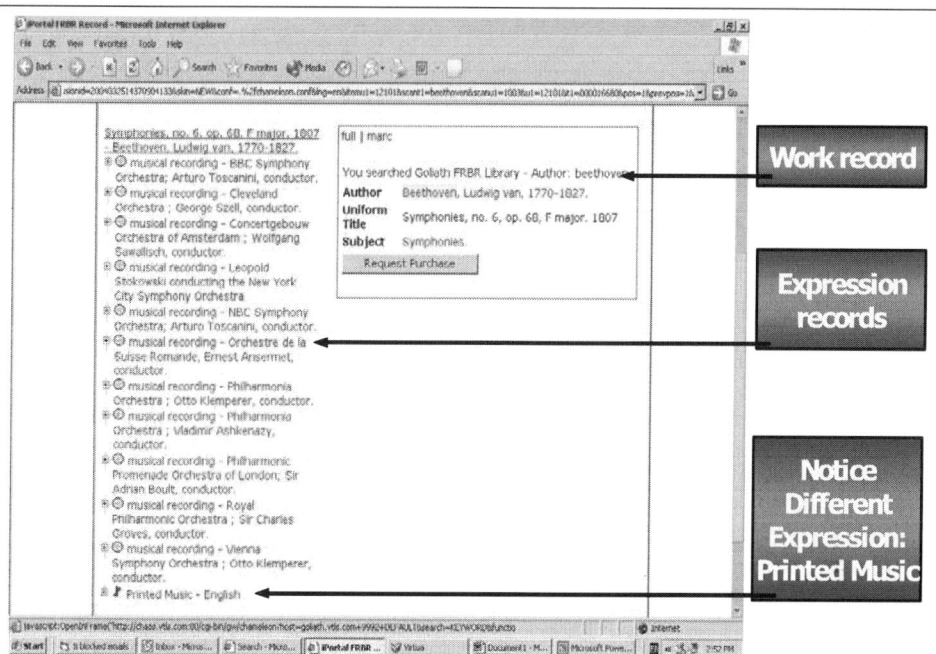

Figure 14.4 VTLS OPAC displaying work and expressions records

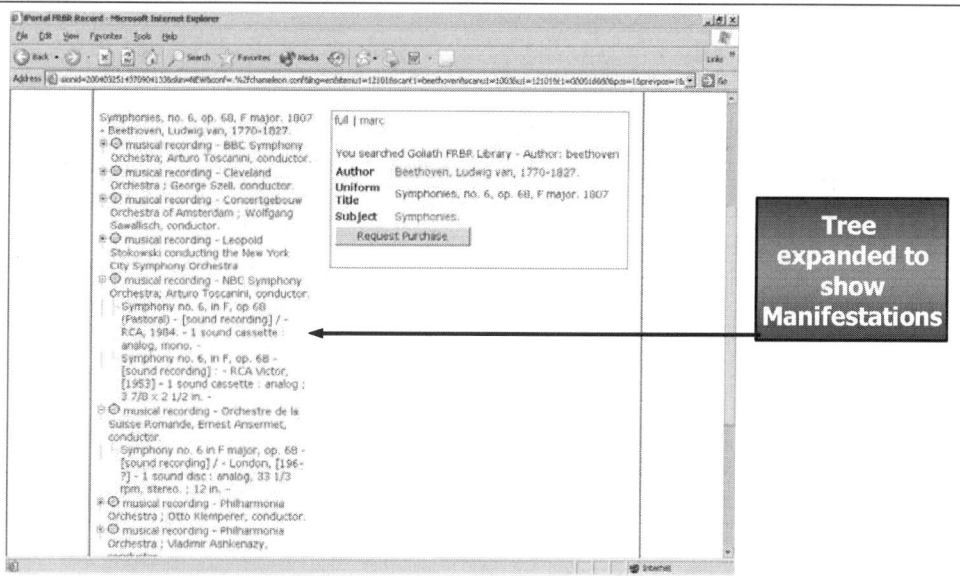

Figure 14.5 VTLS OPAC display expanded to manifestation level

The future for integrated library systems

In integrated library system development, as with all computing applications, the near future very rapidly becomes the present, and, all too soon, the past. The rapidly changing environment in which libraries and other information centres are operating means that new applications are being rushed into the marketplace, where some will stay, but most will sink. One thing is certain, though: the dramatic increase in *interconnectivity* of libraries and of library systems is here to stay. This is probably the single most significant factor we need to consider in relation to the future role of the integrated library system.

Most of the features below are offered by the leading systems available in the market today:

- the ability to operate on a wide range of hardware platforms: the software needs to be portable;
- a user-focused interface: a GUI which can be customised to individual users' needs;
- functionality which is customisable, for example, through macros;
- automated SDI (Selective Dissemination of Information) to users;
- the ability to import, manipulate and export data in a variety of formats;
- the ability to manage and retrieve on a wide range of non-bibliographical data, for example, text, images, line drawings, sound, video;
- effective online documentation and help: for instance, context-sensitive help, online tutorials;
- seamless integration and data transfer: for instance, the ability for users to copy or download search results;
- advanced information retrieval facilities: examples include relevance ranking, hypertext links, fuzzy logic searching, phonetic searching, online thesaurus, full-text display options; and
- networking capability: the ability to access local databases, for example on an intranet, as well as the ability to access external databases and other information resources via the internet.

Some of these features have taken a long time in coming, although one should bear in mind that library system vendors do not make the sort of profits that corporations such as Microsoft do. While the system vendors often have great ideas for the enhancement of their products, they generally possess limited resources for the corresponding development work. The more ambitious their projects, the more difficult it is for them to build on their existing software, and the more frustrated and disappointed become their customers as they wait for a version that properly implements the promised functionality. In short, vendors of library systems have a habit of selling their products before they are fully developed. Thus, librarians are advised not to take at face value any list of features advertised in a brochure.

Experience has shown librarians that although integration of many functions is highly desirable in theory, there are some disadvantages. These arise through poor system design, when the integration has not been well implemented by the system designer. The information professional using such a system may have to put up with a weak, poorly designed module for the sake of other modules in the same library system which are well-designed and well-integrated: an efficient circulation module and OPAC may be available, for example, but the serials control module may be weak or even not available. As integrated library system developers start to aim for a new level of interoperability, this lesson becomes particularly worth remembering. Librarians must be confident that their revamped systems are designed in such as way that they can adapt as the systems operated by their non-library information partners continue to change, and that none of the basic modules are left behind.

Recently, the aim of interoperability has led system vendors to start breaking the mould and to rethink the basis of their system design. While the bibliographic record remains of high importance, systems are now being designed to deal with the resources themselves, as well as their metadata. Today's systems do more than simply point to information in a book that sits on a shelf: they aim to do what they say they do – *provide* the information. The focus is increasingly on the library's ultimate product, information, and less on the library as an institution. Hence many vendors no longer sell 'library systems', but 'information management' systems. In this way, ILS/LMS are beginning to converge with CMS – content management systems (mentioned earlier in chapter 9). As more and more content is digitised, or is born digital, so distinctions between systems for digital libraries and 'regular libraries' will evaporate. Furthermore, the capacity of modern computers to archive enormous amounts of digital data also makes more fuzzy the distinction between libraries and archives, which means that we can expect to see library systems taking on more features of digital repositories. The growing scale of many digital collections has led to an interest in developing open source solutions – packages such as DSpace, Greenstone and Fedora – that borrow from the latest innovations of information retrieval and management, and that can be more readily customised. The future of integrated library systems may therefore lie in their own integration into the wider world of digital information systems.

Conclusion

The integrated library system has transformed the way libraries operate over the past two decades. The more effectively they have been able to integrate the various subsystems, the more successful they have become. They have automated much of libraries' technical services work and have had an enormous impact on end-users. Their interconnectivity has also allowed even the smallest information centres to readily and economically provide an electronic gateway to other information centres throughout the world. This has happened through the development and widespread implementation of the OPAC which, originally conceived as the doorway to the local integrated library system, has rapidly become the gateway to all information resources in a publicly accessible form, as libraries shift from the paradigm of library as collection to that of library as access facilitator.

This shift is now reaching its inevitable conclusion: most of today's libraries aim to offer users access to all kinds of information, not just information to be found in traditional library collections, which means collaborating with other information providers, and designing a new kind of system, not so much an integrated library system as an integrated *information* system. Such a system does not distinguish between 'library information' and other information: it is all information to be managed by the library and provided, as effectively as possible, to its users.

PART V: CURRENT ISSUES IN ORGANISING KNOWLEDGE

Introduction

Part I presented an overview of how information is organised in libraries and information centres, and Part II covered the standards that are used to do this effectively. In Part III the processes and systems involved with providing access to documents through their subject content were described. Part IV was concerned with the standards for exchanging bibliographic data and the organisations that facilitate the sharing of metadata.

In Part V an attempt is made to identify likely developments that will change the way that information is organised in libraries and information centres in the next few years.

CHAPTER 15
The changing role of bibliographic organisation

The starting point of this chapter is the rapid change in bibliographic organisation practice that has taken place over the past decade, particularly as a result of the internet. Perhaps the most obvious example of this change is the transformation of library catalogues from localised finding aids into gateways to global information.

> Going back to Panizzi and Cutter, it has been axiomatic that bibliographic control was a matter of keeping track of, or inventorying, a specific physical object in a specific physical place. Today, these 'objects' are as likely as not to be in a variety of both physical and evanescent formats and in no specific physical place as we have been used to understanding these things … the focus should now shift to where it should have been in the first place – and that is the intellectual content and substance of the work itself (Hensen 2001).

Such change is putting new pressures on what we expect our library catalogues to do, with new expectations about how they present information and how they actively assist users to achieve results. As noted at the start of this book, the significance of conventional bibliographic organisation practice in the digital age is lessening. New mechanisms for organising and controlling digital media and digital information resources are being developed and applied. Conventional practice will not, though, become irrelevant as a result of the widespread use of library computer networks and the digital library revolution. Rather, it forms the basis for future practice, albeit with modification.

This chapter examines some of the significant factors that are altering current bibliographic organisation practice and indicates some of the further changes that are likely to occur.

The major factors

Some trends that will have significant impact on how information professionals organise knowledge in the near future can be readily identified. On some there is general agreement; others are more contentious.

Change is always present. A comment made in 1973 about cataloguing in the future – 'perhaps the only permanent element is change, in the present situation' (Nelson 1974, p.654) – is still germane today, perhaps even more so. However, other commentators (e.g., Oddy 1996, p.83) have pointed out that change for the sake of change is not acceptable to large information centres. These are conservative by definition – for instance they maintain large databases that cannot be changed quickly or frequently because of their size and complexity. Consequently, their inertia acts as a brake on an excessively rapid rate of change to bibliographic standards and practice.

Doing more with less. The economics of operating information centres in the present environment (and for the foreseeable future) indicate that we will continue to be limited in our ability to increase the resources we can devote to organising knowledge.

The OPAC as gateway to global information sources. No longer do users of our information centres expect merely to check whether the information centre owns a particular information resource. They also expect to be able to determine whether that information resource is available for use. Increasingly, they expect to be able to access other catalogues, databases and significant amounts of full-text information and other digital objects through the terminals of the library information retrieval system. Some resources may be available through a library's subscription, other resources, such as those that are part of the 'open access' movement, will be freely available – but users will still expect to be pointed in their direction.

The internet as the primary mechanism for networking information resources and services. Access to global information resources is increasingly being delivered through the internet. This trend will continue, and, increasingly, 'legacy' information resources (those information resources produced originally in analogue form, primarily printed materials, but also including recorded sound and moving images) will be digitised and available through the internet. Also available increasingly via the internet will be the metadata for these legacy collections.

Different kinds of information resources. Traditional bibliographic organisation practice has been developed over many centuries to accommodate information resources that come in specific standard packages. The book and other standard packages such as videos and CD-ROMs are obvious examples. (This is noted in more detail in chapter 2.) Standard codes of practice for bibliographic organisation apply well to such standard packages, particularly packages that are published by conventional formalised processes. They do not, however, work at all well for new kinds of information resources whose characteristics are constantly altering (the website whose address changes, for example).

Library professionals are collaborating with other information professionals to improve the organisation of knowledge. There is growing recognition that there is a significant body of common practice in the ways in which different groups of information professionals organise knowledge. Librarians no longer contemplate only AACR2 and DDC; archivists the concepts of arrangement, description and finding aids; records managers the mysteries of file titling; or museum curators their registration procedures. Forums are now available where commonalities of practice are being developed, debated and refined.

Auto-cataloguing and metadata. The concept that information resources should be designed to be self-cataloguing is being encouraged. This school of thought promotes the idea that creators and publishers of information resources can provide cataloguing data at the point of creation and publication, as an intrinsic part of the information resource. The development of metadata standards and strategies is allowing this to take place.

Users of library information retrieval systems and standards have a strong voice. Information professionals, to remain relevant, are taking more account of user needs to improve library information retrieval systems and standards.

Even the terminology is changing. No longer do we talk about cataloguing, or even bibliographic organisation or bibliographic control: now it is *resource description*. (Hence the *Anglo-American Cataloguing Rules* are to be superseded by *Resource Description and Access*.) This term emphasises one important aspect of the present information/library reality – that we are primarily interested in resources, not only those in our own information centres but also those which we want to bring to the attention of our users, no matter where these resources and our users are located.

Current issues: bibliographic description

Standards for organising information will still have a place in the future – but the problems with our current standards, such as AACR2 and MARC, mean that they are unlikely to survive without significant modification. Fortunately, this modification is now well underway; it involves updating the standards so that they are fully appropriate for online resources and for the creation, or derivation, of their online metadata. Can they be used to describe blogs, wikis and podcasts, for instance? Some of the conventions that the old standards represent are no longer valid, although there are also many which are still relevant. After all, we still often think in terms of the physical world when we describe online phenomena ('desk top', 'windows', 'pages', 'scrolling', etc.). We should not throw the baby out with the bath water; but neither can we sit back and ignore the realities of a new information world, and a new generation of users who know only this world.

The reason why some standards will remain (albeit in modified form), and others will not, is partly linked to the way in which they have been developed, and partly to the way in which they are now firmly entrenched in our current systems. Newer standards might have been developed for the new information world, but they are also less likely to have large amounts of metadata behind them, as have AACR2 and MARC. Despite its critics, MARC is likely to remain relevant over the next decade, although its use as a format for resource description, even in libraries, may well wane, and whether we will ever get to MARC 22 (for the twenty-second century) is highly doubtful. To continue to be applied, in ongoing cataloguing, the standard will need not only to adapt, but also to demonstrate its compatibility with a range of other standards used in modern information retrieval systems (the key to this might be MARCXML). To survive, standards also need their champions – preferably influential institutions (such as national agencies and large companies such as OCLC) as well as energetic individuals. MARC may need more people like Hendrix (1997, p.5): 'I believe … that my friend MARC will escort me from memory lane to Superhighway and probably to the grave. In fact my headstone is already in draft format complete with tags and subfields!' (Hendrix 1997, p.5).

Embedding metadata into standard practice

Librarians have been creating, storing and using metadata for centuries. The major difference between this metadata and the 'new' metadata is that the first is applied to traditional information packets, usually formally published, such as the book, whereas the latter has been developed specifically in response to electronic documents, particularly networked electronic documents. A second significant difference is that the present metadata discussion contains 'an implicit search for ways to go beyond that which is provided by current descriptive practices' (Lynch 1998), extending practice to include new areas such as rights management (who owns, who can use, who pays for use) and the integrity and provenance of resources (where they came from, have they been altered, who altered them, with what authority, when). The metadata concept has also been developed because of the growing realisation of the limitations of current web indexing services – despite their popularity and power – in allowing adequate resource discovery.

Ideally, it is thought, metadata should now be generated at the same time as the information content of the document is created. To put this in traditional library terms, the books should also contain the cataloguing record. Metadata generation needs to be a simple and rapid process in order to encourage all document creators and publishers to participate, but the resulting metadata cannot be so simple that it is useless for its intended purposes of locating information and describing essential parts of the document. To achieve these aims the Dublin Core concept was developed and continues to be refined and expanded.

As indicated in chapter 10, the Dublin Core standard is based on some key principles: simplicity, semantic interoperability, international consensus, and flexibility. It is simple and flexible enough to appeal not only across countries, but also across information communities. It is semantically interoperable so that it accommodates a broad range of content standards.

This does not mean, however, that Dublin Core is the *only* way forward. Its simplicity has led to many local modifications, necessary to meet local users, and it is likely that these will only increase so that even if DC becomes the predominant standard (which is by no means a certainty), the issue of interoperability will become increasingly important. Furthermore, the fact that DC accommodates various content standards means that other problems remain, such as the issue of vocabulary control (otherwise known as authority control).

Nevertheless, the Dublin Core *concept* seems here to stay. That is, librarians and other information communities can no longer afford to develop standards independently of each other. Instead, they must work together and develop standards that are as accommodating as possible. They need to do this because, increasingly, the information they manage will be derived from non-traditional sources and will be transferable to other domains.

What knowledge organisers must be careful to do is to promote a proper understanding of this concept. It does not mean watering down metadata to a few simple, uncontrolled fields. Interoperability does not equate to simplicity. Instead, the challenge of interoperability should lead to ever more complex webs of metadata, held together by crosswalks, multilingual thesauri, and the like; ever more complex to the metadata specialist, that is, but seamless to the end-user.

One platform that might enable both a metadata web and a seamless interface is XML. While XML has been presented as holding great promise, whether XML can improve the chaotic situation we have at present depends less on new XML developments, and more on XML programmers creating applications to meet the specific requirements of knowledge organisers.

Current issues: subject access

Part III noted the ways in which we currently provide subject access to information resources. A balance is being struck between natural language or controlled vocabulary approaches, with both being used to complement each other for maximum effectiveness. There are still many who advocate a fully automated solution to providing subject access, but there remains a long way to go, with results still often less reliable than those produced by systems based on human indexing. However, automatic indexing and abstracting, and automatic classification, can no longer be ignored; rather, they need to be evaluated in the context of particular information environments, users and economics.

The problem can be stated briefly: how can the characteristics of a document be summarised automatically (without human intervention) to facilitate retrieval? This question presupposes, of course, that the documents are in electronic form. Automatic indexing may never be viable for all subject domains, but it provides acceptable results in some domains where knowledge is highly structured. For example, automatic processes can provide adequate access to many electronic documents in the business field where the characteristics sought (company name, activity such as merger or acquisition, etc.) can be readily identified. For other categories of documents, automated techniques can be applied to determine the subjects of documents. Word frequency techniques, for instance, can identify the most commonly occurring words and roots (e.g., *employ** to encompass *employ, employment, employers, employees*). Such techniques will not, however, resolve many of the vocabulary issues that are noted in Part III – at least, they cannot resolve them *yet*. Research is ongoing.

Some commentators suggest that the primary means of accessing information resources in the near future will be full-text searching. The 'default means of searching', suggests Lynch, will be based on 'effective content-based computational techniques [that are] very inexpensive, ubiquitous … available virtually the instant that the content is first distributed or published'. In this scenario there will still be a place for 'information identification support provided by human-based intellectual bibliographic control, which is intrinsically more costly and often available only after some delay following dissemination of a work' and these techniques will be applied only to information resources that are successful or significant enough to justify the expense (Lynch 2000).

Apart from automatic indexing, another way of avoiding the costs of professional indexers, but of supplementing full text with actual metadata, is to foster contributions from authors and users. *Social tagging* has been one of the most studied areas of information organisation in recent years, and has produced some interesting results. Of course, there are again issues of vocabulary control, but there are also some apparent advantages over controlled, and professionally applied indexing – the vocabulary might be inconsistent, but it is, by definition, user-oriented, and accommodates multiple viewpoints of a knowledge resource much better than does a single indexer, however professional.

Perhaps the greatest challenge we are likely to face in providing access to information resources is that of developing effective techniques for non-textual material. Current best practice is based on providing text surrogates for this material. One way we do this is to 'use human intellectual analysis to attach words to them (ideally within a structured descriptive or analytic context)' (Lynch 2000). These words are then searched using the standard information retrieval techniques that we apply to text. Similar techniques that develop textual surrogates include transcribing recorded speech, perhaps using automated processes for turning speech into text, and then searching this surrogate text using standard text-based information retrieval techniques. Images, both still (such as photographs or paintings) and moving (as is film or video), present a much greater challenge. These are likely to continue to require human intellectual input to describe them. Controlling and providing access to non-textual materials is, considers Lynch, 'one of the most complex and controversial areas … [but] a critical area as we think about the context for the new millennium' (Lynch 2000).

Current issues: bibliographic data exchange and management

The battle continues between those who advocate an automated solution to organising knowledge and those who consider that the fully automated approach is inadequate. Automated solutions can only be fully effective if the information to be indexed is in digital form. Is this the norm? When will it become the norm? Is it worth converting printed material to digital form solely for this reason? We cannot yet assume that the only valid information is electronic information, despite the best efforts of Google Books and the digital library movement. However, there can be no question that we are now moving into a truly digital information age, and most information professionals of the future will surely be dealing with online resources much more than physical ones.

More serious objections to the fully automated information retrieval future have already been noted. Vocabulary issues form one group of objections: automatic indexing can only work on the vocabulary present in the document, and this has limitations, as noted in the preceding section, in chapter 8, and elsewhere. Authority control issues are another major concern (see chapter 5). And there are still technical issues to be overcome (see chapter 14). Despite significant early promise, as can be seen in enthusiastic writings in the late 1980s and early 1990s, we should note that expert systems in bibliographic organisation have so far produced few commercial applications (Davies 1992; Hawks 1994; Olmstadt 2000).

This section examines briefly two areas where research into the systems used for organising knowledge in information centres is proving fruitful, even if they are not necessarily leading to a fully automated future:

- information retrieval techniques, and

- the library information retrieval system as gateway.

The section then turns to the progress being made by vendors of library information retrieval systems in some other areas, and ends with a look at the future of metadata exchange.

Information retrieval techniques

Research into information retrieval techniques already has a long and honourable history, and it is impossible to do more than note it briefly here. Some of the research is covered in previous chapters. Areas that appear to be particularly fruitful at present are:

- *alternatives to Boolean systems to improve retrieval* – for example, term weighting and probabilistic retrieval are becoming well established in the current generation of library information retrieval systems; data mining and fuzzy logic techniques are being investigated and applied;

- *document structure to aid retrieval* – investigations into the use of XML and RDF have resulted in some major improvements;

- *developing an optimal query to improve retrieval* – relevance feedback and query expansion are examples; and

- *user studies* – more is becoming known about the characteristics of users of information retrieval systems, the behaviour patterns of searchers, and optimal interface design (particularly through the field of visualisation).

Some of the results of this research are being applied to information retrieval systems used by libraries and other information centres. More will become commonly available in coming years.

Other research with potential application to library information retrieval systems is continuing in many forums and on many topics. One area currently generating interest is auditory display of data (in our case, metadata). There are two main strands of investigation here: auditory output to assist handicapped users, such as the sight-impaired; and audio output to assist in the presentation and comprehension of complex datasets that result from database searches. The major research body in this field is the International Community for Auditory Display. Should we expect to talk and listen to OPACs in the near future?

The library information retrieval system as gateway

Preceding chapters have indicated that the library information retrieval system is no longer merely a tool to provide access to documents in a single collection. Major steps have already been made towards a new networked reality, in which the library information retrieval system is a gateway to a wide range of information resources, regardless of their location. (Not all agree, incidentally, that a single catalogue should perform these functions: the concept of an *access catalogue* as a complement to the traditional *holdings catalogue* has been explored, the impetus for this being Dublin Core and the Z39.50 protocols (Hanson 1998)). Despite this progress, there are still some major obstacles to be overcome and further refinements are needed. Indeed, there are still systems lacking the newer protocols such as OpenURL.

With the advent of Google and a plethora of similar retrieval systems freely available on the internet, library systems have no choice but to continue down this path if they are to remain relevant to users. Libraries are looking to offer their patrons one-stop searching through their websites, instead of users having to interrogate various catalogues and databases in turn. The wider the range of databases libraries have to offer, the greater the technical difficulties. Some commercial solutions are now available, however, which allow direct access to articles and papers, as well as to books and journals.

These solutions also attempt to meet the challenge of aggregated databases, which offer information centres subscriptions across a range of serials, some full-text, others not, and some in part. The problem with these databases is that their contents are highly unstable: full-text articles disappear without warning, as subscriptions are cancelled; and new material appears as new journals are introduced or new issues are made available online. While it is theoretically possible for cataloguers to provide bibliographic access to the journals on these aggregated databases, it has become almost impossible for staff to keep track of a library's virtual holdings and update the catalogue manually. While some vendors are able to supply catalogue records for serials on their databases, the frequent changes mean that this supply has to be ongoing, and may be complicated by multiple subscription options. Even with close collaboration between vendors and libraries, traditional OPACs appear to be losing ground to the aggregators (Martin & Saxton 2001). New approaches utilising online technologies are required.

OPACs and integrated library systems

Chapter 14 discussed the most important issues that need to be addressed in the future in order to improve our library information retrieval systems, especially their OPAC modules. Despite considerable research into improving them, OPACs still frustrate many users. Some libraries have even built their own catalogue interfaces using open source software, demonstrating that attractive, dynamic OPACs *are* possible. If the OPAC is the window to a library's collection and beyond, then it needs to be transparent. Using an OPAC needs to be as rewarding as using Google. Whether it is or not depends to some extent on the library's collection, and on the quality of the metadata, but it also depends on the user's interaction with the system. Some of the standard OPAC modules still need to improve in some basic areas, such as:

- user assistance, for example, spelling feedback;

- information retrieval techniques, as already mentioned in the earlier section; and

- contextual aids, such as assistance with vocabulary choices during the searching process.

Another important issue is multilingual and multiscript handling. As noted in chapter 4 in relation to names and titles, this is of particular interest in Australia where many languages are in common use. The ideal library information retrieval system is one which can be searched using any script and which can display search results in all relevant scripts; the user should have the facility to indicate which script, or scripts, to display. Although today's computers and browsers can handle and display more than one script, thanks chiefly to the Unicode standard, many library information retrieval systems are still much more restrictive.

If library management systems are to survive as a species of information retrieval system, then they must incorporate the latest features that are making other systems so attractive, and, most important, they must allow for *interoperability* – they must fit into the ever more complex network of systems that is evolving on the internet. At a fundamental level, this means being able to work with a range of standards, and metadata based on these standards – not just MARC. Similarly, cataloguers will need to be familiar with a wider range of standards, so that they can make the most of these more accommodating systems.

Metadata exchange

The exchange of metadata has always been driven by economic considerations, and with ever-tightening budgets, libraries and other information centres will continue to seek to cut costs wherever possible. All types of information centre are now involved in the quest for cheaper metadata, and this has already had a large impact on technical services departments. With metadata, at least for some resources, so readily obtainable – that is, downloadable – from all over the world, many libraries are reluctant to have their own staff create detailed bibliographic records: they will wait for someone else to create them. This has meant that many cataloguers now perform much less original cataloguing, and instead have become editors of databases and supervisors of information retrieval systems (Ahronheim & Marko 2000). This presents a paradox, however. If everyone waits for someone else to do the cataloguing, no cataloguing will end up getting done. Already the Library of Congress and other major record suppliers are unable to keep pace with their own collection growth, let alone those of other libraries. The situation seems likely to get worse before it gets better. The need for cooperative cataloguing has never been greater.

With bibliographic data obtainable for free, in many instances, through Z39.50 technology, it would appear that the bibliographic utilities and networks are under threat, even OCLC. However, the ease of exchange is also to their advantage, as it also makes *them* more accessible and affordable. Nevertheless, it would be foolhardy in the extreme for any utility or network to rely on its basic cataloguing service, and all of them now offer additional services and products to safeguard their membership levels. OCLC is, in fact, the leading exponent of this – it is very much a library and information utility, not only a bibliographic utility.

Original cataloguing

For as long as libraries still want quality metadata, created by professionals, then the question remains: *which* professionals are going to do the cataloguing? Many smaller libraries search the web for copy cataloguing not only because its cheap and saves time, but because they simply do not have the expertise on their staff to apply the exacting standards that have been developed for library metadata. However, the larger libraries cannot cover all the original cataloguing, even if they had the staff to do so (which they certainly do not). There are many, many resources, particularly in the online world, which do not form part of their collections, but which might be of great value to the small, specialist library. The metadata for some of these resources may be supplied by a vendor. In other cases, the cataloguing may be outsourced to companies offering cataloguing services. As the technical services departments of even the larger libraries continue to suffer from budget cuts and staff reductions, so it is likely that the use of external cataloguing services will increase. As the resources requiring description will be increasingly digital, the outlook for commercial metadata providers, including freelance cataloguers, would appear to be encouraging. Perhaps the home-based back-of-the-book indexer will eventually become the home-based metatagger.

However, commercial metadata providers cost money that many libraries and other information agencies cannot always afford. The alternative is to make do with less. This could mean accepting whatever metadata the author or publisher can provide, or perhaps, in some situations, relying on user-generated tagging (of the 'folksonomy' variety). It could also mean putting pressure on the existing standards to allow for less detailed cataloguing requiring less expertise and time.

In fact, as it has been noted throughout this book, such pressure is already being applied on the traditional library standards such as AACR and MARC (thus RDA is aiming to be simpler than AACR, and MODS is being offered as an alternative to MARC). Indeed, this pressure is nothing new, far from it, it has existed for as long as the standard – some libraries will always be in less of a position than other libraries to apply detailed standards. However, it does appear that this pressure is building, and that today's libraries are less in a position to apply complex standards, on average, than were those of yesteryear. Along with budgetary squeezes, there is another factor contributing to this building pressure – the greater possibility of alternatives, such as social tagging and full-text searching. This does not mean that original cataloguing will necessarily be 'dumbed down' to a rudimentary level, although some of it is now being performed by paraprofessionals (to the consternation of many professional cataloguers), but it does mean that detailed description by metadata specialists may be reserved for a more select set of resources in future.

With the amount of online information doubling every three years, this selectivity is likely to increase. However, it is worth remembering that library collections have always been selected – they aim to bring together what is deemed *most* valuable to the user, that is part of their value. As collections grow into the online universe, so their treatment may become increasingly differentiated – some resources may be processed by cataloguers with high levels of expertise, some by paraprofessionals for more basic metadata creation, some may have author-created metadata harvested automatically; many resources may have their contents indexed by computers and by users. Materials outside of these collections may still be picked up by search engines and other retrieval mechanisms; but many may simply be ignored – this may be unfortunate, but it means that the more important materials tend to be highlighted. It is also no different from what has happened in the past.

It may become more difficult to decide *what* to select for cataloguing, not only because of the greater amount of information, but also because of increased difficulties in defining *a* resource. Does one catalogue a whole website, or just particular pages; each sound file or a collection of tracks that might in a past era have represented an 'album'? In the online world, bibliographic composition is much more problematic – not that it was all that straightforward previously!

The Semantic Web

Traditional ways of organising knowledge are being challenged by the web, raising questions about how the advantages of quality metadata can be promoted, and how we might integrate traditional bibliographic services with those of search engines. As noted in chapter 9, search engines are changing the way users think about access; the verb 'to google' has entered current parlance.

The Semantic Web is a concept that has the potential to bring together the wide range of approaches to organising web resources and make them more effective at describing and locating online information. 'The information may be there in the web, but currently only in a form that requires intensive human processing' (Miller & Swick 2003, p.8). It is, claimed the SemanticWeb.org website, 'a vision: the idea of having data on the web defined and linked in a way that it can be used by machines – not just for display purposes, but for using it in various applications' (*SemanticWeb* 2003). The aim is to use:

> enabling standards and technologies to allow data on the web to be defined and linked in such a way that it can be used for more effective discovery, automation, integration and reuse across various applications. The web can reach its full potential if it becomes a place where data can be shared and processed by automated tools as well as by people (Miller & Swick 2003, p.8).

The Semantic Web concept brings together many of the ideas noted elsewhere in this book as being of current interest, such as automated cataloguing, and interoperability. It has the potential to harness the energies and interests of a large number of stakeholders in many communities, including the web industry, the library and information science sector, and the archives sector.

Standards are the essential element in turning the concept into a working reality where software agents automatically carry out tasks that are very complex for humans. In the Semantic Web, all content is described in terms of its contextual relationships (e.g., 'hasLocation, worksFor, isAuthorOf, hasSubjectOf, dependsOn', Miller & Swick 2003, p.8) and then the standardised ways in which this is done 'opens doors for a whole new set of effective information integration, management and automated services' (Miller & Swick 2003, p.8). Controlled vocabularies, metadata, ontologies, all have a place. Many of the standards that are required for the Semantic Web to become a reality are already in place, such as XML, RDF, URIs (Uniform Resource Identifiers), and Unicode (Miller & Swick 2003; Greenberg, Sutton & Campbell 2003); Topic Maps is a recent addition to this list (ISO/IEC 13250:2003).

The key to the Semantic Web is having online information that is well described. If this can be achieved and interoperability implemented, we will have web pages, 'databases, services, programs, sensors, personal devices and even household appliances to both consume and produce data on the web' (Miller & Swick 2003, p.11). Consider this scenario of a person travelling to attend a meeting. Currently the process is 'designed to be driven by humans':

> We find that Darmstadt is near Frankfurt. Then we find that there are flights from Glasgow to Frankfurt, and there is a bus from Frankfurt Airport to Darmstadt. Then I search for timetables, make manual comparisons and decide which times best suit my requirements.

In the Semantic Web a software 'agent':

> would recognise from its regular review of my diary that I needed to be at a meeting in Darmstadt on the 21st of January 2003 and it would search out the options, analyse the timetables, identify the optimum travel arrangements, book my non-smoking hotel accommodation, and order the taxi to take me to the airport. (It might

even check the weather forecasts and warn me to bring particular types of clothing.) (Ross 2003, p.7)

The Semantic Web, if it becomes a reality, is likely to revolutionise how information is organised and accessed. Like many concepts, they may take a while to be realised. The jury is still out on the Semantic Web. Or perhaps that should be the population of the online world – ultimately they are likely to be the ones who make it a reality, or not. There have been a raft of refinements of the concept over the last few years (for example, see the activities of SKOS on its website – *Simple Knowledge Organisation for the Web*), but no matter how much refining and sophistication, it will work only if the ideas behind it are applied by a sufficient number of the web's users.

Conclusion

What might the bibliographic organisation (near) future look like? In broad outline it seems likely to be something like this.

- *'self-describing' information resources*. Many information resources will be created with embedded tags that allow for the identification of the metadata elements necessary to provide resource description. XML is the likely standard for such tagging, accommodating a variety of formats and content.

- *more selective use of cataloguing and indexing expertise*. There will still be a need for highly skilled indexers and cataloguers, but they will assign controlled vocabularies and other metadata to more select groups of resources, and possibly more at a 'collection level'.

- *a more complex network of information retrieval systems*. The information resources with which libraries will be concerned will cover a wider range than the average library currently handles, including archival documents, image databases and so on. This will become possible because of the increasing use of metadata standards in all information professions, and because of more interoperable systems based on crosswalks between these standards.

What will be the role of the librarian in all of this? We envisage that it will be similar in essence to the current role, but different in detail. The primary motivation will be as it always has been – to act as an intermediary between information and user, and to organise information resources (wherever they are located) and provide access to them (and to parts of them) so that the user and the information can be brought together. The tools by which this is done will be different. Most of the important standards and systems we will need to master are now in place, although some are in embryonic form. In order to use them effectively we need to keep foremost in our minds the reasons why we organise information. As the preface to this book notes, Ranganathan's five laws of library science encapsulate these reasons. Here is an inelegant updating of those laws:

- information is for use,
- to every user his information,
- to all information its user,

- save the time of the user,
- an information centre is a growing organism.

These laws should continue to guide us into the information future.

Michael Gorman's words at a 1997 conference are a worthy reflection for the end of this book:

> We librarians have the tools, experience, and the capability to preserve and organize recorded knowledge and information on a global scale, to realize the ideals of Universal Bibliographic Control, and to play our vital part in human progress and the advancement and protection of civilization. For cataloguers particularly, the future is challenging and bright. We must maintain the bibliographic structures that we have built and expand and develop them in two ways. First, by ensuring that worthwhile electronic documents are organized and preserved so that they can be made available to future generations. Second, by improving bibliographic standards world-wide and ensuring that they reach a level of standardisation that makes possible a new level of global cooperation. Some have speculated that cataloguing and cataloguers may be obsolete – I firmly believe that the opposite is true and that cataloguers will have an increasingly important role to play in the future of libraries and of society (Gorman 1997).

Abbreviations

AACR	Anglo-American Cataloguing Rules
AACR2	Anglo-American Cataloguing Rules, 2nd edition
ABN	Australian Bibliographic Network
ACS	Australian Card Service
AEI	Australian Education Index
AGLS	Australian Government Locator Service
ALA	American Library Association
AMRS	Australian MARC Record Service
ANB	Australian National Bibliography
ANBD	Australian National Bibliographic Database
ANSI	American National Standards Institute
APAIS	Australian Public Affairs Service
APT	Australian Pictorial Thesaurus
AUSMARC	Australian MARC
BC	Bliss Bibliographic Classification
BNB	British National Bibliography
BNBMARC	British National Bibliography MARC
CAVAL	Cooperative Action for Victorian Academic Libraries
CCF	Common Communications Format
CD	Compact disc
CD-R	Compact disc-recordable
CD-ROM	Compact disc-read only memory
CDWA	Categories for the Description of Works of Art
CIMI	Computer Interchange of Museum Information
CIP	Cataloguing in Publication
CJK	Chinese, Japanese, Korean
CLANN	College Libraries Activities Network of New South Wales
CMS	Content management systems
COMPASS	Computer Aided Subject System
CONSER	Cooperative Online Serials Project (originally Conversion of Serials Project)
CORC	Cooperative Online Resource Catalog
CQL	Contextual Query Language
CSDGM	Content Standard for Digital Geospatial Metadata
CURL	Consortium of University Research Libraries
DC	Dublin Core
DCMI	Dublin Core Metadata Initiative
DDC	Dewey Decimal Classification
DTD	Document Type Definition

EAD	Encoded Archival Description
EdNA	Education Network Australia
ERIC	Education Resources Information Center
ESTC	English Short Title Catalogue
FAST	Faceted Application of Subject Terminology
FRAD	Functional Requirements for Authority Data
FRBR	Functional Requirements for Bibliographic Records
FTP	File Transfer Protocol
GILS	Government Information Locator Service
GMD	General material designation
GUI	Graphical user interface
HTML	Hypertext Markup Language
HTTP	Hypertext Transfer Protocol
ICABS	IFLA-CDNL Alliance for Bibliographic Standards
IEEE LOM	Institute of Electrical and Electronics Engineers, Inc.Learning Objects Metadata
IFLA	International Federation of Library Associations and Institutions
ILANET	Information Libraries Access Network
ILL	Inter-library loan
ILS	Integrated library system
IMS	Instructional Management Systems
ISAAR(CPF)	International Standard Archival Authority Record for Corporate Bodies, Persons and Families
ISAD(G)	International Standard Archival Description (General)
ISBD	International Standard Bibliographic Description
ISBN	International Standard Book Number
ISDS	International Serials Data System
ISO	International Organization for Standardization
ISSN	International Standard Serial Number
KM	Knowledge management
KWIC	Key word in context
KWOC	Key word out of context
LASH	List of Australian Subject Headings
LC	Library of Congress
LCC	Library of Congress Classification
LCMARC	Library of Congress MARC
LCRI	Library of Congress Rule Interpretations
LCSH	Library of Congress Subject Headings
LINNET	Libraries in the Northern Territory Network
LMS	Library management system
LSP	Linked Systems Project
MARC	Machine-readable cataloguing
MeSH	Medical Subject Headings
METS	Metadata Encoding and Transmission Standard
MODS	Metadata Object Description Schema
NACO	Name Authority Cooperative Project

NISO	National Information Standards Organization
NLA	National Library of Australia
NLM	National Library of Medicine (U.S.)
NZBN	New Zealand Bibliographic Network
OAI	Open Archives Initiative
OPA-PMH	Open Archives Initiative Protocol for Metadata Harvesting
OCLC	Online Computer Library Center (originally Ohio College Library Center)
OCR	Optical character recognition
ONIX	Online Information eXchange
OPAC	Online public access catalogue
OSI	Open Systems Interconnection
PCC	Program for Cooperative Cataloging
PRECIS	Preserved Context Index System
RAK	Regeln für die alphabetische Katalogisierung
RDA	Resource Description and Access
RDF	Resource Description Framework
RECON	Retrospective Conversion Project
RLG	Research Libraries Group
RLIN	Research Libraries Information Network
RSS	Really Simple Syndication (originally RDF Site Summary)
SCIS	Schools Catalogue Information Service
SAB	Klassifikationssystem för svenska bibliotek
SACO	Subject Authority Cooperative Program
ScOT	Schools Online Thesaurus
SGML	Standard Generalised Markup Language
SILAS	Singapore Integrated Library Automation Services
SKOS	Simple Knowledge Organisation for the Web
SOAP	Simple Object Access Protocol
SOFI	Supersearch Ozline Friendly Interface
SRU	Search/Retrieval for URL
TCP/IP	Transmission Control Protocol/Internet Protocol
TEI	Text Encoding Initiative
UBC	Universal bibliographic control
UBCIM	Universal Bibliographic Control and International MARC
UDC	Universal Decimal Classification
UKMARC	United Kingdom MARC
UNIMARC	Universal MARC format
URL	Universal Resource Locator
USMARC	United States MARC
VIAF	Virtual International Authority File
VRA	Visual Resources Association
W3C	World Wide Web Consortium
WLN	Western Library Network (originally Washington Library Network)
XML	Extensible Markup Language
XOBIS	XML Organic Bibliographic Information Schema

Z39.50   ANSI/NISO Z39.50 Information Retrieval Service, Definition and
                Protocol Specification for Library Applications
ZING   Z39.50-International: Next Generation

Glossary

Abstracting the process of summarising concisely and accurately the content of an information resource, usually in the context of indexing and abstracting services

Abstracting and indexing service a service, usually offered on a commercial basis, that provides access to surrogate records of information resources (and increasingly to the information resources themselves). The techniques such services apply are closely related to, or often the same as, those used in information centres

Access point a name, term, code, etc. under which a bibliographic record may be searched and identified (*Anglo-American Cataloguing Rules* 2002)

Added entry a characteristic of a document which is useful for identifying that document but which is of lesser significance than a characteristic selected as the primary (main) entry; in a card catalogue or printed book catalogue, a brief version of a bibliographic record. See also *Main entry*

Alphabetical indexing language an indexing language in which the subject terms are selected from words or phrases in common use in the literature of the subject field being described. Examples of alphabetical indexing languages include thesauri and subject headings lists

Assigned indexing indexing in which the terms used are selected from a source other than the document, such as a controlled vocabulary. See also *Derived indexing*.

Author the person chiefly responsible for the creation of the intellectual or artistic content of a work (*Anglo-American Cataloguing Rules* 2002)

Authority control the process of ensuring that the headings for names (of people, corporate bodies and places), titles (of documents and of series) and subjects in an information retrieval system are used consistently

Authority file a mechanism for recording and implementing authority control decisions

Authority records records included in an authority file

Automatic classification classification automatically assigned without human intervention, based on characteristics of the document

Automatic indexing indexing automatically assigned without human intervention, based on characteristics of the document, such as words in the title

Bibliographic classification a classification which is concerned with subjects as they are presented in documents and with the documents themselves, not with the objects and entities which are the primary interest of other kinds of classification schemes

Bibliographic control the organising of the bibliographic information that users of libraries and information centres need in order to find and select the information resources that allow them to acquire the knowledge they seek

Bibliographic data a set of bibliographic elements that describes an information resource; sometimes called *metadata*

Bibliographic database a database containing bibliographic records

Bibliographic description the process, and product, of describing aspects of information resources in sufficient detail to distinguish them from other similar documents and to aid in their selection; the process is also known as *descriptive cataloguing*

Bibliographic organisation the organising of the bibliographic information that users of libraries and information centres need in order to find and select the information resources that allow them to acquire the knowledge they seek

Bibliographic records metadata records produced by cataloguers according to defined standards and included in a library catalogue or bibliographic database

Bibliographic utility a non-profit organisation serving as a source of bibliographic data stored in machine-readable form, which data are available to those affiliated with the utility (usually library members) for such purposes as online cataloguing and interlibrary loan through a telecommunications network (*World Encyclopedia of Library and Information Services* 1993, pp. 119-120)

Bibliography a list (usually exhaustive or comprehensive) of information resources in a specified field, usually with no geographical limitation on where the information resources are located

Brevity the requirement that notation in a bibliographic classification scheme should be as short as possible

Broker network a network which functions as a service centre of a larger bibliographic utility, such as OCLC, and which may, in addition, host local union catalogues and act as a focal point for local activities

Catalogue a list of information resources gathered in a single collection or set of locations, for example, in one library, or accessible from that location

Cataloguing the process of compiling bibliographic records for information resources by identifying and recording certain attributes of those information resources and recording information relating to title, authorship, publication and contents. This process can be divided into two parts: *descriptive cataloguing,* by which information resources are described in sufficient detail to distinguish them from other similar information resources, and *subject cataloguing,* by which the subject content of information resources is described. These terms, as defined here, are usually used in a library context and imply adherence to defined library standards, such as cataloguing rules

Chief access point the primary attribute by which the document can be identified and located; usually the name of a person, or, in some instances, of an organisation or the document's title; one feature of a document which is selected as its identifying access point. See also *Main entry*

Citation order in a faceted classification scheme, the order in which the facets are added together

Classification the process of identifying the subject content of an information resource and of allocating a classification number from a bibliographic classification scheme to that information resource. Classification is closely related to subject indexing

Classification scheme a logical scheme for the arrangement of knowledge, based on the systematic arrangement of entities and concepts into categories

Coextensive entry the concept that terms should be coextensive with subjects covered in the document. For example, a book about marsupials and mammals will require terms for both, not one or the other

Controlled indexing language an indexing language based on predefined terms which are selected from an authority list by the indexer and by the user (who uses them to locate documents about a sought subject). Also known as *controlled vocabulary*

Copy cataloguing the process of locating a metadata record created by another cataloguer for the document you want to catalogue, then making a copy of that record, usually by downloading that record into the local library information retrieval system. See also *Original cataloguing*

Corporate body an organisation or group of persons that is identified by a particular name and that acts, or may act, as an entity. Typical examples of corporate bodies are associations, institutions, business firms, nonprofit enterprises, governments, government agencies, religious bodies, local churches, and conferences (*Anglo-American Cataloguing Rules* 2002)

Corporate responsibility the idea that a group of people (for example a corporation) can act together as one entity and be responsible for creating the intellectual content of a document

Crosswalk a mapping of one metadata schema to another, for the purposes of conversion from one format to another

Derived indexing indexing in which the terms are selected from the title, the abstract or some other part of a document, as distinct from being selected from a controlled indexing language; in other words, the indexing language is a subset of the text of the document. Also known as *derivative indexing*. See also *Assigned indexing*

Descriptive cataloguing the process by which documents are described in sufficient detail to distinguish them from other similar documents and to aid in their selection

Descriptor in indexing, a word or symbol used to designate the subject of a document

Digital library a library which comprises a collection of digital objects, accessed through a computer; sometimes called a *virtual library*

Digital object an object that can be represented by a computer. Digital objects commonly of interest to libraries and information centres include web pages, databases, spreadsheets, word-processed documents, video, audio, images, and maps

Document used here in its very broadest sense of information-bearing medium. The term has traditionally been applied only to printed media, but in this book should be taken to include non-print media as well; information in digital form is also encompassed by the term

Dublin Core a metadata schema developed for the description of a broad range of information resources, but in particular of web resources. The schema is comparatively simple, appropriate for author-generated metadata

Enhanced subject access the addition of subject-indicative terms selected from the contents pages, indexes or other parts of documents to the bibliographic record

Enumerative classification scheme a bibliographic classification scheme which lists (or enumerates) the subjects, loosely grouping related subjects, or aspects of a subject, together

Exchange format a format standard which allows metadata to be exchanged among information retrieval systems

Exhaustivity the level of detail we go to in providing subject access; exhaustive subject indexing means that the number of terms selected from the indexing language is large and attempts to cover most or all of the subjects of the document

Expert system a computer program which uses a knowledge base of facts and rules about a specific area of expertise to perform problem-solving tasks by imitating the processes used by the human experts in that area

Expressive notation a notation used in a bibliographic classification scheme which reflects the structure of the classification: for example, in DDC, 7 is the symbol for fine and decorative arts, 74 for drawing and decorative arts, 746 for textile arts, 746.1 for yarn preparation and weaving, and 746.13 for dyeing yarn

Facet a single concept of a composite subject

Faceted classification scheme a bibliographic classification scheme which is based on identification and representation of facets

Format integration the process of bringing together all the MARC formats for different media into a single format

Free indexing language an indexing language in which any term, whether found in the document or not, can be used to describe the subject of a document

General classification scheme a bibliographic classification scheme which aims to cover all of documented knowledge, usually developed and maintained for use in large libraries where collections cover a wide range of subjects, such as academic libraries or public libraries. Examples are the Dewey Decimal Classification (DDC), the Library of Congress Classification (LCC) and the Universal Decimal Classification (UDC)

Heading an access point to a bibliographic record, originally located at the head of a record, card or page

Hierarchical classification scheme a bibliographic classification scheme which groups related concepts into primary and subordinate areas, attempting to emulate the natural order of the subject as closely as possible

Hospitality the requirement that notation in a bibliographic classification scheme should be able to accommodate new concepts or subjects by allowing them to be inserted into the notation

Hybrid library a library based on both physical and digital collections. See also *Digital library*

Index a list of information resources with a specified limitation, such as their subject coverage, or their existence in one collection; this definition accommodates both bibliographies and catalogues as examples of indexes

Indexing the process of describing an information resource according to specific data elements (such as author, title or subject) in order to provide access to that information resource. The term is used in many different ways, but is used here to encompass more than the term *cataloguing*; it includes not only the largely library-specific process already noted, but also the processes, often less standardised, which are used to build up the metadata records used by indexing and abstracting services

Indexing language terms, along with the rules for combining these terms, which are used to represent the subject content of documents. See also *Vocabulary*

Information centre an organisation which has as its primary function the provision of information

Information resources the *documents* and *digital objects* that are present in the collection of a library or information centre, or to which the library or information centre provides access

Information retrieval system any total system in an information centre used for performing the tasks associated with the intellectual organisation of information resources so that they can be retrieved when required

Integrated library system a computer-based library system which provides at least four basic functions (acquisitions, catalogue maintenance, circulation, and the online public access catalogue) and relies on a single database of bibliographic data to perform these functions. See also *Library management system*

Intellectual access access to the information contained in an information resource by allowing the seeker of that information to locate a reference to the information resource where it is present. See also *Physical access*

Interoperability the ability of two or more systems or components to exchange information and to use the information that has been exchanged (IEEE 1990). Interoperability has become a critical issue since relevant metadata is now available in a range of formats

Inverted order the order in which terms are sometimes used in subject headings: for example the subject heading *Cookery, Singaporean* is in inverted order, rather than in the direct word order *Singaporean cookery*

Known item search a catalogue search performed to determine whether or not the library owns a particular book or document. See also *Subject search*

KWIC (KeyWord In Context) index a permuted title index generated by a simple computer program

KWOC (KeyWord Out of Context) index a permuted title index generated by a simple computer program

Library information retrieval system any total system in an information centre used for performing the tasks associated with the intellectual organisation of information resources so that they can be retrieved when required

Library management system one of a new generation of integrated library systems which include more features and cover more functions, and may combine multiple databases of diverse content. See also *Integrated library system*

Literary warrant the concept that controlled vocabularies should accommodate only those subjects about which documents have been produced (or catalogued), rather than subjects which may exist theoretically but about which no documents have yet been produced (or catalogued)

Main entry the primary attribute by which the document can be identified and located, usually the name of a person, or in some instances of an organisation or the document's title; in a card catalogue or printed book catalogue, the full version of a bibliographic record. See also *Added entry*

Mark-up language A system of codes for indicating layout and style of a file

MARC (Machine-readable Cataloguing) a family of formats used for the exchange of cataloguing data, particularly among computerised library systems. MARC is the main data communication standard in use in libraries

Metadata a set of elements that describes an information resource; library-oriented metadata is traditionally called *bibliographic data*

Metadata elements the building blocks of the metadata record; they are the attributes of the information resource considered necessary to describe it succinctly

Metadata records summaries of information resources which represent those information resources, for example catalogue records, index entries, metadata

Metadata schema a structured format in which metadata elements are organised and exchanged. Metadata are thus downloaded and uploaded into other information retrieval systems which use the same schema. Sometimes called *metadata format*

Mixed notation a notation used in a bibliographic classification scheme which incorporates two types of symbols, for instance ML745 which uses both (Arabic) numerals and letters of the (roman) alphabet

Mixed responsibility the situation where different persons or bodies have made different contributions to the intellectual and/or artistic content of a work; adaptations or revisions of existing works, or the products of collaboration between an author and an artist, are examples of works of mixed responsibility

Mnemonic notation notation used in a bibliographic classification scheme which is intended to be easily remembered, such as the repetition of a particular sequence of notation throughout the classification to represent the same concept. For example, in DDC, the sequence 94 often indicates an Australian aspect of a subject

Natural indexing language an indexing language in which any term from a spoken/written language (such as English) may be selected to represent a subject; the opposite of a *controlled indexing language*. Also known as an *uncontrolled indexing language*

Notation the set of symbols which represent the arrangement of the bibliographic classification. See also *Mixed notation* and *Pure notation*

Original cataloguing the process of creating a bibliographic record from scratch, using standards for this purpose such as AACR2. See also *Copy cataloguing*

Permuted title index an index to documents generated by computer, based on words in the titles of the documents

Personal author the person chiefly responsible for the creation of the intellectual or artistic content of a work (*Anglo-American Cataloguing Rules* 2002)

Physical access access to an information resource by indicating where it is located (for instance, its location on the library shelf as indicated by a classification number, or its electronic address as indicated by its URL (Universal Resource Locator) or other resource identifier). See also *Intellectual access*

Post-coordination one of the ways in which we use terms from controlled vocabularies to create and search indexes. After the single concepts to describe a subject have been selected, they are used separately in turn to carry out a subject search, then the results are combined after the search. See also *Pre-coordination*

Precision the number of documents in the results of a search which are relevant to that search request

Precision ratio the number of relevant documents retrieved divided by the total number of documents retrieved; the precision ratio is a measure of how many documents retrieved are relevant

Pre-coordination one of the ways in which we use terms from controlled vocabularies to create and search indexes. After the single concepts to describe a subject have been identified, they are grouped together and then used to carry out a subject search. See also *Post-coordination*

Pure notation a notation used in a bibliographic classification scheme which uses only one type of symbol, for example all numerals (993.1)

Reader interest classification a classification scheme based on a limited number of general categories (such as Travel, Leisure, Crime fiction), determined according to reader interests

Recall the number of documents retrieved by a search

Recall ratio the number of documents retrieved divided by the total number of documents in the system

Reclassification the process of changing the classification notations used for documents from one bibliographic scheme to another, or from one edition of a scheme to another edition

Relevance in information retrieval, having direct bearing on the subject requested

Resource description the description of information resources for the purposes of their retrieval and selection. See also *Bibliographic organisation*

Retrospective conversion the process of converting into machine-readable versions bibliographic records which have been produced manually, such as on catalogue cards, microfiche or microfilm

See also reference a reference which directs the user from one heading to a related heading: for example, to another of an author's pseudonyms

See reference a reference which directs the user from a term, name or title not used in the information retrieval system to the term, name or title (i.e. the authorised heading) that is used

Shared responsibility the collaboration of two or more persons who performed the same kind of activity such as writing, adapting, or performing in a work

Simplicity the requirement that notation in a bibliographic classification scheme should be as readily comprehensible as possible

Special classification scheme a bibliographic classification scheme which covers a limited field of documented knowledge. Examples include the British Classification of Music, Moys (for law), and Boggs and Lewis (for maps)

Subject cataloguing that part of the cataloguing process which is concerned with describing and providing access to the subject content of a document

Subject headings list a list of terms, arranged in alphabetical order, which have been selected for their ability to indicate subjects and have been authorised for use to provide subject access to metadata records. Such a list usually covers many subjects and is therefore intended for use in information centres whose collections span a wide range of subjects, such as public, academic and school libraries

Subject search a catalogue search performed to identify books or documents that deal with a particular subject. See also *Known item search*

Surrogate records summaries of information resources which represent those information resources, for example catalogue records, index entries, metadata

Switching language a query language, usually a controlled indexing language, into which user queries are converted in order to making cross-database searching more effective

Synthesis the process of synthesising or combining together facets to build up complex subjects

Thesaurus a list of terms, arranged in alphabetical or classified order, which have been selected for their ability to indicate subjects and have been authorised for use to provide subject access to bibliographic records. Such a list usually covers a limited subject field

Uniform title a device whose purpose is to collocate (bring together in one place) documents which are variants of the same work

Union catalogue the *union* of the catalogues of a group of libraries, such as a catalogue of all parliamentary libraries, or of all libraries in one state, or of all libraries in Australia

Uniqueness the requirement of notation in a bibliographic classification scheme that no particular notation can be used to represent more than one concept, so that no subject or concept can be mistaken for another

Universal bibliographic control (UBC) the concept that all of the world's published output can be recorded and thus controlled

Universal Resource Locator (URL) a code or address which enables a site on the World Wide Web to be uniquely identified and provides access to that site

Vocabulary terms (usually words or numbers) used to summarise and describe the subject content of a document; these terms form the vocabulary of the indexing language. See also *Controlled indexing language* and *Indexing language*

References

ABN for Australian Subject Access. (1997). *National Library of Australia Gateways,* 28, p.9.

ABN Handbook Part 1: General Information for New and Existing Users. (1986). Canberra: National Library of Australia.

Ahronheim, J. & Marko, L. (2000). Exploding Out of the MARC Box: Building New Roles for Cataloging Departments. *Cataloging and Classification Quarterly,* 30, pp.217-225.

ACOC. (2006). *Beyond the OPAC: Future Directions for Web-based Catalogues* (online). http://www.nla.gov.au/lis/stndrds/grps/acoc/acocseminar2006.html (accessed 12 December 2007).

Aitchison, J., Gilchrist, A. & Bawden, D. (2000). *Thesaurus Construction and Use.* 4th ed. London: Aslib.

ALA Cataloging Rules for Author and Title Entries. (1949). 2nd ed. Chicago: American Library Association.

Alonso, P.A.G. & Prescott, D.F. (1977). Deweying Maps. *Australian Library Journal,* 26, pp.47-52.

American Institute of Physics (12 December 2007). *Physics and Astronomy Classification Scheme* (online). http://www.aip.org.pacs/

Anderson, D. (1974). *Universal Bibliographic Control: A Long Term Policy, A Plan for Action.* Pullach/Munchen: Verlag Dokumentation.

Anderson, D. (1982). *UBC: A Survey of Universal Bibliographic Control.* London: IFLA International Office for UBC.

Anglo-American Cataloguing Rules (1988). 2nd ed. (1988 revision), eds. M. Gorman & P. W. Winkler. Ottawa: Canadian Library Association; London: Library Association Publishing; Chicago: American Library Association.

Anglo-American Cataloguing Rules (2002). 2nd ed. (2002 revision). Ottawa: Canadian Library Association; London: Chartered Institute of Library and Information Professionals; Chicago: American Library Association.

Annual Review of OCLC Research. (1995) (online). http://www.oclc.org/oclc/research/publications/review95.htm

Another First for the CJK Service. (1997). *National Library of Australia Gateways,* 28, p.4.

At the Coalface: Upper Murray Regional Library. (1992). *ABN News,* 62, pp.14-15.

Attar, K.E. (2000). The Application of the Bliss Bibliographic Classification in Cambridge College Libraries. *New Review of Academic Librarianship,* 6, pp.35-49.

Auld, L. (1982). Authority Control: An Eighty-Year Review. *Library Resources and Technical Services,* 26, pp.319-330.

AUSMARC Bibliographic Format: A Summary of Changes. (1989). Canberra: National Library of Australia.

Australian Bibliographic Network. (1998) (online). http://www.nla.gov.au/abn/

The Australian Cataloguing-in-Publication Program: Information for Co-operating Publishers (1976). Canberra: National Library of Australia.

Australian Dictionary of Biography (1979). Parkville, Vic.: Melbourne University Press, vol. 7. pp.95-96.

Australian Libraries Provide Access to RLG Databases. (6 Feb. 1995) (online). http://www.rlg.org/pr/9502aust.html

Australian Subject Access Project. (2001) (online). http://www.nla.gov.au/kinetica/slash.html (accessed 29 May 2003)

Australian Thesaurus of Education Descriptors. (1996). 2nd ed., eds. E. Miller & M. Findlay. Camberwell, Vic.: Australian Council for Educational Research.

Avram, H.D. (1984). Authority Control and Its Place. *Journal of Academic Librarianship, 9,* pp.331-335.

Ayres, F. (1983). Is There a Future for Cataloguers? *Catalogue & Index, 70,* pp.1-2.

Baker, N. (1994). Annals of Scholarship: Discards. *New Yorker,* 4 April, pp.64-86.

Ballard, T. (1994). Comparative Searching Styles of Patrons and Staff. *Library Resources and Technical Services, 38,* pp.293-305.

Balnaves, J. (1974). Australian MARC Record Service. *Australian Academic & Research Libraries, 5,* pp.127-130.

Barrett, B. & Maticka, M. (1990). An Analysis of User Failure in Subject Searching an Online Catalog. In *Garbage In – Garbage Out: The Need for Quality in the Age of Automation,* eds. A. Bundy & J. Bundy. Adelaide: Auslib Press.

Basic CATSS Description. (1995) (online). http://www.ism.ca/lis/catssdes.htm/

Bates, M. (1996). Indexing and Access for Digital Libraries and the Internet: Human, Database, and Domain Factors (online). http://dlis.gseis.ucla.edu.au/research/mjbates2.html (accessed 29 May 2003).

Bates, M. (2002). After the Dot-Bomb: Getting Web Information Right This Time (online). *First Monday,* 7. http://www.firstmonday.org/issues/issue7_7/bates/index.html (accessed 14 April 2003).

Bates, M.J. (2003). Improving User Access to Library Catalog and Portal Information: Final Report. Version 3 (online). http://www.loc.gov/catdir/bibcontrol/2.3BatesReport6-03.doc.pdf (accessed 12 December 2007).

Beagrie, N. (2003). *National Digital Preservation Strategies.* Washington, D.C.: CLIR and Library of Congress.

Bearman, D. & Trant, J. (2005). Social Terminology Enhancement through Vernacular Engagement: Exploring Collaborative Annotation to Encourage Interaction with Museum Collections. *D-Lib Magazine, 11*(9) (online). http://www.dlib.org/dlib/september05/bearman/09bearman.html (accessed 12 December 2007).

Beatty, S. (1985). An Experiment in Enhanced Subject Access. *Cataloguing Australia,* 11, pp.86-95.

Beatty, S. (1987). DDC to LCC in Eight Weeks. *Cataloguing Australia,* 13, pp.92-100.

Beatty, S. (1991). ESP at ADFA After Five Years. *Cataloguing Australia,* 17, pp.65-92.

Beatty, S. (1993). Tables of Contents or Index Data for Subject Enrichment: Sources and Developments. *Cataloguing Australia,* 19, pp.16-29.

Berners-Lee, T. (1998). Semantic Web Road Map (online). http://www.w3.org/DesignIssues/Semantic.html (accessed 12 December 2007).

BIBDATA Network: A Draft Proposal for an Australian National Shared Cataloguing System. (1976). Canberra: National Library of Australia.

Biskup, P. (1994). *Libraries in Australia.* Wagga Wagga: Centre for Information Studies, Charles Sturt University-Riverina.

Bliel, L.A. & Renner, C. (1990). Copy Cataloguing and the Bibliographic Networks. In *Technical Services Today and Tomorrow,* eds. M. Gorman, & associates. Englewood, CO: Libraries Unlimited.

Borchardt, D.H., Marshall, M.J. & Dunn, L.J. (1955). University of Tasmania Library in a State of Bliss. *Australian Library Journal,* 4, pp.48-52.

Borgman, C.L. (1996). Why Are Online Catalogs Still Hard to Use? *Journal of the American Society for Information Science,* 47, pp.493-503.

Bourke, L. (1992). Contract Cataloguing at CAVAL. *Cataloguing Australia,* 18, pp.22-25.

Bourke, L. & Haby, S. (2001). SCIS in the New World. In *Seachange: Cataloguing in a Dot Com World: 14th National Cataloguing Conference Preprints.* Geelong, Vic.: Organizing Committee of the 14th National Cataloguing Conference, pp.68-71.

Breeding, M. (2002). Understanding the Protocol for Metadata Harvesting of the Open Archives Initiative. *Computers in Libraries,* 22 (8), pp.24-29.

Brodie, M. (1998). *In the Company of Strangers: Challenges and Opportunities in Metadata Implementation* (online). http://www.anu.edu.au/caul/mirror/global/content/repor~29.htm

Browne, G. (1996). Automatic Indexing (online). http://www.aussi.org/conferences/papers/browneg.htm (accessed 30 May 2003).

Bruce, J. (1989). Using RLIN in the Australian National Gallery. *Art Libraries Journal,* 14, pp.17-20.

BS 1629:1989 References to Published Materials. (1989). Rev. ed. London: British Standards Institution.

BUBL Link. (12 December 2007) (online). http://bubl.ac.uk/link/

Buckland, M. (1988). Bibliography, Library Records, and the Redefinition of the Library Catalog. *Library Resources and Technical Services,* 32, pp.299-311.

Buckland, M. (1992). Bibliographic Access Reconsidered. In *Redesigning Library Services: A Manifesto.* Chicago: American Library Association.

Buick, W.G. (1967). The Classification of English Literature: A Faceted Classification Compatible with DDC. *Australian Library Journal,* 16, pp.174-177.

Burgess, M., Thomas, M. & Whitton, R. (1981). *Australian Bibliographic Network Pilot Project User Report, November 1981: Library, Attorney-General's Department.* Canberra: The Library.

Byrne, A. & Micco, M. (1988). Improving OPAC Subject Access: The ADFA Experiment. *College & Research Libraries*, 49, pp.432-443.

Byrum, J.D. (1992). Standard Cataloging Data: The View from the Library of Congress. In *Cataloging Heresy: Challenging the Standard Bibliographic Product*, ed. B.H. Weinberg. Medford, N.J.: Learned Information.

Byrum, J.D. (2000). The Emerging Global Bibliographic Network: The Era of International Standardization in the Development of Cataloging Policy. *Library Resources and Technical Services* 44, pp.114-121.

Byrum, J.D. (2001). The Birth and Re-birth of the ISBDs: Process and Procedures for Creating and Revising the International Standard Bibliographic Descriptions. *IFLA Journal* 27, pp.34-37.

Calhoun, K. (2006). The Changing Nature of the Catalog and its Integration with other Discovery Tools: Final Report (online). http://www.loc.gov/catdir/calhoun-report-final.pdf (accessed 12 September 2007).

Cameron, M. (1992). A Catalogue is a Reader Service. *InCite,* 14 Dec., p.18.

Campbell, D. (2003). Definitions for Web-Based Services (online). http://www.nla.gov.au/initiatives/sg/servicetypes.html (accessed 10 June 2003).

Campion, E. (1999). Paddy-whackery. *The Australian's Review of Books*, 4 (10), p.23.

Catalogue Card Service for Australian Publications. (1967). *Australian Library Journal,* 16, pp.245-246.

Catalogue Card Service for Australian Publications. (1969). *Australian Library Journal,* 18, pp.80-82.

Cataloguing: It's All Greek to . . . (1990). *InCite,* 16 July, pp.4-5.

Cataloguing Rules: Author and Title Entries. (1908). Compiled by Committees of the Library Association and of the American Library Association. English ed. London: Library Association.

Cathro, W. (1980). Developments in the AUSMARC Format and in the Distribution of MARC Records in Australia. *Cataloguing Australia,* 6, pp.56-64.

Cathro, W. (1983). USMARC, ABN and AUSMARC: Changing Structures for Nonbook Cataloguing. *Cataloguing Australia,* 9, pp.7-14.

Cathro, W. (1985). The Politics of Sharing. *Cataloguing Australia,* 11, pp.71-77.

Cathro, W. (1988). The Exchange of Cataloguing Data in the Australian Bibliographic Network. *International Cataloguing & Bibliographic Control,* 17, pp.19-21.

Cathro, W.S. (1991). The Australian Bibliographic Network: A Survey of its First Decade. In *Library for the Nation*, eds. P. Biskup & M. Henty. Canberra: Australian Academic & Research Libraries and National Library of Australia.

Cathro, W.S. (1997). Current Information Technology Activities at the National Library of Australia. *LASIE,* 28(2), pp.6-13.

Cations, W.T. (1978). The Australian MARC Record Service 1974-1977: An Analysis and Evaluation. *Australian Academic & Research Libraries,* 9, pp.81-86.

CAVAL: Collaborative Solutions. (12 December 2007) (online). http://www.caval.edu.au

Chan, L.M. (1994). *Cataloging and Classification: An Introduction.* 2nd ed. New York: McGraw-Hill.

Chan, L.M. (1995). *Library of Congress Subject Headings: Principles and Application.* 3rd ed. Littleton, CO: Libraries Unlimited.

Chan, L.M. (2005). *Library of Congress Subject Headings: Principles and Application.* 4th ed. Westport, CT: Libraries Unlimited.

Chan, L.M. (2007). *Cataloging and Classification: An Introduction.* 3rd ed. Lanham, MD: Scarecrow Press.

Chan, L.M. (2000). Exploiting LCSH, LCC, and DDC to Retrieve Networked Resources: Issues and Challenges. *Bicentennial Conference on Bibliographic Control for the New Millennium, Library of Congress, 15-17 November 2000* (online). http://lcweb.loc.gov/catdir/bibcontrol/chan_paper.html (accessed 6 June 2003).

Chan, L.M., Comaromi, J.P. & Satija, M.P. (1996). *Dewey Decimal Classification: A Practical Guides.* 2nd ed. Albany, NY: Forest Press.

Chan, L.M. & Hodges, T. (1998). Subject Cataloguing and Classification. In *Technical Services Today and Tomorrow*, 2nd ed., eds. M. Gorman & associates. Englewood, CO: Libraries Unlimited, pp.95-109.

Chan, L.M. & Hodges, T. (2000). Entering the Millennium: A New Century for CSH. *Cataloging & Classification Quarterly*, 29, pp.225-234.

Chan, L.M. & Mitchell, J.S. (2003). *Dewey Decimal Classification: Principles and Application.* 3rd ed. Dublin, OH: OCLC.

Chen, H. & Rasmussen, E.M. (1999). Intellectual Access to Images. *Library Trends,* 48(2), pp.291-302.

Chandrakar, R. (2001). Mapping CCF to MARC21: An Experimental Approach. *Cataloging and Classification Quarterly*, 33, pp.33-49.

Chaplin, A.H. & Anderson, D. (eds.) (1963). *International Conference on Cataloguing Principles, Paris, 9th-18th October 1961: report.* München: K.G. Saur. Chen, H.-L. & Rasmussen, E. (1999). Intellectual Access to Images. *Library Trends*, 3, pp.291-302.

Chaplin, A.H. (1966). *Statement of Principles Adopted by the International Conference on Cataloguing Principles, Paris, October, 1961,* Annotated ed. Sevenoaks: IFLA.

Cherry, J.M. (1994). OPACs in Twelve Canadian Libraries: An Evaluation of Functional Capabilities and Interface Features. *Information Technology and Libraries,* 13, pp.174-195.

Cherry, J.M. & Cox, J.P. (1996). World Wide Web Displays of Bibliographic Records: An Evaluation. In *Proceedings of the 24th Annual Conference of the Canadian Association for Information Science.* Toronto: Canadian Association for Information Science.

Chiba, M.V. (1982). *Library Networks, Automation and Computerized Information Services in Academic and Research Libraries in the United States.* Clayton, Vic.: Monash University.

Christian, E. (2001). A Metadata Initiative for Global Information Discovery. *Government Information Quarterly* 18, pp.209-221.

CIC Libraries' Strategic Plan: Strategic Directions for 1998. (1998) (online). http://ntx2.cso.uiuc.edu/cic/cli/statplan98final.htm (accessed 14 April 1998).

Clack, D.H. (1990). *Authority Control: Principles, Applications, and Instructions.* Chicago, IL: American Library Association.

CLANN. (1980). *Annual Report 1979-80.* NSW: CLANN.

Cleveland, D.B. & Cleveland, A.D. (1990). *Introduction to Indexing and Abstracting.* 2nd ed. Englewood, CO: Libraries Unlimited.

Coates, E.J. (1960). *The British Catalogue of Music Classification.* London: British National Bibliography.

Cochrane, P. (1978). *Books are for Use: Final Report of the Subject Access Project to the Council on Library Resources.* New York: Syracuse University.

Cochrane, T. (1988). Living Together in the Australian Bibliographic Network: A Member's View. *International Cataloguing & Bibliographic Control,* Oct./Dec., pp. 3-1–3-3.

Cole, T.W. & Kazmer, M.W. (1995). SGML as a Component of the Digital Library. *Library Hi Tech,* 52, pp.75-90.

Cook, C.D. (1986). Cataloguing in the International Arena. *Library Resources and Technical Services,* 30, pp.23-30.

Copac. (12 December 2007) (online). http://www.copac.ac.uk/

Cromwell-Kessler, W. (1997). Dublin Core Metadata in the RLG Information Landscape. *D-Lib Magazine.* December (online). http://www.dlib.org/dlib/december97/12cromwell-kessler.html

Cristán, A.L. (2003). SACO and Subject Gateways. In *Authority Control: Definition and International Experiences: International Conference, Florence, February 10-12, 2003.* http://www.unifi.it/universita/biblioteche/ac/en/intro_eng.htm (accessed 21 March 2003).

Culkin, P.B. (1992). The MARC Format: Private Road or Public Highway? *Advances in Librarianship,* 16, pp.83-91.

Curriculum Corporation. *Cataloguing/Database News.* (6 May 1998) (online). http://www.curriculum.edu.au/scis/database.htm

Curriculum Corporation (2003). CC News (online). *Connections,* 45. http://www.curriculum.edu.au/scis/connect/cnetw03/45ccnews.htm (accessed 1 May 2003).

Curriculum Corporation. (12 December 2007). *SCIS* (online). http://www.curriculum.edu.au/scis/ (accessed 15 May 2008).

Curwen, A.G. (1991). International Standard Bibliographic Description. In *Standards for the International Exchange of Bibliographic Information: Papers Presented at a Course Held at the School of Library, Archive and Information Studies, University College London, 3-18 August 1990,* ed. I.C. McIlwaine. London: Library Association.

Cutter, C.A. (1904). *Rules for a Dictionary Catalog.* 4th ed. Washington, DC: USGPO.

CyberStacks(sm).(1998) (online). http://www.public.iastate.edu/~CYBERSTACKS/ (accessed 4 April 2003).

Davies, R. (1992). Expert Systems and Cataloguing. In *The Application of Expert Systems in Libraries and Information Centres*, ed. A. Miller. London: Bowker-Saur.

Davis, S.W. (1997). *DDC21 Workbook: A Practical Introduction to the Dewey Decimal Classification.* Wagga Wagga: Centre for Information Studies, Charles Sturt University-Riverina.

Davis, S.W. & New, G.R. (1997). *DDC 13 Workbook: A Practical Introduction to the Abridged Dewey Decimal Classification.* Wagga Wagga: Centre for Information Studies, Charles Sturt University-Riverina.

DCMI. (2006). *Dublin Core Metadata Element Set, Version 1.1* (online). http://dublincore.org/documents/dces/ (accessed 12 December 2007).

De La Motte, B. (2000). Kinetica Annual Users Meeting, 2000 (online). *Gateways*, 47. http://www.nla.gov.au/ntwkpubs/gw/47/p04 (accessed 2 May 2003).

De Smet, E. & Nieuwenhuysen, P. (1997). The DANIS Database System: Integrating Bibliographic and Factual Information Using CDS/ISIS Software and the Common Communication Format. *Journal of Information Science*, 23(4), pp.327-337.

Dean, N. (2002). New world for WorldCat: Bibliographic Store Adds Features and Aims for Globally Distributed System. *Information World Review* 177, p.12.

Delsey, T. (2000). The Library Catalogue in a Networked Environment (online). *Bicentennial Conference on Bibliographic Control for the New Millennium, Library of Congress, 15-17 November 2000.* http://lcweb.loc.gov/catdir/bibcontrol/delsey_paper.html (accessed 6 June 2003).

Description of Dublin Core Elements. (1998) (online). http://purl.oclc.org/metadata/dublin_core/

Development of the Encoded Archival Description DTD. (5 April 2003) (online). http://www.loc.gov/ead/eaddev.html

DESIRE (1999). *Subject Gateways* (online). http://www.desire.org/html/subjectgateways/subjectgateways.html (accessed 10 June 2003).

Dewey Decimal Classification. (1955). *Australian Library Journal,* 4, p.112.

Dierickx, H. & Hopkinson, A. (eds.) (1986). *UNISIST Reference Manual for Machine-Readable Bibliographic Descriptions.* 3rd ed. Paris, Unesco.

Dillon, K. (ed.) (1997). *School Library Automation in Australia: Issues and Results of the National Surveys.* 2nd ed. Wagga Wagga: Centre for Information Studies, Charles Sturt University-Riverina.

Directory of Z39.50 Targets in Australia. (28 May 1998) (online). http://enzo.nla.gov.au/products/alg/adm/vCucadm.html

Dittman, H. & Hardy, J. (1999*). Learn Library of Congress Classification.* Scarecrow Press.

Dobrovits, A. (1971). The Future of Original Cataloguing and the Library of Congress. *Australian Library Journal,* 20, pp.16-19.

Dobrovits, A. (1975). Some Thoughts on MARC. *Australian Library Journal,* 24, pp.20-26.

Dobrovits, P. (1978). Is There a Need for Regional Centres in an On-line Situation? *Australian Academic & Research Libraries*, 9, pp.87-90.

Dobrovits, P. & O'Mara, R. (1979). Searching the OCLC Database for Older Type Research Material. *LASIE,* 10(2), pp.2-9.

Down, D.W. (1982). One Bibliographic Data Base for Australia? In *Challenge and Response: Proceedings of the 22nd Biennial Conference of the Library Association of Australia, held in Adelaide, Aug. 22-26, 1982.* Sydney: Library Association of Australia.

Drabenstott, K.M. & Weller, M.S. (1996). Failure Analysis of Subject Searches in a Test of a new Design for Subject Access to Online Catalogs. *Journal of the American Society for Information Science*, 47, pp.519-537.

Draft Proposal for the Development of an Australian Bibliographic Network. (1981). Canberra: National Library of Australia.

Dublin Core/MARC/GILS Crosswalk. (1997). Library of Congress. Network Development and MARC Standards Office (online). http://lcweb.loc.gov/marc/dccross.html

Dublin Core Metadata. (2 November 1997) (online). http://purl.org/metadata/dublin_core

Dunkin, P.S. (1969). *Cataloging USA.* Chicago, IL: American Library Association.

Dykstra, M. (1988). LC Subject Headings Disguised as a Thesaurus. *Library Journal,* 1 March, pp.42-46.

Edmond, M. (1993). Linking Libraries: The UNILINC Experience. In *Networking & Libraries in Australia,* ed. C. Goodacre. Melbourne: ALIA/Thorpe.

Eichinski, G. (1973). An Analysis of R.M.I.T. Monograph Intakes. *Australian Academic & Research Libraries,* 4, p. 180.

Ellis, A. (1973). The National Library of Australia and MARC. In *Proceedings of the MARC II Seminar Held at the School of Librarianship, The University of New South Wales, 18-20 August 1971,* ed. J.R. Nelson. Kensington, NSW: University of New South Wales.

Ellis, D. & Vasconcelos, A. (1999). Ranganathan and the Net: Using Facet Analysis to Search and Organise the World Wide Web. *Aslib Proceedings*, 51, pp.2-10.

Elrod, J.M. (1976). Is the Card Catalogue's Unquestioned Sway in North America Ending? *Journal of Academic Librarianship*, 2, pp.4-8.

Endeavor Information Systems (2003). *Endeavor Customer List* (online). http://www.endinfosys.com/prods/ifp_custlist.htm (accessed 27 March 2003).

Family Thesaurus: Subject Terms Used in Australian Family. (1996). 5th ed. Melbourne, Vic.: Australian Institute of Family Studies.

Fattahi, R. (1996). A Comparison Between the Online Catalogue and the Card Catalogue: Some Considerations for Redesigning Bibliographic Standards. *Library Review*, 44, pp.44-58.

Ferguson, S. & Hebels, R. (1998). *Computers for Librarians: An Introduction to the Electronic Library.* 2nd ed. Wagga Wagga: Centre for Information Studies, Charles Sturt University.

Ferguson, S. & Hebels, R. (2003). *Computers for Librarians: An Introduction to the Electronic Library.* 3rd ed. Wagga Wagga: Centre for Information Studies, Charles Sturt University.

Fidel, R. & Crandall, M. (1988). The AACR2 as a Design Schema for Bibliographic Databases. *Library Quarterly,* 58, pp.123-142.

Fielding, D. (1978). Regional Centre Not Wanted. *Australian Academic & Research Libraries,* 9, pp.91-97.

Fitch, K. (2002). Taking RDF and Topic Maps Seriously (online). http://ausweb.scu.edu.au/aw02/papers/refereed/fitch2/paper.html (accessed 12 December 2007).

Foskett, A.C. (1996). *The Subject Approach to Information.* 5th ed. London: Library Association.

Fox, M.J. (2001). Stargazing: Locating EAD in the Descriptive Firmament. *Journal of Internet Cataloging,* 4, pp.61-74.

From the Desk of Augustus Slope. (1994). *Australian Library Journal,* 43, p.181.

Franks, A.R.D. (2000). International Cooperation in the Program for Cooperative Cataloging. *Cataloging & Classification Quarterly,* 30, pp.37-50.

Gatenby, J. (1981). The Implementation of Additional and Changed MARC Formats into an Existing System. *LASIE,* 11(4), pp.2-8.

Gatenby, J. (1987). What is the Future of AUSMARC? *LASIE ,* 18(1), pp.4-12.

Gatenby, J. (1991). Fulfilling Promises: Authority Control Today. *Cataloguing Australia,* 16, pp.35-48.

Gatenby, J., Rogerson. M. & Peake, D. (1978). An Investigation into the Feasibility of Using OCLC in Australia, via the MIDAS Service. *LASIE,* 9(2), pp.2-9.

Gatenby, P. (1988). Cataloguing in Publication (CIP). In *ALIAS: Australia's Library, Information and Archives Services.* vol.2. Sydney: Library Association of Australia.

Genoni, P. (1981). LASH. *Cataloguing Australia,* 7, p.75.

George, J. (2003). What Users Are Telling Us: A Symposium. *CLIR Issues,* 33, pp.1-2, 6.

Gilchrist, A. (ed.) (1997). *From Classification to 'Knowledge Organization': Dorking Revisited or 'Past is Prelude',* ed. A. Gilchrist. The Hague: FID.

Gilchrist, A. (2002). Thesauri, Taxonomies and Ontologies: An Etymological Note. *Journal of Documentation,* 59, pp.7-18.

Golder, S. & Bernardo, A. (2005). The Structure of Collaborative Tagging Systems (online). http://arxiv.org/pdf/cs/0508082 (accessed 12 December 2007).

Golder, S. & Huberman, B.A. (2006). Usage Patterns of Collaborative Tagging Systems. *Journal of Information Science,* 32(2), pp.198--208.

Gömpel, R. & Niggemann, E. (2002). *RAK und MAB oder AACR und MARC?: Strategische Überlegungen zu einer wieder einmal – weil immer noch – aktuellen Diskussion* (online). http://www.ddb.de/professionell/pdf/goe_ng.pdf

Goodram, R., Howard, M. & Eaves, D. (1974). The University of Tasmania's Reclassification Programme: The First Year. *Australian Academic & Research Libraries,* 5, pp.101-112.

Gorman, M. (1975). Osborn Revisited; Or, The Catalog in Crisis. *American Libraries,* 6, pp.599-601.

Gorman, M. (1981). The Most Concise AACR2. *American Libraries,* 12(8), p.499.

Gorman, M. (1987). Implementing Changes in Cataloging Rules. *Library Journal,* 15 Feb., pp.110-112.

Gorman, M. (1989). Yesterday's Heresy – Today's Orthodoxy: An Essay on the Changing Face of Descriptive Cataloging. *College and Research Libraries,* 50, pp.630-631.

Gorman, M. (1990a). Descriptive Cataloguing: Its Past, Present, and Future. In *Technical Services Today and Tomorrow,* eds. M. Gorman & associates. Englewood, CO: Libraries Unlimited.

Gorman, M. (1990b). Introduction. In *MARC Format Integration: Three Perspectives: Papers Presented at the Second National Conference of the Library and Information Technology Association, October 2-6, 1988, Boston, Massachusetts,* ed. M. Gorman. Chicago, IL: American Library Association.

Gorman, M. (1991). A New Golden Age?: The Future of Cataloguing. *Cataloguing Australia,* 17, pp.128-134.

Gorman, M. (1992). How Cataloging and Classification Should Be Taught. *American Libraries,* 23, pp.694, 696-697.

Gorman, M. (1993). How Cataloguing and Classification Should be Taught: A Manifesto. In *AACR, DDC, MARC and Friends*, eds. J. Byford, K.V. Trickey & S. Woodhouse. London: Library Association.

Gorman, M. (1997). What is the Future of Cataloguing and Cataloguers? *63rd IFLA General Conference. Programme and Proceedings* (online). http://www.ifla.org/IV/ifla63/63gorm.htm

Gorman, M. (2004). *The concise AACR2.* 4th ed. Chicago, IL: American Library Association; Ottawa, ON: Canadian Library Association; London: Chartered Institute of Library and Information Professionals.

Gorman, M. & Oddy, P. (1997). The Anglo-American Cataloguing Rules Second Edition: Their Historical Principles. In *The Principles and Future of AACR: Proceedings of the International Conference on the Principles and Future Development of AACR, Toronto, Ontario, Canada, October 23-25, 1997,* ed. Jean Weihs. Ottawa, ON: Canadian Library Association.

Gredley, E. & Hopkinson, A. (1990). *Exchanging Bibliographic Data: MARC and Other International Formats.* Ottawa, ON: Canadian Library Association.

Greenberg, J., Sutton, S. & Campbell, D.G. (2003). Metadata: A Fundamental Component of the Semantic Web. *Bulletin of the American Society for Information Science and Technology,* 29, pp.16-18.

Greig, E. (1989). Library of Congress Classification in an Australian Environment. *Cataloguing Australia,* 15, pp.40-44.

Groenewegen, H. (1982). Effective Governance and Management of Library Networks. In *Challenge and Response: Proceedings of the 22nd Biennial Conference of the Library*

Association of Australia, held in Adelaide, Aug. 22-26, 1982. Sydney: Library Association of Australia.

Groenewegen, H. (1988). Australian Bibliographic Network. In *Australian Libraries Summit Discussion Papers*. Canberra: National Library of Australia.

Groenewegen, H. (1992). Warwick Cathro. *InCite*, 17 Feb., p.21.

Groom, L. (1995). The Australian National (Chinese/Japanese/Korean) Project. In *Asia-Pacific Library Conference, 28 May 1995-1 June 1995, Brisbane, Australia*, v. 2. Brisbane: State Library of Queensland.

Grosch, A.N. (1995). *Library Information Technology and Networks*. New York: Marcel Dekker.

Grose, M.W. & Line, M.B. (1968). On the Construction and Care of White Elephants. *Library Association Record*, 70, pp.2-5.

Gu, B. (1994). Essential Elements of Bibliographic Records: An Evaluation of Current ABN Minimum-Level Cataloguing Standards. MA (Librarianship) thesis, Monash University.

Guenther, R.S. (1996). The Challenges of Electronic Texts in the Library: Bibliographic Control and Access. In *Scholarly Publishing: The Electronic Frontier*, eds. R.P. Peek & G.N. Newby. Cambridge, MA: MIT Press.

Haddad, P. (1990). Retrospective Conversion in National and Research Libraries: The Australian Experience. *IFLA Journal*, 16, pp.67-70.

Haddad, P. (2000). National Bibliography in Australia: Moving Into the Next Millennium. *International Cataloguing and Bibliographic Control*, 29, pp.31-32.

Hagler, R. (1997). *The Bibliographic Record and Information Technology*. 3rd ed. Chicago, IL: American Library Association.

Hanson, T. (1998). The Access Catalogue Gateway to Resources (online). *Ariadne*, 15. http://www.ariadne.ac.uk/issue15/main/

Hansson, J. (1997). Why Public Libraries in Sweden did not Choose Dewey. *Knowledge Organization*, 24, pp.145-153.

Harvey, R. (1999). *Organising Knowledge in Australia: Principles and Practice in Libraries and Information Centres*. Wagga Wagga, NSW: Centre for Information Studies, Charles Sturt University-Riverina.

Hawks, C.P. (1994). Expert Systems in Technical Services and Collection Management. *Information Technology and Libraries*, 13, pp.203-212.

Hayes, R.M., Maguire, C. (1980). Cooperation Between CLANN and ABN. *LASIE*, 11(3), pp.2-30.

Hayward, B. (1985). *The Reader at the Catalogue*. Perth, W.A.: Western Australian Institute of Technology Library.

Heaney, M. (1995). Object-Oriented Cataloging. *Information Technology and Libraries*, 14, pp.135-153.

Heiner-Freiling, M. (2000). Survey on Subject Heading Languages Used in National Libraries and Bibliographies. *Cataloging & Classification Quarterly*, 29, pp.189-198.

Hendrix, F. (1997). MARC Harmonisation: Strategies for the Future. *Catalogue & Index*, 124, pp.1-5.

Hensen, S.L. (2001). Quote of the Month. *American Libraries*, 32 (Jan), p.86.

Henty, M. (1986). The Use of the Online Catalogue: A Record of Unsuccessful Keyword Searches. *LASIE,* 17(2), pp.47-52.

Henty, M. & Steele, C. (1988). Automated Systems in Australian Libraries: A 1987 Perspective. *Electronic Library,* 6, pp.100-106.

Hider, P. (2002). A Survey of National Union Catalogues. *Singapore Journal of Library & Information Management*, 31, pp.73-78.

Hider, P. (2004). Australian digital collections: metadata standards and interoperability. *Australian Academic & Research Libraries,* 35(4), pp.289-300.

Hider, P. & Turner, S. (2006). The application of AACR2's rules for personal names in certain languages. *Cataloging & Classification Quarterly,* 43(2), pp.37-52.

HILT (High-Level Thesaurus) Project. (2001). *Final Report: Executive Summary for JISC and RSLP* (online). http://hilt.cdlr.strath.ac.uk/Reports/FinalReport.html (accessed 12 December 2007).

Hine, J.D. (1973). *Cataloguing Practices in Australian Libraries.* Sydney: Library Association of Australia.

Hine, J.D. (1979). LASH: An Exploration. *Cataloguing Australia,* 5, pp.25-37.

Hodge, G. (2000). *Systems of Knowledge Organization for Digital Libraries: Beyond Traditional Authority Files.* Washington, DC: Council on Library and Information Resources.

Hoffman, B. (1990). Establishing New Academic Libraries in Country Areas. In *Coming of Age in Librarianship: A Festschrift for the 21st Birthday of the WAIT Library*, eds. G.G. Allen & I. Zoll. Perth: Curtin University of Technology.

Hoffmann, H. (1977). Cataloguing Codes and Nonbook Materials. *Australian Academic & Research Libraries,* 8, pp.139-146.

Holdsworth, M. (2002). ONIX: A Transforming Standard. *Against the Grain,* 14(3), pp.22-26.

Hopkinson, A. (1983). *UNIMARC Handbook.* London: IFLA International Office for UBC.

Hopkinson, A. (1991). Information Transfer and Exchange Formats. In *Standards for the International Exchange of Bibliographic Information: Papers Presented at a Course Held at the School of Library, Archive and Information Studies, University College London, 3-18 August 1990*, ed. I. C. McIlwaine. London: Library Association.

Horny, K. (1991). Cataloguing Simplification: Trends and Prospects. *International Cataloguing & Bibliographic Control,* 20, pp.25-28.

Horton, W. (1987). The Australian Bibliographic Network. *International Cataloguing,* Jan/March, pp.8-10.

Hu, L.H. (1990). Online Cataloguing Systems for Chinese Japanese and Korean Collections: An Evaluation Report from the University of Melbourne. *LASIE,* 20(4), pp.70-79.

Hunt, R. et al. (1976-77). *PRECIS, LCSH and KWOC: Report of a Research Project Designed to Examine the Applicability of PRECIS to the Subject Catalogue of an Academic Library*. Wollongong: Library, University of Wollongong.

Hunter, E.J. & Bakewell, K.G.B. (1991). *Cataloguing*. 3rd ed. London: Library Association.

IFLA Study Group on the Functional Requirements for Bibliographic Records. (1998). *Functional Requirements for Bibliographic Records: Final Report*. München: K.G. Saur. (Also available online. http://www.ifla.org/VII/s13/frbr/frbr.htm)

IFLA UBCIM Core Programme. (11 October 1997). *Annual Report 1997* (online). http://www.ifla.org/VI/3/annual/ann97.htm

INNOPAC Chosen for the Australian National CJK Project. (1994). *LASIE*, 24(6), p.104.

Innovative Interfaces. (2003). *Notable OPACs*. http://www.iii.com/customers/notableopacs.shtml (accessed 27 March 2003).

Integrated Library Information Systems in ARL Libraries. (1983). Washington DC: Systems and Procedures Exchange Center.

International Community for Auditory Display. (28 August 2003) (online). http://www.icad.org.

International Council on Archives. (2004). *ISAAR(CPF): International Standard Archival Authority Record for Corporate Bodies, Persons and Families*. 2nd ed. Paris: ICA. (Also available online. http://www.icacds.org.uk/eng/ISAAR(CPF)2ed.pdf)

International Council on Archives. (2000). *ISAD(G): General International Standard Archival Description*. 2nd ed. Ottawa, ON: ICA. (Also available online. http://www.ica.org/biblio/cds/isad_g_2e.pdf)

International Federation of Library Associations and Institutions (1996). *Names of Persons: National Usages for Entry in Catalogues*. 4th rev. & enlarged ed. München: K.G. Saur.

International Federation of Library Associations and Institutions. (2001). *Guidelines for Authority Records and References*. 2nd ed. München: K.G. Saur. (Also available online. http://www.ifla.org/VII/s13/garr/garr.pdf)

Intner, S.S. AACR2 Forever. *Technicalities* 22, pp.3-5.

Introducing SOFI. (1993). Canberra, ACT: National Library of Australia.

ISBD(CR): International Standard Bibliographic Description for Serials and Other Continuing Resources. (2002). München: K.G. Saur. (Also available online. http://www.ifla.org/VII/s13/pubs/isbdcr-final.pdf)

ISBD(M): International Standard Bibliographic Description for Monographic Publications, 1st standard ed. (1974). London: IFLA Committee on Cataloguing.

ISMIR. (12 December 2007). *The International Conferences on Music Information Retrieval and Related Activities* (online). http://www.ismir.net.

ISO 690 : 1987 Documentation – Bibliographic References – Content, Form, and Structure. (1987). Geneva: ISO. (Extracts also available online. http://www.nlc-bnc.ca/iso/tc46sc9/standard/690-1e.htm)

Jacob, E.K. (2003). Ontologies and the Semantic Web. *Bulletin of the American Society for Information Science and Technology*, 29, pp.19-22.

Jacob, M.E. (1972). MARC in the University of Sydney Library. In *Progress and Poverty: Proceedings of the 16th Biennial Conference held in Sydney, August 1971*. Sydney: Library Association of Australia.

Jacob, M.E.L. (1974). Reviews: Australian MARC Specification. *Australian Library Journal*, 23, pp.196-197.

Janes, J. (2002). Librarianship after Google. *American Libraries,* October, p.84.

Jeffreys, A. (1993). AACR2 After 1978. In *AACR2, DDC, MARC and Friends: The Role of CIG in Bibliographic Control*, eds. J. Byford, K.V. Trickey & S. Woodhouse. London: Library Association.

Johnson, B.C. (2001). XML and MARC: Which is "Right"? *Cataloging and Classification Quarterly* 32, pp.81-90.

Joint Steering Committee for Revision of AACR. (1997). Report on the International Conference on the Principles and Future Development of AACR held October 23-35 1997 in Toronto, Canada. *Catalogue & Index*, 126, pp.6-10.

Jorna, K. & Davies, S. (2001). Multilingual Thesauri for the Modern World: No Ideal Solution? *Journal of Documentation*, 57, pp.284-295.

Kellsey, C. (2002). Cooperative Cataloging, Vendor Records, and European Language Monographs. *Library Resources and Technical Services*, 46, pp.105-110.

Ketley, A. (1988). Australian MARC Record Service. In *ALIAS: Australia's Library, Information and Archives Services*. v.1. Sydney: Library Association of Australia.

Kilgour, F.G. (1984). The Online Catalog Revolution. *Library Journal,* 15 Feb., pp.319-321.

Kinetica (2001). *Progress Review of Kinetica: Australia's Library Network* (online). Canberra, ACT: National Library of Australia. http://www.nla.gov.au/Kinetica/ProgressReview.html (accessed 15 May 2003).

Kinetica (2002). *Future Development* (online). Canberra, ACT: National Library of Australia. http://www.nla.gov.au/Kinetica/future.html (accessed 15 May 2003).

Kinetica and Australian Bibliographic Network Annual Users Meeting. (1998) (online). http://www.nla.gov.au/abn/committees/annuala/98mins.html

Kinetica Implementation Project: Consolidated Q&A's (11 May 1998) (online). http://www.nla.gov.au/nsp/amicqar.html

Kinetica Vision (2002). Canberra, ACT: National Library of Australia.

King, G.W. (1963). *Automation and the Library of Congress: A Survey Sponsored by the Council on Library Resources.* Washington, D.C.: Library of Congress.

Kingscote, A. (2003). The Australian Pictorial Thesaurus in 2003. *Aiming for Access: the Australian Committee on Cataloguing Seminar, Sydney, 25 July 2003* (online). http://www.nla.gov.au/lis/standards/grps/acoc/papers.html (accessed 3 August 2003).

Klassifikationssystem för svenska bibliothek. (2006). 8th rev. ed. Lund: Bibliotekstjänst.

Lambrecht, J.H. (1992). *Minimal Level Cataloging by National Bibliographic Agencies.* München: K.G. Saur.

Lancaster, F.W. (1979). *Information Retrieval Systems.* 2nd ed. New York: Wiley.

Lancaster, F.W. (1989). The Perspective – Natural Language versus Controlled Language: A New Examination. In *Perspectives in Information Management 1*, eds. C. Oppenheim, C.L. Citroen & J. Griffiths. London: Butterworths.

Lancaster, F.W. (1993). *If You Want to Evaluate Your Library . . .* 2nd ed. Champaign: University of Illinois, Graduate School of Library and Information Science.

Lancaster, F.W. (1999). Second Thoughts on the Paperless Society. *Library Journal,* 125, pp.48-50.

Lancaster, F.W. (2003). *Indexing and Abstracting in Theory and Practice.* 3rd ed. Champaign, Il.: University of Illinois, Graduate School of Library and Information Science.

Langker, R. (1974a). ISBD: Another Step in the Right Direction. *Australian Library Journal,* 23, pp.99-103.

Langker, R. (1974b). Two Phoenix, Too Ill-Done: A Critique of the Eighteenth Edition of the Dewey Decimal Classification. In *Outpost: Australian Librarianship '73: Proceedings of the 17th Biennial Conference held in Perth, August 1973.* Perth: Library Association of Australia.

Langridge, D.W. (1989). *Subject Analysis: Principles and Procedures.* London: Bowker Saur.

Langridge, D.W. (1992). *Classification: Its Kinds, Elements, Systems and Applications.* London: Bowker-Saur.

Langville, A.N. & Meyer, C.D. (2006). *Google's PageRank and Beyond: The Science of Search Engine Rankings.* Princeton, NJ: Princeton University Press.

Lesk, M. (1997). *Practical Digital Libraries: Books, Bytes & Bucks.* San Francisco: Morgan Kaufmann.

Lewis, T. (1993). LINNET: The Networking Vision for the Northern Territory. In *Networking & Libraries in Australia*, ed. C. Goodacre. Melbourne: D.W. Thorpe/ALIA Press.

LibLink Launches Access to Library Catalogues. (1997). *InCite,* Dec., p.22.

Library Association of Australasia (1896). *Account of the Proceedings of the First Australasian Library Conference held in Melbourne on the 21st, 22nd, 23rd and 24th April 1896.* Melbourne: Government Printer.

Library Networks in Australia: A Survey for ACLIS. (1992). Canberra: Peter Judge and Associates.

Library of Congress. (1992). *Subject Cataloging Manual: Classification.* Washington, DC: Cataloging Distribution Service, Library of Congress.

Library of Congress. (2001). Cataloging in Publication Celebrates 30th Anniversary. *Information Bulletin,* 30 (5) (online). http://www.loc.gov/loc/lcib/0105/cip.html

Library of Congress. (12 December 2007a). *MARC Standards* (online). http://www.loc.gov/marc/

Library of Congress. (12 December 2007b). *PCC* (online). http://www.loc.gov/catdir/pcc/

Library of Congress. (12 December 2007c). *Series at the Library of Congress* (online). http://www.loc.gov/catdir/cpso/series.html

Library 2000: Investing in a Learning Nation: Report of the Library 2000 Review Committee. (1994). Singapore: SNP Publishers.

Lindlan, K., Beacom, M. & Attig, J. (2003). *The Future of AACR* (online). http://www.libraries.psu.edu/iasweb/personal/jca/ccda/future1.html (accessed 5 April 2003).

Line, M.B. (1969). White Elephants Revisited. *Catalogue & Index,* 13, pp.4-6.

[LINNET]. (22 Oct 1997) (online). http://www.nt.gov.au/ntl/linnet.html

List of Canadian Subject Headings. (1968). Ottawa: Canadian Library Association.

Little, K. (1993). Constructing a Thesaurus of Environmental Protection Terms. *Cataloguing Australia*, 19, pp.222-232.

Llewellyn, R. (1982). The Role of Library Cooperatives in an Australian Bibliographic Network. *Australian Library Journal,* 31, pp.14-20.

Lodewycks, A. (1953). The Self-Cataloguing Book. *Australian Library Journal,* April, pp.29-34.

Lodewycks, A. (1961). The Cataloguing in Source Experiment: An Appraisal. *Australian Library Journal,* 10, pp.157-160.

Lodewycks, A. (1990). A Contribution to the History of Cataloguing in Publication. *Australian Library Journal,* 39, pp.245-246.

Long, C.E. (2000). Improving Subject Searching in Web-based OPACs: Evaluation of the Problem and Guidelines for Design. *Journal of Internet Cataloging*, 2, pp.159-186.

Lopes, M.I. & Beall, J. (1999). *Principles Underlying Subject Headings Languages (SHLs).* München: K.G. Saur.

Lubetzky, S. (1953). *Cataloging Rules and Principles: A Critique of the A.L.A. Rules for Entry and a Proposed Design for their Revision.* Washington: Library of Congress.

Lynch, C. (1998). Metadata: Moving from Planning to Implementation (online). http://www.anu.edu.au/caul/mirror/global/content/repor~28.htm

Lynch, C. (2000). The New Context for Bibliographic Control in the New Millennium. *Bicentennial Conference on Bibliographic Control for the New Millennium, Library of Congress, 15-17 November 2000* (online). http://lcweb.loc.gov/catdir/bibcontrol/lynch_paper.html (accessed 6 June 2003).

McCallum, S.H. & Roberts, W.D. (eds.) (1989). *UNIMARC in Theory and Practice: Papers from the UNIMARC Workshop, Sydney, Australia, August 1988.* London: IFLA UBCIM Programme.

MacEwan, A. (1999). Working with LCSH: The Cost of Cooperation and the Achievement of Access. *International Cataloging and Bibliographic Control*, 28, pp.94-97.

MacEwan, A. (2000). Crossing Language Barriers in Europe: Linking LCSH to Other Subject Heading Languages. *Cataloging & Classification Quarterly*, 29, pp.199-207.

McGarry, D. (2000). An Interview With Elaine Svenonius. *Cataloging & Classification Quarterly*, 29, pp.5-17.

McIlwaine, I.C. (1996). New Wine in Old Bottles: Problems of Maintaining Classification Schemes. *Advances in Knowledge Organization*, 5, pp.122-136.

McIlwaine, I. (1998). UDC – Into the 21st Century. *Aslib Proceedings*, 50, pp.44-48.

McIlwaine, I.C. (2000). UDC in the Twenty-first Century. In Marcella, R. & Maltby, A. (eds) (2000). *The Future of Classification*. Aldershot: Gower, pp.93-104.

McIlwaine, I.C. & Williamson, N.J. (1999). International Trends in Subject Analysis Research. *Knowledge Organization*, 26, pp.23-29.

McKiernan, G. (comp.) (20 April 1998). Onion Patch(sm): New Age Public Access Systems (online). http://www.public.iastate.edu/~CYBERSTACKS/Onion.htm

McKiernan, G. (11 May 1998). The Next WAVe(sm): Auditory Browsing in Web and non-Web Databases (online). http://www.public.iastate.edu/~CYBERSTACKS/Wave.htm

McKiernan, G. (1999). Points of View: Conventional and 'Neo-Conventional' Access and Navigation in Digital Collections. Journal of Internet Cataloging, 2, pp.23-41.

McKiernan, G. (2001). Beyond Bookmarks: Schemes for Organizing the Web (online). http://www.public.iastate.edu/~CYBERSTACKS/CTW.htm (accessed 4 April 2003).

McKinlay, J. (1970). Australia and the Classificationists. *Australian Library Journal*, 19, pp.334-338.

McKinlay, J. (1974a). Subject Headings for Australia. *Australian Academic & Research Libraries*, 5, pp.131-136.

McKinlay, J. (1974b). The User's Catalogue. *Australian Library Journal*, 23, pp.172-177.

McKinlay, J. (1976). DC and Australia. *Cataloguing Australia*, 2, pp.19-41.

McKinlay, J. (comp.) (1978). *A List of Australian Subject Headings*. Preliminary ed. Bundoora: Cataloguers' Section, Australian Library Association.

McKinlay, J. (1980). Classification in Australian Libraries. *International Classification*, 7, pp.131-134.

McKinlay. J. (ed.) (1981). *A List of Australian Subject Headings*. 1st ed. Sydney: Library Association of Australia.

McMillan, S. (1989). Cataloguing Rules Revisited. *InCite*, 24 April, p.7.

McMillan, S. (1991). AUSMARC to USMARC. *Cataloguing Australia*, 17, pp.113-119.

McMillan, S. & McMillan, J. (1984). Reclassification and the University of Queensland Library. *Australian Academic & Research Libraries*, 15, pp.135-142.

Maddick, P. (1997). The Role of SCIS Cataloguing Agencies: The NCEC. In *School Library Automation in Australia: Issues and Results of the National Surveys*, ed. K. Dillon. 2nd ed. Wagga Wagga: Centre for Information Studies, Charles Sturt University-Riverina.

Maguire, C. (1993). Automation in Australian University Libraries at the end of 1992. *LASIE*, 23 (4 & 5), pp.56-61.

Malinconico, S.M. (1984). Catalogs & Cataloging: Innocent Pleasures and Enduring Controversies. *Library Journal*, 15 June, pp.1210-1213.

Mann, T. (2003). Why LC Subject Headings Are More Important Than Ever. *American Libraries*, 34(9), pp.52-54.

Mann, T. (2006). What is Going On At the Library of Congress? (online). http://www.guild2910.org/AFSCMEWhatIsGoingOn.pdf (accessed 12 December 2007).

Mann, T. (2007). The Peloponnesian War and the Future of Reference, Cataloging and Scholarship in Research Libraries (online). http://www.guild2910.org/Pelopponesian%20War%20June%2013%202007.pdf (accessed 12 December 2007).

Marcella, R. & Maltby, A. (2000). *The Future of Classification*. Aldershot: Gower.

Marcella, R. & Newton, R (1994). *A New Manual of Classification*. Aldershot: Gower.

Martin, C.K. & Saxton, E.L. (2001). Do We Catalog These or Not?: How Research Libraries are Providing Bibliographic Access to Electronic Journals. *Serials Librarian*, 40, pp.355-360.

Martin, S.K. (1987). Library Networks: Trends and Issues. *Journal of Library Administration*, 8, pp.27-33.

Martin, G. (1996a). Bibliographic Control and Access. In *Librarianship and Information Work Worldwide 1995*, ed. M. Line. London: Bowker Saur.

Martin, G. (1996b). Email to CATLIBS list, 3 December.

Martin, G. (1997). The DDC in the Asia-Pacific Region. In *Dewey Decimal Classification: Edition 21 and International Perspectives*, ed. L.M. Chan and J.S. Mitchell. Albany, NY: Forest Press, pp.59-66.

Martin, G. (2001). DC and Australia from the 19th to the 21st Century. In *Seachange: Cataloguing in a Dot Com World: 14th National Cataloguing Conference Preprints*. Geelong, Vic.: Organizing Committee of the 14th National Cataloguing Conference, pp.54-57.

Medeiros, N. (2004). Repurposed Metadata: ONIX and the Library of Congress' BEAT Program. *OCLC Systems & Services*, 20(3), pp.93-95.

The MetaWeb Project. (16 June 1998) (online). http://www.dstc.edu.au/RDU/MetaWeb/

Metaweb Project Update. (1997). *National Library of Australia Gateways*, 31, pp.5-6.

Metcalfe, J. (1959). *Subject Classifying and Indexing of Libraries and Literature*. Sydney: Angus & Robertson.

Miller, E. (1998). An Introduction to the Resource Description Framework. *D-Lib Magazine*, May (online). http://www.dlib.org/dlib/may98/miller/05miller.html

Miller, E. & Swick, R. (2003). An Overview of W3C Semantic Web Activity. Bulletin of the *American Society for Information Science and Technology*, 29, pp.8-11.

Millsap, L. & Ferl, T.E. (1997). *Descriptive Cataloging for the AACR2R and the Integrated MARC Format*. Rev. ed. New York: Neal-Schuman.

Missingham, R. (2002). Report to the Annual Users' Meeting 2002 (online). http://www.nla.gov.au/kinetica/aum/aum02/report.html (accessed 4 June 2003).

Missingham, R. (2003). Kinetica. In Ferguson, S. and Hebels, R. (2003). *Computers for Librarians: An Introduction to the Electronic Library*, 3rd ed. Wagga Wagga, NSW: Centre for Information Studies, pp.263-266.

Missingham, R. (2004). Reengineering a National Resource Discovery Service: MODS Down Under. *D-Lib Magazine* 10(9) (online). http://www.dlib.org/dlib/september04/missingham/09missingham.html (accessed 12 December 2007).

Mitchell, J. S. (1997). The Road Ahead for Library Classification Schemes. *Cataloguing Australia*, 23, pp.41-51.

Mitchell, J.S. (2003). DDC 22: An Introduction. *World Library and Information Congress: 69th IFLA General Conference, 1-9 August 2003, Berlin* (online). http://www.ifla.org/IV/ifla69/papers/121e-Mitchell.pdf (accessed 12 July 2003).

Moorcroft, H. (1992). Ethnocentrism in Subject Headings. *Australian Library Journal*, 41, pp.40-45.

Morrison, E. (1982). FLASH in the Pan or in the Fire. *Australian Academic & Research Libraries*, 13, pp.217-230.

Morrison, I. (1993). The Australia's Book Heritage Resources Project. *Bibliographical Society of Australia and New Zealand Bulletin*, 17, pp.113-124.

Mortimer, M. (1997). *Learn Dewey Decimal Classification (Edition 21)*. Canberra: DocMatrix.

Mortimer, M. (2002). *Learn Descriptive Cataloguing*. 4th ed. Canberra: DocMatrix.

Mortimer, M., Lochhead, K. & Hyland, M. (1994). *CatSkill: A Multimedia Course on AACR2 and MARC (CD-ROM)*. Canberra: Learning Curve Pty and DocMatrix.

Morville, P. & Rosenfeld, L. (2006). *Information Architecture for the World Wide Web: Designing Large-Scale Web Sites*. 3rd ed. Beijing: O'Reilly.

National Archives of Australia (2003). *AGLS Metadata Element Set: Part 2, Usage Guide*. Canberra: National Archives of Australia.

National Bibliographic Database. (1998). Report to Annual Users Meeting, August 1997-June 199*8* (online). http://www.nla.gov.au/2/abn/committees/annuala/aum98papers.html

National Library of Australia. (1994). *Survey of Music Collections in Australian Libraries, August 1994*. http://www.nla.gov.au/libraries/hosted/musurvey.html (accessed 4 April 2003).

National Library of Australia. (2000). Report to the [Kinetica] Annual Users' Meeting 2000 (online). http://www.nla.gov.au/kinetica/aum/annualreport2000.html

National Library of Australia. Expert Advisory Group on Authority Record Delivery (NLA. EAGAD). (2002) *Final Report of the Expert Advisory Group on Authority Record Delivery* (online). http://www.nla.gov.au/kinetica/EAGADReport.doc

National Library of Australia. Expert Advisory Group on Authority Record Delivery (NLA. EAGAD). (5 April 2003) (online). *Summary of User and Vendor Surveys*. http://www.nla.gov.au/kinetica/eag_ad_reports.html

National Library of Australia. (12 December 2007). Libraries Australia (online). http://www.nla.gov.au/librariesaustralia/

Nederlandse Basisclassificatie (1998). 3rd ed. Den Haag : Koninklijke Bibliotheek.

Nelson, J. (1986). Cataloguing Theory and Practice in Nineteenth Century Australian Libraries. *Cataloguing Australia*, 12, pp.18-38.

Nelson, J.R. (1967). The Blue Book versus the Red Book: Some Reflections on the New Cataloguing Code. *Australian Library Journal,* 16, pp.119-123.

Nelson, J.R. (ed.) (1973). *Proceedings of the MARC II Seminar Held at the School of Librarianship, The University of New South Wales, 18-20 August 1971.* Kensington, NSW: University of New South Wales.

Nelson, J.R. (1974). Cataloguing in Australia; Past, Present and Future. In *Outpost: Australian Librarianship '73: Proceedings of the 17th Biennial Conference held in Perth, August 1973.* Perth: Library Association of Australia.

NetFirst: The Authoritative Directory for Internet Resources. (1998) (online). Dublin, OH: OCLC. http://www.oclc.org/oclc/netfirst/netfirst.htm

Networked Services Project. (1998) (online). http://www.nla.gov.au/nsp/

New Future for Ozline. (1998). *National Library of Australia Gateways,* 33, pp.17-18.

New National System – AMICUS Comes in First. (1998). *National Library of Australia Gateways,* 31, pp.1-2.

The New NSP Project. (1997). *National Library of Australia Gateways,* 26, pp.6-7.

Newton, R. (2000). Information Technology and New Directions. In Marcella, R. & Maltby, A. (2000). *The Future of Classification.* Aldershot: Gower, pp.43-57.

Nicholson, S. (2000). A Proposal for Categorization and Nomenclature for Web Search Tools. *Journal of Internet Cataloging*, 2, pp.9-28.

Notess, G.R. (12 December 2007). *Search Engine Showdown* (online). http://searchengineshowdown.com

O'Brien, A. (1994). Online Catalogs: Enhancements and Developments. *Annual Review of Information Science and Technology,* 29, pp.219-242.

OCLC Authority Control. (1998) (online). http://www.oclc.org/oclc/menu/auth.htm

OCLC CAT CD450 in Australian Libraries. (1992). *LASIE,* 22(5), pp.119-124.

OCLC/CJK and the Australian National University. (1990). *LASIE,* 20(4), p.69.

OCLC Link Proposal. (1974). *Australian Library Journal,* 23, p. 380.

OCLC Office for Research. (1999). *The Scorpion Project.* http://orc.rsch.oclc.org:6109/ (accessed 4 April 2003).

OCLC Online Computer Library Center, Inc. (12 December 2007) (online). http://www.oclc.org

OCLC Profile. (18 Sept 1997) (online). http://www.oclc.org/oclc/splan/profile.htm

OCLC Reference Services /OCLC FirstSearch. (31 March 1998) (online). http://www.oclc.org/oclc/fs/service.htm

Oddy, P. (1996). *Future Libraries, Future Catalogues.* London: Library Association.

Oddy, P. (1999). The Case for International Co-operation in Cataloguing. *Program*, 33, pp.29-39.

Olding, R.K. (1954). A System of Classification for Music and Related Materials. *Australian Library Journal,* 3, pp.13-18.

Olmstadt, W. (2000). Cataloging Expert Systems: Optimism and Frustrated Reality. *Journal of Southern Academic and Special Librarianship,* 1(3) (online). http://southernlibrarianship.icaap.org/content/v01n03/olmstadt_w01.html (accessed 28 August 2003).

Olson, H.A. & Boll, J.J. (2001). *Subject Analysis in Online Catalogs.* 2nd ed. Englewood, CO: Libraries Unlimited.

O'Mara, R. & Peake, D.G. (1985). OSI – The Open Systems Interface or 'The Building Block of the 80s'. *LASIE* 16(3), pp.2-5.

Open Systems Interconnection and the National Library of Australia: The Official View. (1986). *LASIE,* 16(6), pp.9-11.

Orna, E. & Pettit, C. (1998). *Information Management in Museums.* Aldershot, Hants: Gower.

Osborn, A. (1979). The Professional Excellence of AACR2: Its Implementation in Australia. *Australian Library Journal,* 28, pp.301-304.

Osborn, A.D. (1941). The Crisis in Cataloging. *Library Quarterly,* 11, pp.393-411.

PADI: Preserving Access to Digital Information: Metadata. (11 May 1998) (online). http://www.nla.gov.au/padi/metadata.html

Parker, D. (1987). LIBNET: A Victorian College Library Network. *LASIE,* 18(1), pp.13-17.

Patton, G. & Weiss, P. J. (1993). Cataloging After Format Integration. In *Format Integration and its Effect on Cataloging, Training, and Systems: Papers Presented at the ALCTS Preconference 'Implementing USMARC Format Integration' American Library Association Annual Conference, June 26 1992,* ed. K. Coyle. Chicago: American Library Association.

PCC. (2006). *Annual Report FY06.* http://www.loc.gov/catdir/pcc/PCCAnnualFY06.pdf (accessed 12 December 2007).

Peake, D.G. (1976). *Library Networks and Changing Library Service: A Quiet Revolution.* Sydney: Information Resources Section, N.S.W. Institute of Technology.

Peake, D.G. (1996). The Heroic Age of Australian Library Automation and its Immediate Aftermath. *LASIE,* 27(4), pp.4-17.

Permanent UNIMARC Committee. (15 Aug 1997) (online). http://www.ifla.org/ifla/VI/3/puc.htm

Peterson, E. (2006). Beneath the Metadata: Some Philosophical Problems with Folksonomy. *D-Lib,* 12(11) (online). http://www.dlib.org/dlib/november06/peterson/11peterson.html (accessed 12 December 2007).

Petersen, T. & Molholt, P. (eds.) (1990). *Beyond the Book: Extending MARC for Subject Access.* Boston, MA: G.K. Hall.

Piggott, M. (1988). *A Topography of Cataloguing: Showing the Most Important Landmarks, Communications and Perilous Places.* London: Library Association.

Potter, W.G. (1990). The Evolving Online Catalogue in Academic Libraries. In *Technical Services Today and Tomorrow*, eds. M. Gorman & associates. Englewood, CO: Libraries Unlimited.

Pouchard, L. (1998). Cataloging for Digital Libraries: The TEI Scheme and the TEI Header. *Katharine Sharp Review*, 6 (online). http://alexia.lis.uiuc.edu/review/6/pouchard.html

Powell, S. & Missingham, R. (2003). Kinetica Developments Customer Input Shapes Future Work. *Gateways*, 62 (online). http://www.nla.gov.au/ntwkpubs/gw/62/p06a01/html (accessed 29 April 2003).

Prabha, C. (1996). Office of Research Studies Copy Cataloging Throughput for CIP Titles. *OCLC Newsletter,* 219, pp.13-14.

Pre-Cataloguing. (1971). *Australian Library Journal,* 20, p.27.

Prytherch, R. (1995). *Harrod's Librarians' Glossary.* 8th ed. Aldershot: Gower.

Qin, J. & Paling, S. (2001). Converting a Controlled Vocabulary into an Ontology: The Case of GEM. *Information Research*, 6 (online). http://information.net/ir/6-2/paper94.html. (accessed 27 June 2003).

Rachmananta, D.P. (1990). Bibliographic Standards of Indonesia. *International Cataloguing & Bibliographic Control,* 19, pp.37-40.

Radebaugh, J. (2003). MARC Goes Global and Lite. *American Libraries,* 34, pp.43-44.

Rajapatirana, B. (2002). Kinetica: Subject Headings Review Panel Update. *Gateways*, 60 (online). http://www.nla.gov.au/ntwkpubs/gw/60/p09a01.html (accessed 3 May 2003).

Ramsden, M.J. (1978). A New Life for Bliss. *Australian Academic & Research Libraries,* 9, pp.210-214.

Ramsden, M.J. (1979). Travels With a Cataloguing Code. *Australian Library Journal,* 28, pp.308-309.

Reggie - The Metadata Editor. (29 May 1998) (online). http://metadata.net/dstc/

Richardson, C. & Exon, M. (1990). Garbage Out: The Quality of Library School Graduates. In *Garbage In – Garbage Out: The Need for Quality in the Age of Automation*, eds. A. Bundy & J. Bundy. Adelaide: Auslib Press.

Richardson, E. (1982). The Administration of Technical Services in Australian University Libraries. *Australian Academic & Research Libraries*, 13, pp.95-106.

RLG Services for Information Access and Management. (1994). Mountain View, CA: Research Libraries Group.

RLG's RedLightGreen Project: Mining the Catalog (2003). http://www.rlg.org/redlightgreen/mining.html (accessed 12 June 2003).

Robinson, G. (1999). Abridging the UDC: the Compiling of the Pocket Edition. *Knowledge Organization*, 26, pp.149-156.

Roe, S. (1999). Online subject access. *Journal of Internet Cataloging*, 2(1), pp.69-78.

Ross, S. (2003). Position Paper. In DigiCULT Project (2003). *Towards a Semantic Web for Heritage Resources: Thematic Issue 3* (online). http://data.digicult.info/download/ti3_high.pdf. (accessed 5 September 2003).

Rowley, J. (1994). Making the Right Choice: Strategies and Pointers for the Selection of Library and Information Systems. *Managing Information,* 1, pp.26-30.

Rowley, J.E. & Farrow, J. (2000). *Organizing Knowledge: An Introduction to Managing Access to Information.* 3rd ed. Aldershot: Gower.

Rowley, J. & Hartley, R. (2007). *Organizing Knowledge: An Introduction to Managing Access to Information.* 4th ed. Aldershot: Ashgate.

Rules for Descriptive Cataloging in the Library of Congress (1949). Washington, DC: Library of Congress.

Rusch-Feja, D. (2002). The Open Archives Initiative and the OAI Protocol for Metadata Harvesting: Rapidly Forming a New Tier in the Scholarly Communication Infrastructure. *Learned Publishing,* 15, pp.179-186.

Saeed, H. & Chaudhry, A.S. (2002). Using Dewey Decimal Classification Scheme (DDC) for Building Taxonomies for Knowledge Organisation. *Journal of Documentation,* 58, pp.575-583.

Saffady, W. The Status of Library Automation at 2000. *Library Technology Reports,* 36, p.3.

Sapiie, J. (1995). Reader-Interest Classification: The User-Friendly Schemes. *Cataloging & Classification Quarterly,* 19, pp.143-155.

Satija, M.P. (1997). The Revision and Future of Colon Classification. *Knowledge Organization,* 24, pp.18-23.

Saye, J.D. (2000). *Manheimer's Cataloguing and Classification.* 4th ed. New York: Dekker.

Sayers, W.C.B. (1967). *A Manual of Classification for Librarians.* 4th ed., rev. A. Maltby. London: Deutsch.

Schabas, A.H. (1982). Postcoordinate Retrieval: A Comparison of Two Indexing Languages. *JASIS,* Jan., pp.32-37.

Scharf, D. (2002). XML under the Hood. *Information Outlook,* 6, pp.20-23.

Schauder, C. (1991). Library of Congress Subject Heading Reference Structures and OPACs. *Cataloguing Australia,* 17, 44-64.

Schmidmaier, D. (1975). Machine-Readable Data Bases in Australia: A State of the Art Report. *LASIE,* 5(6), pp.2-34.

Schmidmaier, D. (1978). Are Regional Processing Centres Necessary? *Australian Academic & Research Libraries,* 9, pp.98-100.

Schools Catalogue Information Service. (1 April 1998) (online). http://www.curriculum.edu.au/scis/

Schools Online Thesaurus. (12 December 2007) (online). http://www1.curriculum.edu.au/scis/

Schwartz, C. (2001). *Sorting Out the Web: Approaches to Subject Access.* Westport, CT: Ablex.

SCISWeb Information (2003) (online). http://www.curriculum.edu.au/scis/handouts/00web.htm (accessed 1 May 2003).

Seal, A. (1983). Experiments with Full and Short Entry Catalogues: A Study of Library Needs. *Library Resources and Technical Services,* 27, pp.144-155.

Sears List of Subject Headings. (27 April 1998) (online). http://www.hwwilson.com/searslst.htm

SemanticWeb (2003) (online). http://www.semanticweb.org

Sherrie, H. & Mander Jones, P. (1950). *Short List of Subject Headings.* Sydney: Angus and Robertson.

Simpler Charging Structure. (1998). *National Library of Australia Gateways,* 33, pp.14-16.

Slavic, A. (2006). UDC in Subject Gateways: Experiment or Opportunity? (online). http://dlist.sir.arizona.edu/1556/01/UDCSG_AS_preprint.pdf (accessed 12 December 2007).

Slavic, A. (2006) Use of the Universal Decimal Classification: A Worldwide Survey (online). http://dlist.sir.arizona.edu/1555/01/UDCuse_aidaslavic_preprint.pdf (accessed 12 December 2007).

Smiraglia, R.P. (1987). The Consolidated Reprinting of AACR2. *Cataloging & Classification Quarterly,* 8, pp.3-6.

Smith, E.H. (1991). Enhancing Subject Accessibility to the Online Catalog. *Library Resources & Technical Services,* 35, pp.109-113.

Some Electronic Classification Schemes. (1998) (online). http://orc.rsch.oclc.org:6109/classification/

Special Report: 1971–1991. (1991). *OCLC Newsletter,* 191, pp.13-35.

Stecher, G. (1976). Shared Cataloguing: An Exercise in Costing OCLC. *Australian Academic & Research Libraries,* 7, pp.1-11.

Steele, C. & Jensen, J. (1993). The State of the Nation: An Overview of Australian University and Research Library Annual Reports. *Australian Academic & Research Libraries,* 24, pp.116-126.

Stockdale, R. (1981). National Union Catalogues. In *Bibliographical Services to the Nation: The Next Decade: Proceedings of a Conference Held in Sydney 26-27 August 1980,* eds. D.H. Borchardt & J. Thawley. Canberra: National Library of Australia.

Studwell, W.E. (1990). *Library of Congress Subject Headings: Philosophy, Practice, and Prospects.* New York: Haworth.

Svenonius, E. (1983). Use of Classification in Online Retrieval. *Library Resources & Technical Services,* 27, pp.76-80.

Svenonius, E. (ed.) (1989). *The Conceptual Foundations of Descriptive Cataloging.* San Diego, CA: Academic Press.

Svenonius, E. (2000). *The Intellectual Foundation of Information Organization.* Cambridge, MA: MIT Press.

Talbot, M. (1985). The Library Association of Australasia: A Professional Body? In *Books, Libraries & Readers in Colonial Australia: Papers from the Forum on Australian Colonial Library History held at Monash University, 1-2 June 1984.* Clayton, Vic.: Graduate School of Librarianship, Monash University.

Taylor, A.G. (1999). *The Organization of Information.* Englewood, CO: Libraries Unlimited.

Taylor, A.G. (2000). *Wynar's Introduction to Cataloging and Classification.* 9th ed. Englewood, CO.: Libraries Unlimited.

Taylor, A.G. (2004). *The Organization of Information.* 2nd ed. Westport, CT: Libraries Unlimited.

Taylor, A.G. (2006). *Introduction to Cataloging and Classification.* 10th ed. Westport, CT: Libraries Unlimited.

Technilib [brochure]. (1993). Richmond, Vic.

Tedd, L. (1993). *An Introduction to Computer-based Library Systems.* 3rd ed. Chichester: Wiley.

Tennant, R. (2002). MARC Must Die. *Library Journal,* 15 Oct., pp.26, 28.

Thesaurus Usage in Australian Libraries. (30 October 1996). Towards Federation 2001 Working Group on High-Priority Cross-Sectoral Projects (online). http://www.nla.gov.au/dnc/tf2001/austhes.html

Thomas, S.E. (2000). The Catalog as Portal to the Internet. *Bicentennial Conference on Bibliographic Control for the New Millennium, Library of Congress, 15-17 November 2000* (online). http://lcweb.loc.gov/catdir/bibcontrol/thomas_paper.html (accessed 10 June 2003).

Tillett, B.B. (1995). Cataloguing Rules and Conceptual Models for the Electronic Environment. *Cataloguing Australia,* 21, pp.67-103.

Towards a Common Vision in Library Networking: Proceedings of the Library of Congress Network Advisory Committee Meeting, December 9-11, 1985. (1985). Washington, DC: Library of Congress.

Trainor, J. (20 February 1998). The Future Direction for Australian Subject Access (online). http://www.nla.gov.au/abn/committees/982subj.html

TU Goes LC. (1973). *Australian Library Journal,* 22, p.272.

Turner, J. (1991). The SUN Trial: Improving Retrieval of Books from the Library Catalogue. In *OPAC and Beyond: 6th Biennial Conference and Exhibition, Victorian Association for Library Automation, 11-13 November 1991.* Melbourne: VALA.

Turner, P. & Crowe, R. (1996). RLIN Trial: State Library of New South Wales Librarians Evaluate the RLIN Database for Cataloguing Copy Using the ABN Gateway Service. *Cataloguing Australia,* 22, pp.48-54.

UKMARC Manual (1975). 1st standard ed. London: British Library.

UKMARC Manual (1980). 2nd ed. London: British Library.

Undy, G.C. (1978). Regional Centres in General – CLANN in Particular. *Australian Academic & Research Libraries*, 9, pp.101-106.

Unicode, Inc. (26 May 2003). What is Unicode? (online). http://www.unicode.org/standard/WhatIsUnicode.html

UNILINC Limited Annual Report 1996. (1996) (online). http://www.unilinc.edu.au/annual.htm

UNILINC Limited Annual Report 2002. (2003) (online).
http://www.unilinc.edu.au/annualrep/annual02.htm (accessed 4 June 2003).

UNILINC. (2007) (online). http://www.unilinc.edu.au/ (accessed 12 December 2007).

UNIMARC manual. (1987). London: IFLA UBCIM Programme.

VALA 1991: State of the State & Territories. (1991). *Australian Library Journal,* 40, pp.270-288.

Van Orden, R. (1990). Content-Enriched Access to Electronic Information: Summaries of Selected Research. *Library Hi Tech,* 31, pp.27-32.

Vizine-Goetz, D. (1996). *Using Library Classification Schemes for Internet Resources* (online). http://www.oclc.org/oclc/man/colloq/v-g.htm (accessed 25 June 2003).

Vizine-Goetz, D. (2000). Exploiting LCSH, LCC, and DDC to Retrieve Networked Results: Comments. *Bicentennial Conference on Bibliographic Control for the New Millennium, Library of Congress, 15-17 November 2000* (online).
http://lcweb.loc.gov/catdir/bibcontrol/vizinegoetz_paper.html (accessed 11 June 2003).

Vizine-Goetz, D. (2002). Classification Schemes for Internet Resources Revisited. *Journal of Internet Cataloging,* 5, pp.5-18.

Wade, R. (1988). OSI in Australia: Potential, Planning, Progress. *Paper 015-INF-2-E Presented at 54th IFLA General Conference, Sydney, Australia, 30 August-3 September 1988.*

Wade, R. (1993). Overview of Regional Networks and Their Future. In *Networking & Libraries in Australia,* ed. C. Goodacre. Melbourne: ALIA/Thorpe.

Wang, A.H. (1992). OCLC Services in Asia, the Pacific Region, and Latin America. *OCLC advertising brochure.*

Ward, M. (1994). Expanding Access to Information with Z39.50. *American Libraries,* 25, pp.639-641.

Webb, K. (1993). Overview of Concepts of Data Communications and Networking. In *Networking & Libraries in Australia,* ed. C. Goodacre. Melbourne: ALIA/Thorpe.

Weibel, S., Godby, J., Miller, E. & Daniel, R. (1995). *OCLC/NCSA Metadata Workshop Report.* (online). http://www.oclc.org:5046/conferences/metadata/dublin_core_report.html

Weiss, A.K. & Carstens, T.V. (2001). The Year's Work in Cataloging, 1999. *Library Resources & Technical Services,* 45, pp.47-58.

Welcome to ISM Library Information Services. (29 Feb. 1996) (online).
http://www.ism.ca/lis/

SCIS. (12 December 2007). *Schools Catalogue Information Service* (online).
http://www.curriculum.edu.au/scis/scis.htm

What's New: Strategy Cataloguing Client, Strategy Public Access Catalogue. (4 June 1998). Stowe Computing Australia (online). http://www.stowe.com.au/index.htm

Williams, J.W. (1987). Serials Cataloging with AACR2: The Primary Problems and Concerns. *Serials Librarian,* 12, pp.27-42.

Wilson, P. (1983). The Catalog as Access Mechanism: Background and Concepts. *Library Resources and Technical Services,* 27, pp.4-17.

WLN Cataloging Services (1998) (online). http://www.wln.com/wlnprods/catalog.htm

Wood, F. (1984). *Evaluation of a University Library's Catalogue: Patron Usage, Problems and Policy Directions*. Canberra: Australian National University.

Workshop on Electronic Thesauri (1999). *Report* (online). http://www.niso.org/news/events_workshops/thes99prt.html (accessed 29 May 2003).

World Encyclopedia of Library and Information Services. (1993). 3rd ed. Chicago, IL: American Library Association.

Wright, B. (1996). PALINET Celebrates 60 Years of Pioneering Technology to Serve Libraries and Library Users. *OCLC Newsletter,* 220, pp.8-9.

Wright, J. (1992). An Australian Z39.50 Implementation. In *Networking & Libraries in Australia*, C. Goodacre ed. Melbourne: ALIA/Thorpe.

Xu, A. (1997). *Metadata Conversion and the Library OPAC* (online). http://web.mit.edu/waynej/www.xu.htm

Yeung, T. & Tam, O. (2003). Enhancing the Library Online Catalogue with Value-Added Information from Online Bookstores. In Ferguson, S. & Hebels, R. (2003). *Computers for Librarians: An Introduction to the Electronic Library*, 3rd ed. Wagga Wagga, NSW: Centre for Information Studies, pp.258-262.

Younger, J.A. (1997). Resources Description in the Digital Age. *Library Trends*, 45, pp.462-481.

Yu, H. & Young, M. (2004). The Impact of Web Search Engines on Subject Searching in OPAC. *Information Technology and Libraries*, 23(4), pp.168-180.

Z39.14-1997. Guidelines for Abstracts (1997). Bethesda, MD: NISO Press.

The ZedWeb Project. (30 April 1998) (online). http://www.dstc.edu.au/RDU/ZedWeb/

Zumer, M. & Zeng, L. (1994). Comparison and Evaluation of OPAC End-User Interfaces. *Cataloging & Classification Quarterly,* 19, pp.67-98.

Index